Forensic Nursing and Multidisciplinary Care of the Mentally Disordered Offender

Forensic Focus

This series, now edited by Gwen Adshead, takes the currently crystallising field of Forensic Psychotherapy as its focal point, offering a forum for the presentation of theoretical and clinical issues. It will also embrace such influential neighbouring disciplines as language, law, literature, criminology, ethics and philosophy, as well as psychiatry and psychology, its established progenitors.

Forensic Psychotherapy
Crime, Psychodynamics and the Offender Patient
Edited by Christopher Cordess and Murray Cox
Forensic Focus 1
ISBN 1 85302 634 4 pb
ISBN 1 85302 240 3 slipcased 2 vol hb

A Practical Guide to Forensic Psychotherapy
Edited by Estela V. Welldon and Cleo Van Velsen
Forensic Focus 3
ISBN 1 85302 389 2

Remorse and Reparation
Edited by Murray Cox
Forensic Focus 7
ISBN 1 85302 452 X pb
ISBN 1 85302 451 1 hb

Psychiatric Assessment
Pre and Post Admission Assessment
Valerie Anne Brown
Forensic Focus 8
ISBN 1 85302 575 5 A4

Managing High Security Psychiatric Care
Edited by Charles Kaye and Alan Franey
Forensic Focus 9
ISBN 1 85302 581 X pb
ISBN 1 85302 582 8 hb

Working with Sex Offenders in Prisons
and Through Release in the Community
A Handbook
Alec Spencer
Forensic Focus 15
ISBN 1 85302 767 7

Psychiatric Aspects of Justification, Excuse and Mitigation
The Jurisprudence of Mental Abnormality in Anglo-American Criminal Law
Alec Buchanan
Forensic Focus 17
ISBN 1 85302 797 9 pb

Forensic Focus 14

Nursing and Multidisciplinary Care of the Mentally Disordered Offender

*Edited by David Robinson
and Alyson Kettles*

Jessica Kingsley Publishers
London and Philadelphia

This edition published in the United Kingdom in 2000 by
Jessica Kingsley Publishers Ltd,
116 Pentonville Road,
London N1 9JB, England
and
325 Chestnut Street,
Philadelphia, PA 19106, USA.

www.jkp.com

Copyright © 2000 Jessica Kingsley Publishers

Library of Congress Cataloging-in-Publication Data
Forensic nursing and multidisciplinary care of the mentally disordered offender / edited by David Robinson and Alyson Kettles.
    p. cm. -- (Forensic focus 14)
Includes bibliographical references and index.
ISBN 1-85302-754-5 (pb : alk. paper) -- ISBN 1-85302-753-7 (hb : alk. paper)
1. Forensic psychiatric nursing. 2. Mentally handicapped offenders. 3. Forensic nursing. I. Robinson, David (David K.) II. Kettles, Alyson, 1956– III. Series.
[DNLM: 1. Psychiattric Nursing. 2. Forensic Psychiatry. WY 160 F7155 1999]
RA1155.F67 1999
610.73'68--dc21 99-042863

British Library Cataloguing in Publication Data
Forensic nursing and multidisciplinary care of the mentally disordered offender. - (Forensic focus ; 14)
1.Forensic psychiatry nursing
I.Robinson, David, 1952– II.Kettles, Alyson, 1956–
610.7'368

ISBN 1 85302 753 7 hb
ISBN 1 85302 754 5 pb

Printed and Bound in Great Britain by
Athenaeum Press, Gateshead, Tyne and Wear

For Mr Alan and Mrs Margaret Kettles

Contents

Acknowledgements

Very many thanks must go to Mrs Bridget Bower and Mrs Sally McCracken without whom this text would never have come to fruition. Their hard work to strict deadlines and for fraught editors has made life so much easier.

Preface

It was from our interest and general discussion about the so-called profession of the forensic nurse and the growing contrasting literature, which appears uncertain about whether or not the profession exists, that we embarked upon this book. Seeking empirical evidence along the way along with international and cross-cultural contributions we offer a first account of forensic nursing in relation to the mentally disordered offender.

What we offer is not exhaustive and merely scratches the surface of a complex multi-professional role and, indeed, a complex and demanding group of patients. Where possible, we have drawn upon the latest research, some of which is ongoing and, outside of this text, unpublished. We hope we have set the scene and answered some questions about the nature and role content, the dilemmas and difficulties, and the lack of opportunities in a growing profession. We raise many questions along the way and hope we contribute to answering some of the questions being discussed in what we believe is a very much under-recognised and exciting growing profession. Clearly, more research-based texts which can inform and contribute to the further growth of the profession are required.

Secure facilities to care for and treat a group of patients labelled as mentally disordered offenders are growing in number each year. Informal inquiries identify more than 60 units in the United Kingdom alone offering such provision, not including provision for those being treated within the prison service. No one knows the exact number of patients or units, as there is no official central register of units, patients or staff. Services, as we write, are expanding every week. As we have identified in this book, there are also many forensic and related units in other countries, all of which have forensic nurses.

There are considerable numbers of nurses as well as other professionals working with a large, sometimes difficult and challenging, group of patients and an emerging profession is without question developing. More importantly it is under-recognised and often acknowledged not as a profession but only as a sub-speciality. This is evidenced through the growing quantity of academic posts, research, publications, books and conferences and academic courses directed to develop nursing and other related professions' skills, not just within the United Kingdom but also on an international basis.

This book therefore examines the role of the emerging profession of the forensic nurse and explores some of the multi-professional boundaries. It is not an attempt to clearly define the role, but rather it describes some of the empirical content and discusses key contemporary issues which can inform not only nurses within the profession but also those in training and, equally important, other professionals who work with and alongside the forensic nurse.

At times we think the title forensic nurse is perhaps misleading and can be confused with more detailed forensic issues particularly discussed in the American chapter, and this indeed calls for some clarification. What we do believe, however, is that there is this evolving profession which demands often quite different and advanced skills from more traditional mental health workers – although these are fundamental and extremely important to the role. We also believe that this book will raise more issues than it will attempt to resolve. What we hope it will do most of all is to provide a first detailed account about some of the key issues in recognising an emerging profession. In addition it will help move forward the profession by informing those entering and those already in the profession as well as germinating ideas, thinking and further research on a national and international basis.

David Robinson and Alyson Kettles

CHAPTER 1

Educational Aspects of Forensic Nursing

Lawrence A. Whyte

There is a story that Handy (1995) tells about the road to Davy's Bar. He relates that whilst touring in the Republic of Ireland he was *en route* to a place called Davy's Bar. Those of you who are familiar with driving in Ireland may have had some experience of the confusion of the road signs. Handy found himself well and truly lost and being unsure of direction, decided to ask a local for advice. The local advised him of the direction and the route, but emphasised that he needed to turn off the main road before he reached a well-known landmark. It was only when he drove off, apparently confident of where he was going, that he realised a fundamental error. Not knowing the country at all, he had to idea where the well-known landmark was. Not knowing where the landmark was made it, therefore, impossible for him to know where to turn off before reaching it.

The moral of this story is that if you do not know where you are coming from you cannot have much idea about where you are going. This moral could equally apply to the sub-speciality of 'forensic nursing'. Trying to base informed judgement about the future direction of the educational and training needs of 'forensic' nurses can be little more than speculative until some clear estimate of the present position of 'forensic nursing' can be established through an empirical base, rather than a desire to be perceived as a specialist branch of nursing.

There are too many unanswered questions about the present position of 'forensic nursing' that need addressing. This chapter examines some of these unanswered questions. Three main issues will be addressed. First, the extent to which a clear and relatively unambiguous definition of 'forensic nursing' exists. Second, the extent to which 'forensic nursing' can differentiate itself from mainstream mental health nursing. Third, and fundamental to the debate, is the extent to which 'forensic nursing' is nursing at all, and how the nature of the relationship between the nurse and the patient in a 'forensic' setting may be different.

These three issues will form the basis of an examination of the present position of 'forensic nursing'. Having explored and examined these issues, the chapter will then attempt to make some speculative comments upon the future training and education needs of this group of nurses. It will be useful though to keep in mind the moral of Handy's story; concentrate primarily upon establishing where you are before making steps on your journey.

IS THERE SUCH A THING AS 'FORENSIC NURSING'?

In an earlier piece of work (Whyte 1997), it was argued that the emergence of a sub-specialism of mental health nursing, generally referred to as 'forensic nursing', was based upon a desire on behalf of 'forensic nurses' to be perceived as different and unique, rather than on any firm empirical basis. This argument was constituted on two main premises: first, that the term 'forensic' was being inappropriately applied and had been modified in its pure meaning to incorporate a wide variety of nurses working with the mentally disordered offender. That is to say that merely coming into contact with mentally disordered offenders somehow made your nursing work 'forensic' in nature. Second, that 'forensic nursing' can differentiate itself from other nursing. Strict definitional meaning of the term 'forensic' refers to 'belonging to courts of law ... loosely of or pertaining to scientists connected with legal investigation' (Onions 1977). Modified to incorporate 'forensic psychiatry', Pollack (1980) defines it as 'the application of psychiatry to evaluations for legal purposes. Psychiatric evaluation of the patient is directed primarily to legal issues in which he is involved and consultation is concerned primarily with the end of the legal system, justice, rather than the therapeutic objectives of the medical system.'

Several aspects of these two definitions are important in the debate about the existence of 'forensic nursing'. First, it is apparent within the definition that there is a relationship between the purpose of health interventions and criminal justice. That is to say, it is not merely contact with mentally disordered offenders that constitutes 'forensic-ness', but what you do with them. 'Forensic' work is primarily involved with the investigation and evaluation of a person's mental state to determine which system of care, criminal or health, most equitably and fairly meets an individual's needs. Second, the primary emphasis is to achieve justice within a broader system of equity. Health care services are therefore accountable, within a 'forensic' conceptualisation, to the criminal justice system.

What are the implications of these points to the present position of 'forensic nursing'? The first objective of 'forensic nursing' is to define itself. As Meleis (1991) suggests, defining helps to delineate the dimensions of a concept, clarifying any ambiguities within a concept and enabling a clearer and more precise definition of what that concept means. So, for example, in the case of 'forensic nursing', Lynch (1993, 1995b) offers a typology of 'forensic nursing' that suggests that 'forensic nursing' is more of an umbrella term for a wide range of nursing activity rather than a single conceptualisation.

From an American perspective, Lynch suggests that there are four different areas of 'forensic nursing' which each imply a special form of nursing work. 'Clinical forensic nursing' is involved with 'the application of clinical and scientific knowledge to questions of law and the criminal and civil investigation of survivors of traumatic injury and for patient treatment involving court related issues' (Lynch 1993). This is an area of nursing work that is much more developed in the USA and whilst there may be nurses working within the UK employed within the legal context, they may not wish to perceive themselves as being 'forensic nurses'.

Similarly, in relation to Lynch's typology the Sexual Assault Nurse Examiner (SANE) has not emerged within the UK context. This area of work is concerned with the clinical examination of sexually assaulted victims and the employment of therapeutic interventions to enable the process of healing, after the traumatic attack, to begin. Within the UK context this area of work has primarily emerged within the criminal justice system with specially trained police officers engaging with adult individuals who have been the victims of sexual assault, and working in partnership with medical interventions and investigation.

The forensic psychiatric nurse that Lynch (1993) refers to has commonalities with court diversion and liaison schemes that have developed within the last decade in the UK (Parry 1991; Kitchener 1996). This area of work involves the assessment of criminal defendants before court hearing. This assessment may be used by the police or the courts in deciding the most appropriate means by which an individual can be managed and fits most comfortably with the definitions of 'forensic' identified.

By far the largest area of 'forensic nursing' activity within the UK is what Lynch refers to as 'correctional/institutional nursing' where the nurse specialises in the care, treatment, rehabilitation and management of individuals who have either violated criminal law or been deemed to pose a high level of dangerousness to themselves or others. Nursing within these environments has a dual role in providing secure facilities and engaging in therapeutic nursing work. Within the UK correctional/institutional nursing is dominated by the four high security hospitals of Broadmoor, Carstairs, Ashworth and Rampton and by the system of regional and medium secure units. These are complemented, or confounded depending upon opinion, by hospital facilities in prisons to the extent that in 1992 NACRO estimated that there were an estimated 14,000 people in prison who should be in hospital, and less than 50 per cent of these needed to be in high security hospitals requiring maximum security (Marchant 1992).

Predominantly, it has been the assertion that it is nurses who work within these secure environments who constitute the majority of 'forensic nurses'

(Burrow 1993a; Tarbuck 1994a; Kinsella and Chaloner 1995). Whilst this may be the largest group of nurses working with the mentally disordered offender, it is the furthest away in conceptualisation from the original definitions of 'forensic' that were offered. That is to say, in relation to definition, it is difficult to sustain an argument that suggests that those who practise in correctional facilities can realistically refer to themselves as 'forensic nurses' unless they can clearly determine that they are predominately involved in the assessment and evaluation of clients that inform the decision-making process of the criminal justice system. Whilst some of their work may include this, such as assessment of people from prisons and courts, or crisis intervention, the vast majority of their work is with a relatively stable, long-term population.

Those nurses, therefore, that seem to be most assertive in the use of the term 'forensic nursing' are most likely to be those who are furthest away in definitional terms from a 'forensic' meaning. This would suggest that the first premise that the term 'forensic' was being applied inappropriately was strongly indicative of not supporting the existence of 'forensic nursing' other than in specifically located areas of practice such as court diversion or liaison schemes.

The second premise that argued against the emergence of 'forensic nursing' as an emerging sub-speciality argues that there has been little work that supports that 'forensic nursing' is substantially different from other forms of mainstream mental health nursing. According to Meleis (1991) differentiation refers to the process whereby the similarities and differences between a new concept and other similar ideas are identified. In the case of 'forensic nursing', therefore, if it were possible for 'forensic nurses' to empirically identify what distinguishes them from other mental health nurses, then the case for the emergence of the sub-specialism of 'forensic nursing' could be made.

An early attempt to differentiate between the knowledge and skills of the mental health nurse working in 'forensic' settings was undertaken in Canada by Niskala (1986). She was concerned with developing a curriculum from a research base, using both a workshop and survey approach. Through this process she was able to identify 13 main competencies thought by her sample of 'forensic nurses' to be the core skills required. These core skills were:

- maintaining security;
- communicating effectively;
- maintaining records;
- counselling;
- performing the nursing process;
- planning and participating in groups;
- planning and participating in programmes;

- administration;
- diagnostic and treatment procedures;
- maintaining the professional role;
- psychiatric nursing approaches;
- research skills; and
- ability to teach.

Of these 13 core skills, the most important were considered to be those of:

- maintaining security;
- communicating effectively;
- performing the nursing process; and
- maintaining the professional role.

Regarded as the least important were:

- ability to teach;
- administrative skills; and
- research skills.

Whilst Niskala should be complimented upon this systematic attempt to differentiate the knowledge and skills required by nurses working with 'forensic' areas, there is little here that would support differentiation. All of these skills might equally be applicable to mainstream mental health nursing in a residential setting. It fails to establish sufficient differentiation between the two related ideas. Similarly, Scales, Mitchell and Smith (1993) used a survey method to elicit the present position of 'forensic nursing' in 67 per cent of forensic facilities in the USA. Whilst providing a great deal of useful information on the employment, education and professional orientation of qualified nurses within 'forensic settings' there is little to indicate differentiation from mainstream mental health nursing other than a desire to be perceived differently. Thus:

> There is a palpable sense that forensic psychiatric nursing is unique, and as such would benefit from sharing strategies, successes, failures and quality initiatives in caring for dually stigmatised, mentally ill offenders. It is time to 'come out of the closet' and share the difficult, challenging and rewarding work we do with patients and for society. (Scales *et al.* 1993, p.43)

Hurst, Whyte and Robinson (1998) undertook a comprehensive review of nursing activity within one high secure hospital in the UK. By using a multiple method approach of patient dependency ratings, nursing quality measures and observed nursing activity, some interesting data emerged that was comparable to other data generated from a similar methodology for more mainstream mental health nursing settings. Based upon almost 7000 nursing assessments and observation of over 15,300 nursing activities over a four-week period across 15 wards, some evidence of the activities of 'forensic nurses' developed:

- Nurses within the high secure setting spend less time in face-to-face contact with patients than their peers on non-high secure settings (53% compared with 57%).

- They also spend less time in indirect care (patient-related but not face-to-face) care, 12 per cent compared with 16 per cent.

- These activities that delineate patient-related care from associated work and personal time show that in total those nurses in high secure settings spend about 65 per cent of their time in patient-related work as compared with 73 per cent of nurses in non-high secure settings.

- Conversely, nurses in high secure settings spend more time, 35 per cent as compared with 27 per cent, on associated tasks (two steps removed from patient care such as administration) and personal time than nurses in non-high secure settings.

- Encouragingly, the high secure nurses spend more time in therapeutic activity than their non-high secure peers (8% as compared with 6%).

- The higher the grade of the nurse (and therefore implicitly the more skilled), the more time they spend away from patient-related activity; and conversely the lower the grade the more time spent in patient-related activity – a trend that operates in most nursing environments.

Whilst the data from this study highlights some interesting areas of differences, there is nothing strikingly different that would suggest that 'forensic nursing' was radically different from its mainstream counterparts. In terms of attitudes to care, Kinsella and Chaloner (1995) attempted to test the assumption that 'forensic nurses' (defined as those working within one regional secure unit) were more custodial orientated in their work in comparison with staff working within other treatment settings. However, they conclude that there is no significant difference between the groups of staff in relation to attitudes to treatment.

The second premise, therefore, that it is possible to differentiate the work of the 'forensic nurse' from more mainstream mental health nursing, has not been supported by the evidence produced. What then of the third premise upon which the existence of 'forensic nursing' might be questioned? This relates not to changes in secure care generally, but to changes in more mainstream psychiatric and community provision. It is becoming increasingly more likely that mainstream mental health nurses are coming into contact with people with a criminal background and with challenging behaviour and for whom security is an issue. Security is a variable in most aspects of mental health nursing and the initial dilemma between being agents of control in a custodial role and agents of therapy, as has been argued by proponents of 'forensic nursing' (Burrow 1993a; Fisher

1995; Dhondea 1995), are as much an issue with most other forms of mental health nursing care (Reynolds and Cormack 1990; Whyte 1985).

Suffice to say that the existence of a sub-specialism known as 'forensic nursing' does not seem to be supported by evidence from research. The attempt by those nurses who have the desire to develop the sub-specialism has been impeded by a limited amount of empirical evidence to support their aspirations up to this point.

IT MAY BE FORENSIC, BUT IS IT NURSING?

Whilst the arguments presented in the preceding section may be criticised for their semantic limitations, a more fundamental question that needs to be addressed, particularly in secure settings, is the extent to which this activity constitutes nursing. Traditionally, nursing theory has been centred around core elements or meta-paradigms associated with (Fawcett 1989):

- personhood;
- health;
- environment; and
- the purpose of nursing.

Nursing models, for example, will generally make implicit or explicit statements about each of these meta-paradigms. There are attempts to describe and explain nursing practice (Aggleton and Chalmers 1986). The crucial point is, therefore, to what extent it is possible to explain and describe the practice of correctional/institutional nursing within the framework of these meta-paradigms and establish it as nursing.

Five major points will be explored. These are:

- the underlying principles on which the nurse–patient relationship is based;
- the purity of the nurse–patient relationship within the confines of the criminal justice system;
- the nature of nursing interventions employed for criminogenic behaviour and their relationship to concepts of health;
- the classification of some problem populations as a health problem; and
- environmental factors within secure settings that militate or facilitate therapeutic conditions for health.

The central premise is that if it is difficult to locate these issues from forensic correctional/institutional nursing within existing nursing theory, then it may be difficult to sustain the notion that forensic correctional/institutional nursing is nursing as it is known.

The underlying principles on which the nurse–patient relationship is based

Central to the theory and practice of nursing is the importance of the nurse–patient relationship. For example, Peplau (1952) uses terms such as 'a significant therapeutic process' to describe the relationship. King (1971) suggests 'purposeful interaction with clients mutually to establish goals and to agree means of meeting goals'. Roper, Logan and Tiernay (1996) point out that 'each person is in the health care system for a purpose, seeking help with health problems, actual or potential'.

Such notions of nurse–patient relationships are located within a broader conceptualisation of the relationship being based upon co-operation between the parties, collaboration in planning and patient and nurse compliance to participate in the process of getting better. As such they tend to draw upon the concept of the 'sick-role' developed by Parsons (1951). Within this concept ill-health is perceived as an undesirable state in which the individual sufferer will be motivated to get well through seeking competent help.

Topologies of helping relationships in health tend to draw upon this concept, such as that developed by Szasz and Hollander (1956). They suggested that the relationship between helper and helpee in health fell into three broad types, with each type of relationship being regarded as being influenced by the patient's illness or health state.

The first type of relationship they identified is referred to as the activity–passivity model. This is generally found in circumstances where the patient is in a state of helplessness in which they are the passive recipient of the helper's expertise, having little or no participation in the negotiation of care or its implementation. The helper as the 'active' agent determines the level of care required and effectively does for the patient those activities that are necessary to sustain and restore functioning. Examples are the unconscious patient or the severely withdrawn depressed person.

The second type of relationship is the guidance–co-operative model, where the helper offers guidance and advice to the patient, with the patient co-operating in being accepting of these interventions. For example, in the care and management of phobic states there might be structured activities that the nurse suggests that the patient co-operatively agrees to, trusting the judgement and expertise of the nurse.

The third type of relationship is the mutual–participation model in which the helper enables the helpee to help themselves, but acts as a guide on the path to wellness or well-being. Predominately, counselling relationships would be an example of this type of model.

Reflections of this model are used to underpin most nursing models which generally have variables such as dependence–independence (Roper *et al.* 1996), co-operation and independence (Peplau 1952). Whilst it would be possible for nurses working in secure settings to encounter each of these types of relationship, they are also likely to encounter relationships of non-compliance and non-co-operation. That is to say, a fourth type of model may operate in secure settings where there is conflict between the wants and needs of the patient and the duties and responsibilities of the nurse. The dilemma of custodian and therapist that several authors have identified (Burrow 1993a; Fisher 1995; Dhondea 1995) is an example of this potential conflictual relationship that nurses working in correctional settings may encounter as part of their everyday work.

Patients admitted to secure settings may feel that they do not require treatment, they are not ill, they would be better off in prison or that they have a differing set of rationales for engaging in the types of behaviour which may have prompted their admission. How nurses in secure settings cope with, deal with, manage and change such perceptions is rich and fertile ground for developing a knowledge base and set of skills that is unique in the world of nursing. A challenge lies here.

The purity of the nurse–patient relationship

Whilst most nursing models and theorists emphasise the centrality of the nurse–patient relationship in nursing, they do not cite the fact that this particular relationship occurs within a network of other therapeutic and social relationships such as doctor–patient, patient–patient, nurse–nurse, psychologist–patient, etc. In a sense there is no nurse–patient relationship that remains pure, that is not affected or influenced by the wider professional and social relationships that both parties are involved with. A major compounding relationship within secure settings is likely to be the relationship between the patient and the criminal justice system (Gunn and Taylor 1993). That is to say, the patient's therapeutic progress may be subject to controls other than those found in a more conventional health care relationship. At some stage within the therapeutic process the patient may have attained a state of wellness compatible with movement to a less secure environment. However, the existence of mental health or criminal justice legislation may prevent this progression occurring. How 'forensic nursing' manages to negotiate and manage the therapeutic relationship within the confines of this powerful external control of the criminal justice system is a further area of potential differentiation that sets it apart from mainstream mental health nursing. Within conventional nursing theory, termination of the nurse–patient relationship occurs at wellness, independent functioning or maturity.

The nature of nursing interventions employed for criminogenic behaviour

Crucial to an understanding of nursing theory, and explicit in nursing models, is a conceptualisation of health or wellness as major forms within health care. Leading on from the last section, it is possible for a patient within secure settings to achieve wellness or health in the conventional sense of being free of symptoms. That is, conventional psychiatric treatments and therapeutic processes may stabilise or minimise a person's symptomology. But, by virtue of their possible criminal activity whilst ill, there may be other risk factors about future behaviour that may inhibit or prevent movement away from a secure setting or discharge from the criminal justice system. This may call into question whether nurses working in secure settings should involve themselves in programmes that seek to address index offences such as arson, assault, murder and sexual offending. Whilst psychiatric symptomology may have been contributory factors within the index offence or as a result of recognition of the index offence, such as guilt and remorse, the central question is whether intervening in programmes for these offences constitutes a health issue. That is, are 'forensic nurses' clear about their role in relation to index offences, or do these sometimes fall outside a health concept? A clearer exploration of the relationship between index offence work and nursing work needs to be undertaken to integrate these areas of practice within nursing knowledge.

The classification of some problem populations as a health problem

It is estimated that 25 per cent of the high secure hospital population is detained under the legal category of psychopathic disorder (SHSA 1995). 'Psychopathic disorder' is a legal classification under the 1983 Mental Health Act that is clinically used to embrace a number of personality disorders. This group of patients does not form a homogeneous group, with individual patients showing considerable clinical complexity and often having one or more additional diagnoses. There remains considerable debate with psychiatry about the aetiology, the scientific basis for the concept, its epidemiology, its diagnosis and the potential for effective treatment. There is also considerable debate about treatability (Dolan and Coid 1993). The discussions and debates about whether personality disorder or psychopathic disorder constitute a health or social issue will be decided by people other than nurses. However, the prevalence and referral rates of people with personality disorders is increasing within secure hospitals and units and it is nurses who are being asked to manage the care and treatment on a day-to-day basis. How far such disorders can be incorporated within existing nursing theory has been relatively unexplored. Certainly, the emphasis within theorists such as Peplau (1952) upon developmental psychology, interpersonal communication and the movement towards maturity may be useful starting points to inform nursing practice.

Environmental factors within secure settings that militate or facilitate therapeutic conditions for health

The extent to which treatment and care is inhibited or promoted by a secure environment has been relatively unexplored. Topping-Morris (1992) argues that treatment provided in secure settings is classically delivered by a powerful institution to a powerless patient. Dale (1995) contends, however, that it is the role of nursing, especially in controlled environments, to establish therapeutic alliances that attempt to redress power imbalances. Tarbuck (1994a) challenges nursing by contending that they tend to take a security world view of their work, where security overrides all else and the individual patient feels displaced or disempowered. A lack of focus upon nursing meta-paradigms would be one way for nurses to address this, he maintains. Whatever the view, the environment plays a major part in the care and management of patients in secure settings.

Fundamental to its importance are the dilemmas that are purported to be experienced by nurses in their custodial versus therapeutic roles. A central question for the development of 'forensic nursing' must be about the extent to which nurses can act within these two conflicting roles. Earlier arguments about the definition of 'forensic' health care were that it is to serve the ends of the criminal justice system. Is it therefore contentious to contend that the primary role of those who work within the secure environments is the maintenance of security and the protection of the public? If this is not contentious, the question should then be whether or not nurses are best employed in a security capacity or whether this is better left to other groups. Within correctional/institutional facilities within the USA, for example, there is a clear division of responsibility between security staff who manage security and nursing staff who have responsibility for the quality of the environment, advocacy and therapeutic engagement (Scales et al. 1993). The therapy versus custody dilemma has been created by the curiously developed hybrid system of employing health educated and trained staff to act in a capacity which holds too many dilemmas between their socialisation as health professionals and their everyday work as security personnel. Both aspects of the work are important, but are we justified in placing nurses in the position of carrying out both roles? Part of the frustration that emanates from nurses working within secure environments is the cognitive dissonance that they experience between what they have been socialised to believe and the practical everyday nature of their work as custodians.

Little wonder, then, that authors such as McDougall (1997) contend that the concept of partnership, collaboration and power-sharing, so implicit in nursing theory and emphasised within nurse–patient therapeutic relationship, is an idealistic principle within secure environments that is rarely translated into practice. Rather, the normative form of nurse–patient relationship involves an imbalance of power around issues of control and compliance, with nurses colluding in schemes of care and coercing patients to participate in allegedly therapeutic activities with little focus upon health outcome.

SPECULATING ABOUT THE FUTURE

What has been argued in this chapter is that there are too many unanswered questions about 'forensic' health care and nursing. This leaves unaddressed answers as to whether the role of the nurse is based upon nursing knowledge or informed by emerging practice. Rather than focusing upon the professional development of a role that, if established, is established on tenuous principles, nurses working within secure environments might be best served by 'going back to the basics of nursing work'. An absence of good clear nursing case studies is a major inhibitor to preventing practice development. These might serve to inform and influence debate and discussion about the nature of nursing within secure settings.

Furthermore, more extensive research, at a national level, into the role of the nurse working in secure environments might be a useful starting point to establish the diversity and similarities in practice. As Lynch (1993, 1995b) identifies from the American experience, there is much more diversity within forensic nursing that we may be failing to identify.

Clearly, the patient groups that are entering secure facilities are diverse and often with complex needs. There is little homogeneity within mentally disordered offenders and the complexity of history and multiple diagnosis would suggest that nurses working within secure environments would need more defined and comprehensive assessment skills to elicit information from the patient, and more knowledge about the wide variety of agencies that the patient is likely to have encountered prior to their admission to secure facilities.

The relationship between the criminal justice system and the health care system, plus the relationship between secure care and the wider NHS, needs to be more fully understood. This is not just in relation to the legislative acts and public policy, but also the ethical and moral dilemmas that nurses and patients may experience as a result of them.

The greatest challenge for the population group is that of care and management of people with personality disorders. The irony is that as a patient group they are increasing, yet in terms of education and training programmes there is the least provision.

Above all, and very much from a personal perspective, the future education and training of nurses working in secure settings will focus upon a rediscovery and return to some of the underlying principles and theories that underpin nursing practice and a re-emphasis upon the centrality of the nurse–patient relationship from a nursing perspective. The challenge I throw down to nurses wishing to be perceived as 'forensic' in speciality is to provide me and your peers with good case study material and empirical research evidence to support your assertions. As Handy (1995) suggests: 'Know where you are coming from before you know where you are going to.'

CHAPTER 2

Overview and Contemporary Issues in the Role of the Forensic Nurse in the UK

Alyson M. Kettles and
David K. Robinson

THE MENTALLY DISORDERED OFFENDER

Before we move onto the forensic nursing role it is important to briefly set the scene in relation to the patients, since this dictates the existence of the forensic nurse.

It is widely recognised that the provision of nursing care within secure environments requires staff with considerable expertise (Reed 1994). Such units or hospitals are uniquely different from mainstream mental health in that they care and treat men and women who are compulsorily detained under the 1983 Mental Health Act. The bottom line for being detained under this Act is the propensity for violence to oneself or others whilst suffering from a mental illness. Termed as mentally disordered offenders (MDOs), this patient group receives care and treatment in a range of secure and non-secure facilities from high through to medium and low secure units until they are deemed well enough to be integrated back into less secure or community settings. Some may be transferred back to prison. Within these wide and varied settings has emerged a new professional role for mental health and learning disability nurses who are developing a vast range of advanced skills and competencies whilst working for this challenging group of patients.

A number of authors have attempted to give a definition of the mentally disordered offender and there is much disagreement about this (e.g. James 1996; Peay 1996; Bailey 1996; Berkely 1995). The National Association for the Care and Resettlement of Offenders do, however, offer a broad definition: '...those offenders who may be acutely or chronically mentally ill; those with neuroses, behavioural and/or personality disorders; learning disabilities; alcohol and substance misusers and sex offenders' (NACRO 1993).

It is, however, clear that two requirements must be met: (a) the person must be deemed to have presented offending behaviour; and (b) the person must be deemed to be mentally disordered. Badger *et al.* (1998) state that for a person to be considered as presenting offending behaviour at least one of three criteria must be met: (i) the person has been convicted of a specified criminal offence; (ii) the person has been charged with a specified criminal offence; and (iii) the person's behaviour has involved either violence towards others, or arson. He goes on to state that of the three criteria the third is the most arbitrary.

What is clear with this group of patients is that they present a danger to themselves or to the general public. The National Health Service Act 1977 (section 4) requires the Secretary of State to provide a special hospital service for detained mentally disordered patients 'who in his opinion require treatment under conditions of special security on account of their dangerous, violent or criminal propensities'. The role of the nurse in these conditions of security is to provide, co-ordinate and integrate care of the highest standards with regard for individual rights, available resources and needs. This is often a difficult task, continually juggling the intricate balance of therapy with security.

Different levels of security exist. Mentally disordered offenders are within the prison system, the special hospitals (Ashworth, Broadmoor, Rampton and Carstairs State Hospital) offering maximum security, through to more than 60 units dealing with medium and low secure facilities as well as community homes and units.

Patients within secure facilities have at some stage had major difficulties, which make co-existing with others sometimes extremely problematic. Some exhibit specific behavioural problems, including self-mutilation, verbal and physical aggression and refusal to form therapeutic relationships. Offences include paedophilia, arson, manslaughter, attempted murder, wounding, assault, rape, indecent assault and robbery. Therapy is often sabotaged by avoidance techniques employed by patients who do not see the need for it and/or are unable to co-operate with it. Forming therapeutic relationships can be further hindered as some may be damaged, especially women, to the extent that they are unable to have confidence in others. Many of the women have been the victims of physical, emotional and sexual abuse.

IS THERE SUCH A PERSON AS A FORENSIC NURSE?

There has been little written on the nature and role of the 'forensic nurse', that is, nurses working with the mentally disordered offender. Whilst some texts and chapters exist, these are merely speculative accounts which tend to lack any empirical basis. Furthermore, nurses often write these texts with little reference to cross-cultural issues and the contribution of nurses within the multi-professional team.

Forensic care and especially high secure services have been crisis-led, going from one political investigation to another with little vision and a decided lack of social policy. Such a lack of policy has restricted the growth of the profession with only general models being applied, which are often difficult to adopt with the needs of this special client group. The complexity of this client group is represented by staff who work in a variety of care settings, including the prison service, high, medium and low secure areas and the community.

There are currently more than 60 forensic units throughout the UK alone, with many more secure services attached to prison services. Every country, particularly the North American continent (Canada and the USA), Australia, the Netherlands and Germany, has its own forensic units that deal with people who suffer from a wide range of mental health problems and who present a danger to themselves or others.

There are several components which comprise the role of the forensic nurse and which are under examination here. The nature of the role itself is of primary importance, but as role underpins function this cannot be examined without recourse to the education and training which forensic nurses require in order to be fit to practise. In addition to this, the contribution to the multi-professional team and the dilemmas they face must also be addressed as a part of the examination of the overall role. The outcome of examining role is that it enables forensic nursing staff to be clear about the particular competencies related to their area of practice.

Few empirical studies into the role of the forensic nurse have been conducted and those which have been tend to use questionnaire methodology or survey design (Phillips 1983; Niskala 1986, 1987; Kitchener and Rogers 1992; Kitchener et al. 1992a; Scales et al. 1993).

Whilst conflict of role exists, what does appear to be happening is that the work of mental health nurses is being increasingly influenced by the forensic or legal aspect of mental health care. Role can be defined as 'actor's part; one's function, what a person or thing is appointed or expected to do' and role playing as 'behaving in accordance with specified function' (Sykes 1988). If we examine these definitions then we can see that the specified function does not exist, as it has never been defined through the use of the application of competencies to forensic nursing as either a specialty in its own right or as a form of advanced practice.

If the role of the forensic nurse is not clear, this leads to the question of how forensic nursing is affected by the education and training directed towards producing a nurse who is fit to practise in this complex area. None of these roles have been addressed, in the literature, in relation to training, education or subsequent career pathways.

Competence, or fitness to practise, in mental health nursing has been addressed over recent years with educational reviews (Runciman 1990; Sharp *et al.* 1995) and reports (Carlisle, Kirk and Luker 1996; McAleer and Hamill 1997; National Board for Nursing, Midwifery and Health Visiting for Scotland (1998)), but these are related to basic nurse education. What have not been discussed are the competencies related to post-basic or advanced practice such as forensic nursing.

Other disciplines, such as psychology and psychiatry, have unmistakeable postgraduate education and career pathways to specialise in forensic care. However, for forensic nurse education this kind of clear pathway is not evident. There are elective programmes at post-basic level and in the Diploma programmes, but any such inclusion of specialist modules can at best only introduce the student to the area and at worst skim the surface. This does not prepare the student adequately to work in such an area.

Post-registration courses, such as the Diploma in the Care of the Mentally Disordered Offender and the Diploma in Forensic Health Care, address some of the issues within forensic care such as: social policy for the mentally disordered offender; crime and mental disorder; forensic care delivery; assessing risk; and include issues such as ethnicity, empowerment, power, control, and anger management. However, they only address issues in terms of either top-up training or in terms of multi-professional care, rather than in the context of forensic nursing care as a speciality in its own right which offers pre-registration training resulting in career pathways into the profession.

As a result of this confusion, lack of direction, vision and career pathways for forensic nursing, it was considered essential to conduct an empirical study, which would assist in clarifying the situation. The following describes the funded study the authors conducted to attempt to clarify the predicament (Kettles and Robinson 1998).

A STUDY INTO ISSUES OF FORENSIC NURSING

Aims of the study

There were several aims of the study:

1. To describe the nature and content of forensic nursing.

2. To identify the subtle differences between fundamental mental health nursing and the advanced practice of specialist care, i.e. forensic nursing.

3. To find out how staff in forensic nursing were prepared for the role they now play.

4. To find out what training and education forensic nurses believe that they need in order to carry out their role.

5. To identify how forensic nursing differentiates from and contributes to multi-professional care.

Methodology

The study was conducted in ten study sites in Scotland and England. These units offer distinct discrete differences in education, legal provision and health care. The sample consisted of mainly nurses with the input from some multi-professionals (n = 72). Characteristics of the sample are shown in Table 2.1.

Table 2.1 The characteristics of the sample population (n = 72)

	Men	Women	RMN	EN	Unqualified	OT	Psychologist	Diploma/Project 2000 qualified RMN
Scotland	14	14	19	2	4	2	1	4
England	34	10	43	0	0	1	0	9 (3 students)
TOTAL	48	24	62	2	4	3	1	13

A focus group approach was taken in order to elicit qualitative data. Eight questions were asked as outlined in Figure 2.1. Data analysis was conducted through qualitative thematic analysis.

1. Is there such a person as a forensic nurse?

2. What makes a forensic nurse different from a mental health nurse?

3. What are the key characteristics of the forensic nursing role for:

   (a) qualified nurses?

   (b) nursing assistants?

4. What sort of training/preparation have you had that enables you to work with mentally disordered patients?

5. What sort of training is required?

6. What are the dilemmas facing you when caring for and treating the mentally disordered offender?

7. How does the forensic nurse differ from other disciplines?

8. What do forensic nurses contribute to the multi-professional team?

Figure 2.1 The eight questions asked in the study

Findings

Despite the potential for discrete differences in health care, legal provision and education between the two countries there were few differences in the responses to the questions. Unless stated otherwise, the responses given are representative of all groups.

Is there such a person as a forensic nurse?

Responses are shown in Figure 2.2. The forensic nursing role was viewed as qualitatively different from that of the mental health nurse due to factors such as the complex nature of the client group being offenders and the secure environment. There are several issues related to this, such as seeing themselves not only as mental health nurses but as 'more so' because the level of clinical skill has to be more advanced because the client group is often different and more complex.

	Scotland	England
Yes	28	38
No	0	5
Unsure	0	1
Total	28	44

Figure 2.2 Responses to the question: 'Is there such a person as a forensic nurse?'

Staff indicated that they are being asked to become more expert without training and education. They think that there is a forensic nurse 'in as much as there is any other kind of nurse' such as an acute mental health nurse or an elderly care nurse. Nursing staff see themselves as being at the interface between mental health nursing and criminology, as if it is a balancing act between therapy and custody. They see themselves as pivotal in relation to links with the courts and the judicial system, evidence, assessment and other professionals.

Judicial issues are a strong component of being a forensic nurse and this was shown both in the implicit use of terms such as 'index offence' and 'offenders' as well as explicitly, for example 'forensic means the legal system'. The term 'more sophisticated' was used about how relationships are different and in terms of the balance between safety/security and therapy.

Adaptation in terms of personal qualities and application of self to the client group is involved, because the client group is more demanding than other groups. In-depth knowledge of offenders is part of the role and as a consequence the thinking of the staff is different. They were also aware of the perceptions of others about the nature of the client group (they are seen as more extreme) in terms of both the person and the offence, and of others' lack of understanding of the role: nurses acting as jailers holding keys and wearing types of clothes which are perceived as 'the uniform of forensic nursing', i.e. trousers and boots.

What makes a forensic nurse different from a mental health nurse?

This elicited a very specific response about forensic nurses being 'more so'. The term 'more' was used in relation to fifteen items, such as: more backup; more aware of the patient's potential; dealing with more violence; more complex; cope with more; and more team-based. These examples were given separately but the key here is the word 'more' in relation to the way the client group is viewed.

The client group, the nature of the index offence, the potential of the clients to commit heinous offences, their history and the complexity of the person were all seen to make forensic nursing different. Additionally to this, staff feel they need to be more stable to cope with the demands and stresses of both the client group and the environment. They need to be 'stronger people'. The environment is controlled, custodial, secure, safe and provides protection of the public.

Core skills are those of the mental health nurse but the skills of the forensic nurse are differentiated by the type of environment from high security to community forensic nursing. An example of this is that mental health nurses do not anticipate risk in the same way. Some of the staff see a narrow band of skills that are particular to forensic nursing, such as being more assertive, more confronting and more challenging. They also believe that the balance between security and therapy is not always even.

What is interesting is that they see that forensic services are well funded generally and act in a much more multidisciplinary way.

What are the key characteristics of the forensic nursing role in relation to groups of staff?

For qualified staff the responses are based on mainly personal qualities which have been described rather than competency-based outcomes or structure. For example, personal qualities such as honesty, maturity, nerve, awareness, reliability and common sense were seen as the basic material of a forensic nurse.

Process issues were also described, such as restrictions/security/prevention of self-harm, dangerousness, continuous assessment, risk/risk-taking, legalities and implementation.

However, qualified staff were thought to require much more than unqualified staff in being able to handle and take on responsibility and decision-making, especially split-second decision-making in risky situations. Also, that other professionals rely on nurses for knowledge, security, safety, assessment and focus. There is also a greater focus on clinical issues, with the capacity to assimilate, to process ideas and to be eclectic.

Unqualified staff were also thought to need personal qualities and these were viewed as the most important thing an unqualified member of staff could bring to forensic nursing. Their degree of mature self-awareness was perceived as valuable by staff. They were seen as being given more responsibility than in other areas but were not thought to be adequately rewarded, recognised or trained for it.

Qualified staff state that they depend heavily on the unqualified staff and that they have a vital role to play.

However, one group of respondents saw unqualified staff as only following procedures and orders, with little or no initiative involved; while all other groups valued their contribution and saw them as having more independence and being able to challenge.

What sort of training/preparation have you had for the role?

Nurses indicated that training and education is patchy and poorly done. Staff in the sample say they have received little or no formal training with even the basic, such as control and restraint, being inconsistent, in that not everyone does the course and not everyone who does the course does both parts. Project 2000/Diploma courses give only a passing mention to forensic nursing and placements are generally elective so not everyone experiences the area. People do not get exposure unless they are already interested. There is a perceived negative attitude from education.

In the special hospitals it was felt that in-service education was done on the job and that you learn as you go along. Staff recognise that there are courses but there are few places and there are few opportunities (especially in Scotland). The resource issue needs to be urgently addressed. Tutors with forensic experience were seen as being outside the hospitals in the higher and further education establishments. Informal training and education was also patchy with a variety of in-service or on-the-ward training ranging from very short periods of time, e.g. half an hour, to six-week induction courses. Although there are increasing numbers of Diploma and some Master's courses in forensic care, these are at post-registration level.

Medical forensic education and nursing forensic education were viewed as worlds apart with the medical education being seen as far superior to that received by nurses.

What sort of training is required?

Here a considerable list was generated. Much of it has been identified elsewhere in the literature, such as specific issues in forensic nursing: e.g. sexually inappropriate behaviour and how to deal with it; women's issues; rehabilitation models of care; the THORN Psychosocial Nursing Programme and its relationship to forensic care; inter-agency working; personality disorder and related offending behaviour.

However, some had not been previously identified in the literature and it is in this area where 'chronic crises' are identified by staff that the issue of advanced competencies needs to be addressed. For example, staff require more knowledge and information about: the prison sub-culture; contacts with the Prison Service;

legalities such as the Criminal Procedures Act and homicide inquiries; danger-ousness; manipulation and how to deal with it.

There were a few surprising items that staff felt they required and which are not usually part of forensic courses, either nursing specific or multidisciplinary. Examples include cost restriction and the issues around replacement costs; crisis intervention; the need for direction in relation to skills and their use; and the need to educate other professionals about nursing. Perhaps the most surprising answer came from only one unit, that of 'literacy'.

What are the dilemmas facing you?

In forensic care, dilemmas are seen as being greater in scope than in other areas of mental health nursing. Three categories were generated with several subgroups in each. The first category is that of legal/judicial dilemmas with two subgroups. Legal/Home Office/judicial dilemmas relate to the balance between the patient's rights versus society, or patient detention; for example, when a patient commits or attempts to commit suicide whilst in the forensic care and waiting to go to court. Consequence dilemmas relate to the decisions made and the question of 'What happens when I …?' This is about living with the consequences of split-second decisions, such as the decision to restrain a patient. Hostile or aggressive behaviour is seen as the foundation for much of this type of dilemma.

The second category of dilemmas is that of interpersonal/professional dilemmas, with four subgroups. Internal resources dilemmas relate to the internal functioning of the staff, such as 'giving unconditional positive regard,despite the index offence' and 'having to leave morals at the door'. By this we mean, how do you care for and treat someone who has committed a horrendous crime and can you develop caring relationships when the non-professional side of you may be saying that this person should be locked away, not treated? This also relates to the ways in which they see themselves coping: 'It's a sign of weakness if you can't' and 'Staff have to work harder to see the patient underneath.' This can clearly lead to stress issues, which we cover later.

Some dilemmas are about things staff feel they can do nothing about but which they are required to do, for example: 'gut reaction versus consensus decisions' or 'locking people up' in seclusion.

Treatment dilemmas relate to specific issues such as: refusal of treatment by patients; restraint; oral medication versus intra-muscular medication (this item related very much to the staff in medium secure facilities); 'forcing' treatment on people who do not want it; treatment of paedophiles and use of the Penile Plethysmograph (PPG) machine.

Dilemmas related to working with other professionals were mentioned, particularly doctors and psychologists coming in to the clinical area and leaving the nursing staff to pick up the pieces after that professional has left. Nurses want to be 'up front' about issues with patients but are often told not to by the other professionals so that when the patient is finally told this causes problems.

The third category of dilemmas is a miscellaneous category with a variety of issues such as patients presenting differently to different disciplines, often manipulating staff, particularly against each other, and the inconsistent labelling of patients.

How does the forensic nurse differ from other disciplines?

Nurses felt that they are the core of the clinical team, providing the link between all other disciplines. They undertake the provision of care to this complex and challenging group of patients 24 hours a day, 365 days per year and in some ways they 'endure the intensity of the ward which other disciplines do not'. They can provide a first-hand holistic view of the patient and feel that their day-to-day interactions with the patient are particularly important when dealing with severe behavioural and risk-related issues.

Forensic nurses also pick up the pieces when other professionals give patients bad news, possibly results of discharge reviews.

They juggle the roles of therapist and gatekeeper. Other professionals are only responsible for their own safety whereas the nurses are responsible for everybody. This is a particularly important issue when protecting patients, staff and public whilst trying to maintain the optimum therapeutic environment. They feel they have the ability to manage the environment and that they require a particular brand of detachment in order not to overreact, i.e. a calmness which allows them to be in control but not over-controlling.

Often nurses believe that they have least status in the clinical team, which is reflected in the pay, as well as less autonomy than other professions. They often feel ruled by the medical model and that they have to live with the decisions of others.

What do forensic nurses contribute to the multi-professional team?

There were two groups of responses. The first was decidedly positive about their contribution and impact. It ranged from single-word descriptions, such as opinion, ideas, truth, realism, and counselling, to more detailed phrases such as the provision of 'balance – a balanced view; a pragmatic view' and 'holistic view of the individual and ward/collective impact'. They see themselves providing 'a link between disciplines, which is a pivotal role and is central to communication'. As well as being co-ordinators of care, they provide support for the patient, simple language, therapeutic activity and education about nursing for other professionals. For example, 'some didn't know that nurses work to a Code of Conduct'.

However, the second group of responses related to the ways in which nurses had difficulty in contributing to the team. They see themselves as needing professional credibility as specialist nurses. This is illustrated in the way that being listened to varies so much. They feel they contribute to the team but have the least influence and that it 'is not an exchange of equals as nursing staff are manipulated by other professions'. They feel that they are still seen as 'handmaidens'. Each profession has different agendas and different views on the roles of the units so that the need for consensus can only be addressed through education of all concerned. Nurses are more willing to take risks than the other professions yet some staff still feel under-used.

DISCUSSION

Role underpins competence to practice. It is role that enables us to examine the difference between basic competence as described in three-year RMN courses and the advanced practice of the forensic nurse.

What runs through every part of this study is the lack of any clear education and career pathway either into or within forensic nursing. Yet every nurse and the other professionals who took part in this study could identify the ways in which the other professions have identified routes if they wish to specialise in forensic care. Nurses on the other hand have to rely on very basic 'competencies' as the jump-off point to self-education in forensic nursing.

Competencies at basic level tend to make general statements such as the student shall 'demonstrate knowledge and understanding to meet the requirements of legislation which is relevant to his or her professional practice'. It is that which is taken to mean that students will, at the end of three years, understand and know about the Mental Health Act (Scotland or England as appropriate) or the Nurses, Midwives and Health Visitors Act. However, the forensic staff clearly identified other issues not addressed at basic level. These included a working knowledge of the Criminal Procedures Act and Homicide Inquiries. Homicide Inquiries are not legislation in themselves but are legal procedures which are not covered, either at basic or advanced level.

Competencies related to dilemmas always ask students to have knowledge and understanding of dilemmas. However, the forensic staff wanted to take this much further and to be competent in relation to management of the many dilemmas they saw themselves facing on a daily basis.

Other issues were seen as more complex and sophisticated than those at basic level. For example, in the *Pulling Together* (Sainsbury Centre for Mental Health 1997) document it clearly states that mental health nurses should have as a competency 'knowledge and skill in effective inter-personal communication' yet the forensic staff saw themselves as having to be 'more so' than mental health nurses. This related particularly to skills such as challenging, dealing with manipulation, dangerousness, confronting and confrontational aspects of care and attitudinal work with both patients and staff.

It is interesting to note here that staff did feel they could handle manipulation by patients but not manipulation by other professionals. Maybe this is related to the power gradient in forensic care and the rule of the medical model, which they see themselves as unable to break away from. The power gradient is where the power between nurses and patients is unequal with nurses holding the power to lock up and direct patients at all times of the day and night. The power between professionals is also unequal with doctors at the top of the heap and others at varying points on the gradient.

In relation to qualified staff the responses tended to bear out some of Glen's (1996) ideas that competence is based on personal qualities and that those qualities are used differently to the personal qualities of the unqualified staff. Glen (1996) views nursing as being underpinned by different powers and capacities with the implication that there are four stages of professional development which range from the minimally acceptable level of competence to excellence.

The four stages lead from 'nursing as labour' at the basic level of competence. This is the capacity to follow and correctly apply a programme of rules and procedures which are the source of competence. Then the second stage is 'nursing as craft' where a nurse requires a repertoire of specialised techniques and knowledge, including a knowledge of how to use these skills. The third stage of 'nursing as profession' requires not only the repertoire of skills but also the exercise of judgement about where the skills should be applied. The source of competence here resides in the nurse's own capacity to control his/her own performances which are regulated by conscious decisions and action plans.

The fourth stage, 'nursing as art', is where the nurse reaches excellence through reflective practice and is at his/her most competent. The techniques and procedures of nursing are personalised because the nursing situation is seen as unpredictable and needs frequent departure from usual techniques; these are expressions of the personality and personal insight of the individual nurse. In this context, competence involves the development of emotional and motivational states, which are appropriate to the nursing task.

It is interesting to note here that some forensic nurses saw 'adaptation, in terms of personal qualities and application of self to the client group' as fundamental to the role. Hence personal qualities, in Glen's view, can justifiably be viewed as a fundamental source of nursing competence.

It must be asked here which stage forensic nursing is at. Has it reached the stage of becoming 'nursing as profession' with its repertoire of skills and the exercise of judgement about where those skills should be applied or is it still at 'nursing as craft' where the source of competence resides in the capacity for processing contextual and situational information as a basis for performances?

This idea of advanced competence is not addressed in the education or training which is available. Indeed, staff were particularly critical of the way in which current education is carried out. They feel that it is patchy and poorly done, unlike medical and psychology forensic courses. Staff were able to identify deficits in training and education. They also knew where courses were but identified the resource issue as a limitation (especially in Scotland).

CONCLUSION

It is becoming clear how staff see themselves differentiating from other professions and contributing to the multi-professional team. It seems, from this study at least, that forensic nurses are a reality rather than a myth, and that what they now require includes: a clear career pathway; clearly defined competencies relating to the care and treatment of the mentally disordered offender; and education and practical training linked in to pre-registration programmes into forensic nursing and an in-depth, comprehensive account of who they are, what their roles are and what direction forensic nursing is taking.

ACKNOWLEDGEMENTS

The authors would like to thank the Mental Health Divisional Research and Audit Steering Group of Grampian Healthcare NHS Trust for their support and for funding this work. We would also like to express our thanks to all those who participated in the study.

CHAPTER 3

The Practitioner New to the Role of Forensic Psychiatric Nurse in the UK

Mick Collins

INTRODUCTION

Registered psychiatric nurses care for patients who suffer from a mental disorder under differing conditions of security. This is a fact. These people have become collectively known as forensic nurses. The purpose of this chapter is to introduce the elements of the forensic psychiatric nursing role. It is applicable to those who are considering a career in the area or are about to take up a new post. Both newly qualified and experienced psychiatric nurses are included. Gaining some basic 'hands on' knowledge offers the potential for a more informed choice about what could be a long-term career decision. This is also an 'experiential chapter'. It concentrates on the experience of the author and other professionals working in the field of high security forensic psychiatric care. The text that follows represents a selection of the often taken-for-granted issues (for those that nurse in a high security environment) that present as different from nurses working in the field for the first time.

There has always been substantial debate surrounding the 'forensic nurse' ever since the term came into regular use – are they different? What is it that is different about them? Criticisms of the role range from 'glorified custodians', to a homogenous group who strut around swinging a capacious bunch of keys, in a quest for domination of those under their care (this latter and more severe accolade generally being unfairly reserved for nurses working within the special hospital system). Others suggest the role of the forensic psychiatric nurse does not exist.

This debate has led the champions of the forensic role to attempts at substantiation via increasingly complex theories and models. High level theorising of this nature seems to be 'putting the cart before the horse'. It appears to avoid explicitly stating the pivotal issues that surround those nurses working in the forensic environment. Services that come under the 'forensic' umbrella are expanding and more people are beginning to call themselves a forensic nurse. The role of the forensic psychiatric nurse in the United Kingdom has its pedigree (however unpalatable this may be for the critics) within the special hospitals. The term did not receive attention in any great detail until the establishment of medium secure services. These developing services at times desperately seemed to want to dissociate themselves from the special hospitals. This is hardly surprising considering the criticism and negative media attention that has been, and still is, levelled at these particular units. Obviously things were wrong, as different reports during the last 18 years illustrate. However, if they devoted similar effort to publicising some positive work, they would provide a more equitable picture. The role is still arguably at its most different, difficult and complex within the special hospitals.

Some basic tenets that guide the existence of secure forensic psychiatric care facilities have remained the same since their inception. These principles are sometimes ignored because they are necessarily mechanistic: the treatment of people with a mental disorder under conditions of security for the protection of the individual and the public. It is the challenge for all professionals within forensic psychiatric care to develop continually the services on offer within the confines of these principles.

Debate will continue, and it is not the purpose of this chapter to stifle the views of others. Such discussions are healthy and, if constructive, will only serve to advance patient care. The differences in role exist in reality and do not need inventing or complicating at this level of discussion. Any nurse new to a forensic environment will find many areas of difference and different expectations of them as practitioners. Neither is it the intention of this chapter to present nurses working in forensic psychiatry as an élite (a criticism levelled at this emerging group of professionals as they try to stake a claim to their identity), but merely to clarify the elements that make the role different. Any nurse returning to general psychiatry from the forensic branch would find similar role differences and would need to make necessary adjustment. Critics have described the life of the forensic psychiatric nurse as an easy one or an 'opt out'. Sadly, such descriptions sometimes come from individuals who have almost no experience of the 'front line of patient care' (particularly regarding high security). Nurses working within forensic psychiatry have a very demanding role to fulfil, in difficult circumstances, with a high level of commitment. It is all too easy to criticise from a distance.

At the time of writing this text, policy change in the care and treatment of certain groups of mentally disordered offenders was under debate. These changes may have extensive implications for forensic care and some areas outlined in this chapter. This is particularly true of those patients classified as suffering from psychopathic disorder for whom the provision of service may change. This patient group is covered later in this chapter.

Some following text may seem simplistic and obvious, but deep consideration is necessary on how individuals will cope with each theme outlined. When amalgamated these themes form what is a demanding and challenging role, and one that some nurses find does not suit them.

Accordingly, elements are chosen which are different and in their most extreme form (at the highest level of security). This will enable people considering a career in the forensic area to examine these to see how they would function. Their chosen area of practice, however, may have role expectations in much more diluted form. Detailed areas, such as which sections of the Mental Health Act are specific to forensic care, are avoided. These are covered very well within other modern texts (for example, Kirby and McGuire 1997). It would also be a sincere hope that all practitioners can accept these role differences and move towards collaboration and a seamless service of care. This will allow patients in the rehabilitation process a more trouble-free progression through the forensic system.

CORE PSYCHIATRIC NURSING SKILLS

There are, of course, major similarities in the core role of the psychiatric nurse in general or forensic psychiatry. Perhaps the most important example is the ability of the psychiatric nurse working at any level of security to use the skills necessary to form a nurse–patient relationship. This has long been seen as one of the most subtle, yet defining, elements of the psychiatric nursing role. A successful nurse–patient relationship is the basis for a high standard of care, and is the vehicle by which many other care processes can be brought to successful conclusion. Some core elements of the nurse–patient relationship are affected in forensic psychiatric nursing. These will be examined throughout the chapter.

Two strikingly obvious, but vital, phenomena exist for the forensic psychiatric nurse: *security* and *patients suffering from a mental disorder who have offended and are detained against their will for purposes of treatment and protection of them and others*. The two phenomena are interrelated and contain many important themes. These will be examined separately along with their effect on the nurse–patient relationship. The nurse new to the forensic role will have to adjust to these areas and learn new skills.

So, in summary: the forensic psychiatric nurse is expected to care for *patients with a mental disorder who have offended* (or patients whose behaviour is so extreme that secure care is necessary for their own protection and that of others – these latter patients could be regarded as non-forensic because often they have committed no criminal offence). This requires their care under conditions of *varying security* to minimise the risk that they present to themselves or others.

This care scenario adds complexity. The forensic nurse may provide nursing care for patients who have committed some very serious offences, which may include, for example, murder, rape, paedophilia, arson, and aggravated violence. Traditionally, psychiatric nurses are taught the skills of unconditional positive regard. This involves the treatment of every patient as an individual despite what might have occurred in their past, or, not making value judgements of their behaviour. Conceptually this is ideal, but putting it into practice may be much more difficult and require high levels of support for even the most experienced practitioners. Psychiatric nurses are often seen as 'bullet-proof' individuals who can take anything thrown at them. They are, however, human beings with individual thoughts, feelings and a set of moral values. Imagine the following scenario:

> John, a first level registered nurse, is to act as named nurse for Bill, a patient suffering from psychopathic disorder. Bill has been convicted of a particularly bizarre and vicious murder of a young person. John has children of the same age as the victim. His thoughts turn to how he would feel about the situation if it were his child involved. This is possibly a by-product of the core psychiatric nursing skill of empathy within the nurse–patient relationship. In this situation the nurse may find it all too easy to empathise with the victim of the offence but have very little common ground with the perpetrator. Critics would say that John should remain unaware of the offences committed by Bill. Realistically, this would be practically impossible for any number of reasons. For example, part of the intervention strategy for Bill may be therapy that is directly related to the offence and John would be involved as part of the multidisciplinary team. John will also need a full knowledge of the risks that Bill may pose to others when making care decisions with Bill. It is even possible that Bill may gleefully discuss elements of the crime to gain a reaction. This can be an extremely distressing phenomenon.

A further core skill of the psychiatric nurse is that of self-awareness. This is particularly important. The forensic nurse must carefully examine his/her feelings about the patients with whom he/she comes into contact and how these will affect the care he/she can offer. This is a difficult area and one that often seems covert within forensic care. Support is required along with honesty. The situation may arise where a nurse feels that he/she will be unable to offer care as a named nurse for a particular individual in the way that he/she should. Certain patients may provoke feelings of fear in even the most experienced nurses. These situations require acknowledgement. They should not be seen as a weakness of the nurse. Careful reflection is required by the individual with regard to his/her ability to cope with such situations.

This begins to emphasise some difficulties and differences in the forensic psychiatric nursing role and the series of ethical and moral issues that are unique. The nurse new to the role will deal with security in many ways, states and forms, which he/she will not generally have encountered before. Security is a pivotal issue but not a simple one.

Security exists to enable legal detention of patients with a mental disorder for the purposes of treatment by the multidisciplinary team of which the nurse is a member. Examination of security issues reveals a number of distinct procedural and conceptual differences for the forensic psychiatric nurse.

SECURITY

The forensic psychiatric nurse is responsible for security to a very high degree. A very basic, but often neglected, concept needs emphasis at this point. Often it is not just the patients that security restricts. Nurses may find that movement within the area of work may be much more restricted than that which is familiar. Freedom of interventional strategies may be subject to certain restrictions. Forensic psychiatry is not therapeutically restrictive, indeed it is entirely the opposite. However, safeguards may have to be in place before certain interventions can safely occur.

Forensic psychiatry welcomes newly qualified nurses. However, their enthusiasm and innovative ideas can sometimes feel stifled if they are not prepared for the procedural necessities that exist in putting some things into practice. The environment can feel oppressive, by virtue of the security, to the point whereby nurses begin to feel that they are the ones subject to detention. Which to a degree they are! This is a useful exercise in empathy in examining the feelings of the patients under your care. Panic attacks are possible among nurses new to a maximum security environment.

Contemporary psychiatric nursing see the nurse–patient relationship as that of two people who are equal. The nurse enters a professional relationship with the patient, by which each party makes equal contribution. This presents the nurse with some obvious dilemmas when he/she is one of the people who is responsible for the patient's detention. Psychiatric nurses are used to the detention of patients within general psychiatry. This is usually short-term under sections of the Mental Health Act that deal with assessment and treatment in the acute hospital setting. In the forensic environment detention is often long-term and, in certain circumstances, much more structured. This presents a whole range of difficulties and skill development requirements and sometimes places considerable strain on the nurse–patient relationship. This chapter can only provide a thumbnail sketch of the areas involved; texts for further reading are suggested on p.302.

Let us return to the concept of security. In the maximum secure environment the nurse new to this situation will find that security affects almost everything that he/she does, either directly or indirectly. Theoretically, security comes in two forms: physical and relational. Physical security refers to the objects or systems in place. Examples include locks, fences, closed circuit television and regular procedures that prevent breaches. Relational security is much more complex. This is a state of mind. The everyday practice of the forensic psychiatric nurse is governed by reference to how they may relate anything that happens to security or breaches of it. Relational security entails a deep individual knowledge of patients gained through an effective nurse–patient relationship, which is at times very difficult. Every situation has to be regarded with reference not only to the actual risks, but also the potential ones, and how they will be minimised. This concept is examined in more detail in the section on detained patients (pp.46–50).

These definitions are necessarily brief. Nevertheless, years of debate have focused on the balance between therapy and security or care and custody. Innovations continue to achieve a therapeutic balance. A nurse new to forensic psychiatric care will undoubtedly become part of this debate and will be aware of the dualistic role with which he/she is now faced.

PROCEDURES! PROCEDURES!

Any organisation has procedures, but maximum security forensic psychiatric care has more than its fair share. Obviously, they exist to safeguard the interests of everyone within a given situation, yet some are exceedingly invasive. The issue of the forensic psychiatric nurse is twofold. First, there is the procedure itself. Second, there is the execution of whatever elements the procedure may entail within an effective nurse–patient relationship (which is arguably the most important of the two). This is not an easy skill to learn, and some of the procedures that follow may put some potential forensic nurses off seeking a career in the field. Remember, however, that some of these may not be an expected part of the role in environments of lesser security. The following items are some core examples only, as providing an exhaustive list is unrealistic.

Keys

It may be simplistic, or blatantly obvious, for this to be first or even to state it at all, yet forensic nurses carry keys (or associated items such as electronic pass cards). They are responsible for them and for using them in the correct manner. Keys govern movement of anyone around the environment. This is a simplistic idea. However, with the possession of such keys the locus of control shifts very much on to the keyholder, which produces interpersonal dynamics which are much less simplistic. These dynamics in turn can have some marked effects on the nurse–patient relationship.

Searching of patients/premises

It may come as a surprise to nurses unfamiliar with forensic psychiatric care that patients, their effects and living environment are subject to routine or reactive searching procedures. Members of nursing staff usually carry these out. Anybody can blunder into a search procedure with little thought or reference to the recipient. However, to carry out such a procedure within the confines of a nurse–patient relationship that is based on equality is a very difficult skill to develop. Insensitivity can potentially damage the results of weeks of effective interpersonal work. Searching people or their effects/living space involves an invasion of personal space. The reader may be familiar with that awful situation when passing through the airport metal detector and it registers positive. Subsequently a member of security staff 'frisks' you. This is an uncomfortable experience, as is having your luggage searched by customs staff. These are useful parallels that many patients in forensic psychiatric care have to face on a regular basis. The forensic nurse may also have to counter the results of less experienced staff having carried out similar procedures. These particular phenomena once again revolve around the issues of power and control. Not only do nurses possess a set of keys, but they also have the authority to carry out the above searches.

Most psychiatric nurses will be familiar with the unfortunate situation where they have had to administer medication against a patient's will. This can involve similar problems and is why it is not included as a domain reserved for those in the forensic field.

Some nurses would feel very uncomfortable having to carry out any of the above and may decide that on this basis forensic care would not be an option for them.

Specialist training/procedures

A number of procedures exist that will be new to the nurse within forensic psychiatry. Again, it may be a surprise that, on occasions, forensic nurses will be in charge of an escort outside the forensic environment (if they are a first level qualified nurse). This may be for attendance at out-patients or crown court, or for a home visit. The patient may present certain risks that need to be minimised. Overall responsibility remains with the person in charge while out of the secure area. In extreme circumstances the use of handcuffs may be required during an external escort. This raises two issues: how the interpersonal aspects of such a situation are dealt with (training on the mechanical usage would be given); and possible additional external factors such as members of the public making assumptions, asking awkward questions or attempting to interfere. Such situations present an array of risks that require continual evaluation and decision-making based on that evaluation.

Most psychiatric nurses are used to mandatory procedures involving control and restraint training, though within forensic care these may be more advanced. Further opportunities for skill development exist at the more senior level, for example in areas such as hostage negotiation. This presents a picture of the different skills needed within the forensic psychiatric field, where something as seemingly simple as carrying a set of keys can drastically affect many other phenomena. The dualistic role between maintaining security and therapy is an extremely difficult one. Professional dilemmas will arise on a regular basis where a decision has to be made that maintains security for all involved but minimises any detrimental therapeutic effect. This can be at times very frustrating. The following imaginary situation presents the elements of security and therapy in conflict:

> Jane is named nurse to patient Claire. Claire is a new admission to the hospital and has been particularly suspicious and withdrawn. Over a period of weeks Jane has spent long periods with Claire carefully explaining routine procedures and building up a relationship. Claire is beginning to talk more openly with Jane and some level of trust has begun to be established. It is obvious to Jane, however, that this relationship is still very fragile. One day Jane receives a phone call from an occupational therapy suite where a pair of scissors has gone missing. Unfortunately, Claire has been in that area and will have to be searched on return to the ward, as will all patients who have been in the suite. The task of searching Claire has all the hallmarks of ruining the careful work carried out by Jane. It will be very difficult to give the assurance and explanations necessary, despite how logical they may seem, that will prevent Claire from believing that she has been singled out and is under suspicion. Jane will know this, yet security must be maintained and the scissors must be found for the safety of everyone. Further weeks may have to be spent re-establishing trust just to get back to the same point. It is, of course, possible that Claire may have the scissors. This would lead to a different situation.

Security is not just locks, keys and associated physical elements. The relational skills of the forensic psychiatric nurse are as important as the correct use of the physical elements.

DETAINED PATIENTS

Patients suffering from a mental disorder within forensic psychiatric care are usually subject to longer periods of detention than those encountered in general psychiatry. Often they are subject to different sections of the Mental Health Act. A proportion of forensic psychiatric patients may have been admitted directly from prison or from crown court. In addition many will be subject to restriction orders. This means that their movement in and out of the hospital and eventual discharge is generally subject to approval from the Home Office.

The long-term nature of detention may have an inextricable effect on the nurse–patient relationship. Detention and security may make the patient's view of the nurse different from that which is familiar. Nurses provide twenty-four hour care for patients and unfortunately are often seen as the main custodians. This presents obvious complications to establishing a nurse–patient relationship, and the nurse can often be used as an antagonist when the patient is trying to vent some frustration. For example, the author has often heard something similar to the following statement from patients who are under particular stress. 'You're not really bothered, you're only interested in keeping me locked up.' This can be distressing, particularly when such a statement is the culmination of extensive intervention. A capacity for self-awareness is very important, in addition to support from colleagues, when handling a situation like this and many other subject areas that follow. These phenomena are very important, particularly with patients new to the environment.

It is important to remember that some patients will have come directly from prison and will be used to a much more custodial focus. Other patients will have had very little or no experience of security. Introducing the concept of a psychiatric nurse is often difficult enough to a newly admitted patient in any psychiatric setting. Positive feedback is not a usual feature from patients who are acutely ill and the addition of differing levels of security can increase this difficulty significantly. The possibility of a small number of patients who will never fully accept forensic nurses, except as custodians, exists despite any amount of effort.

Other areas relate to detained patients, although most psychiatric nurses will be familiar with them at some level.

Patients classified as suffering from psychopathic disorder

This group of patients has been the subject of intense debate for many years. Within high security forensic psychiatry the nurse will encounter a range of patients detained under this Mental Health Act legal classification. It is not the purpose of this chapter to enter the treatment/classification debate; other texts provide comprehensive coverage of the issues (e.g. Dolan and Coid 1993). This group of patients can present some extreme challenges to the nurse new to forensic psychiatric care. To try to cover the range of therapeutic regimes that exist, or the range of clinical presentations, would be unrealistic. However, in the extreme, forensic nurses can be faced with severely manipulative and predatory individuals whose care needs are often very long term. This long-term nature of care can also provide a source of extreme frustration for the forensic nurse (not only those new to the environment but experienced staff also). There will be occasions when very little change can be seen in the patient despite intense intervention over a long period. This, of course, is not reserved for this group of patients alone. Other patients may exhibit similar long-term treatment challenges. Nurses unused to caring for this group of patients often describe similar feelings.

Patients classified as suffering from psychopathic disorder sometimes seem to have 'magnetic personalities' and seeing anything wrong with them at all is very difficult. The exact opposite is also possible. Some patients may be extremely difficult in any number of ways. The key to this area, as with all the other areas of forensic psychiatric care, is experience, support and the teaching necessary to gain that experience.

Self-harm

Psychiatric nurses may be familiar with the concept of patients who self-harm. A group of patients exist within forensic psychiatric care who exhibit very serious levels of self-harming behaviour. This can involve serious multiple attempts to self-ligate or cause injury in any number of ways. Nursing and coping with these patients is very intense, often requiring specialist supervision of nurses new to the area. It is without doubt extremely stressful.

Violence

Similarly, psychiatric nurses will be familiar with patients who exhibit violence. Within forensic psychiatric care there will be a number of patients who are extremely violent. Violence may also be carefully premeditated with the intention of severe harm either to other patients or staff. Coping with being the recipient of any type of violence is very difficult, even when it is a spontaneous outburst.

The possibility exists that forensic psychiatric nurses may be the recipients of such carefully premeditated attacks. They will have to cope with the aftermath of such a situation, part of which will be continuing to offer a high standard of care to a patient who may, at worst, have tried to cause serious physical harm. This is a good example of relational security as part of the skills repertoire of the forensic psychiatric nurse. Knowing that such eventualities exist allows a level of awareness that can enable the observation for various subtle warning signs.

Seclusion

A further controversial practice exists within the forensic environment. This is the process of seclusion: the supervised confinement of patients in a locked room for the protection of others. This raises many dilemmas, previously discussed, such as effects on the nurse–patient relationship and the dualistic problems of custody and therapy. This practice exists and the potential forensic nurse needs to question carefully whether they can initiate such a procedure.

Multidisciplinary working

The forensic psychiatric nurse plays a full role in the multidisciplinary care team that includes the full range of disciplines that would be expected within general psychiatry. One interesting difference is that the forensic nurse may be in regular contact with the patients' legal representatives. They can also play an active role in

Mental Health Review Tribunals that are an important part of long-term detention.

Patients' relatives and visitors

It is not just the patients with whom the security/therapy issues are an important topic. Patients' relatives and other visitors cannot freely go in and out of the hospital. Obviously, they will need escorting. A member of the nursing staff usually supervises visits to patients, and this can be uncomfortable for all parties concerned so discreet handling is required. Friction is a possibility, yet relatives and friends can also form a major part of the multidisciplinary team. Perseverance and interpersonal skills are needed to ensure that people see the nurse 'behind the keys'. Such situations do exist in general psychiatric nursing, but the added complexity of security can put additional barriers in place. Other factors such as supervised patient phone calls and screened mail can exacerbate situations. It is also a feature of high security establishments that visitors will be subject to searching procedures. Additional strains can be placed upon relationships in these circumstances.

Risk assessment and management

The forensic psychiatric nurse faces an extended role in risk assessment and management. The potential of many patients for dangerous and life-threatening behaviour exists. This applies both within the care environment and to the problems associated with recidivism. As part of the multidisciplinary team your reports and assessments can have a significant effect on patient progress.

Directly related to the factors of risk/danger is another phenomenon worthy of consideration. Most people are familiar with those 'notorious' patients who have received high levels of media attention. The possibility exists that forensic nurses may meet such patients. The public do have an interest, and friends and relatives outside forensic psychiatry may press for the revelation of individual details. This, of course, can present additional unwelcome stress.

Safeguarding patients' rights

The presence of such a string of restrictive phenomena means that the individual rights of patients need to be subject to safeguard. Local procedures exist to ensure such rights are met. Patient councils and advocacy services exist in forensic psychiatric care just the same as in general psychiatry. Allegations from patients are not uncommon, and these are treated very seriously on all occasions. For the safety of all concerned this is an inescapable fact. Two stress-provoking situations can arise from allegations in their most severe form. A member of staff may be suspended from duty on full pay during an investigation for their own protection.

This is a very lonely time requiring high levels of staff support. Second, the possibility of being interviewed by the police in an investigation, either as a witness or as the subject of an allegation, is a further consideration. This again can be a time of extreme personal anxiety and can affect domestic life.

REWARDS

A very gloomy picture may have emerged of a career in forensic psychiatry. The intention of this chapter is, in fact, entirely the opposite. The purpose has been to outline the very real differences that exist for the forensic nurse and to show that it is not a career decision to be taken on the basis of the often-quoted, but misinformed, negative perception of the role. Forensic psychiatric nursing presents some excellent and highly rewarding opportunities. The decision of the interested individual lies in the examination of each area to assess that they will be able to offer, or develop, the skills. It is an impossibility to cover every area in such a short chapter, or offer a great deal of detail about the areas covered. The basic areas are presented for anyone that wishes to pursue them by further in-depth examination.

Each area represents opportunities for a rewarding job. The challenges of effectively balancing security and therapy are not easy ones but, when achieved, present a great deal of job satisfaction. A career in forensic psychiatric nursing has many unique areas of practice on offer. There are an increasing number of settings in which to work, ranging from maximum security to community work. The ability to work within differing patient groups with a variety of needs provides specialist opportunities. Movement into a career in high security offers the benefits of preceptorship, supervision and considerable attention to your induction into what may initially seem a very strange environment. Learning to balance the therapeutic needs of patients with security is an experiential skill that is part of this supportive process. Opportunities exist for further professional development from dedicated courses that deal with the prevalent issues to therapeutic strategies such as forms of behavioural therapy. Vast opportunities exist for those interested in research and evidence-based care, and many hospitals have dedicated research departments that include opportunities for nurses. Forensic psychiatric nursing is a demanding career pathway that now may be discarding some myths that surround it. However, not everyone will find it suitable for their own career opportunities. If this chapter has served to whet some appetites and put others off, by virtue of the information within, then it will have achieved its aim.

CHAPTER 4

A Two-Nation Perspective on Issues of Practice and Provision for Professionals Caring for Mentally Disordered Offenders

Carol Watson and Stephan Kirby

INTRODUCTION

This chapter will explore the different perspectives of the roles which Scottish and English forensic nurses have evolved, and also how that perspective affects the services provided and their practice(s). This will be in particular reference to the therapeutic relationships they establish and maintain with patients who display very challenging and, at times, extremely violent behaviour. Strategies to prevent, monitor and manage such behaviour will be discussed. Also addressed will be some of the ethical dilemmas facing the nurse (and the clinical team) caring for this difficult and highly stigmatised patient group. In most instances the authors realise that there is no (nor should there be any) distinction between English and Scottish forensic nurses. Issues related to the maintenance of a secure and therapeutic environment and effective nurse–patient relationships are the same across the UK, and in both high and medium secure settings. Only at times of obvious diversity, or specific examples, is a distinction made between the two nations, using two specific establishments and their staff.

HISTORY

Since the Act for Regulating Madhouses (1774), Britain has had legislation controlling the activities of institutions for the mentally ill, and since 1890 there have been laws regulating compulsory detention (Chiswick 1993). The most significant changes in recent years were driven by the need to support and recognise the rights of individuals suffering from mental disorders. Chiswick noted that good legislation must strike a balance between these rights, the loss of liberty of the mentally ill, and the right of society to be protected from the consequences of untreated illness. There is a perception that mental health legislation in respect of those diagnosed as having a personality disorder is different in the two countries, which is not borne out in reality. The Mental Health (Scotland) Act 1984 does not recognise personality disorder as a primary diagnosis, but does allow compulsory detention for 'dangerous, violent or criminal propensities' and 'aggressive and/or seriously irresponsible conduct'. The semantics may be different but the outcome is the same.

Care of the mentally disordered offender in Scotland was established in legislation as early as 1840; the Criminal Lunatic Division of Perth Prison was administered as a hospital, separate from the prison, and had its first medical superintendent in 1878. The State Hospital, at Carstairs, was created by Parliament in 1935, completed in 1939 and transferred patients from Perth after the war in 1948. It has continued to be the sole provider of high secure psychiatric care for the populations of Scotland and Northern Ireland with a primary remit to provide in-patient services for approximately 250 patients suffering from mental disorder, who present with 'dangerous, criminal or violent propensities' (Mental Health (Scotland) Act 1984). The hospital currently has eleven wards supported by an active patient services department comprised of workshops which concentrate on off-ward therapeutic activities. Care is managed by a multi-professional clinical team, including occupational therapists, social workers and psychologists, in addition to nursing and the responsible medical officer (RMO). During the 1960s and 1970s the hospital had developed a progressive approach to holistic care, until the violent incident in 1976 in which a nurse, a policeman and a patient were killed. This defining moment in the hospital's history interrupted a relatively enlightened phase, the effects of which were felt for more than a decade, particularly the misperception that any increase in therapeutic activity had a related decrease in safety and security. In 1995 the hospital became part of the NHS, with the status of a health board directly responsible to the Scottish Office. For staff and patients, if not the public at large, this was another defining moment. Though patients had never been subject to the 'penal discipline' described in the 1952 Rules for Prisons, and the focus of care had been toward health, the hospital had to develop nursing practice which was more treatment oriented, and fill what was, in effect, a therapeutic vacuum. A subtle shift in philosophy towards the 1990s Health Service norms, values and practices had to be internalised and acted upon. This included the broad principles of the Patients' Charter, consumerism and greater user involvement in care.

These changes had a major impact upon staff, in particular upon their conception of the nature and function of their roles during and following this transition period. The changes in roles, and the staff's adjustment in their perceptions of them, remain an influence on both the culture and the therapeutic nurse–patient relationships that develop within the institution. Throughout the rest of the UK other high and medium secure facilities have their own distinct histories and cultures. These are firmly embedded within health care frameworks and philosophies. However, within Scottish forensic care the philosophy has primarily been shaped from a correctional perspective, albeit in the Scottish tradition of common well-being and managed care.

One such English establishment which has been in existence long enough to have created its own very distinct and unique identity, history and care philosophy is the Hutton Centre. This medium secure unit which is in the grounds of St Luke's Hospital in Middlesbrough was the first purpose-built regional secure unit in the country and was officially opened in November 1980.

As there were no other medium secure facilities at that time against which it could be benchmarked, the Hutton Centre initially modelled its approach on high secure principles, erring towards a custodial approach to care at the expense of the treatment agenda. This led to a struggle to develop a health care foundation for the treatment of those first patients, which was compounded by the forensic experience of the key staff, primarily recruited from the English special hospitals. With them came the custodial constraints to therapeutic relationships, which were steeped in history and tradition. Within the decade this (high secure) tradition was to come under some very close scrutiny, not only by the staff who were working within and without these establishments, but also by the Government and, more powerfully, the media.

Nearly twenty years on the Hutton Centre is one of the lead providers of medium secure care in the country. It has grown to 58 beds with a wide and diverse range of support services, CPN service, prison health care provision, and an active academic and research facility. These endeavours were recently rewarded when the Hutton Centre was awarded practice development unit status by the University of Teesside, the first medium secure unit to achieve this.

DEVELOPMENT OF SERVICES

As already stated, the State Hospital was integrated into the NHS in 1995. Around this time the English special hospitals (Rampton, Ashworth and Broadmoor) were responding to the challenges of the Reed Report (Department of Health and Home Office 1992) and the State Hospital was moving towards a therapeutic agenda of care and treatment.

The State Hospital was designed to care for approximately 200 patients and this number continues to be the optimum that can be managed effectively. Patients are referred from the courts, the prison service and other hospitals. As is common within forensic services across the country, members of the clinical team from the admission/assessment ward will visit referred patients in hospitals or prisons to determine if they meet the criteria for admission. Patients referred from court are generally only seen by the responsible medical officer (RMO) as Scotland has, at present, no well-developed system of court liaison/diversion. Unlike England and Wales, which have, at last count, in the region of 50+ medium and low secure facilities (NHS and private), there is no similar, centrally planned forensic infrastructure. Services are unevenly distributed and not generally located in the major cities, having been developed because of the drive of local product champions rather than in response to local needs. Many patients with lesser security requirements have no alternatives for referral or admission, for either assessment or treatment. This obviously impacts upon the patient's clinical progress, when their clinical condition improves, or their need for secure conditions decreases. As such, the State Hospital addresses the needs of patients from admission through rehabilitation to discharge, tailoring the level of security according to individual need, albeit within a high secure environment.

This lack of medium secure facilities has meant that almost one-fifth of the patients at any one time within the State Hospital do not require conditions of maximum security, though they have no available appropriate discharge route. They may wait on average almost two years for an appropriate place. This is especially problematic for patients with learning difficulties and those patients who require supported community placements.

Whilst this situation paints a picture of acknowledged, limited resources, this is not a phenomenon limited to Scotland. There are few medium secure units in England which could boast a diverse range of facilities into which their patients could be discharged. There are many problems associated with establishing some form of community placement for people who have the triple stigma of being not only mentally disordered, with a criminal record, but also come from a secure in-patient setting. There are very few instances where society's NIMBY (not in my back yard) attitude has been overcome effectively. It could be suggested that forensic services, be they high or medium secure, should work and liaise closely with the local communities when planning to set up any form of community housing for this particular client group.

Whilst this may risk drawing even more attention to this client group, it could also be viewed as a proactive method of including local community groups in developments. This kind of initiative may, over time, lessen society's withdrawal from, and potential antagonism towards, any proposed development involving mentally ill people.

Generally, patients who return to local hospitals from the State Hospital are placed in an intensive psychiatric care unit (IPCU), or in other acute units, to be nursed alongside a patient group which is suffering from florid mental illness and distress. For patients accustomed to their own room, and a quiet rehabilitation unit with a range of off-ward activities for both occupational and leisure pursuits, this can be viewed as a traumatic backward step. This environment can compound the stress of re-integration and seriously constrain ongoing rehabilitation, particularly for longer-term patients. In Scotland, there are a limited number of small specialist units, which cater for patients discharged from the State Hospital in Aberdeen, Perth and Glasgow, but there is a need for a broader spectrum of facilities to enable a more needs-led service. In addition there are very few forensic community psychiatric nurses, one outreach service and no specialist teams to deal with this group of patients after discharge.

The recent publication in Scotland of the consultation paper on the Review of Services for Mentally Disordered Offenders (Scottish Office 1999) recommends the development of a range of services to support the work of the high secure hospital and enable patients to move more quickly to more appropriate facilities. The next two years will see the development of a number of facilities designed to make forensic services more accessible and responsive to the local needs of service users and their families.

The picture in the north of England, within the medium secure network, is not very different. Patients discharged from the Hutton Centre invariably return either to prison or to their parent general psychiatric hospital which means, similar to the State Hospital, they return to an acute ward. However, the small number of patients who are discharged to the community in the immediate locality are supported by a team of forensic community psychiatric nurses, social workers and other members of the multidisciplinary team.

Considerable change in the provision of care for mentally disordered offenders in England and Wales is again on the agenda, as a result of yet another inquiry, chaired by Judge Fallon 1998 (Fallon et al. 1999). Few would argue against the need for this, though it is unclear as yet how this specialist care provision will look following this reformation, or how it will impact upon local medium secure facilities. The Scottish picture is also about to change, though for different reasons. Against this background, and given the historical precedents, it seems probable to expect changes in the professional identity and nature of forensic mental health nursing.

THE CARE CONTEXT AND THE CULTURE OF FORENSIC NURSING

The profession of nursing has its own discrete culture, consisting of meanings, roles and rituals; myths and maxims; and practices and theories which are all distinctive and thereby differentiate nursing from other health care professionals (Street 1995). Within each branch or specialism, and indeed each institution, is a subculture within which other subcultures develop. These enable nurses to define and appraise their role, support and motivate each other, form norms and values, and validate the performance of the nursing function. The development of the profession, particularly within institutions, must be managed with great care, so that staff can review and update their skills and knowledge in a positive way. It is important to recognise and value the existing skills base of staff and integrate new skills upon that base, so as to avoid staff feeling undervalued or distanced from professional developments. It is also necessary to emphasise the maintenance of existing competencies to the same degree as the acquisition of new ones.

Many forensic mental health nurses feel alienated by the trend within mental health care generally towards consumerism, user involvement, and the nursing models, which lean heavily on humanistic psychology (Clarke 1996). Empowerment, autonomy and positive unconditional regard have superseded traditional concepts of caring which were philosophically grounded in paternalism, supported as it is by the principle of beneficence. However, Atkinson (1991) argues that autonomy is not the only ethical imperative and that an exaggerated regard for this may well risk therapeutic relationships. Whilst unrestrained paternalism can deny autonomy, without it unnecessary harm would be caused. A clinician's professional responsibility and skill lies in understanding the patient's position within this tension at any point in time.

Though forensic mental health nurses clearly operate within a dichotomy created by their (paternalistic) custodial role and their role as agents of therapeutic change, mainstream mental health nurses are also uncomfortable with certain assumptions about their therapeutic relationships and 'role ambiguity' (Ryan 1997, p.118). Chan (1998) argues that nurses may have to reconcile the public expectations of their control (i.e. custodial) function with those professional assumptions and principles. In addition, nurses in high security hospitals, medium and low secure units and prisons find their approaches under constantly increasing scrutiny. Crabbe (1988) states that 'nurses working in special hospitals have to tread a tightrope between providing therapeutic treatment and maintaining a secure environment', a conflict which is made more difficult by the absence of any clear theoretical or conceptual models of the relationship between the constructs of therapy and custody. This conflict has led to a misperception and perceived acceptance that any model of therapeutic custody must place these two at opposite ends of a scale or continuum, the implication being that one increases or decreases only at the expense of the other.

All nurses, however, regardless of specialism, have a responsibility within their role for the maintenance of patient safety, and the adaptation of the physical environment to promote patient health and well-being. This is generally viewed as contributing to, and enhancing, therapy which is an integral part of the therapeutic process. It is consistent with the hierarchy of human needs as described by Maslow (1970) where physical and safety needs must be met before addressing the higher order psychosocial needs. Nightingale herself reminded nurses that the individual patient is not the whole of what must be managed if he is to be cared for, and that the nurse must control the environment on his behalf (Ryan 1997). Within secure environments, such is the degree of risk to patients, staff and members of the public that a broader, more prescriptive, range of measures must be employed. These are aimed at ensuring the safety of the environment prior to, and continuously during, the development of any therapeutic alliances, and as essential components of therapy.

Nursing has traditionally been delivered within systems and processes which were conceptual, e.g. models of nursing, the nursing process, or theoretical, e.g. using Rogerian or cognitive approaches (Reynolds and Cormack 1990). These generally highlight the role of the nurse in managing the environment as legitimate aspects of care design and delivery. There is a custodial element in most in-patient settings; the nurse will actively sanction or prohibit certain behaviours to promote health and encourage compliance with treatment. For example, the effectiveness of oxygen therapy for a breathless patient is maximised by nursing interventions on the environment (use of upright bed position or chair, multiple pillows, etc.) and the custodial element prevents the patient (and his family) from smoking. This can include direct observation to ensure safety, especially if the patient is in an altered state of consciousness for any reason. The nurse may use a range of strategies to achieve compliance: education regarding needs and consequences, counselling and support, and may even remove and store cigarettes and matches away from the patient. Many patients may resent this, even though they know it is in their best interests. Most will co-operate and comply.

These principles apply to the patient who presents as a danger to him/herself and/or to others including the public. Non-compliance poses a greater risk to both patient and nurse, especially if the environment becomes less safe. Not only will therapy be less effective, it may need to be abandoned as the environment would no longer be capable of supporting the therapeutic risk-taking within the alliance. The nurse, in particular, finds it impossible to function in any of the caring roles such as a resource person, teacher, leader, surrogate, counsellor (Peplau 1952). If they perceive the environment to be unsafe then they will not feel safe utilising non-verbal and verbal strategies within the nurse–patient relationship; for example, to challenge, confront, role model de-escalate or reassure. The nurse must have confidence in the systems and processes designed for personal and professional safety and environmental security. Equally, therapeutic risk-taking is unpredictable and thus unmanageable.

The collaborative nature of modern-day forensic health and social care demands a care arena where alliances between client and carer are seen as cornerstones of the treatment process. This is not only to promote a culture of client empowerment where the client takes more responsibility for their lives and their actions, but also to support and facilitate greater client engagement with their condition. Professionals within care teams need to see patients in relation to their social and personal reality, and address the needs presented accordingly. This supportive, patient-centred environment offers the patient hope by providing the means for him to develop his individuality. The therapeutic alliance is also the vehicle within which individual responsibility is monitored. This emphasis on individual empowerment must remain within the utilitarian principles of benefit to the common good in order that all in the care arena remain safe. This leads to a much more complex three-dimensional conceptual model of forensic nursing care in which the maintenance of a safe and secure environment is the essential basis for all other psychotherapeutic work, rather than its antithesis.

CORE COMPETENCIES

There are several elements to the maintenance of effective safety and security, which are within the domain of nursing practice. Discrete competencies can be described and training targeted at all trained and untrained staff, especially during their 'induction period'. This ensures that nurses acquire the knowledge that underpins their practice and provides a credible professional rationale for these activities. It helps nurses to develop the skills and the ability to demonstrate the internalisation of appropriate attitudes to carry out these procedures within the framework of the nurse–patient relationship. Implicit in that framework is the professional code of conduct, and its ethical principles of beneficence and duty to care (UKCC 1992a). All nursing staff within secure environments should acquire these core competencies related to maintaining this environment within their first year. Regular auditing of practice and competency-based appraisal ensure that this knowledge and skill base become internalised and firmly enmeshed in clinical practice. These competencies include searching, both areas and people, monitoring visitors, escorting patients both internally and externally, and dealing effectively with aggressive behaviour (see Table 4.1).

Table 4.1 Maintaining patients in a secure environment: core competencies

Title of unit	Teaching/learning strategy
Fire	Computer-assisted learning programme
Hostage management	One-day seminar
Misuse of substances	Half-day seminar/supervised practice
Escorting patients	Role-modelling/supervised practice
Visitor control	Role-modelling/supervised practice
Observation	Seminar/supervised practice
Communication	Seminar/supervised practice
Preventing and managing aggressive behaviour	Five-day course/supervised practice
Security breaches	Half-day seminar

The Patients' Charter (see Appendix) is a local example of the responsibilities of the hospital (in this instance the State Hospital, Carstairs) to maintain a secure, safe environment for all patients, staff and members of the public. This document clearly lays out for public scrutiny the strategies that are taken to ensure the integrity of the environment, as well as the standards of best practice, which patients and their families have a right to expect.

Dynamic and robust guidance must support nursing practice. The design and implementation of policies and good practice guidelines are the remit of senior clinical staff. The development of systems which can be monitored and audited contribute to maintenance of confidence in the integrity of the environment. Regular and random searching of personnel, living and working accommodation, the control of visitors (family and professional), escorting of patients, and random urinalysis for illicit substances must have practical guidelines and rationale and regular reviews as to their effectiveness. The use of constant observation must also be monitored for its effects on patients and staff, and especially during those visits that are assessed to be of a high risk to the safety of the environment for the patient, staff and/or the public.

Nurses must develop a range of interpersonal skills which enable them to carry out these procedures in a caring, professional way. But, as with all adult experiential learning, they must internalise the legitimacy of the competency (Steinaker and Bell 1979) and trust both the profession and their employers to support their practice. The professional isolation which forensic nurses feel may in part stem from the perceived conflict of this custodial role with more easily identifiable concepts of caring. However, such a narrow view of caring must be challenged. The duty of care implicit in all nursing encompasses this custodial element, as without it the promotion of a safe, secure and ultimately therapeutic environment cannot be achieved. If we are unable to create a therapeutic environment then any attempt to create a therapeutic alliance with our individual patient or patient group is doomed to fail.

Gaining the co-operation of the users of forensic services within the NHS is a complex issue, but they are patients and as such have a right to participate in their care. In addition their families, who in many cases have to travel great distances, especially in regard to those patients in high secure hospitals such as the State Hospital, must have a range of mechanisms to enable them to fully participate in care and treatment. A carefully drafted Patients' Charter, practical and realistically able to meet local needs, will address these mechanisms while making clear the responsibilities everyone carries in supporting the therapeutic agenda.

Throughout the therapeutic process nursing staff have the day-to-day responsibility, and are best placed to maintain and enhance relationships with patients and their families, and to build up a degree of mutual respect which enables a working therapeutic alliance within the constraints of the environment.

PROFESSIONAL DEVELOPMENT

Health care and its provision is a dynamic process, which should continuously evolve in order to remain responsive to the needs of individuals and groups within a changing society and care arena. To respond to these changes, staff within forensic settings continually require and request educational, professional and managerial support. In England there is a plethora of post-basic courses, at diploma, first and higher degree status, available to the full range of multidisciplinary forensic staff. An example of this is the recent collaboration between the Hutton Centre and the University of Teesside who are jointly hosting a multidisciplinary diploma level course, ENB A71 'Care of the Mentally Disordered Offender', as well as a BSc (Hons) in 'Forensic Health Social Care'. As the collaborative nature of forensic health and social care expands, so must the collaborative nature of educational provision. Pre-registration courses must also reflect the reality of in-patient care for the whole range of individuals with mental health problems, including mentally disordered offenders. The nature of in-patient provision has changed considerably, and mental health students must have the opportunity during basic courses to explore both their attitudes towards this patient group and the more diverse concepts of caring which must be applied to them.

In contrast, Scotland suffers from a lack of post-basic education in mainstream mental health, and forensic mental health in particular. The first forensic nursing degree within Scotland was established in collaboration with Robert Gordon University in Aberdeen only three years ago. There is no forensic CPN training and no educational infrastructure similar to that which is offered by the English National Board with accredited stand-alone courses and modules, in the wide range of therapeutic approaches. The University of Dundee has a substantial history of postgraduate diplomas in skills-based courses such as cognitive behavioural therapy, but other educational institutions are only now developing courses which may meet the needs of advanced practitioners in both mental health and forensic mental health.

This lack of a broad education and practice base has led to the identity of forensic nurses, particularly, within the context of this chapter, being historically linked to the contextual environment of care (the State Hospital, prison nurses) rather than to its content. Whilst this is by no means exclusive to Scotland, it has been prevalent and relevant across the UK forensic network, a situation that is only now beginning to change.

Of greater significance is the likelihood that many nursing staff working in forensic settings view the tension between custodial and therapeutic aspects of their role as a diametric split. This may be because, as individuals, they are oriented either empathically towards therapeutic interventions or uncompromisingly towards custodial considerations (Burrow 1993b). Their stance on these issues will derive from the diffuse social and political values they hold as members of a broader culture.

Each individual nurse must come to terms with, and examine, the attitudes he or she holds as a citizen towards offenders, deviant behaviour and other social deviations. It demands a great deal of professionalism and competence from nurses to avoid the application of differentiating criteria to the mentally disordered offender. Our patients are also members of society with a stake in the community, and are therefore entitled to participation in a care alliance which restores them to this community, on either a micro or macro level.

Forensic nurse managers, educationalists and leading clinicians cannot wait for such tensions in role and attitude conflict to resolve themselves. Strategies must be developed and a forum provided for the active exploration of these issues. In addition, research into nurses' conceptualisation of the relationship between care, treatment and custody is urgently required.

The majority of courses leading to registration are philosophically grounded in humanistic Rogerian approaches. They are theoretically underpinned by concepts such as trust, consumer-focused care, empowerment, self-governance and unconditional positive regard (for examples, see Brooking, Ritter and Thomas 1992; Thomas, Hardy and Cutting 1997) with little opportunity to explore, either theoretically or practically, alternative modes of caring related to this patient group.

The reality for many mental health nurses is of working with the mentally ill in environments which are far from safe, either within institutions or in the community. Pre-registration education must equip nurses to work within that reality, and some basic principles of secure care and core competencies in maintaining safe care environments must be given more prominence and thus legitimised in curricula.

Advanced clinical competencies for nurses working in secure environments have been suggested, though have yet to be validated. It is extremely difficult to develop evidence-based practice where nurses are unsure of the nature of the competencies. Muir Gray (1997) argues that evidence-based practice requires two elements: motivation and competence. Lack of clarity on competencies does not facilitate the development of projects and initiatives to test the clinical effectiveness of care and treatment strategies.

Examples of these advanced competencies can be found in Kirby and Maguire (1997) where they cite and expand upon the work of Tarbuck (1994b). These can be further developed into a competency framework by adapting the work of Benner (1984) to the forensic arena. This broad framework enables clear professional development through achievement of competence, as well as competency-based appraisal. Such frameworks should have a common theoretical base, but be flexible enough to meet local needs. Clinical staff must be involved in identifying the actual demonstrable skills and knowledge for them to be relevant to their care environment.

CONCLUSION

The circumstances of forensic nursing highlight the invidious role conflict in which nurses find themselves trying to fulfil both therapeutic as well as custodial criteria. Individual practitioners must have a clear and unambiguous philosophy about their occupational purpose, and view the dichotomy as a tension rather than a split. It must not be forgotten, though, that one of the primary purposes of containing patients in secure settings is to assess and contain any residual, or potential, dangerousness (Burrow 1993b). The control of the environment and the forensic mental health nurse as an agent of social control has clear historical and professional antecedents, which contribute to an understanding of contemporary practice.

While the function of forensic psychiatric nursing seems, superficially, fairly obvious, the role is highly complex. The overall function could be described as providing health care (as opposed to a custodial care and containment) for mentally disordered offenders within the varying conditions of security which are required to contain their dangerous, violent or criminal propensities.

While this view may appear to be simplistic, it captures the essence of the forensic psychiatric nurse's role and function. By providing health care to people who have a mental illness whilst also being agents of social control for their deviant and antisocial behaviour, the nurse's role is caught up in contradictory issues. Within such a controlling environment, there is the potential for self-esteem, self-worth and personal identity to be eroded. This can lead the patient to withdraw further into his/her own reality, becoming disengaged from individuality as well as surroundings, with the associated increase in the use of medication. It becomes very important for forensic nurses to strive to show faith in, and respect for, their patients despite past and present behaviour. The conceptualisation of a range of competencies which integrate the therapeutic alliance within a safe and secure environment enables clinical staff to promote engagement, individuality and growth.

Forensic nurses have a responsibility to raise the status of forensic patients as deserving of appropriate health care facilities and treatments. The mentally disordered offender is more likely thereby to be seen as a human being rather than a tabloid-generated monster.

CHAPTER 5

The Role of Forensic Nurses in the Community

Phil Woods, Charles Brooker and Edward White

INTRODUCTION

This chapter describes the role of the nurse who specialises in providing care and treatment for the mentally disordered offender in the community: the forensic community mental health nurse. Brought together here is the literature on forensic community mental health nursing and an empirical base.

The community mental health nurse census 1996 in England and Wales collected, for the first time since the census began, data from forensic community mental health nurses as a specific group. The total data set is too large to report fully here, but evidence will be provided following secondary data analysis on their:

- service base;
- patterns of work;
- specialist therapeutic approach and client group;
- caseload; and
- working pattern.

Mentally disordered offenders are those mentally disordered persons who have broken the law or who are alleged to have broken the law (Department of Health and Home Office 1992). However, they are perhaps more fully defined as:

> Those offenders who may be acutely or chronically mentally ill; those with neuroses, behavioural and/or personality disorders; those with learning difficulties; some who, as a function of alcohol and/or substance misuse, have a mental health problem; and any who are suspected of falling into one or other of these groups. It also includes those offenders where a degree of mental disturbance is recognised, even though that may not be severe enough to bring it

within the criteria laid down by the Mental Health Act 1983. It also applies to those offenders who, even though they do not fall easily within this definition – for example, some sex offenders and some abnormally aggressive offenders – may benefit from psychological treatments. (NACRO 1993, p.4)

The forensic community mental health nurse is a registered nurse working in the community, whose primary remit is to address the needs of people with a mental health problem who have offended, are likely to offend, or who are the subject of detention, within terms of legislation (Brooker and White 1997). They are further described as advanced nursing practitioners who provide skilled care for clients within community settings (Royal College of Nursing 1997).

The basic principle of government policy is that, wherever possible, mentally disordered offenders should receive care and treatment from the health and social services, rather than in the criminal justice system (NACRO 1993, p.7). This was further reaffirmed in the Reed review (Department of Health and Home Office 1992). This review called for continuity of care with multi-disciplinary care teams consisting of general practitioners, forensic and general psychiatrists, nurses, approved and generic social workers, probation officers, clinical psychologists, occupational therapists, speech therapists, other therapists, interpreters, and education staff. Specific recommendations also included that there should be a nationwide provision of properly resourced court assessment schemes where a psychiatrist, community psychiatric nurse or approved social worker assesses suspected mentally disordered offenders and advises the court on non-custodial alternatives (Phipps 1994). Further recommendations were for the forensic training of community psychiatric nurses.

Despite these explicit social policies, mentally disordered offenders often fall between service provision and are the individuals that services do not like. Indeed, Grounds (1996) states how currently local psychiatric services struggle in their attempt, often without the availability of local forensic services, to either reject or manage difficult patients – the ones having varying combinations of offending and violent behaviours/histories, drug and alcohol abuse, personality disturbance and mental illness. Moreover, mentally disordered offenders in the community require a higher than average amount of support and supervision (Lloyd 1995).

REVIEWING THE LITERATURE

There is a paucity of literature on the role of the forensic community mental health nurse. What has been written often has little or no empirical base, with a forensic community mental health nurse describing his or her own specific role.

The first to try and define the role was Pedersen (1988) who indicated that this was primarily to act as an ambassador by enhancing and improving working relationships between the forensic and other services, thus reducing stigma, misconceptions and alienation of mentally disordered offenders and their services. Later Cook (1991) described developments in forensic community mental health nursing specifically in relation to court assessment.

Kitchener, Wright and Topping-Morris (1992b) mailed a questionnaire to an opportunistic sample of two hundred forensic health care workers all over the United Kingdom (84 per cent were forensic community mental health nurses). The questionnaire examined role perceptions of knowledge, skill, management, educational and personal issues. One hundred and three questionnaires were returned and the constant theme on analysis was that all issues were felt to be important. Further analysis conflated the themes into two categories – therapy and control. Within the therapy issues 85 per cent felt that forensic community mental health nurses should be self-aware, 79 per cent communicate effectively and 78 per cent be able to develop close therapeutic relationships. In the control issues 84 per cent felt they should have knowledge of assessing dangerousness, 76 per cent be able to handle violence and 69 per cent be able to deal with hostility.

In the same year Banerjee *et al.* (1992) described a model that integrated psychiatric services for mentally disordered offenders in south east London where, as part of their court liaison service, a community psychiatric nurse and a research psychiatrist assessed defendants referred for psychiatric opinion at four magistrates' courts. Further developments are discussed as the creation of formal links both inside and outside the service catchment area, specifically with the community psychiatric nurse developing links with district teams to facilitate community follow-up.

Kennedy and Ward (1992) examined training aspects of a Birmingham-based court diversion scheme from a medical perspective. The primary role of the two forensic community mental health nurses was discussed as undertaking initial screening of all prisoners in police custody. The forensic community mental health nurse was described as being able to make recommendations to the court: either a remand for psychiatric report (bail or custody); or informal admission to the local psychiatric hospital. One year on, Gina Hillis (1993), a forensic community mental health nurse in the above scheme, describes her own role. This is reported to be equally divided between court diversion work and clinical responsibilities at the local regional secure unit. The nurse's role in the scheme is:

- to identify individuals with a mental illness as soon as possible after arrest and before court appearance;
- to offer advice to criminal justice agencies to assist in making recommendations to the court;
- to make arrangements for referral for assessment, treatment and admission if necessary;
- to liaise with the court and all other appropriate services.

Close liaison takes place with probation officers, solicitors, medical staff and staff from other services, the crown prosecutor, and the forensic community mental health nurse. Hillis was clear in stating that although forensic community mental health nurses are unable to make medical diagnosis, their in-depth assessments provide the court with presenting symptoms. Moreover, the autonomous nature of the role means they are responsible for making decisions regarding any appropriate courses of action.

The role of two community psychiatric nurses in a project team, along with a probation officer and approved social worker in north Humberside, are described by Staite (1994). The team members assess prisoners in police custody and court, identifying mentally disordered offenders and consequently arranging packages of care. Close working relationships are reported with the local prison.

Doyle (1996) explored practice and culture differences between a sample of six forensic community mental health nurses and six generic community mental health nurses when assessing risk of client violence. He found that forensic community mental health nurses placed greater emphasis on past history of violence and the views of the multidisciplinary team as a whole. Differently from their generic counterparts, forensic community mental health nurses placed little value on information from significant family and friends. There was no reference made to use of established psychometric tests and intuition was felt to be important in assessing risk. Both groups felt that good rapport and interpersonal relationships were important, and felt that little training or education was given to assist in the process but access to facilities did not differ.

One hundred and twenty forensic community mental health nurses were mailed a 55-item questionnaire, consisting of five-item Likert scales (strongly agree through to strongly disagree) by Kitchener and Kidd (1996). The response rate was 52 per cent. Responses revealed that 71 per cent were attached to forensic psychiatric services, with the remainder spread across others. Half of the forensic community mental health nurses had been practising for up to three years. The age range for 92 per cent was 25–49 years and 61 per cent were female. In relation to nursing grade, 13 per cent were E or F; 55 per cent G; and 32 per cent H or I. A variety of skills and interventions were reported to be used: 89 per cent counselling, 61 per cent behavioural, and 69 per cent cognitive therapy. All respondents felt that they were skilled in the assessment of risk and 96 per cent in assessing dangerousness. Fifty-three per cent reported that they were skilled in the care of sex offenders, 62 per cent in group therapy and 47 per cent in family therapy. In all three of these skill areas respondents reported the need for more training.

Rowlands et al. (1996) demonstrate through their study in Rotherham that diversion schemes can run successfully, with a forensic community mental health nurse as the main focus, when supervised by a consultant forensic psychiatrist. The role of the forensic community mental health nurse is described as contacting the local police stations at the start of each day and examining the custody records. Each prisoner held in custody overnight is discussed with the custody sergeant and, using a broad and what is described as an over-inclusive criteria, those with possible mental health problems are identified. Other routes of referral are self, probation officers and lawyers. The forensic community mental health nurse undertakes a standard psychiatric history to determine the presence, or absence, of psychiatric symptoms. Further assessment can be requested from the consultant psychiatrist or senior registrar. The forensic community mental health nurse is said to have established a high profile within the court system, local police and probation services.

Vanderwall (1997) examines his own role as a forensic community mental health nurse based within a remand prison in Bedford. He further describes a second role as operating a court diversion scheme with colleagues in the Luton area. Within the prison he describes the job purpose as threefold: first, to identify and implement care strategies for mentally disordered offenders; second, to offer training and advice to prison staff; and third, to promote effective inter-agency relationships. The role is further conflated into key objectives:

- to assess prisoners' mental health needs, plan care, or refer to other professionals as necessary;
- to offer support and counselling; to establish and maintain the service; to liaise with, and offer support to, the family; to establish links with other caring agencies;
- to promote good working relationships with prison staff.

Indeed Kitchener (1995) describes the fundamental requirements of penal system links for health service organisations as:

- to create a good working relationship with prison staff;
- to build up trust with the prisoners;
- to retain professional independence.

Vanderwall (1997) further discusses how the establishment of clear client boundaries are central to his work, and that tact is required when recording information (i.e. mental health status and dangerousness) as although the primary objective of the forensic community mental health nurse is mental health care, they may also have some say in judicial outcomes. Personal supervision is essential, as manipulation for secondary gain is rife and risk to self or the reality of hostage situations is always present due to the interpersonal nature of the job. Kitchener (1996) warns of the possible misuse of the forensic community mental health nurse by potential criminals or their solicitors as a way of bypassing custody, while Vaughan and Badger (1995) consider the risk to the worker.

Taylor (1998), examining his specific role as a forensic community mental health nurse, describes this as ensuring that police, courts, social workers and mental health services are aware of their own role and that of others, or potential contribution, in the assessment and treatment of mentally disordered offenders. He informs us that he is in great demand and response has been favourable. Future developments may even include joint assessments with the police surgeon. Finally, Wilkinson (1998) describes the role of the first forensic liaison nurse service in Kent. This service provides nursing input to eleven prisons in the area, where the nurse liaises with prison health care staff and the wider multidisciplinary team. Central to the role is:

- mental health screening and assessment;

- organising support and follow-up for prisoners with mental health needs on release;

- support and education for prison staff.

Also encompassed in the role is working within the local court diversion scheme and liaison with the local regional secure unit.

The above review has highlighted that forensic community mental nurses appear to have a diverse role which is intrinsically linked with the work of other agencies and disciplines. Often they are working autonomously, influencing decision-making processes for mentally disordered offenders, and educating others. Indeed, Backer-Holst (1994), reporting on the implications of the Reed report, stated that 'the educational benefits to the custody sergeant of a forensic community mental health nurse should not be underestimated'. Moreover, in prison, the role of the forensic community mental health nurse is reported as contributing to the process of health assessment of prisoners at reception, by screening for signs and symptoms of mental disorder or potential suicidal behaviour.

THE FORENSIC COMMUNITY MENTAL HEALTH NURSE CENSUS

As mentioned above, the secondary analysis of data that was received during the fourth quinquennial census of community mental health nurses will inform this chapter. This was the first time since the series started that data was collected from forensic community mental health nurses as a discrete target group. In a sense this then offers considerable data to continue to map their role. Data is provided here from both the quantitative and qualitative indices. One hundred and five responses were received and it was estimated that this was approximately a 46 per cent return rate (Brooker and White 1997).

Information about individual patterns of work

A diverse range of main service bases was reported by the responding forensic community mental health nurses. However, not surprisingly, a high percentage were based at a regional secure unit, court, and prison (see Table 5.1).

Table 5.1 Main service base

Service base	n	%
Psychiatric hospital	6	5.7
Health centre/clinic	2	1.9
Community mental health centre	4	3.8
Rampton Hospital	3	2.9
Regional secure unit	45	42.9
Prison	4	3.8
Police station	7	6.7
Court	17	16.2
Social services department	1	1.0
Medium secure unit	2	1.9
Local secure unit	2	1.9
Other community base	5	4.8
Out-patient settings	1	1.0
Low secure unit	1	1.0
High dependency unit	1	1.0
Police station/court	1	1.0
Psychiatric intensive	1	1.0
Missing	2	1.9
Total	105	100.0

A high percentage (74) reported that liaison arrangements and joint working was a major component of their work patterns. This involved both formal and informal working with generic community mental health nurses, community mental health teams, probation services and criminal justice agencies to provide or deliver care and treatment for mentally disordered offenders. For instance, this may involve managing and advising the other professionals involved about key issues related to treatment and management of mentally disordered offenders. Indeed, one forensic community mental health nurse reported that they facilitated a mental health clinic within the probation service.

For many forensic community mental health nurses, arrangements exist whereby non-forensic community psychiatric nurses can refer their clients for specific risk assessment and advice on management issues, when they are presenting with disturbed behaviours:

- on appropriate placement issues;
- on clinical strategies for managing periodically assaultative patients;
- crisis intervention;
- advice and guidance on Mental Health Act legislation.

Many of these nurses aim to provide a period of intensive support and assessment service which incorporates a follow-up service of support, as necessary, after clients are transferred back to the generic community mental health teams.

Supervision is contractual for many of the forensic community mental health nurses, but for others less formal. The process is reported as providing supervision to other non-forensic mental health professionals who have difficult-to-manage offender patients on their caseload. Inherently, this includes providing advice, support and guidance. Many of the forensic community mental health nurses reported informal arrangements which involve attendance at regular meetings, or when clients are transferred between forensic and generic teams. Others will contact the community mental health team in the relevant area to ascertain if the client is already known to the team – if so they will liaise with the community psychiatric nurse/other community workers. Yet others regularly maintain contact with patients' catchment area teams to appraise them of progress, with a view to eventually handing over certain cases.

We can observe, from the above, seven key themes emerging:

1. Joint working;
2. Advice;
3. Assessment;
4. Supervision;
5. Support;
6. Guidance;
7. Maintaining contact.

However, it is difficult to actually separate one of these themes from another, or indeed all, at times. Moreover, perhaps this is because they are not, and could never be, separate entities – which indicates just how diverse working patterns are for forensic community mental health nurses. Hence they may be better described as key issues as opposed to themes.

A high number reported that they held a caseload (83 versus 17 per cent). The mean caseload was 17.4 clients. This has been shown (Brooker and White 1997) to be a significantly lower number of clients than non-forensic community mental health nurses (17.4 versus 38.2). The caseload composition is shown in Table 5.2. It can be observed here that the nurses work mainly with clients who have had a previous hospital admission, with a chronic or severe mental illness and a diagnosis of schizophrenia. They are also key-worker for nearly half of the clients on their caseload.

Table 5.2 Caseload composition of forensic community mental health nurses

Clients on caseload	Mean %
With previous admissions	70.3
With chronic/severe mental illness	59.9
With a diagnosis of schizophrenia	47.6
Where the nurse is CPA key-worker	46.5
Clients on supervision register	15.1
Clients on supervised discharge	6.1
Clients on leave of absence	3.8
Clients on restriction order	26.9

Differing descriptions of the role of those nurses who did not hold a caseload were described. The assessment of mentally disordered offenders in the regional secure unit prior to discharge, ongoing assessment and follow-up was a constant response. This role may involve the supervision of discharged patients to monitor mood, mental state and behaviour, and to administer treatments, where appropriate, and provide support. Others reported taking referrals from within the prison where they were based. This would, as above, be an assessment and follow-up service of mentally disordered offenders in prison.

This again, as with the liaison arrangements which the forensic community mental health nurses reported, involves specifically risk assessment, advice or an educational role. It can perhaps, at times, involve passing referrals to the appropriate agency, or joint working following the initial assessment or discharge of the mentally disordered offender.

Other forensic community mental health nurses reported that they carried short-term caseloads for more lengthy assessment or intervention before referring on. This appears to be more intrinsically linked to those which have a diversion from criminal justice system role, where at the point of arrest, or as soon as possible thereafter, mentally disordered offenders are diverted from prison or the criminal justice system. Central to the role of these nurses is criminal justice system liaison, by providing an assessment and liaison service to the courts, police stations and probation service.

From the above responses we can observe some key themes to the role of the forensic community mental health nurse who does not carry a caseload. The themes emerging appear to be in relation to the role of:

1. Education;
2. Advice;
3. Co-ordination;
4. Assessment;
5. Liaison;
6. Diversion.

Only a small number of the forensic community mental health nurses reported that they specialised in a particular therapeutic approach (32 versus 67 per cent). The most widely used approach, by far, is counselling (30 per cent), followed by brief intervention (15 per cent). A high number reported that they had formal qualifications to specialise in their approach (71 versus 29 per cent). However, less than half reported that their employer recognised their specialised approach (47 versus 44 per cent). In contrast, a high percentage reported that they specialised in working with a particular client age group (66 versus 33 per cent). Probably not surprisingly from those who reported that they specialised, 97 per cent were with adult clients (18–64 years) and only 3 per cent with elderly clients (65+ years). Interestingly, for 86 per cent their employer recognised this form of speciality.

Forty-three per cent of the forensic community mental health nurses reported that they specialised with a particular client group (see Table 5.3). It can be seen from this table that a high number of them specialise in dealing with clients who have a history of violence. Again, for a high number, their employer recognises this speciality (89 versus 11 per cent).

The forensic community mental health nurses were asked to report approximately what percentage of their normal working week they usually spent in certain activities (see Table 5.4). Here we can observe that they spent the highest percentage of their working time during the week in face-to-face client contact. The next most time-consuming activity is travel. Interesting to note is that the two clinical liaison activities only total 22 per cent of their working week, far less than face-to-face client contact. From the previous responses given, of an extreme liaison role, we could have expected that this would have been a more time-consuming activity than reported. Moreover, this is even more interesting considering the small client caseloads. Further, it is interesting to note that staff development amounts for only 6 per cent of the working week.

Table 5.3 Specialised client group

Client group	n	%
Rehabilitation/severe mental illness	1	2.2
Forensic clients	3	6.7
History of violence	17	37.8
Sex offenders	1	2.2
Personality disorder	2	4.4
Learning difficulties	1	2.2
Deliberate self-harm	1	2.2
Women with a history of violence	1	2.2
Mentally disordered offenders	5	11.1
Other	1	2.2
Missing	12	26.7
Total	45	99.9

Table 5.4 Time allocation to specific activities in a normal working week

Activity	Mean (%)	SD	Min (%)	Max (%)
Face-to-face client contact	35.33	14.95	10	80
Travel	16.79	8.99	0	40
Clinical liaison	11.62	8.85	0	40
Clinical liaison with colleagues	10.36	7.27	0	30
CPA administration	7.21	7.31	0	35
Other administration	10.43	8.27	0	40
Staff development	5.57	5.83	0	40
Other	2.69	9.02	0	50

DISCUSSION

Within this chapter we have provided evidence specific to the role of the forensic community mental health nurse. Debates around the role and speciality of forensic nursing have ensued for many years. Whilst these debates continue, fundamentally focused around what exactly they do which is different from mental health nurses in general, the forensic community mental health nurse has evolved. It is probably fair to say that community mental health nurses have cared for mentally disordered offenders in the community for many years. However, with governmental principles of caring for these mentally disordered offenders in conditions of the least security as is feasible, there has been the development of more specific forensic community mental health nursing. Furthermore, whilst forensic nurses working in secure conditions have continued to debate their role with a view to developing the profession, the forensic community mental health nurse appears to have taken their role into a specialism: they are specialist practitioners who work autonomously and contribute fully to multidisciplinary care. The care/custody debate, although paramount to forensic nurses within institutional care, has little bearing on the role of the forensic community mental health nurse. The role here needs to paradoxically focus on risk assessment and management for individuals from whom society may be at greatest risk. This is not to say that these are not important issues for forensic nurses in general, but are predominately more important for forensic community mental health nurses.

Recent RCN guidelines for purchasers of forensic mental health nursing (RCN 1997) put forward twelve expectations that purchasers should have of forensic community mental health nurses and it is perhaps useful to consider these alongside what we have provided above and are discussing here:

1. Effective communication between forensic and non-forensic services.

2. Client assessment.

3. Pre-discharge assessment and care planning.

4. After-care for those discharged from secure units.

5. Skilled supervision.

6. Responsible and discrete care co-ordination, risk reduction and relapse prevention.

7. Advocacy on behalf of clients.

8. Liaison between health, social and probation services.

9. Involvement with court diversion schemes.

10. Assessment of individuals held in police custody.

11. Crisis intervention and management services.

12. Provision of advice and support to generic service colleagues.

It appears from the evidence we have found, both within the literature and from our own empirical base, that the forensic community health nurses are certainly achieving most, if not all, of these. If we compare them with our findings we can see considerable similarities. We have found strong evidence of an extensive liaison role that they have, involving joint working both with other forensic and non-forensic services. They provide advice on aspects of management, but more specifically risk assessment. Further, they educate, supervise, support and guide non-forensic community mental health nurses and other professionals. Moreover, important aspects of their role are the maintenance of contact with other professionals and the clients themselves, and co-ordinating care.

We have provided here some of the data from the first systematic attempt to provide a baseline census of forensic community mental health nurses. Further details of data not included can be found in Brooker and White (1997). Not surprisingly, forensic community mental nurses predominately work from regional secure units, prisons or courts. There are, however, two diversities to their role, with some sharing components of both and others only one.

The first distinctive role is that of carrying a caseload of clients. These are predominately individuals with a previous admission, chronically mentally ill, and a diagnosis of schizophrenia. They are also key-worker for many of these. Many of their clients have a history of violence and are subject to restriction orders. Working with such clients as the known violent can obviously face the forensic community mental health nurse with dilemmas, foremost, perhaps, for their own safety but also for the safety of others. The second, however, do not carry caseloads and their role is to identify mentally disordered offenders as soon after arrest as possible, either in court or prison, diverting these to the mental health services which are appropriate. Then there are the nurses that share aspects of both roles.

From the literature review we have indicated some of the dilemmas which the forensic community mental health nurse faces. These seem to be more specific to those whose role encompasses working in the penal system. They must be aware of secondary gain that others get from them; their input can be misused both by other professionals and the clients themselves. Further professional boundaries and standards must be maintained when working in such strict and regimented establishments; where trust is paramount for effective assessment, however, this must be balanced with issues of professional independence.

CONCLUSION

Within the confines of this chapter it is difficult to consider fully the complexities and diversities of the role of the forensic community mental health nurse. What we have indicated is that they work as autonomous and specialist practitioners; are predominately based in forensic establishments, courts and prisons, working with a challenging and difficult client group; and are truly multidisciplinary in their approach, and place strong emphasis on liaison activity. The clients with which they practise means they are involved in the assertive follow-up and monitoring of mentally disordered offenders, where the interface between professions is flexible and versatile and there is understanding of complementary interests and skills.

CHAPTER 6

A Forensic Psychiatry Perspective

Christopher Cordess

INTRODUCTION

This chapter is written from my experience of training in psychiatry and forensic psychiatry, then as a consultant forensic psychiatrist leading a multidisciplinary team (MDT) in a Regional Secure Unit – each spanning periods of over ten years – and, now, my experience in academic forensic psychiatry, including work within a maximum secure hospital.

I have written elsewhere (Cordess 1996) about the MDT in forensic psychiatry and specifically within a forensic Regional Secure Unit, from my particular perspective also as a psychoanalyst. A main interest for me continues to be that of the development, nourishment and maintenance of a psychodynamically informed culture of care which allows thought, reflection and discussion within the MDT in traditional (but changing) forensic clinical settings. At an institutional, regional and national level – spurred by the recommendations of numerous and fairly catastrophic hospital inquiries – there is now a developing awareness of the importance (and necessity) of a psychotherapeutic culture and the integration of the 'talking treatments' into forensic care at many different levels – from day-to-day clinical interactions either in the ward or in community practice, to specific programmed psychotherapy sessions. The evidence base in forensic care, however, for the socio-therapeutic and psychodynamic method is thin, largely because of the extreme difficulties of methodology. Whilst the rigours of the randomised control trial (RCT) are indispensable, say, in the evaluation of drug efficacy, issues of best working models, best nursing practice and MDT function are necessarily based upon more complex criteria and upon experience.

This chapter is *not* written with the advantages of any specifically professional nursing knowledge, nor with the possible disadvantages of an attempted 'honing up' on developments in nursing theory and practice. I am, however, aware of some of the advances and reversals in conceptualisation – and funding – of nursing education, and the relative lack hitherto of formal, specifically forensic, nurse training, although recent developments in 'competency-based training', for example, at the University of Central Lancashire give hope in this respect. As such, this account represents the views of a colleague but nonetheless an outsider. What is, I hope, thereby gained in freshness of perspective may run the risk of some personal idiosyncrasy of viewpoint, but not – I hope – of doctorly prejudice.

The traditional or 'old' model of the MDT is one which gathers a variety of different disciplinary skills around the 'lead' Responsible Medical Officer (RMO). This model is the most common in in-patient psychiatric practice and has largely been accepted within forensic clinical practice, partly because of the statutory requirements and expectations placed upon the RMO by the criminal justice system.

A newer version of the MDT is essentially more democratic, but most importantly allows for a far greater balance of multidisciplinary perspectives and values. It recognises that the 'medical' or psychiatric conceptualisations and constructions of mental 'illness', and certainly personality disorder, are not necessarily the 'best', and certainly that they should not necessarily seek to be dominant. Such a representative system of different viewpoints aimed towards achieving a balance of values within mental health services and specifically within the MDT, rather than the familiar, continually competing, oppositional one, can be traced back to the work of philosophers of the mind and of moral theory, especially to the work of R.M. Hare.

It seems quite possible that many of the RMO functions within law which underwrite the medical dominance of the MDT will change in the future, for example with the proposed new legislation and the 'third way', announced in skeleton form in February 1999 and to be expanded later in a joint report of the Department of Health and the Home Office. The hegemony of the psychiatrist in forensic psychiatric care may be about to give way to nursing and psychology prominence, especially in relation to the management of personality disorders.

FUNCTION AND ROLES

It seems to me that there are at least three ways conceptually of dividing up the forensic nursing function and roles:

1. The specifically nursing role, with its essential forensic aspects of providing not merely physical but also essential emotional security (the 'containing' and 'holding environment' functions of Bion (1970) and Winnicott (1960) respectively). There are major burdens of stress and issues, of 'counter-transference' which pertain. For some purposes this role may, artificially, be considered independently of the functions of other MDT members since it can conceivably be practised independently of others, at least temporarily. I shall leave the detailed exegesis of key tasks and competencies of the different levels within the nursing career structure

to others: a good overview is contained in Tarbuck (1996). Clearly, the competencies required of the ward manager are greater, but include those carer competencies of less senior posts.

Williams, in a paper entitled 'Risks to the worker in dealing with disturbed adolescents' (1983), described some of the different roles expected of those working in a residential adolescent unit. We may extend those categories to certain forensic nursing situations with adult patients. The categories he selected were those of guardian, care giver and 'continuity figure'. Williams considered that workers could usually fulfil two of the roles, but all three roles only rarely and with difficulty. What is so rarely emphasised in contemporary services is the pivotal role of the 'continuity figure', especially with offender/patients whose lives have frequently been characterised by the absence of a stable, reliable figure, or where such a figure has often been lost early in life.

2. The nursing role within, and interacting within, the multidisciplinary forensic team.

3. Super-specialised' roles, which will depend upon particular aptitude, talent, opportunity and training. These might include: research and education; audit; management, and a specialised role in pharmacotherapy; or – what will provide the backbone of this chapter – the opportunities within forensic nursing to practise the psychological treatments and psychotherapy.

I shall take these in turn.

The specifically nursing role

The time has clearly come for due recognition of the crucially important, if not primary, place that forensic nursing plays in good forensic care (Cordess 1996). This is evident at many levels but is perhaps expressed most clearly in the phrase 'the other 23 hours' (Stanton and Schwartz 1954), which refers to that amount of time within the in-patient's day outside of specific therapies and of what then was assumed to be the one hour of specific (psychoanalytic) treatment. A contemporary version is the consideration that the effective therapeutic working of the ward occurs from Monday to Friday, in working hours. The important question is: what is a system doing which assumes that the professional interactions which make up the majority of the patients' day (and evening), i.e. those with nurses, are somehow not those of major significance? This recognition has been long in coming – and is partly marked by the fact of this volume.

Still, other disciplines – man (and possibly 'forensic man' especially) being a naturally hierarchical beast – can still be 'snippy' or superior about the nursing role, and nurses can in turn feel, or be made to feel, unappreciated, unrecognised and lowly in whatever hierarchy pertains. Poor pay and conditions, shift patterns incompatible with normal domestic and social life – including opportunities for personal or educational pursuits – as well as lack of a proper career structure have all been ingredients in producing the frequently low morale amongst forensic nursing staff. Of course, personal characteristics – aims and motivation, expectation and intellectual and emotional capacities – contribute crucially to the making of a competent, even exceptional, forensic nurse, as they do in other clinical professions. I exclude from this the ambition merely to be custodial – which is another function, *possibly* for another place, like prison. It should be said in this regard, however, that with the increasing recognition of the full range of psychopathology, and especially of personality disorders and substance abuse within prison populations, few nowadays would argue against the need for major therapeutic initiatives, including the nursing function, within prisons. As is well known, it is the juggling of the mix, and the interface between the therapeutic and the custodial (or the 'patient or prisoner' balance) at any given time, and within any given interaction, which poses some of the profoundest difficulties (Killian and Clark 1996). Whilst clearly, too, there is a balance to be found between the clinical skills and training of nursing staff on the one hand, and the costs thereby entailed, there is frequently a rhetoric of 'skill mix' nowadays which actually translates to the saving of funds by employing lesser-trained staff because they are cheaper. It seems likely to prove a false economy, although the recruitment or return to work of older people with life experience may bring with it increased capacities for understanding and emotional containment. Indeed, a précis of the person specification for the forensic nurse has been described as that of 'a mature, interested, person with lots of time' (Blackburn 1995).

The other side of the coin of nurse–patient interaction, however, is that nurses, along with occupational therapists, bear the brunt of direct patient contact, undiluted often for the duration of their shifts. Aside from the risks of violence from some patients, this is where there can be an overwhelming *emotional* burden with consequent attrition as a consequence of the intensity of nurse–patient interaction. I take the view that the offender (forensic) patient is 'captive' within the actual physical system but that more significantly he/she is a 'captive' of his past (and often a grossly abusive past) in an emotional and psychological sense, and that he/she also is a potential emotional and psychological 'captor' of others. In in-patient/residential settings this implicates the nurses as front-line staff. I use this term 'psychological captor' to refer to the unconscious re-enactment of interpersonal relations which the patient brings about with staff – i.e. the 'transference'. Put another way, nurses are the recipients of intense and extreme projections of gross psychopathology, which inevitably takes its toll if it is not properly 'dealt with' by good support, communication between staff and appropriate supervision.

'Burn-out', the term first used by Freudenberger (1974) to describe his own emotional exhaustion as a mental health professional, has been elaborated upon for those working specifically with 'forensic' offender patients by West (1996). He includes sub-headings entitled: 'On the effects of listening to violence'; 'On being frightened'; 'On the effects of mood'; 'On facing a negative work setting'; and, finally, 'The effects of working with sex offenders'. All these have especial relevance for the forensic nurse and yet largely they remain unexplored, at least in the clinical settings that I know. West quotes Winnicott (1949): 'To help...[one] must study the nature of the emotional burden which the [clinician] bears...in doing this work... However much he loves his patients, he cannot avoid hating them and fearing them, and the better he knows this the less will hate and fear be the motive determining what he does to his patients.'

At its extreme, records of Inquiries in Psychiatric Hospitals, including Special Hospitals, and in Children's Homes attest to the actual abuse of patients by some staff: what is invariably apparent is a failure of staff support and good supervision. However, far less recognised is what is effectively the 'abuse' of patients by passive withdrawal of staff across the professional spectrum from emotionally painful and difficult interactions. The forensic psychotherapy literature is rich in the 'reaction' which we have to patients, or, in psychodynamic parlance, 'the counter-transferential' effect of patients on staff, and the range of possible responses evoked in staff. For example, Symington (1980) describes 'the response aroused by the psychopath', specifically a common sequence, first of collusion (with his frequent 'charm'), then disbelief (at what he does to us) and then of consequent rejection of him. In this he will often have brought about a repeat of the very situation which is at the root of his and other people's suffering.

Searles (1979) has written of the negative effect that self-protective emotional 'cutting off' by staff can have upon patients (or anyone) who is emotionally needy and needs to make an emotional connection. Cox (1996), too, has described the phenomenon: 'All are caught between the Scylla of voyeuristic hyper-involvement on the one hand and the Charybdis of hyper-defended professional "distance" on the other.'

Most relevant of all at the level of the functioning of the hospital – and particularly of the near-total institution – itself, is the work of Jaques (1955). He writes:

One of the primary cohesive elements binding individuals in institutionalised human association is that of defence against psychotic anxiety. In this sense individuals may be thought of as externalising those impulses and internal objects that would otherwise give rise to psychotic anxiety, and pooling them in the life of the social institution ... [This implies] that we would expect to find in group relationships manifestations of unreality, splitting, hostility, suspicion, and other forms of maladaptive behaviour.

'Psychotic anxiety' in this context refers to our (the staff's) own central existential insecurities which we seek relief from, and comfort for, through our work. The workplace in this reading carries our own psychological anxieties and burden. Add to that the anxieties of the patients and we get a heady brew indeed. Menzies Lyth (1960, 1988a, 1988b) has written of the frequently defensive and therefore ritualised responses of nursing management and staff to the anxieties of a general hospital, and Hinshelwood (1996) to those of staff within a prison. He summarises this way of thinking as follows:

> The work task creates specific anxieties that disturb the people engaged on the work to a greater or lesser extent. Individuals may seek to protect themselves against those anxieties – to make them unconscious – by using *psychological defences*. In the working institutions those psychological defences may be supported by collective agreements to perform the work task in specific ways; and that will involve the development of certain attitudes to the work, often unrealistic, and certain work practices, called *defensive techniques*. This configuration of collective anxieties, with the unconscious organisation of collective attitudes and defensive techniques within the work practices is termed *the social defence system*.

He concludes, tellingly:

> In effecting change it is important to recognise, and then to apply a leverage to, the unconscious psychodynamics that are revealed. It is necessary to intervene in the balance between frustration and the frightened clinging to the defensive protection of the *status quo*. Whereas consciously it makes sense to address the frustrating limitations of the social defence system; unconsciously an alternative point of leverage is to address the anxieties themselves which are protected against. This entails an institution, and specifically a management, that can allow staff to suffer their anxiety without immediate relief; the pain of helplessness and the fear of violence need a currency within the prison as much as brutality and competitive trickery. We need consciously to forego technical tinkering with bits of the offender system, that avoid addressing the unconscious conflicts and suffering.

Most recently Hinshelwood (1999) has compressed an enormous body of thought in this subject into a short paper. He comments: 'With difficult patients, staff typically retreat emotionally from their patient, and from their experience ... [which] very specifically blinds us to what is happening subjectively in the patients – and indeed in staff. With these specific patients, that blind spot crucially feeds back directly into the patients' difficulties.' That is to say that we can have a negative effect upon the difficult patient by mirroring his emotional deficits and giving him a repeat experience of his (possibly unconscious) expectations.

Following on from these considerations, it is my view that the milieu in which the psychiatric in-patient is cared for – forensic or not – should aspire to the maximum degree of 'therapeutic community' which the mix of patients makes appropriate. The conventional social structure of the medically dominated mental hospital, with doctors and nurses striving to uphold forms of medical and nursing hierarchy, has only a limited – and diminishing – place, and that only for the acutely psychotic patient. It has none for the primarily personality disordered patient. Equally, the preoccupation, taken from traditional general medicine, of the numbers of 'beds' (with patients often quite unnecessarily *in* them (see Asher 1972)) should have been superseded long ago. Now we think in terms of levels of emotional (psychological) and physical support and containment, emphasising the goal of the patients' greatest possible autonomy.

Since the common denominator and central deficit of 'forensic' patients is in social, interpersonal (or, to use the jargon, 'object') relations, the practice of interpersonal social (and day-to-day, psychological) interventions should, in my view, move from being what currently is at best an added dimension to being the central and integral core of all forensic care. At the very least it is important that we pay attention to the *narrative* of a patient's life which provides meaning, context and perspective for his/her predicament. Even contemporary general medicine now exhorts clinicians to avoid 'the relentless substitution … of skills deemed "scientific" – those that are eminently measurable but unavoidably reductionist – for those that are fundamentally linguistic, empathic and interpretative … At its most arid, modern medicine lacks a metric for existential qualities, such as the inner hurt, despair, hope, grief and moral pain that frequently accompany, and often indeed constitute the illnesses from which people suffer' (Greenhalgh and Hurwitz 1999). If this is true of physical illnesses and appropriate clinical responses, how much more true of forensic clinical practice.

It is probably the case that the overall 'leader' of the clinical team in forensic psychiatry will continue to be the Responsible Medical Officer (RMO) in cases of mental illness, although different lead functions can be delegated, so long as professional boundaries are preserved. I have commented above upon possible (and necessary) changes in this medical hegemony in relation to the personality disorders.

It is one of the striking characteristics of the 'new NHS' by comparison with former times that a number of nurses have risen to positions of senior academic status and of high management responsibility – and are seen to have been disproportionately successful as, for example, Chief Executives of Trusts. Whilst this is not evidence of practical and clinical day-to-day nursing 'success', it does underline the high potential of some nursing staff. Equally, it emphasises the need to offer suitable career structures within clinical nursing – as well as management and research – if excellent staff are to be not only recruited, but retained within mainstream nursing practice. There appears to be a danger that clinical nursing practice is 'time limited' for many. Burn-out looms early, and, then, typically, after a period of community nursing (which gives greater professional freedom and allows room for personal initiative often subdued within in-patient management structures), a radical change follows away from the mainstream to a non-clinical role. Fortunately these problems are beginning to be addressed in the UK, as the significance of not only recruitment but also staff retention focuses the minds of hitherto unthinking or reluctant management to take staff supervision, staff well-being, and its opposite, staff burn-out, seriously.

We would all agree that the aim of forensic clinical practice is to give back to the dependent, detained offender/patient as much personal responsibility and autonomy as he is able to cope with and use, preferably pro-socially, but at least not anti-socially. On a personal level the task echoes that one we all have (and, no doubt, relatively, fail in) in the larger world within which 'nothing will change for the better in our being as humans, and the catastrophe towards which our world is headed ... will be unavoidable [whilst] we are still incapable of understanding that the only genuine backbone of all actions – if they are to be moral ... is responsibility, responsibility to something higher than my family, my firm, my success, responsibility to the order of being' (Vaclav Havel, address to US Congress, 1990). This begs the question of what is the 'order of being', but for our purposes we can agree, for example, that our responsibility is *not* merely a responsibility to 'management', political fashion, or other social construction, but to what we genuinely and conscientiously feel to be the right and moral order. Ethical questions are becoming increasingly important as the third party, public protection agenda sidelines the primacy of individual patients' interests and rights.

The nursing role within the multidisciplinary team

An account of the multidisciplinary team, and specifically a view of the forensic nurse's role within it, has already been referred to (Killian and Clark 1996). In their account they focus upon the nursing role, whilst in related chapters other disciplines – social work (Wrench), psychology (Hilton), occupational therapy (Finnegan), and psychiatry (Cordess) – all give accounts (Cordess 1996) from their own professional perspectives.

As a forensic psychiatrist leading the MDT within a RSU, I most valued those nurses who in, say, weekly meetings were able to communicate their experience and interactions with the patients, their own feelings and, so far as possible, verbatim accounts of what both the patient and the nurse had actually said to each other. Sometimes when asked for their experience over the week and for their views, nurses would make statements like: 'No change', 'Nothing in particular to report', or 'The patient has had an uneventful week.' This would invariably say more about the nurse than the patient, i.e. disengaged, passive, unmotivated and demoralised – for whatever reason. I took this, too, to be important information that needed understanding and needed addressing. This could, for example, be seen as the effect, by projection, of this particular patient's psychopathology, or it may be representative of the total ward situation, or of possibly an ongoing mental state in a particular nurse. Each would need addressing differently. Far more often, however, a narrative could be given, not only of the activities which the patient had undertaken during the week, but also of interactions – whether benign, or difficult, or even offensive – with staff. Sometimes an incidental event might have precipitated a very 'live' interaction, with heavy emotional loading sometimes present, which may be described as 'the past in the present and the present in the past' (Sandler and Sandler 1984).

Example 1

A nursing assistant was accompanying the occupational therapist of the team on a gardening group. As one of the male patients dug the garden he turned over a large stone – and found, to his alarm, that a toad had been accidentally decapitated by his spade. *His* horror was specific, and the nurse (who knew him well) realised that to her own alarm this man had been confronted unexpectedly by an only too vivid reminder of his own index offence (a homicidal attack on his wife) which actually involved her partial decapitation. This had occurred during an episode of profound depression, and although he had initially been fully amnesic for the attack and the surrounding events, lacunae of memory were gradually returning. There followed silence; discomfort; and an atmosphere which was very tense. This was a critical moment – amongst many others. The nurse, finding emotional resources and courage – as she said later 'with difficulty' – eventually said, simply, 'That's pretty awful.' The patient, in tears and dropping his spade, shaking, said, 'I didn't *mean* to do it.' After some time (during which the nurse felt it appropriate to preserve her silence) he continued, 'It was like that with my wife … but it couldn't have been just an accident … I mean I didn't want to hurt her.'

This seems to me – in condensed form – a fine example of how those clinical staff in direct patient contact may have the opportunity for highly significant interactions which may never come the way of more 'hands-off' clinical staff – like psychiatrists and psychologists. I do not wish to button-hole such an interaction as *necessarily* psychodynamic – for there is no particular theory involved. What the interaction shows is a capacity to stay *in emotional contact with the patient and continue thinking at the same time* which is a feature essentially of a fully human interaction as well as a therapeutic one: it happens to be one that can be fostered by psychodynamic psychotherapy supervision. Many staff faced with a similar (difficult) situation may have taken the socially acceptable (but professionally unproductive) route of 'pretending' or covering over the intense feelings out of a (misplaced) sense of embarrassment – of their own and on behalf of the patient. Clearly, if such interactions are to arise, and be encouraged, and be followed through, then there needs to be a commitment by the team and by a trained supervisor (whether a member of the team, or a psychotherapist appointed within the institution at a supra-team level) to offer the required level of supervision and training.

There is a fine balance between the allowance of such intense interactions and, on the one hand, more management-based nursing functions and, on the other, the more formalised specifically psychotherapeutic functions of the psycho-therapist.

Example 2

A nurse from the team spent sessions with a large group of patients in art therapy. During the third session he commented that a patient – who had hitherto not spoken of his offence in two years of in-patient care – had repeatedly drawn multiple versions of the same house and front porch with many details in common. The nurse commented that the patient seemed preoccupied with this scene. He rejoined that it was the picture of the front of the house where he had lived with his wife and children for 30 years: it was the porch where they had their final, fatal, row, and the threshold upon which he had killed his wife as she threatened (not unreasonably, as he acknowledged) to leave him.

Moment of choice: what to say? The nurse, to his later chagrin, found himself going into ultra-defensive mode, indicating that he need not continue with the same scene, that if he preferred he could 'do a landscape or a portrait, or anything'. This was a highly significant and 'live' moment lost. What is far more important, however, is that the nurse felt that this was a significant matter and felt able to discuss it with the MDT.

The patient did move on from that repeated scene of the crime – and went silent on his offence again. With time, however, he returned to repeating the familiar scene, and the art therapist (who by now had been party to the discussion) could later make use of it in an interactive and exploratory way.

These two examples both refer to nurses working *outside* of the day-to-day routine of nursing practice. Possibly this is significant; possibly it is easier for nurses to be able to think dynamically (and laterally) when they are away from the frequently operationalised, and too frequently over-bureaucratised, humdrum of their daily work.

'Super-specialised' roles

There was a time when psychiatric nurses in Britain were not expected to play any part in a patient's specifically psychological treatment. As Marks *et al.* (1977) remark: 'Surprise is sometimes expressed that nurses *treat* as well as *care* for patients.'

According to my anecdotal sources, this changed favourably with the first engagement and training of nurses at the Maudsley Hospital in the early 1970s as 'Behavioural Nurse Therapists' (Marks *et al.* 1977). Like much psychotherapy provision, in my view, the influence that this initiative has exerted has been more a consequence of general factors rather than of the specific relevance of the purely behaviour therapy formulations and technique. Indeed, few would seek to justify the isolated use merely of behavioural treatments (i.e. without a cognitive component) for any mental disorder, nowadays, and certainly not in the forensic sphere. The point, however, is that this initiative was good for the staff, who were thereby empowered as 'therapists'. That many went on to train further and now occupy influential posts in related fields is not in doubt. That is, it provided a first stepping stone for career growth within mainstream nursing practice.

In my experience at the Maudsley Hospital, there was around this time, too, encouragement given to nurses to specialise in psychodynamic psychotherapy with in-patients on what was then Ward 6 under the consultant leadership of Dr Murray Jackson (Jackson and Cawley 1992). This was an acute in-patient ward for mostly young psychotic patients: the milieu was psychodynamic offering in-depth understanding of the predicament and 'madness' of the patient – with the provision of all the other usual treatments, including medication. This ward sadly closed – a victim to some degree of the *realpolitik* of the 'internal market' and the NHS 'reforms' of the 1980s; and but one example, amongst many, of a contemporary culture in mental health of a wish to find impossibly 'quick fix' solutions to distressing, ingrained and highly complex failures of human development (i.e. personality disorder and major mental illness). These examples apply to the mainstream, albeit in a highly privileged and rarefied hospital. The therapeutic community development by contrast (and definition) was always more respectful of, and made better use of, nurses – but in a resident social therapist role (Jones 1952) – along with those whose disciplines or origin were different; for example, social work or psychology.

New forms of psychotherapy have been developed in recent years, and have each been applied in some form or other to patients in forensic care. Each had originally been developed primarily by psychologists, but nurses increasingly play a prominent part in the delivery of such treatments. They have the pragmatic advantage over the psychodynamic psychotherapies that they are definitionally more focused, and, as a corollary, have far more focused trainings. In other ways they are less ambitious, require less time duration for delivery (and for training) and, therefore, are often delivered by therapists of relatively less experience.

Any members of the MDT (or pairs, in the case of joint therapy with families or in groups) are free to practise specific, circumscribed dynamic or systemic therapies either outside of the MDT (thereby avoiding conflict of roles) or with patients within their team (so long as manageable boundaries are negotiated). These include individual and group psychodynamic therapies, as well as systems-based family therapy.

Confidentiality is not possible in absolute terms in these situations: there can be no important 'secrets' within the MDT, without their proving to be potentially divisive. However, *relative* confidentiality can be preserved in that only 'bare-bones' reports and summaries need to be fed back into the team's general information, plus any *critical* details which team members rightly need to know.

The whole area of these various psychotherapies is a large and specialised subject, which is summarised by Cordess (1998).

CONCLUSION

I have confined myself largely to the in-patient role of the forensic nurse within the secure institution with only few comments about practice within the community. I have concentrated predominantly upon the interactions of (nursing) staff with patients, the possible effects of those interactions and, in turn, with the interrelations of the members of the MDT clinical team.

In my view, one of the major tasks of the forensic nurse – as of other practitioners, in the settings I have described – is that of striving to maintain emotional contact with the patient, whilst at the same time maintaining a certain degree of objectivity.

There are clearly very different problems in the role of nursing the forensic patient within the community. For one, there is (relative) release from the demands (and projections) of others in what can be an intense crucible, or 'hot house', of the secure ward and the 'madness' of all human beings in such situations, let alone that of the designated patients. In many ways a major challenge for the future will be that of bringing the skills of the forensic nurse and the forensic MDT to bear within community practice.

Such is the failure of confidence of non-secure non-in-patient psychiatric care that the new mental health strategy for England and Wales, *Modernising Mental Health Services*, asserts that 'community care has failed' (Department of Health 1998). It goes on to describe a strategy for providing a service 'in which patients, carers and the public are safe and where security and support is provided to all'. As Marshall (1999) comments: 'This strategy has two key elements: increased investment and increased control (over patients and clinicians).' Others have commented that the strategy errs in claiming that 'community care has failed' and that is would be more true to say that 'it has not been properly tried' for lack of funding, poor services, overburdening of families, problems in recruiting and retaining staff and an outdated legal framework. We can agree, however, that the stage is set for attempts at far greater social control and legislation to 'ensure compliance with appropriate treatment' (Department of Health 1998). It will be for nurses, and specifically forensic nurses, along with other members of the MDT, to decide what part they wish to play in this far more coercive (and ethically dubious) policy, and to find whether they can shape it, and claim for it the therapeutic function, rather than the restrictive punitive and marginalising one it is in danger of becoming.

Indeed, in community forensic practice the anxieties of both patients and staff have some similarities to each other. For both they are largely those of isolation and of insufficient support from their management structures, the health and welfare infrastructure, and from other members of the community team – even though it is part of the job of the community nurse to look as if he/she is confidently coping, and the 'privilege' of the forensic patient to feel more or less unpredictable or vulnerable. Greater team support for staff, and maximum 'voluntariness' for the patient, is needed, not increased imposition and therefore alienation.

CHAPTER 7

Clinical Psychology and the Forensic Nursing Role

Nigel Hopkins and Leah Ousley

INTRODUCTION

This chapter is about what a forensic nurse is, and how forensic nurses can use psychological knowledge. Written by both a nurse and a psychologist, the chapter also aims to make the point that by learning to understand and work with psychologists, the nurse may be able to facilitate these colleagues in what is without doubt a very difficult role. Four previously unpublished studies are used to illustrate some of the issues involved.

WORKING TOGETHER

George Kelly, the founding father of personal construct theory psychology, argued that playing a role with another person meant that we 'subsumed' their construct system (Kelly 1955). This means that we need to understand how the other person (or discipline) sees things: what their priorities are, how they view their own work in terms of purposes and goals and how these are to be achieved. Basically, if we are to work together, each party needs to be able to describe not only their own role (hard enough), but also the role of other disciplines.

WHAT IS FORENSIC NURSING AND WHAT IS FORENSIC PSYCHOLOGY?

One way of answering this question would be to ask nurses and psychologists themselves. A recent study of nursing staff by Sally Wilson, a psychologist from York University, has made a start on doing just that. She sought the opinion of the three ward managers at Wathwood Hospital Regional Secure Unit, on the question of what characteristics go together to make a good forensic nurse (Wilson 1998). Using a repertory grid measurement technique based on personal construct theory (PCT), Wilson asked each ward manager to describe their staff in terms of bipolar constructs. Wilson correlated these constructs with each other and with a supplied bipolar construct 'very good practitioner' versus 'some way to go yet'. A cluster analysis was carried out on the resulting correlation matrix. This cluster analysis produces results broadly equivalent to those of a principal components analysis.

Table 7.1 sets out the ward managers' ideas as to the characteristics of an effective forensic nurse. There are many similarities between the clusters of the three ward managers, whilst some variation is expected. In general the person they describe appears to have a mature outlook, be clear-thinking and well-organised, with a definite notion of their objectives, but they are not strident or rigid in the way they go about their work. The importance of being responsive to individual patient need is paramount.

Table 7.1 Characteristics of an effective forensic nurse (Wilson 1998)

Ward Manager 1	Principal construct	Significantly related constructs
Cluster One	Common-sense versus prone to make mistakes	Ability to change, maturity, innovative, respected, laid-back, decisive, never threatening
Cluster Two	Patient-focused versus offence-focused	Patience, focuses on illness (rather than offence), maturity
Cluster Three	Commitment versus not committed	Laid-back, decisive
Cluster Four	Life experience versus little life experience	Respected, never threatening
Ward Manager 2	Principal construct	Significantly related constructs
Cluster One	Fair versus irrational	Relaxed, intelligent, interested, committed, calm
Cluster Two	Firm versus not firm	Detachment (ability not to take things too personally), professional
Cluster Three	Efficient versus lazy	Focus (on an individual patient rather than the group), structured (plans things for the day)
Ward Manager 3	Principal construct	Significantly related constructs
Cluster One	Confident versus feels insecure	Organisation, social skills, work rate, experience, can relate to patients, self-aware, open and objective mind
Cluster Two	Composed versus panics	Open and objective, optimistic, work rate, self-aware
Cluster Three	Parameter setting* versus relaxed attitude	Demarcation line (patient and staff)*
Cluster Four	Caring versus not caring	(No significantly related constructs)

* Note that in Cluster Three of Ward Manager 3, 'parameter setting' and 'demarcation' were negatively related to being a good practitioner.

This study tells us about the *kind of people* nurses are, especially ones who work within a controlled environment. Being able to define the 'person specifications' for such a nurse is part of what is needed, but it is still necessary to ask the question: 'Is there such a person as a *forensic* nurse?' This suggests the absence of any role definition. Blackburn (1996) addresses this issue and brings another dimension to our query regarding the difference between a forensic nurse and a mental health nurse. He asks not only whether the type of work involved justifies the use of the term 'forensic', but he also questions the desirability of workers within controlled environments thinking of themselves in this way (Blackburn 1996). Traditionally, activities are properly thought of as forensic when they relate to the workings of a court of law. It is certainly true that secure hospitals care for patients who are most often held there by direction of a court under a section of the Mental Health Act (1983). It is also true that workers within controlled environments provide information for the court, in the form of the Mental Health Review Tribunal, in regard to the ongoing risk posed by a particular patient. To this degree then the work can be seen to be 'forensic', but these aspects aside, Blackburn would ask, could it be said that the rest of the work is forensic in nature?

It is clear that Blackburn is not being overly fussy about the linguistic correctness of the term's use. He wants us, that is nurses, psychologists and the rest of the clinical team, to think about who we are working for. Are we working primarily for the interests of our patients or for the purposes of the court? We may begin to think that the paternalistic, but undoubted, need to protect the public is our main objective rather than it being only one of them. This ethical dilemma 'control versus care' is one shared by all those involved in the care of the mentally disordered, but it is an ongoing problem for those of us working in the secure hospitals. Of all the characteristics that differentiate between the psychiatric nurse working in a general psychiatric ward and the one working in a controlled environment it is this one that justifies the distinction above any other.

CONTROL VERSUS CARE OR CONTROL WITHIN CARE?

Control versus care or control within care? One way of dealing with this potential conflict of interests is to 'reframe' the issue by observing that whilst our patient's judgement is impaired we need to act on their behalf in some areas. We need to protect them from themselves, and we can do this by observing that we do them no favours if we were to contribute to their release before they were ready and they were to re-offend, for 'the key would be thrown away'.

It is possible that someone will come up with a more appropriate descriptive term for this genuinely different type of work, but for now people are describing the work as 'forensic', inviting the dangers inherent in that.

CORE PURPOSES IN FORENSIC MENTAL HEALTH: DESCRIBING OUR WORK

Monitoring met and unmet needs

Learning to work together requires the clear identification of our common aims and these can be usefully expressed in terms of a patient's needs. Forensic patients ought not be thought of as different in this respect. At any one time, a given patient may have several unmet needs and therapeutic care plans can be administered sequentially or in parallel.

One of the authors (NJH) has experience of using an instrument that is designed to identify both a patient's met needs and their unmet needs (a need being defined as a deficit or a symptom for which there is a demonstrably effective intervention). The needs for care assessment schedule (NFCAS) is 'prescriptive', that is, it tells us what the care plan should contain for a given patient. The NFCAS (Brewin *et al.* 1987) was applied in Rotherham, England, to compare the levels of care being received by two populations of day patient: those attending a local authority day centre and those attending a National Health Service day hospital (Raleigh *et al.* 1997).

The study concluded that the two populations were very similar in terms of their needs. But interestingly, although not surprisingly, the day hospital was better at meeting needs arising out of psychiatric symptomatology whereas the day centre tended to be more focused on responding to their clientele's perceived needs rather than some of the prescriptive needs identified by the NFCAS. This difference reflected a contrasting philosophical approach that probably had its roots in the core purposes of the two agencies. In the NHS the person is a patient with an illness; in the local authority its clients are citizens with problems. How we think about our patients does make a difference to what we do.

Mentally disordered offenders

This last observation brings us to our case in point: just how are we to view the central person in our professional world, 'the mentally disordered offender'? This category of person typifies the patients of forensic workers. Strictly speaking, many are not fairly described by the term 'offender'. For whilst they may have committed an offence, and have been found by a court to have done so, they have been excused from an attribution of blame due to their being also found to be incompetent or 'insane', under the McNaughten rule, at the time of the crime. The latter is an important point, as it is vital that we attempt to minimise that punitive tendency in all of us that is triggered on hearing details of, say, a person's violence to another. It is more difficult for us to aid someone if we fear them or are disgusted by their past actions. When the court makes a hospital order the expectation is that the perpetrator of the crime will be given treatment that will lead to them being freed from the affliction that largely caused them to behave as they did. If we are to be a constructive force in the healing process we need to regard the secure hospital patients themselves as victims, in this case of their history and biology.

Should the patient tune into our negative evaluation of them it is virtually certain that they will be far less open to the idea of change during our work with them. In fact, they could become even more rigid and contrary than they were to begin with, erecting obstacles to the process we are trying to set into motion. With this type of consideration in mind we need to choose our words with great care as we work with the patient to orient them towards the adoption of a constructive perspective. For example, calling a group a 'sex offender group' poses an immediate problem. A large proportion of the patients selected for such a group would initially reject the idea that they belonged to such a category of person, which after all is perilously close to being a description of a group for 'bad persons'! Starting off in therapy with such an insult is likely to be counter-productive. This of course does not mean to say that during the course of the therapeutic process the patient will not come to view their behaviours of the past with horror. Owning a negative behaviour has a very different impact from being invited to own a dysfunctional personality. 'Hate the sin and love the sinner' seems an appropriate sentiment (see Jenkins 1998).

This 'mentally disordered offender group', in itself an unflattering descriptive category, is a very varied group indeed. It covers people who suffer from many different types of dysfunction. Here we have patients with 'mental impairment' or learning disability, 'mental illness', which generally is referring to a diagnosis of schizophrenia or manic-depressive psychosis, and 'psychopathic disorder' which is described legally to the effect that it is an enduring condition which gives rise to especially aggressive or seriously irresponsible behaviour. These definitions come from the attempts of various governments of the day to put into legal terms those psychological states of mind that modify the type of legal action that will be taken. The forensic worker needs to be aware of this and not confuse legal jargon with clinical categories stemming from evidence-based classification systems.

Dysfunctional cognitions: a unifying perspective

Often, patients from within all these legal categories also demonstrate disorders of their personality. To the mainstream psychologist and nurse this means that they operate on the basis of extremely dysfunctional cognition. Hence the problems experienced by individuals in these broad legal categories are sometimes very similar to each other and at other times very different. These legal definitions give no really reliable guide to what might be targeted by our interventions – for example, Blackburn et al. (1990) found that two-thirds of each of their two groups of patients, one mentally ill and one psychopathic, had personality disorders of one kind or another.

Often, it seems likely that a person's delusional system has contributed to (or 'driven') their antisocial behaviour – this could be, say, arson or violence. Taylor (1985) suggests that between one-fifth and one-half of her cohort of delusional prisoners acted under the direction of their delusional beliefs, or were directed by 'command' hallucinations. Whilst evidence suggests there is reason to believe that the majority of people who have a serious mental illness are at no greater risk of offending than the population at large (Blackburn 1996), some aspects of a person's psychosis can sometimes lead to violence, as Taylor may have highlighted. It could turn out that it is partially the content of the delusion or hallucination that prompts the behaviour. This content, in turn, is probably shaped by the sufferer's developmental and other life experiences. What might be at work here are tendencies to release a sense of deep hurt, resentment, sense of injustice, and an all-pervading suspicion of others, in the form of retribution or retaliatory violence.

Not surprisingly, there is evidence that antisocial beliefs and attitudes are strong causal factors in the production of socially deviant behaviours (Andrews, Bonta and Hoge 1990). If a person who has developed this sort of mindset should become psychotic, then could the threshold to express their anger be lowered even further by whatever psychological changes have taken place as a result of this psychotic process?

Problems with empathy

An interesting suggestion has been put forward by Frith (1992) who is investigating whether or not our ability to put ourselves in the place of another person, and experience the world as they do, is damaged in people experiencing a psychosis. Frith goes as far as to speculate that psychosis itself is the result of our loss of this ability to empathise.

If we are not distressed by the likely effects of our behaviour on others, then of course it becomes that much easier for us to damage another person or their property. It also becomes easier for us to develop our fantasies about their likely responses to our behaviour, for we are no longer taking accurate account of their true reactions.

People who are diagnosed as falling within the 'autistic spectrum', and this includes those exhibiting 'Asperger's Syndrome', have a similar problem with empathy. The difference is that they have had this problem all their life, unlike the psychotic person who wrongly believes they still have the skills, and so get their 'mind reading' wrong. Again, there are other people who have this ability to understand what another person might be experiencing, and yet do not respond by holding back their aggressive or exploitative behaviour. These people may have an incomplete or only partially functioning empathic system. They may know of the distress they are causing and yet they do not feel it themselves. This is perhaps because they have learned not to identify with others strongly, or in particular their victims, whom they may de-personalise, rather as soldiers are said to imagine that the enemy are not human beings but belong to some other perhaps monstrous or despicable species. Why this happens is not yet known. Often, such people have been the victims of terrible abuse themselves and they may have learned to suppress the awareness of their own earlier deep distress. In doing so they may have also rendered inoperable the mechanism for experiencing not only their own distress, but also that of other people. Psychopathic behaviour may fall into this category.

The patients of forensic workers have a greater proportion of such people within their ranks than do patients elsewhere in the mental health services. This is another distinguishing characteristic of our work.

Improved coping with cognitive therapy

Therapeutic efforts need to be directed towards the suppression of the psychotic process and anti-psychotic medication is by far the most successful technique available. The supplementary cognitive behavioural techniques being developed are designed both to give the patient a framework for understanding their experience, and to teach them improved coping skills to reduce the distress caused by their disordered thoughts and perceptions. This is exceptionally difficult work, but with training and good supportive supervision, both nurse and psychologist can provide this form of therapy. Nelson (1997) has produced a practice manual for this type of intervention and also offers a three-day workshop.

Going for the holistic approach

Whilst we are naturally concerned that a patient's harmful behaviour should not be repeated, and whilst we work to achieve such a positive outcome, our assessments will have identified many problems that may or may not have contributed to a particular antisocial act. We wish to argue that our rehabilitation of people in controlled environments needs to look at the person as a whole and not in a restricted way as we would do if we think of them as primarily being offenders. Blackburn (1996) agrees with this stance and he targets the goal as increasing personal effectiveness, by dealing with those psychological deficits that prevent a full and satisfying involvement in social life. It is important also to remember that the patient themselves may come to be traumatised by their own act of human destruction. This may well need to be addressed if the patient is to progress. This position is not necessarily at odds with the view of Burrow (1993a) who identifies the focus of forensic nursing as being the targeting of behaviour that links offending activity to psychiatric symptomatology. The fact is that we do not yet know for sure what these causal links are.

Risk assessment and management

The psychologically disturbed offender adds the characteristic of dangerousness to their list of needs. These patients need help to become less dangerous. We work with them to reduce the risk they pose to others and part of this work requires the measurement of risk.

Dynamic versus static risk analysis: a basic model

The prediction of risk is an ongoing activity and the forensic nurse and psychologist make a contribution here. As a team, we are on the look-out for *analogue* behaviours; that is, activities that are similar to those seen in the patient's offending behaviour or were likely part of the 'lead up' repertoire of the offender. It is often said that nothing predicts behaviour better than previous behaviour and analogue activity is a powerful example of this as generalisations can be made using this sort of sampling of the patient/offender's continuous writing of their 'behavioural autograph'.

The nurse draws on observations made in a broad spectrum of settings and the report back to the multidisciplinary team often makes a powerful contribution to the final appraisal of the multidisciplinary team, which is embodied in the form of the review summary. For maximum usefulness, generalisations are accompanied by clearly described events.

The psychologist works to try and identify the developmental stages that led up to the index offence and previous offences. 'Person' states and/or traits (or construct systems) interact with situational influences, or triggers, to create the ingredients that add up to the committing of socially unacceptable behaviours. The vehicle for offences against the person may involve the progressive development of fantasies and the ever-escalating extent of partial 'try-outs'. Some offences against property, such as arson, may reflect a person's desperate attempt to influence the direction of factors affecting their life, when they cannot identify any other alternative method of coping. The arsonist's mental state may involve an intense sense of injustice and deep hurt or powerfully felt rejection.

An underlying assumption of risk management is that an estimate of a person's increasing level of safety can only be gained by the gradual easing of restrictions on the patient, accompanied by high levels of observation. At the first suggestion of there being analogue behaviour the microscope is turned onto that area, and a re-assessment made in the light of the emerging information. Thus, someone who has committed a sexual offence against an elderly person will need to be asked why they seemed to be so distracted by a group of older people in a restaurant. A person who killed whilst deluded and under the influence of drink will need to re-visit their work on alcohol abuse, if they become drunk whilst out on community leave. And a person who cannot tolerate noisy neighbours, to the point of using a knife to back up their complaint, is a continuing source of concern if they repeat this intolerance within the controlled setting. There are a large number of factors to take into account when evaluating the risk posed by a patient, and it is important that the team pay attention to all these issues. When things have gone wrong in the past it has often been because some procedure had been omitted from the team's activities or dealt with inadequately. Risk assessment like this is a continuous process, and is in contrast to the static 'one-off' checklist approach that is insensitive to fluctuations and situational observations that occur daily.

Matching up to good practice in risk assessment

The audit group at Wathwood Hospital Regional Secure Unit, South Yorkshire (Hopkins *et al.* 1997, 1998), set about an evaluation of the unit's effectiveness in accurately assessing the level of risk posed by the patients cared for there.

From a parent list of 'good practices', the audit group selected eighteen examples that seem to sample the various categories of risk management activity. These 'good practices' became the basis of the 'standards' that had to be achieved. For each of the eighteen items there was an analogue scale with 'anchors' at five points. These were 'very poor', 'poor', 'adequate', 'good', 'very good' and were placed at 0", 1.5", 3", 4.5" and 6" intervals along the six-inch scale. The standard set for all items on the first cycle of the audit was a scale measurement of 3.5"; this was a third of the way along the interval between 'adequate' and 'good'.

The subjects were nurses, occupational therapists and psychiatrists. Psychologists were excluded, as there was only one of these!

Differences amongst disciplines

Although none of the item scores were on average significantly less than 'adequate', only six were numerically equal to or greater than the 'standard'. Psychiatrists were in general more optimistic in their perceptions of the unit's risk assessment procedures and their scores very often approached 'good', whereas nursing staff and occupational therapy staff scores hovered around the 'adequate' mark. The source of such a difference was of interest and a factor analysis of the data was carried out in an attempt to shed light on this. A three-factor solution was chosen and this seemed to indicate that psychiatrists 'tuned into' a dimension of outcome prediction, nurses were more concerned with a dimension that looked at the application of therapeutic procedures, and occupational therapists' scores indicated variation around an axis dealing with the accuracy of the assessment process.

The value of having a variety of opinion

The first audit report concluded by suggesting that each discipline's perception could be viewed as meaningful, but that these perceptions were made from the points of view of each profession's perspective which differed due to the nature of the work undertaken, and the varying opportunities for certain sorts of observations to be made. This conclusion was taken to represent a validation of the need for there to be a team evaluation where different views could be documented and debated.

A repeat audit was made one year later. This second time around the audit loop confirmed the previous results. Whilst there was statistically significant evidence of there being a general improvement in scores, the rank position of each item remained fairly constant. The differences between the disciplines were maintained even down to there being a comparable factor structure that differentiated the three professions. The instrument appeared to be reliable even though there has to be uncertainty as to what was in fact being measured.

Other professional characteristics and differences between the disciplines

Having seen, in the audit of risk assessment and risk management, that the three disciplines varied in their retrospective evaluation of Wathwood's risk assessment procedures, one of the authors (LO) explored whether there were differences between disciplines in another respect. She attempted to measure their perception of the relative importance of the various risk factors routinely identified in this regional secure unit (Ousley 1998). She found considerable variation in levels of agreement *within* each discipline's rank ordering of the importance they attach to the risk factors put before them. However, there was a good level of agreement *between* the disciplines concerning the most important risk factors when an average was taken of the ranking.

All three qualified disciplines ranked 'insight into offending behaviour', 'response to therapy', 'history of offending' and 'compliance with medication' in their first five most important risk factors. Nurses and psychiatrists identified a history of aggression; occupational therapists ranked this seventh. Interestingly, only occupational therapists ranked psychopathy in their first five. All disciplines ranked having a regular and continuous risk assessment process highly (in contrast to having less frequent snapshot assessments).

When it came to the rest of the thirteen risk factors considered, the levels of agreement amongst the qualified staff falls off as expected. An overall rank order of importance was calculated, by averaging the ranks of all three qualified disciplines, and the nurses' rank ordering correlated 0.92 with this. Psychiatrists' rank ordering correlated 0.77 and occupational therapists' 0.89. When the rank orderings of each discipline were compared with the other two, nurses' priorities were found to correlate 0.56 with those of psychiatrists, and 0.84 with occupational therapists. Psychiatrists correlated 0.41 with occupational therapists. These figures indicate that there are clear differences between disciplines in the weighting they give to many risk items. It is of note that only the unqualified care assistants ranked the presence of psychotic symptoms highly. Occupational therapists and psychiatrists ranked this eleventh and nurses tenth.

A factor analysis of the results identified five important dimensions of risk. Factor 1 could be labelled *co-operation and engagement*, and included compliance with medication, response to therapy, and the development of insight. Factor 2 seemed to relate to membership of a *delinquent and under-socialised subculture*, and included the use of drugs and alcohol, acts of delinquency, poor family networks, and immaturity. Factor 3 involved a *history of aggressiveness, hostility and suspicion*, and offending behaviours. Factor 4 included *age* as a risk-reducing variable. Factor 5 concerned the development of insight into offending behaviour, and *participation in offence-related interventions* that might achieve this.

Studies such as this help to explain the richness of the multidisciplinary interactions that take place in controlled environments. In a well-functioning unit opinion will be sought after and any differences in view debated and ultimately documented. Due to their profession's unique role within the team, each discipline's observations and interpretations are of potential value and care must be taken to ensure that these differences are not obscured in the multidisciplinary team review summaries.

Specific interventions

Teaching the patient alternative methods of meeting their own needs is an obvious form of intervention and is directly associated with a strengthening of that person's well-being as well as contributing to a reduction in the risk that they pose to others.

Help to see the point of changing can be given using the techniques of *motivational interviewing*, and *cognitive–behavioural therapy* (CBT) interventions. But these need to be suitably modified for work with a more resistant and damaged personality disordered population than is seen in OP settings (Young 1994). Young, a past student of Aaron Beck, founder of the cognitive approach, argues for the modification of CBT to fit with the special characteristics of the personality disordered patient. These are the patients we work with in controlled environments. Their problematic characteristics are, firstly, their rigidity – they will tend not to be able to work in the collaborative way CBT practitioners hope for. They also tend to be people who think that their personality is fine. Secondly, they practise avoidance, of some of their most painful beliefs and cognitions, to a degree not seen amongst most neurotic people. They are experts at defending against the deeply disturbing feelings that they anticipate will destroy them if they make it into full consciousness, to use one or two psychoanalytic terms.

Finally, personality disordered people classically also have dysfunctional interpersonal relationships. CBT workers tend not to expect that they will need to utilise any special interpersonal skills in their therapy, but Young points out that in-depth involvement with interpersonal issues will often be a prerequisite when working with the personality disordered patient.

Given the great difficulties in achieving lasting personal change, much hope is currently pinned on the possibilities promised by *relapse prevention* programmes. Here the goal is to reduce the likelihood of repeating the undesired behaviours by working to minimise the replication of the *conditions* under which such behaviours occurred in the past.

Both psychologist and nurse can, with training, undertake many of the specific highly focused interventions discussed above, but the forensic nurse is best placed to undertake the *milieu* work that may well constitute the most potent form of change induction available.

Milieu interventions

The 'RAID' approach of Will Davies of the Association of Psychological Therapies (APT) presents itself as an almost ideal backdrop to the everyday running of a secure environment. RAID stands for 'Reinforce Appropriate, Ignore Disruptive' behaviours.

The emphasis is on 'building the individual', encouraging their development of a sense of their own future and achieving this, in the main, by using social reinforcement whenever appropriate behaviours are spotted.

The idea can be visualised by thinking in terms of the accumulation of positive behaviours simply taking up the space of inappropriate challenging behaviour as the person experiences less and less need to use challenging behaviours to meet their needs.

Psychosocial Intervention (PSI) models provide further ideas that help to develop our milieu schema or mindset that generates a holistic view of our work. The stress vulnerability model (Zubin and Spring 1977) underpins much of the thinking in this PSI area. One powerful source of stress identified arises through intense interpersonal interaction that produces relapse-inducing exchanges known as high expressed emotion (EE), those with coercive and critical contents being amongst the most damaging of these.

The development of communication skills and problem-solving ability and techniques, which reduce EE, figure amongst the needs of the social participants in these types of programme. Many other needs can be identified and generating interventions tailored to meeting these is part of the therapy process.

The forensic nurse as a therapist

It is important to note that the one-hour-per-week therapist may find it hard to compete with the sort of influence that a residential worker can have, interacting with the patient as they do, hour after hour, day after day. The message here is that workers in this position *can* be major forces for change. But, to be in this position, such workers need to be trained and this training will be ongoing and supported through individual and group supervision. The forensic nurse is currently massively under-utilised in this respect. A major factor here is lack of opportunity due to other clinical and administrative pressures. The frustration many psychiatric nurses feel when they see other smaller professions, such as psychology, struggling to meet the demand for therapeutic interventions that they themselves could be involved in, if only they had consistently available time for this, needs to be addressed.

The forensic nurse as researcher and evidence-based practitioner

Three of the four studies described above were carried out by nurses, sometimes in collaboration with a psychologist and sometimes with an occupational therapist or psychiatrist; a fourth study was by a psychologist studying nurses. Research and other projects are fun as well as often being required of us, as in the case of audit. They are also ways of keeping up our interest in the work we do. The literature reviews keep us up-to-date in relation to good practice, and of course it is research that moves our professions on through the development of more effective forms of intervention. Research provides a window on what we do, and we can often see the wood for the trees for the first time! Evidence-based working is now the established way we all operate in the modern health service.

FUTURE HORIZONS

In 1989, the Manpower Advisory Service report on psychology services pointed out that it could be 30 years before there was a sufficient number of psychologists to enable the discipline to offer an independent service to patients that was uniform across the National Health Service. Many in the clinical psychology profession decided in the interim to define their objectives as the dissemination of psychological knowledge and interventions throughout the health service. This strategy can only work if there is a willingness on the part of other professions to enter into some form of collaborative interchange. The teacher–pupil relationship is an inappropriate one, since other professions have their own training plans and personnel, but psychologists could have something to offer forensic nursing on an exchange basis. Collaborative projects in the areas of therapy, training and research could (and already do) bring together the two professions, both of whom have much to gain from subsuming each other's professional construct system.

CHAPTER 8

Transfer of Case Management from Forensic Social Worker to Forensic Nurse

Jean Jones, Karen Elliott and Rachael Humpston

INTRODUCTION

This chapter describes the work of a multidisciplinary team in a high security forensic setting providing care for people with learning disabilities, and demonstrates the transition of responsibility of case management from forensic social worker to forensic nurse in the resettlement process.

It also reflects the change in attitudes towards people with a learning disability and severe challenging behaviour, both within an institution and the community.

The format is a case study of a long-term learning disabled male patient, with a classification of severe mental impairment, as defined in the Mental Health Act 1983, who was resettled directly from high security forensic care into the community.

CASE STUDY

John had been in high security forensic care for twenty-nine years and had been in institutional care since the age of four months. He had been abandoned by his mother at the age of two and had no known relatives. Care was provided from birth by hospital services within his Regional Health Authority. At the age of three years John was certified as an imbecile under the Mental Deficiency Act 1913–1958 and described as:

> He cannot feed himself and has to be fed with slops. His habits are faulty and he has to be washed and dressed. He salivates all the time and touches everything. He loves to make a noise and pulls the chairs or rocks them. He shouts and screams in a temper if restrained and puts his mouth to everything and likes to feel

it with his tongue. He has no control of his actions, pitches toys about and is a danger to other toddlers. He will not play with other children and some appear terrified of him.

At the age of ten years he was described as uncontrollably violent and an increasing source of danger to patients and staff.

John remained from the age of ten to twenty-two years in the same hospital until his transfer to high security forensic care, when he was transferred under Section 26 MHA 1969. The criteria for his detention were:

He makes no response to any formal testing. He has a vocabulary of a few mispronounced words and can only recognise a few simple commands. His uncooperative and aggressive behaviour has persisted throughout his life; he has learnt very little, but, growing bigger and stronger, his aggressiveness has become more difficult to control ... intellectually he has made no progress ... For years he has been nursed in a strong side room, from which he can only be taken out when in a quieter phase. On these occasions he can sometimes be exercised between two members of staff, if his arms are restrained ... He kicked down the door of his room when it was fastened with 3 cast iron bolts, and when these were replaced with bolts of tempered steel, he succeeded in bending these ... etc., etc.

On admission to high security forensic care John was considered to be the most difficult, dangerous patient in the hospital. The years that followed until his planned resettlement reflect progress in an institution where the provision of care was primarily containment for persons who had committed criminal offences. It could be considered that he became lost in a system with provision for more than a thousand patients. Following a restructuring of services, at the age of forty years John was transferred to the mental handicap services and the first improvement in his behaviour was noted. This was attributed to being allowed to smoke and was an attempt to prevent his then established pica behaviour.

Four years later John was 'no longer considered a management problem' by the multidisciplinary team. A resocialisation programme was instigated and he was allowed to be escorted outside maximum security. He was also referred to the speech and language therapist who introduced him to Makaton. A year later, aged forty-five, John's case notes read, 'He no longer requires care in maximum secure services.' The then Special Hospital Services Authority, responsible for the commissioning of beds, made a very clear statement that patients with a classification of severe mental impairment were considered to be inappropriately placed and should be the focus of resettlement. At the same time, day services within the hospital had concentrated on improving the provision of care for learning disabled patients.

The first action, in response to the multidisciplinary team decision that John no longer required secure care, was taken by the senior social worker of the team who wrote to the identified responsible local authority (place of origin) requesting information on policy in rehabilitating long-stay patients into the community. The responsible medical officer referred to the existing services in the responsible health authority, who had last provided hospital care twenty-five years earlier, requesting an assessment. The local authority and health authority were located in different regional areas. Responses to both these requests directed them to other services. The local authority advised the most appropriate route back into the community would be into one of the health authority's care in the community schemes and the health authority advised referral to his place of origin where care had last been provided forty-five years previously. From then on all correspondence was directed to the same local authority and health authority.

In the years to follow, the issues presented by both health and social services which effectively prevented resettlement were: who was to be the lead agency and responsible for the provision of care; funding, both authorities presenting a strong argument for joint funding but with no mechanism or policies to enable this; and limited available resources with no development planning.

Meanwhile, the learning disability service underwent a further restructuring which closed John's ward and the patients were decanted throughout existing services. The ward designated to provide services to meet the needs of patients with severe mental impairment classification and challenging behaviour had limited capacity, as it was providing for both male and female patients. As a consequence John was decanted to a main building maximum observation ward which drastically reduced his quality of life. His peer group was mainly young men with a classification of psychopathic disorder, therefore he was vulnerable to teasing, ridicule, harassment and intolerance, which provoked challenging behaviours. The regime of the ward was inappropriate to meet his special needs and he had no immediate access to an open door and enclosed garden. His resocialisation programme virtually ceased. The most significant changes, which occurred within the multidisciplinary team, were within the nursing team, and in particular the named nurse, who did not support the resocialisation programme. A consequence of the environmental and multidisciplinary changes was a deterioration in behaviour; the opinion of the previous multidisciplinary team was disregarded and no further action was taken in the resocialisation programme, other than that the social worker continued to correspond with the local authority to determine responsibility for the provision of care and funding.

There was no flexibility within the system to transfer John to the appropriate ward and he remained inappropriately placed for a further eighteen months. During this period a further restructuring occurred within the Special Hospital Services Authority and further pressure was placed on the special hospitals to resettle inappropriately placed patients. This assisted in John's transfer to the appropriate ward providing for patients with special needs, where his newly allocated named nurse strongly advocated a care programme which prioritised his needs in communication and resocialisation. Speech and language therapy was re-introduced, and the speech and language therapist proposed a programme which gave the named nurse daily responsibility for practising Makaton with John for the purpose of developing his repertoire of words and ensuring the use of Makaton in everyday life, in order to give him the experience of transferring his skills to other communicative environments.

At the same time, a day programme at the new day services centre was instigated, which included opportunities for art, social skills and integration. The occupational therapists liaised closely with nursing staff and the speech and language therapist. The speech and language therapist and the patient's named nurse started a small Makaton communication group at ward level. The habilitation, rehabilitation and resettlement process had finally been co-ordinated and was supported by the multidisciplinary team, the ward manager and the service management team.

The administrative wrangle with the local and health authorities continued, but it did not deter the multidisciplinary team from continuing to focus on John's resettlement programme. The social worker explored alternative resources outside the responsible authority's area and located a small, established, private hostel who, after a full assessment of needs, offered a trial leave placement. John's care plans continued to prioritise communication, developing speech and language skills and resocialisation, which included a four-day holiday. A referral was made internally and accepted by the rehabilitation resource unit located external to the high security perimeter. Although they were unable to offer a full-time placement, because of the incompatibility between John and the existing resident group, they provided day care one day a week. This ensured a weekly community programme and facilitated access to the proposed hostel placement. The day care services continued to provide a comprehensive programme with clearer objectives to improve communication, interaction and social skills and encourage new interests and leisure options. Contributors to the development of this programme were the speech and language therapist and occupational therapist, whose continued aim was to integrate John's day care programme with his ward-based programme.

Progress in the negotiations with the responsible local and health authorities were tedious and largely unproductive. The local authority agreed to undertake a needs assessment but this was primarily for the purpose of providing a report for the Mental Health Review Tribunal. The health authority also agreed to undertake a needs assessment. Both reports concluded that continued detention in maximum secure care was inappropriate and that John should be resettled into the community, providing his need for a high level of personal support was met. Neither offered resources or funding. Both were informed of the continuing contact with the private hostel and that this action was based on their lack of local provision and the multidisciplinary team opinion which they now concurred with. The senior social worker was responsible for arranging the resettlement programme, including overnight stays, successfully facilitated by staff from the rehabilitation resource and the named nurse.

All multidisciplinary reports continued to record progress. However, two worrying antisocial behaviours developed: inappropriate sexual fondling of females; and a significant increase in John's pica behaviour, initially of cigarette ends and then any rubbish or objects which could be easily swallowed. John responded positively to verbal reprimands when he engaged in inappropriate sexual behaviours, but ignored all staff intervention to control his pica behaviour. The multidisciplinary team decision was that the resocialisation programme should continue and this now included outings to football matches. This had become his primary leisure interest. John then began to express his frustration at being brought back into the secure perimeter from these outings through self-injurious behaviours, by scratching his face and aggression towards staff. Eventually, the combination of these behaviours began to impinge on his treatment programme as day care resources were often under-staffed and could not ensure his personal or staff safety. Consequently, his frustrations increased, as did his antisocial behaviours. The named nurse, speech and language therapist and occupational therapist maintained his ward-based programmes.

The financial and resource issues with the authorities had reached an impasse and the senior social worker proposed three actions: a tribunal; a complaint by John against the local authority; and legal advice on instigating a judicial review against the local authority. This was supported by the multidisciplinary team. It had been necessary to suspend the resettlement programme to the private hostel whilst the funding issue remained unresolved. The tribunal was the first action to be heard. It was adjourned for six months in order to allow both authorities to explain their intended provision of care, having themselves strongly recommended John's transfer from high security care.

A further restructuring in the learning disability service resulted in the closure of the high dependency integrated ward. Within three weeks John was transferred to an all-male ward providing services for mild to severe learning disabled patients. The multidisciplinary team, however, remained intact including the named nurse. Within one month of John's transfer a treatment planning meeting was convened and representatives of the responsible health and local authorities attended. The health representative had been instructed to carry out a needs assessment, to inform the health authority of the services required in respect of environment, staffing and support funds, to produce costings for an appropriate service. Simultaneously, both authorities accepted financial responsibility;

however, they had not decided what proportion of the costings each would have to contribute.

It was acknowledged by the multidisciplinary team that there had been considerable slippage in the implementation of the treatment plan because of the increase in John's inappropriate sexual and pica behaviours. The pica behaviour was considered to be life-threatening and his resocialisation programme had ceased. The speech and language therapist reported John as being co-operative and he had achieved comprehension and a good range of Makaton, which he could use but chose not to. In a six months' study an increase in the pica behaviour was recorded. The psychologist recommended that future monitoring should focus on the periods when the frequency level was zero. The occupational therapist recommended maintenance of communication skills to provide clear clues to facilitate the development of socially desirable behaviour.

The outcome of the treatment planning meeting was a comprehensive care plan which ensured that the skills of the multidisciplinary team addressed the three necessary components for working with people with a learning disability (Lally 1993):

- *Societal issues* – knowledge of how people with a learning disability are regarded by society and the sociological consequences.

- *System issues* – knowing how services are designed and organised to promote desirable experiences and outcomes for the service user.

- *Individual issues* – knowing how to relate and interact with the service user in all aspects of their daily life, emotional and physical needs.

A month later the health authority provided an updated assessment report and a service specification, with costings. The assessment report concluded:

This fifty year old man with a severe learning disability, who had spent his entire life in institutional care and his adult life in maximum secure accommodation, had a basic need of a place to live, relationships and occupation. As well, he had special needs in communication, skills learning and management of behaviour. That he did not require any form of hospital or physical security, and that he could be placed in a well-supported community facility with a moderate level of clinical/health support.

The service specification reflected the recommendations of the needs assessment. As responsibility for funding had not been resolved, the recommendations of the health assessment could not be acted upon.

Despite this continued uncertainty, the care plans remained operational, even though the pica behaviour continued to present major management problems. The ward manager supported the programme by ensuring staffing levels allowed the named nurse to fulfil her responsibilities according to the multidisciplinary treatment plan.

The social worker continued to negotiate with the local authority, supported by the patient's solicitor and the tribunal office. Three months later, joint funding between the local authority and health authority was agreed. A further assessment was undertaken by the local authority which endorsed the resettlement plan proposed by the health authority.

A meeting between the local and health authorities and the multidisciplinary team recommended a link person was identified. A member of the multi-disciplinary team took responsibility for this task. This had been the social worker's role for the last five years; however, it was considered more appropriate to the patient's needs that the responsibility transferred from the social worker to the named nurse. The primary responsibility invested in the named nurse was to develop a framework which would ensure the resettlement plans could be facilitated and progressed. The framework presented by the named nurse, accepted by the multidisciplinary team and the external resettlement team, included: direct communication with the authority's resettlement team, to ensure the resettlement programme progressed to the point of discharge and beyond; establishing a contact programme between the designated external care team and John; advising on risk management in the community, both during the resettlement programme and post-discharge; assessing accommodation for appropriateness and compatibility of other potential residents; and advising on the appointment of care staff. Within this framework the named nurse had responsibility to advise on the frequency of meetings between the two teams, in order to evaluate the care plans and initiate appropriate changes according to need. Alongside these organisational responsibilities, the named nurse continued to ensure the internal care plans were adhered to.

During the ten-month period until discharge, there was a further serious deterioration in John's pica behaviour and an increase in his antisocial behaviours, including public urinating and smearing faeces, increased aggression towards staff and destruction of furnishings. He was admitted to the local general hospital on two occasions for surgery to remove foreign bodies. Level three nursing observations were necessary for certain periods to ensure his personal safety and mittens were introduced in an attempt to control the pica behaviour to reduce the risk of further surgery, which had been advised could prove to be fatal. The named nurse continued to be innovative in meeting the needs of the patient and ensured that services within the hospital were not withdrawn because of his presenting behaviours, as had occurred on previous occasions. During the resettlement process, twenty-one face-to-face contacts between John and the receiving care team were facilitated and there were four multi-agency team meetings. Importantly, the named nurse maintained enthusiasm, motivation and drive to ensure the resettlement process continued, despite John's persistent challenging behaviours. The named nurse continued in this role post-transfer and monitored and advised for a further three months. John was then living in the community on a private housing estate. He was the only resident and was provided with a twenty-four hour residential care team, who had access to on-call facilities. An appraisal of the named nurse indicated a high level of skills in utilising the experience and expertise embodied within both multidisciplinary teams, and an ability to manage serious risk within a maximum secure environment and the community.

DISCUSSION

This case study demonstrates the difficulties which still prevail in resettling long-stay learning disabled forensic patients and how this is more easily achieved through multidisciplinary working and utilising the care programme approach as it was intended, 'to meet the needs of the service user', through the skills of the case manager.

The care programme approach was not fully operational within the hospital; however, the multidisciplinary team decided to apply the principles of care programming in John's case when the problems in engaging local services became apparent. By applying these principles John was entitled to a local authority assessment of need and a responsibility to purchase care if unable to provide it (Cunningham 1990).

The time taken to achieve John's rehabilitation and resettlement was six years. An analysis of the process highlighted the following factors as to why it took so long and how resettlement was eventually achieved.

It is evident that there was a significant period when the multidisciplinary team lost its ability to work as a team: a team in this case being a group of professionals with responsibilities and function as defined by the World Health Organisation 1984 as 'a group who share a common health goal and common objectives, determined by community needs, to the achievement of which each member of the team contributes in accordance with his or her competence and skill and in accordance with the function of others' (World Health Organisation 1987). This occurred when John was inappropriately placed within the hospital system and only two members of the original multidisciplinary team remained responsible for his care. They were the social worker and responsible medical officer who continued to advocate for John's rehabilitation and resettlement. They failed in engaging the new members of the team to implement the established care plans. This could be contributed to a lack of leadership within the team, or the inability of the multi-professional team to collaborate and agree on the previously identified common goal, related objectives and the distribution of tasks. Another factor may have been the named nurse's insecurity in his/her own competence to implement the care plans, given that it would have challenged ward policies and subsequently the ward manager.

Through John's eighteen-month placement on this ward it proved too difficult for the new team members to implement the previous multidisciplinary team's decisions. To have done so would have required subordinate change, a willingness to be prepared to challenge colleagues' institutionalised attitudes and the bureaucracy and politics of the system, as well as acquiring the competence for team collaboration (Engel 1994).

Leiba (1994) recognises that inter-professional teamwork and collaboration in mental health services is complex and difficult due to the wide range of agencies and the lay individuals and professionals who provide services. Feelings expressed by the service user may lead to feelings experienced by staff, which can in some cases cloud their interactions. In order for teams in mental health services to achieve inter-professional collaboration they need to be aware of available specialist skills and use them effectively and share their different perspectives on the service users' problems in order to help provide different solutions. It is vital to develop and maintain communication across the professional boundaries and to give and receive inter-professional support.

Inter-professional teamwork is an unavoidable social construction in mental health services. It is to no avail unless, according to Leiba (1994), there is a flexibility and willingness to modify or even exchange roles according to the needs of individual cases, and the existing barriers, status differentials, authority and proper structures are recognised and overcome. The difficulties of integrating members of different status has been identified as a major problem in inter-professional teams (Hunt 1983). In this case, although the doctor by law (Mental Health Act 1983) remained the responsible medical officer until John's discharge into the community, the named nurse was totally responsible as case manager to implement the care programme, including the internal and external rehabilitation programmes.

Another barrier which permeates inter-professional teamwork in mental health services, and was evident in this case, is sexism and gender issues. Mental health services are steeped in a patriarchal social structure and such an environment can engender the reproduction of relationships in which the power of men over women is sustained (Hearn 1982). There were periods during the management of John's care when this fact impinged on progress. At one stage the only female member of the team was the social worker, who was also subjected to the strong negative stereotype perceptions of the other professionals. The period when progress continued without these professional barriers was when the female named nurse took responsibility for case management, fully supported by a male ward manager who was newly appointed from the community.

Once John was transferred to the appropriate ward, the multidisciplinary team gelled and inter-professional collaboration was achieved. Confidence in their own competencies allowed them to manage the change in John's challenging behaviours and convert or modify the negative aspects of the work which were both internal and external. This ensured easier adaptation of the care plans and gave way to the introduction of new ideas. What followed reflects the developments in social work and nursing over the last twenty years (Pietroni 1994) and the changes both professions have been subjected to via NHS reforms and policy statements, in particular the NHS and Community Care Act (1990).

The Community Care Act 1990 was applied externally to ensure John's rights to a needs assessment and the provision of services and internally to ensure the designated case manager was the most appropriate team member. Traditionally, the management and liaison with the community team and the implementation of the resettlement care plan would have remained with the social worker; however, it was recognised that in John's case the likelihood of a successful resettlement would be dependent on communication (Engel 1994). It was agreed by the multidisciplinary team that the person best placed with the practical knowledge and ability to advocate John's needs was his named nurse and so the decision was made to transfer the responsibilities of case management from the social worker to the named nurse. The responsibilities of the named nurse as case manager were extremely complex and she was in the position of having to balance the needs of John with the needs of high security care and the community. This in itself was unusual as the pattern of resettlement for forensic patients is usually via a medium secure hospital provision. An added pressure was the political sensitivity and the hospital's vulnerability to publicity if untoward incidents occurred in the community, both during the rehabilitation process and post-resettlement. There were periods during the rehabilitation process when the goal of resettlement appeared unachievable and the named nurse had to convince management of the importance of maintaining the rehabilitation programme which was benefiting John. She designed individual packages of care which also focused on his positive mental health (Offer and Shabshun 1966) and used direct observation of John's behaviours for continual assessment. This was meticulously recorded and used as a reference manual following his discharge. In using this model she abandoned the institutional approach of 'block treatment methods' (Goffman 1961), which freed her as the case manager to work with John and the receiving team in such a way that they could accommodate the changes which occurred in his behaviours.

CONCLUSION

In the process of recording the rehabilitation and resettlement of John it became apparent there were numerous obstacles that had influenced and slowed down the process, some of which have been referred to in detail. With hindsight the process was embarked upon without any focused preparation for all those involved. There were periods of fragmentation within the multidisciplinary team when they were inconsistent in advocating on John's behalf. For more than twenty-five years John was subjected to extreme changes affecting his care, relationships and environment. During this time the authorities were unaware of his existence. Resettlement only became a possibility for John when there was continuity of care, stability and trust within the multidisciplinary team and a named nurse, as a care manager, who had the skills to manage and communicate with all those involved in the process.

CHAPTER 9

Reclaiming the Soul

A Spiritual Perspective on Forensic Nursing

John Swinton

INTRODUCTION

Forensic nursing has a long tradition of caring for patients in secure environments. Such a context demands very specific skills, attitudes and role perceptions if care is to be offered which is appropriate, humane and patient centred. In order to offer effective care which is *re*-humanising rather than *de*-humanising, it is crucial that forensic nurses have a clear perception as to the full extent of their role. If nurses in secure psychiatric settings fail to define their role, serious difficulties can occur in the rehabilitation of patients. There is evidence to suggest that if the forensic nurse does not have a clear perception of what his or her role is, forms of practice can emerge which attempt to fit 'average' patients into traditional patterns of institutional care regimes without due regard to the uniqueness of the individual (Robinson, Whyte and Fidler 1997). The dangers of depersonalisation and abuse which can result from such an approach was revealed paradigmatically in the brutalising and damaging regime found in Ashworth Special Hospital in Merseyside (Dale, Rae and Tarbuck 1995; Department of Health 1999), but is often present in less extreme forms in everyday attitudes and practices within many institutions.

These observations concerning the important connection between role perception and the type of care forensic nurses provide raise a number of important questions about the professional, institutional and interpersonal role of the forensic nurse. Whilst some of these questions are effectively answered elsewhere in this book, for current purposes the important thing that will be focused on is the suggestion that: *lack of role definition can lead to models of practice within which the unique individual is lost to the blanket demands of security and impersonal regimentation.* Poor role definition can lead to the person becoming engulfed by their diagnosis, their behaviour and/or overly restrictive routines and strategies designed to *control* rather than *enhance* the life of the individual.

There is therefore the need for a perspective on care which holds the forensic nurses' focus on the centrality of the person, whilst at the same time allowing them to develop an approach which is realistic and practical enough to deal effectively with the specific challenges which arise within the forensic context. It is the intention of this chapter to offer a framework within which forensic nurses can reflect on their practice, and work towards the development of forms of care which can maintain and creatively work within the critical tension between *therapy* and *security*. In so doing it is hoped that forensic nurses can be enabled to work towards a holistic model of care that seeks to take seriously the full gambit of experiences, feelings and emotions which form the life experience of mentally disordered offenders. This chapter will argue that forensic nursing practice that takes seriously the importance of spiritual care can help to actualise such a goal and provide a new and innovative perspective on forensic nursing care.

DEVELOPING A SPIRITUAL PERSPECTIVE

One might be tempted to ask why, in a 'post-Christian', materialistic and technologically oriented society, health professionals should take seriously the therapeutic implications of something as apparently ethereal and 'unscientific' as spirituality? Surely, one might ask, in an 'age of science and reason' such an intangible human quality as spirituality cannot hold a central place within the complexities of contemporary health care practice! What could a focus on spirituality offer within a forensic context that is often marked by violence, behavioural disorder, risk and the need for control? Understandable as such questions might be, this chapter will argue that it is precisely *because* of the specific context within which forensic nursing takes place that an understanding of the importance of spirituality is so important, both for carer and cared for. In order to justify such a suggestion, it is necessary to begin by clarifying what is meant by the term 'spirituality', and explore how it relates to mental health in general, before drawing out its specific implications for forensic nursing.

Defining spirituality

Whilst there is convincing evidence pointing towards the therapeutic benefits of spirituality for mental health (Nolan and Crawford 1997; Swinton and Kettles 1997; Richards and Bergin 1997; Smucker 1996; Twibell *et al.* 1996; Kroll 1995; Landis 1996; Morris 1996; Mickley, Carson and Soeken 1995; Shuler, Gelberg and Brown 1994; Frankl 1964; Jung 1933), there is a distinct lack of clarity when it comes to agreeing on what the term 'spirituality' actually means (McSherry and Draper 1998; Martslof and Mickley 1998; Dyson, Cobb and Forman 1997; Oldnall 1996; Ross 1994). The general assumption seems to be that everyone knows intuitively what spirituality is. However, in reality the wide spread of definitions within the literature would suggest that spirituality very often means whatever the particular writer wishes it to! This being so, before this chapter can explore the benefits of forensic nurses incorporating a spiritual focus within their practice, it is necessary to be as clear as possible about what we mean by the term 'spirituality'.

Joann Wolski Conn (Wicks, Parsons and Capps 1985) offers an understanding of spirituality that will prove helpful for present purposes. She notes that conceptions of spirituality seem to oscillate between a distorted dualism and naïve religious assumptions. Whilst some define spirituality in opposition to matter, others define it in terms of what God is and from this conclude that spirituality is a specifically *religious* phenomenon. However, if one recognises the vital fact that spirituality is a *philosophical, relational* and *psychological* as well as a *religious* term, these distortions are corrected. Put simply, spirituality refers to: *that aspect of human existence that gives it its 'humanness'*. It concerns the structures of significance which give meaning and direction to a person's life and helps them deal with the vicissitudes of existence. As such it includes such vital dimensions as the quest for *meaning, purpose, self-transcending knowledge, meaningful relationships, love* and *commitment,* as well as the sense of the Holy amongst us. A person's spirituality is that part of them which drives them on towards their particular goals, be they temporal or transcendent. Renetzky (in Ross 1994) separates spirituality into three primary components:

(a) the need to find meaning, purpose and fulfilment ... in life, suffering and death;

(b) the need for hope/will to live;

(c) the need for belief and faith in self, others and God.

Understood within this framework, it becomes apparent that spirituality is not an optional extra for 'the religious client', but is in fact an integral part of every human being's striving to make sense of their lives and their world, irrespective of the absence or presence of religious commitment. Although institutionalised and ritualised within particular religious traditions, spirituality is *not* an exclusively religious concept. Whilst certain forms of formal, organised religion have been shown to be beneficial for the development and maintenance of mental health (Fitchett, Burton and Sivan 1997; Mickley *et al.* 1995; Sims 1994; Gartner, Larson and Allen 1991; Stark 1971), it is only one of many vehicles for the expression of a person's spirituality.

Like religion, spirituality, essentially, in all of its diverse forms, strives to answer fundamental questions about what we are as human beings, why we are here and what we can and should become. However, unlike many forms of religion, spirituality does not necessarily find its primary focus in the transcendent aspects of existence. Understood in this way, it becomes clear that spirituality is not a concept which is the property of the chaplain or the religious professional. Spirituality is a fundamental human need that is essential for the development of the type of physical, psychological and social well-being which is central to the goals of all forms of nursing.

Spiritual needs

It is possible to divide spiritual needs into six main categories, as shown in Figure 9.1 (Emblen and Halstead 1993).

Religious needs
- Prayer
- Bible reading
- Confession/catharsis
- Facilitation of discussions about the transcendent aspects of human existence

Values/structures of meaning
- Hope
- Faith
- Search for meaning/purpose to life
- Dealing with guilt

Relationships
- The need for human presence
- The possibility of intimacy

Transcendence
- Dimensions other than physical/mental
- Assurance of God's presence
- Inner need–inner person

Affective feeling
- Reassurance
- Comfort
- Peace
- Happiness

Communication
- Talking
- Listening and being listened to

Figure 9.1 Six categories of spiritual needs (adapted from Emblen and Halstead 1993a)

Those needs that are specifically religious may be best met by religious professionals or mental health professionals with a particular giftedness within this area. However, reflecting on the wider aspects of spirituality, it becomes clear that they fall firmly within the remit of the multidisciplinary team and as such should be of the utmost importance to all forensic nurses.

Spiritual distress

Patients in secure environments are particularly prone to spiritual distress and the experience of acute and chronic spiritual need. However, the particular context of the forensic setting means that there is a very real risk that such needs are not taken seriously or are inappropriately pathologised by being wrongly attributed to illness or disease processes. It is therefore vital that forensic nurses are aware of what might constitute spiritual distress, and be equipped with the tools to deal with it when it arises. Spiritual needs/crises (whether expressed or unexpressed) would include (Taylor, Amenta and Highfield 1995):

- *Fear or anxiety* – relating to treatment or diagnosis; the possibility of permanent or long-term incarceration; the behaviour of self or others; their future possibilities.

- *Depression, sadness and grief* – relating to issues of diagnosis or hospitalisation; fear of other inmates; inability to develop and maintain meaningful relationships with self or others.

- *Hopelessness and despair* – no hope of 'getting better'; an awareness of the apparent hopelessness of their condition.

- *Anger* – frustration at self or others.

- *Expressions of helplessness* – verbal and non-verbal; feelings of powerlessness over the situation.

- *Mention of God or faith.*

- *Searching for meaning* – a focus on questions of why particular experiences/afflictions are happening to this individual.

- *Expressions of guilt* – implicit or explicit, searching for forgiveness.

The thing to note about this list is that these are not aspects that necessarily relate directly to a person's diagnosis or clinical treatment. As such they are not necessarily taken into consideration in terms of treatment planning and therapeutic goals. This is an important observation. By developing a focus on the spiritual aspects of patient care, the forensic nurse can be enabled to look beyond the expected norm, and begin to explore realms of the person which are often hidden, simply because mental health practitioners fail to ask the appropriate questions in their assessments of patient needs.

Spirituality and mental health nursing

A number of researchers have highlighted the positive role that spirituality can play within mental health nursing (Carter 1998; Nolan and Crawford 1997; Morris 1996; Byrne *et al.* 1994). Kirkpatrick *et al.* (1995) found that the engendering of a sense of hope and meaning was central to recovery from chronic schizophrenia. Morris links spiritual distress with depression and presents a spiritual well-being model within which the experience of depression can be understood and appropriate nursing care carried out. Fitchett *et al.* (1997) found that religion was an important source of comfort and support for a significant majority (72%) of the psychiatric patients who participated in their study. Significantly, they conclude that religion is important for psychiatric patients, but that they may need assistance in finding resources to address their religious needs. Tuck, Pullen and Lynn (1997) conclude from their research that 'in order to provide holistic care to clients in mental health settings, it is imperative that spirituality be addressed … If mental health nurses genuinely believe in holistic nursing, then nursing practice should reflect spiritual interventions.' Similarly, Mickley *et al.* (1995) found religion to be an important variable in the health development of a significant number of people. Whilst one might not wish to limit spirituality to the realms of religion, research findings such as these point towards the importance of taking seriously the spiritual aspects of patient care and the spiritual experiences and needs of patients.

Spirituality and forensic nursing

Reflecting on such evidence, one might think that spirituality would be naturally assumed important for forensic nursing. Its context of unwelcome incarceration, security, boredom and confusion means that spiritual distress, feelings of hopelessness, meaninglessness, uncertain identity and lack of a positive life-direction are very much a part of the everyday experience of forensic patients. However, when one turns to examine the place of spirituality within the literature relating to forensic nursing practice, one very soon discovers that there is a virtual absence of books or articles relating to the practice of spiritual intervention by nurses for the benefit of patients in secure environments. In the light of the research evidence pointing towards the benefits of taking spirituality into the psychiatric caring process, as well as calls from within the profession for forensic nurses to adopt a more person-centred approach to care (Thompson and Mathias 1994, p.556), this is an unusual situation. Surprise quickly moves to concern when one reflects on this situation in the light of the observation that the philosophical basis of nursing is concerned with enabling the individual to achieve and maintain 'optimum physical, psychological and social well-being' (Department of Health 1993b). To omit careful reflection on the place of spirituality in forensic nursing practice is to fall seriously short of this philosophical foundation, and risks offering forms of care which neglect vital aspects of the experience of mentally disordered offenders.

How then might we go about incorporating spirituality within the theory and practice of forensic nursing? A useful place to begin to answer this question is through a critical exploration of the concept of mental health.

UNDERSTANDING POSITIVE MENTAL HEALTH

'Nursing is an activity licensed by society concerning assessing, planning, implementing and evaluating strategies of care designed to assist individuals to return to a state of health, or to assist with an acceptable adjustment to a state of disability or loss' (Thompson and Mathias 1994, p.561). Likewise, the primary goal of forensic nursing is to enable patients to develop the maximum level of health possible. The forensic nurse is thus called to offer forms of care which adequately meet the holistic needs of individuals. Such care will necessarily include those aspects of the person that this chapter has described as 'spiritual'. However, whilst this may be the ideal, the particular context of the secure environment offers a serious challenge to the practical possibility of attaining such a goal. Forensic nurses are called upon to care for people who have committed acts that are often horrific, frightening, repulsive and extremely difficult for most people to understand or identify with. They are frequently called upon to offer care to patients whose aggressive and unpredictable behaviour means that the primary therapeutic goal may be to develop and maintain some kind of workable equilibrium rather than to explore the inner realities of their spiritual life. Under such circumstances, it is often difficult to think of some individuals as having anything resembling a sense of spirituality in any kind of conventional sense, particularly when they are acting in ways that are seriously threatening to themselves or others.

Under such circumstances the forensic nurse is faced with at least two possible options:

1. Nurses can exclude the possibility that spiritual care is a realistic prospect for a particular client or client group, and work with models of care which 'protect' them from having to deal with this aspect of their client. This approach functions effectively in structuring secure environments and authoritarian regimes that defend the nurse from 'the challenge of the personal'. However, by ignoring the person-as-person, forensic nurses run the risk of locating their practice primarily within the pathological aspects of the individual. A focus on pathology and control inevitably means that personal needs become subsumed to control and security needs, leading to the disempowerment of the client, the development of models of care which can be oppressive and abusive, and the types of institutional tyranny which Goffman highlighted in his study of mental institutions

(Goffman 1991). Within such a situation, therapeutic risk-taking and patient empowerment, two of the central tenets of contemporary forensic nursing practice, cease to be realistic options.

2. Alternatively, and in this author's opinion, most healthily, forensic nurses can *reframe* their understanding and practice in such a way as to remain open to the possibility that, despite the outward manifestations of illness and disturbance, there remains a valued individual with basic human rights, needs and desires not radically dissimilar to their own. In order to achieve such an approach, it is necessary to find a way of conceptualising mental health and illness which will enable forensic nurses to *reframe* their perceptions of mentally disordered offenders, and in so doing open up new possibilities for truly person-centred care which deals effectively with the spiritual dimensions of patients. We need to find a way of shifting the focus of care from illness to health, or, better, from *illness* to *person*.

POSITIVE MENTAL HEALTH: FROM MENTAL ILLNESS TO MENTAL HEALTH

Reframing psychopathology

Trent (in Tudor 1997) offers a model of mental health that will provide a useful framework within which we can begin to understand the role of spirituality in the process of forensic nursing and overcome some of the difficulties highlighted previously. Trent notes that

> it is commonplace to view the relationship between health and illness [and, by implication, mental health and mental illness] as two ends of the same continuum … According to Euclidean physics it is impossible to be in two places at the same time, for example two places on a continuum of mental health–mental illness at once. Equally it is impossible to be moving from two points in two different directions at the same time. It follows that on a single continuum it is impossible to be healthy and ill at the same time or to be mentally healthy with a diagnosed mental illness. (Tudor 1997, pp.22–23)

As an alternative, Trent suggests that a more appropriate way of defining the relationship between mental health and illness is by viewing each one as a separate continuum: the one, a mental disorder continuum and the other, a mental health continuum (Tudor 1997, p.23). (See figure 9.2.)

This conceptualisation enables one to clearly separate health from illness and in so doing, to focus on issues of mental *health*, rather than simply on mental *illness*. In this way it is possible to consider notions of mental health, distinct from notions of mental ill-health and disorder, and to consider what it might mean in practical terms to talk about developing the mental health of people with severe mental illness. Trent's model comprises of two parallel bipolar continua. The first continuum runs from maximal mental disorder/illness at one pole, to minimal mental disorder/illness at the other. At this level the focus is on mental *illness*. However, running parallel to this is another bipolar continuum that moves from minimum mental health to optimum mental health. At this level the focus is on mental *health*. These continua form the essence of the experience of people encountering psychological distress. At one level the person does have a mental illness, and it does have to be treated. However, this is not *all* that there is to the person. By focusing on the mental health continuum, it is possible to separate the person from the illness, and in so doing to create a space wherein specific issues of mental health can be conceptualised and incorporated within the process of caring. This model also enables us to see that there is much more to treating mental illness than simply controlling or eradicating symptoms.

**Range of diagnosis from
severe to mild**

| Maximal mental | ——————————————— | Minimal mental |
| disorder/illness | | disorder/illness |

| Minimal mental health | ———————————— | Optimum mental health |

including, for example:

subjective distress	subjective well-being
impaired or	optimal development
underdeveloped abilities	

Figure 9.2 The two continua of mental health and mental illness

According to this understanding, a person with, for example, schizophrenia may be relatively free from the major symptoms of their illness, and yet still be mentally unhealthy, in that their relational capabilities and opportunities are poor or non-existent, and their possibilities for the construction of a hopeful future equally as minimal. Their mental illness may be under control, but their mental health is very poor. The sense of hopelessness experienced by many people suffering from schizophrenia has been attributed by some as a primary cause of the negative symptoms of schizophrenia, not only for those who are institutionalised (Wing and Brown 1970; Kirkpatrick *et al.* 1995), but also for those within a community setting where their possibilities for meaningful social interaction are often minimal (Barham and Hayward 1995). The important point to highlight here is that whilst a person may appear to be well, in that their symptoms are controlled and they seem reasonably mentally healthy from a clinical point of view, in reality the *lived experience* of the individual would suggest that they were mentally unhealthy and seriously spiritually deprived.

Similarly, a person who is diagnosed with a severe and unremitting personality disorder, whilst maintaining the clinical label of mental ill-health, may still be able to develop some degree of mental health if they are given the opportunity to appropriate supportive relationships and encounter situations and experiences which enable them to develop confidence, self-esteem and a sense of possibility for their lives (Noak 1995a and 1995b).

Separating person from illness

Whilst there is an inevitable overlap between the two continua, this model nevertheless offers a constructive approach to mental health and illness and opens up new vistas of hope and possibility, particularly for those people whose illness is interminable. By focusing attention on the humanity of the individual, whilst at the same time taking seriously the manifestations of pathology, this model allows forensic nurses to develop a balanced approach which holds in tension illness and person. Rather than simply 'leaving morals at the door', in a way which can only be psychologically damaging in the long term, this model enables the nurse to find a positive way of understanding and reframing their encounter with disturbed individuals. Importantly, the practice and understanding, whilst incorporating and taking seriously disturbance and violence, is not defined by it. Within this model, *the person does not become their illness or their behaviour, but remains a person with particular needs, hopes and desires.* The health/illness continua provide a perspective from within which the forensic nurse can remain focused on the person even in the midst of dangerous and frightening encounters with disturbance and chaos.

Reclaiming the person

A model of mental health and illness such as this goes some way towards healing the split in the forensic nurses' perception of their clients as *persons* to whom they desire to relate, and *offenders* whom they may struggle to control. It also allows forensic nurses to concentrate on how they might understand and seek to develop *mental health*, quite apart from mental illness. Rather than mental health being judged according to the level of a person's illness, it can now be understood in terms of growth and personhood, which, whilst obviously affected by the person's illness experience, is not necessarily defined by it. In this way it is possible to define mental health in terms of the whole person, rather than simply one aspect of themselves or their experience. Mental health care can thus be viewed in terms of a person being provided with adequate resources to enable them to grow as unique individuals and to live their lives humanly as persons-in-relationship. Understood in this way, mental health inevitably incorporates spiritual aspects such as:

1. The capacity for growth (Rogers 1961).

2. Adequate sources of meaning (Frankl 1964).

3. Hope for the future (Byrne *et al.* 1994; Kirkpatrick *et al.* 1995).

4. A sense of empowerment (Lartey 1997).

5. An ability to accept challenges and grow in the midst of struggle and illness (Moltmann 1985).

6. A future orientation (Thompson and Mathias 1994).

7. Adequate resources to ensure that one has the possibility of sustaining healthy interpersonal relationships with self and other (Maslow 1970).

8. An experience of feeling that there are possibilities for the future irrespective of one's circumstances (Swinton 1999).

All of these contribute to enhancing the personhood of the individual and allowing them to develop the strength to live their lives humanly, even in the midst of illness. As one reflects on these aspects of mental health in the light of the description of spirituality which was presented earlier, it becomes clear that a person's spirituality, far from being epiphenomenal to issues of mental health and illness, is in fact intricately bound into the nature and development of mental health and authentic mental health care.

NEW ROLES FOR FORENSIC NURSING

It has become clear from the previous discussions that what this chapter is asking for is a critical reframing of the forensic nursing role, which will acknowledge and seek to embrace those aspects of the person which are often overlooked in our quest for security, control and effective patient management. In closing the chapter I will attempt to tie together the various strands which have been presented, by offering a series of metaphorical images which forensic nurses can use as they try to work out the implications of what it might mean to take seriously their role as spiritual carers. By exploring the role of the forensic nurse as *prophet*, *priest* and *friend*, it will be possible to enflesh the spiritual perspective developed by this chapter, and begin to point towards ways in which spirituality can be effectively incorporated within the caring process.

The forensic nurse as prophet

At first glance the suggestion that the forensic nurse should have a prophetic role may appear rather strange. However, the practice of the type of spiritual care which has been outlined above is wholly dependent on the provision of structures, staff, management and facilities which adequately enable the nurse to provide the type of care which respects the deeper aspects of her patients. In order to ensure such service provision, it is necessary that the forensic nurse be prepared to adopt a prophetic stance that is willing and able to speak out against oppressive structures and values as they impinge upon their practice. The image of the prophet gives the nurse a role that makes it possible to move towards actualising such a form of practice.

Prophets speak new truths to situations that are exhibiting injustice, or systems that have lost their way and are now functioning in a way that is a fundamental distortion of their original intention. The prophet recognises the weakest and most vulnerable within a community and takes a public stance against injustices which are perpetrated against them by unjust individuals and/or systems. Prophets recognise the personhood of the weak and adopt a powerful stance as advocate for the needy. Despite, or perhaps because of, the nature of their crimes and misdemeanours, the types of people with whom forensic nurses work can be extremely vulnerable to personal and political abuse. For example, those who have committed serious sex crimes are unlikely to receive public support, even if gross injustices are perpetrated against them within institutions, and politicians are unlikely to take up their cause if it is liable to damage their public profile and vote-drawing potential. Yet, if we take seriously the spiritual, person-centred perspective outlined within this chapter, irrespective of the nature of their crimes or the particular manifestations of their disorder, forensic patients remain persons with specific needs – it is the responsibility of authentic forensic nursing to attempt to meet them. Prophetic forensic nursing recognises the vulnerability of its client group and seeks to defend their rights and ensure that their personhood is maintained in the midst of public and professional cries for punishment or retribution.

In the light of recent reports highlighting the possibility of abuse within the forensic nursing context (Blom-Cooper 1995; Strong 1997; Department of Health 1999), it is critical that forensic nurses consider this aspect of their role with great seriousness, both on a personal and a political level. On a personal level, the forensic nurse is called to reveal oppressive structures within wards and within structures of management, which might be acting to abuse, dehumanise or depersonalise clients at a material or spiritual level. On a political level, the forensic nurse is called to interpret public policy which may have an agenda quite at odds with the fundamental principles of nursing: *optimum physical, psychological, spiritual and social well-being*. Forensic nursing as a relatively recent specialisation within the field of psychiatry has still to wrestle with many important aspects of its role within the public/political arena. The nature of forensic nursing and the way in which its professional practice is constructed at the interface between the medical and legal services means that, perhaps more than any other group of mental health professionals, forensic nurses function on the thin but critical boundary between politics and therapy. As Mason and Mercer (1996) correctly point out, 'The expanding loci of forensic expertise beyond traditional institutional and health service settings calls for a critical appraisal of present and proposed provision.' Prophetic forensic nursing which genuinely seeks to incorporate patients' spiritual needs demands a form of practice which includes critical reflection on policy and practice in order that the regimes, techniques and forms of relationship which form forensic nursing care enhance rather than detract from the personhood and spiritual direction of mentally disordered offenders.

Understood from this perspective, spirituality is much more than an ethereal, irrelevant, abstracted concept. Spirituality is a personal and political concept that offers a radical approach to the task of forensic nursing. A focus on spirituality lifts forensic nurses beyond the safety of the one-to-one interpersonal relationship, and forces them to gaze towards a prophetic-political stance which infuses a dangerous rehumanising force into forensic nursing practice.

The forensic nurse as priest

If the image of the forensic nurse as prophet appears unusual, the suggestion that forensic nurses have a priestly function appears utterly ridiculous! Nevertheless, reflection on this as a potential role will prove fruitful. Traditionally, a priest is 'one who functions officially to establish or preserve contact between the human community and the Deity; thus a mediator between God and humankind' (Hunter 1990). In terms of the role of the forensic nurse as a 'spiritual carer', this definition of the priestly function is highly suggestive. The forensic nurse is often the primary source of spiritual sustenance for forensic patients. This is so whether or not the nurse acknowledges the fact. The only question is whether this spiritual care is offered implicitly or explicitly. It is the forensic nurse who mediates between the outside world and the world of the incarcerated individual. It is the forensic nurse who communicates the opinions and attitudes of the wider society to the individual. It is the forensic nurse who has the power to build or break the self-image of the individual client and mediate hope or hopelessness.

The forensic nurse can mediate wholeness or she can mediate brokenness, but she will mediate! For many forensic patients, there will either be no possibility of release, or that possibility will be dependent on numerous intermediary factors including response to treatment, attitude towards staff, behaviour and ability to cope with self and others. Within such a context the possibility of institutionalisation in all of its variant forms becomes a very real one if there is no mediating agency which can point beyond the confines of the present, towards new possibilities for the future. Such new possibilities may simply mean the possibility of developing a trusting relationship with a 'significant other', a task that may have been previously considered impossible. It may mean modelling the possibility of forgiveness through the acceptance of the individual, irrespective of their past. It may mean offering someone what we might call an 'unanalytical space': a relational space which is not bounded by therapeutic analysis and preconceived expectations; a safe place where individuals can explore aspects of themselves without those aspects being open to critical analysis. It may mean offering the simple gift of *friendship*.

The forensic nurse as friend: spiritual care as interpersonal encounter

A common thread which runs through much of the research into the relationship between spirituality and health is the theme of interpersonal relationships. A number of studies have highlighted that interpersonal relationships are one of the primary conduits for the outworking of spiritual care (Nolan and Crawford 1997; Twibell *et al.* 1996; Morris 1996; Harrington 1995; Zerwekh 1993; Emblem and Halstead 1993). Whilst contemporary trends within psychiatric nursing have tended to interpret the role and practice of interpersonal relationships within the boundaries of the psychoanalytic paradigm, in terms of the type of spiritual care and development argued for within this chapter, it would seem appropriate to introduce another equally important caring relationship: *friendship*.

Friendship is one important and oft-overlooked relationship within which forensic nurses can meet the spiritual needs of mentally disordered offenders. Friendship embodies the type of spirituality pointed towards by this chapter, and represents a timely and necessary corrective to contemporary definitions of the nurse's role that equate professionalism with ideas of distance and detached specialist knowledge. Its features of companionship, shared understanding and common journeying characterise much about forensic nursing practice which cannot be captured by narrowly rationalistic definitions (McKie and Swinton 1998).

Of course, an immediate reaction to the suggestion that the forensic nurse has a role as the friend of the client might be to begin to highlight the dangers of losing boundaries, the importance of professional distance and other such defences which the medical model has taught us to use to protect ourselves from 'over-involvement'. As nurses we are trained to think clinically, detachedly and to be wary of so-called 'non-therapeutic' relationships. Yet, there is convincing evidence to suggest that friendship is a fundamental human requirement and a primary channel for the working out of human spirituality and mental health (Kirkpatrick *et al.* 1995; Byrne *et al.* 1994; Gurdin 1986; Patterson and Bettini 1993; Derlega and Winstead 1986). Friends accept one another for what they are and seek to offer support and guidance in times of unhappiness and brokenness. Friendship embodies community and acceptance and can provide a safe space for growth and change. Friendship mediates hope, hope fires spirituality, spirituality encourages mental health. Whilst acknowledging the very real dangers of over-involvement, manipulation, loss of security and the importance of effective risk assessment, it is nonetheless vital that forensic nurses do not feel compelled to cloak their essential humanness in such a way that they can no longer function towards patients as fellow human beings. Forensic nurses must begin to think seriously about their potential role as friends, and the spirituality and rehumanising power which is inherent within the relationship of friendship. It may be that this particular role, when developed and worked through within the forensic nursing context, could prove to be a primary means of rehumanisation which can take forensic nursing beyond the medical model, to a new way of looking at professional relationships and a revised model of therapeutic intervention (Swinton 1999).

THE FREEDOM OF INCARCERATION

In conclusion, it is important to note that the type of spirituality this chapter has called forensic nurses to acknowledge, as well as being a potential source of growth and wholeness, is also a powerful medium for *liberation*. Many within the care of forensic nurses may never enter society again. A focus on spirituality enables the reframing of the hopelessness of interminable incarceration. By focusing on issues of meaning, possibility, hope for the future and ultimate possibilities, there is a real sense in which the forensic nurse can bring a form of freedom even in the midst of incarceration. By reframing the patient's situation and embodying new possibilities within the types of relationships that have been highlighted, the forensic nurse can release the individual from their hopelessness and guide them towards a positive sense of future possibilities. In this way forensic nurses can provide *sanctuary*, or *asylum* in the best sense of the word. Within the Christian tradition, sanctuary was understood as a safe place where people could go to escape the persecutions of society. It was also a place where they could escape not only the condemnation of society, but also, through the ordinances of confession and forgiveness, a person could receive absolution for their own failings. In this way sanctuary dealt effectively both with the social pressures as well as the internal pressures of troubled human beings. Whilst the sanctuary experienced by offenders may be enforced rather than freely chosen, the forensic nurse can nevertheless provide a context within which such acceptance, forgiveness and protection can become a reality. By developing a spiritual perspective that incorporates the reality of the need for human relatedness and transcendence with the reality of human brokenness, forensic nurses can enable a positive understanding of the institution as a place of sanctuary. Spirituality leads to inner freedom; inner freedom leads to hope; hope leads to mental health. The primary aim of forensic nursing must be the enhancement of the mental health of the individual. Spirituality is one aspect of care that enables forensic nurses to maintain that focus and to offer compassionate care to some of the most troubled members of society.

CHAPTER 10

Autonomy and Personhood

The Forensic Nurse as a Moral Agent

John Swinton and John Boyd

INTRODUCTION

Health care ethics is an ever-expanding field which has produced some excellent resources for nurses (e.g. Gillon 1986; Wulff, Pedersen *et al.* 1990; Beauchamp and Childress 1994; Downie and Calman 1994; Mason and McCall Smith 1994, to name but a few). To try to cover the whole of the field in a relatively short chapter such as this would be to fail to take seriously the complexities of ethics within a health care context, and to risk understating its importance for forensic nursing practice. This being so, we have decided to narrow the focus of this chapter to two specific areas of forensic nursing ethics: *autonomy* and *respect for persons*. By offering a distinctive and original perspective on these two ethical principles, and exploring some of the ways in which these important areas of moral discourse relate to the practice of forensic nursing, we hope to offer a constructive contribution to the continuing debate into the role and function of ethics in the process of forensic nursing and to introduce forensic nurses to areas of further debate and development.

The forensic nurse as a moral agent

Many of the comments on the distinctive nature of forensic nursing in this book, particularly those in Chapter 2 by Kettles and Robinson describing their role study research, focus on the forensic nurse as a professional and the problems described often derive from the role of the forensic nurse as a moral agent. Much of what makes forensic nursing distinctive can be conceptualised in terms of process skills rather than task outcomes, and in this context it is as well to lay our cards on the table from the outset: ethical behaviour, whether personal or professional, cannot be taught as a competency or collection of competencies. It is only through education in the *practice* of ethical thinking and acting that it may be acquired: it is a type of knowledge through acquaintance and not a series of procedures.

As a profession, forensic nursing shares with other professions the following features:

1. The professional has skills or knowledge which proceed from a broad knowledge base.

2. He or she provides a service to clients by means of a special relationship which consists of an attitude (a desire to help plus a sense of integrity) and a bond (constituted by the role relationship which he or she has with the client). The relationship is authorised by an institutional body and legitimised by public esteem.

3. To the extent that the public does recognise the authority of the professional he or she has the social function of speaking out on broad matters of public policy and justice, going beyond duties to specific clients.

4. In order to discharge these functions he or she must be independent of the influence of state or commerce.

5. He or she must be educated as distinct from merely trained in a narrow sense.

6. In so far as [the above points] are satisfied a profession is morally and legally legitimate. (Downie 1990)

Arguably, most of us spend much of the day making ordinary moral judgements of right and wrong or good and bad. Daily, often minute by minute, ethically 'charged' decisions are taken by nurses; thus they themselves, with their fellow health care professionals, have paramount claim on the practice of health care ethics. Unfortunately, we as a society are all to easily persuaded that it is somebody else's business, that it is the business of the expert or academic ethicist to inform practice and 'keep us on the right track', people who arguably treat such problems with technical precision and expertise, but who lack the aforementioned 'knowledge through acquaintance' and do not face the daily necessity of assuming personal responsibility for their moral actions.

A fortiori, the forensic nurse is both personally and professionally 'at the coal face' of everyday ethical practice.

Understanding autonomy

Many of the dilemmas faced on a day-to-day basis by the forensic nurse involve the treatment of the patient without capacity, which we will take to mean the person lacking in autonomy, and in the treatment of an individual against their wishes, or without their meaningful consent. We shall discuss the concept of autonomy as it applies to health care ethics and then proceed to look at some of the issues the principle of respect for autonomy raises in the delivery of care to mentally ill people.

Definition

The fundamental concept of autonomy may be defined as: *the principle of deliberated self-rule* (Gillon 1986; Downie and Calman 1994). It is a special attribute of all moral agents, and here we use it in the sense in which a person may be said to be acting autonomously if he or she determines his or her own life by rational decisions based on their own beliefs and values without interference. These are the necessary and sufficient conditions for autonomy.

The first point arising from this definition is the question of what is meant by 'determining one's own life'. By this we mean a person's ability to determine his or her own intentions or actions by themselves. To do this rationally or in a deliberated way also involves the ability to evaluate one's proposed aims or conduct with reference to principles or rules. Thus, someone may be considered autonomous if they understand the choices facing them, are rational (that is, they employ reasoned thought in reaching decisions), act on the basis of desires and beliefs normally formed, and are free from coercion.

It will be clear that autonomy is not an 'all or nothing' attribute of a person, and that there exists a spectrum of autonomy with different people possessing different degrees in relation to their individual differences, their particular circumstances and depending on the particular question, problem or situation being considered.

Principle of respect for autonomy

In health care ethics this principle is the moral requirement to respect the autonomy of other persons in so far as this is compatible with equivalent respect for the autonomy of every agent implicated in a given situation. This includes, and fundamentally involves, the application of the principles of *beneficence*, *non-maleficence, justice* and *utility* in dealing with patients, though a comprehensive treatment of these principles is beyond the scope of this chapter.

On a practical level, respect for autonomy involves a number of subordinate principles: taking the wishes of patients into account, not being deceitful, not breaking promises, obtaining meaningful consent to treatments and maintaining confidentiality.

RESPECT FOR AUTONOMY IN FORENSIC NURSING

Introduction

We will consider those facets of nursing practice relevant to the principle of respect for autonomy in the treatment of the mentally ill adult forensic patient and will concentrate on the treatment of the patient against his or her will. Coercive treatment of the autonomous patient for the benefit and safety of others is morally mandated in so far as the patient presents a danger to others and legally and professionally legitimised in the law (in this we are respecting the autonomy of others as, for instance, potential victims, and holding this to be of paramount concern); we will not attempt a treatment of jurisprudential issues here.

Paternalism and forensic nursing

We will assume that the point of psychiatric care is to deliver treatments which assist in restoring some of the qualities, activities or abilities, lost through psychiatric ill health, which typically, when present, make the life of the afflicted individual valuable (Gillon 1986; Beauchamp and Childress 1994; Downie and Calman 1994). However, it may be argued that in forensic nursing one finds in some respects many more potential moral snares and pitfalls than in other areas of nursing practice. This reflects the seldom easy, constantly problematic and antagonistic relationship between patient autonomy and psychiatric paternalism within the field (Clare 1980; Reznek 1991). Paternalism may be thought of as conceptually divisible into three types: *genuine* paternalism, *solicited* paternalism and *unsolicited* paternalism (Wulff, Pedersen *et al.* 1990). *Genuine* paternalism may be defined as occurring when the practitioner himself or herself decides on the patient's treatment, thus imposing his or her will, when the patient is seriously deficient in autonomy. This involves value judgements on the part of the professional that we argue are justifiable in these circumstances and, indeed, may well be unavoidable. *Solicited* paternalism is defined as paternalism where the autonomous patient has given, implicitly or explicitly, their consent; there are no moral difficulties inherent in this. Morally wrong, we contend, save as mentioned above where it is mandated through legal social remedy for the protection of the public, is practice of the third type – *unsolicited* paternalism. This involves the action of the practitioner against the consent of the patient, who is held to be (sufficiently) autonomous.

In 1996/97 (1.4.96 to 31.3.97) in Scotland there were in total 879 patients made liable to detention under the terms of Section 18 of the Mental Health (Scotland) Act, 1984, which does not include those already liable to detention and also implies that those concerned may be legally treated, subject to certain provisions, in instances contrary to their expressed desires (Mental Welfare Commission for Scotland 1997). This statistic alone suggests that there is a large number of fundamentally important decisions being made on a daily basis which have direct implications for the right to autonomy of the psychiatric patient.

If autonomy is not an all-or-nothing attribute, then it follows that there must be a minimum amount present for the principle of respect for autonomy to be applicable. One of the principal problems is that of determining how much autonomy, given it is a variable (affected and diminished, for instance, by illness), is sufficient for the patient to be considered competent to decide for themselves whether to give or withhold consent in any given clinical situation. The question of how much autonomy one need possess to be considered an autonomous agent poses another question: who decides how much autonomy a person has and needs in any given situation?

In psychiatry, impaired autonomy usually takes the form of impaired autonomy of thought, or of intention or, more likely, some admixture of the two. Impaired autonomy of thought may occur without cognitive impairment, in that a person afflicted with a psychotic illness, for instance, may reason wholly correctly in a logically valid way, though reach erroneous conclusions due to the premises being false as a result of the illness. Impaired autonomy of intent may be due to internal or external factors. These are some of the issues considered below in the context of involuntary treatment and hospitalisation.

Involuntary treatment and hospitalisation

Causing patients to be hospitalised against their wishes is, as mentioned already, an example of paternalism. Certainly, in Scottish Law this intervention is legally justified if the patient in question suffers from a treatable mental illness and their health or safety or the safety of others is at risk by virtue of this illness and the patient refuses treatment (Clare 1980; Reznek 1991; Mason and McCall Smith 1994).

Suicide

The act of self-destruction is often used as a paradigm to highlight ethical issues in non-consensual treatment. Let us consider the case of a patient who intends to kill himself and who suffers from a depressive illness. The risk of suicide in depressive illness is high, perhaps thirty times the background lifetime risk of the average man or woman. We argue that psychiatric intervention is justified in treating the suicidal patient against his will, though we first attempt to expose some flaws in commonly encountered arguments in favour of such paternalistic treatment.

The argument that it is justified to treat the suicidal patient due to the fact that often patients thank one for doing so on recovery from illness is, *prima facie*, a sound one. However, it is countered by considering the fact that the said treatment may be held to be unduly influencing the patient's thinking towards this view –

seen as a type of thought reform, for instance. Such a rebuttal is difficult to accept by those who practise compassionately and sincerely to 'save' the patient, but compassion and sincerity are, in themselves, no assurance of ethical behaviour.

Advance directives indicating a wish for such life-saving treatment seem to offer stronger justification for paternalistic intervention but, if such a patient had made an advance directive setting down his or her wishes not to be treated if depressed and suicidal, then we suggest the practitioner would have little problem in considering that the patient may have changed his or her mind before the illness worsened, thereby legitimising treatment against his or her will despite the directive. This considerably weakens the interventionist position.

A third line of reasoning is to argue that there are grounds for genuine paternalism because the behaviour (suicide) is caused by the disease (depression) – this is also superficially sound reasoning. But the crux here is not the presence of or causal link with disease *but* the competence (i.e. autonomy) of the patient. One can conceive of a situation in, for instance, palliative care, where suicidal intent is formed competently by the sufferer in a rational decision based on the desire to escape a protracted, painful and undignified death, perhaps also sparing their nearest and dearest months of unresolved grieving. Our point here is that although the desire to die is caused by the illness, nevertheless any intervention to prevent suicide, say by the prescription of euphoriant medications, would not be justified against the wishes of the patient. Just so in some psychiatric cases where the decision to kill oneself may be rationally taken in considering the avoidance of future suffering and debility consequent upon a chronic mental illness. A patient may form rational and self-deliberated desires with respect to their future and treatment, knowing and understanding the alternatives open to them, if, despite mental illness, they are sufficiently competent (i.e. have sufficient autonomy).

Following from this our main thesis is that it is because we value patient autonomy so highly that we are justified in intervening against the will of the patient only where they lack sufficient autonomy to decide rationally for themselves. Thus, we see that, in the case of suicide, paternalistic intervention is justified if the patient is so depressed that they cease to understand fully what they are doing and therefore cease to be rational. Real respect for the patient's autonomy demands intervention to restore it. Thus, a necessary condition for the justification of paternalistic intervention is that the patient lacks full autonomy.

There is no doubt that some cases of suicide are rational; however, we contend that the moral practitioner must treat all potential suicides as non-rational and intervene on that basis until they are proved otherwise. This is justified on two counts: first, the consequences of suicide are irreversible and those of intervention reversible, so being mistaken in intervening is remediable while being mistaken in not intervening is not; the patient is dead. Second, it is an empirical fact that about

90 per cent or more of completed suicides are mentally ill a short time before the act, and many are known to be so at the time of death.

Psychosis

These arguments apply equally well in the case of psychotic illness, where the patient, by definition, fails to understand rationally the alternatives facing them and thus is impaired in autonomy. For instance, such an afflicted person may irrationally consider that they have the choice of 'brainwashing' through treatment or of staying in touch with reality through refusing treatment. No matter that their beliefs about reality are formed abnormally through the action of mental disease and their conception of it is thus pathologically distorted. This states the second morally necessary condition: to justify psychiatric treatment against the patient's wishes it is necessary that their autonomy is impaired as a result of mental illness. An example where this is not so illustrates the case: in a case where a terminally ill patient irrationally holds an optimistic view of prognosis, there would not be justification for intervening and, say, lowering the patient's mood with depressant medications, as irrational optimism is not mental illness.

Harms and benefits

Interventions against the will of the non-autonomous patient are justified only in so far as their results convey more benefit than harm. This was implicit in the foregoing paragraphs. It may be argued that, in general, the continuation of an episode of any sufficiently damaging or disabling mental illness constitutes sufficient harm to justify the interventions of treatment and hospitalisation. This view will never cease to be controversial, however, as the opposing view which argues that mental illness is not sufficient reason for removing people's liberty is widely held (Illich 1985). That is, the removal of liberty is the greater harm when compared with the benefit of treating the mental illness against the wishes of the sufferer.

This argument, albeit imperfectly paraphrased, is seriously flawed. The liberty to be ill can in no sense be held to be ethically preferable to treatment that results in the restoration of the patient's autonomy. The freedom to choose is surely valueless if the chooser does not understand the choices. Autonomy is what is valuable, not hollow liberty. This exemplifies the third ethically necessary condition for genuine paternalism in psychiatry as is enshrined in United Kingdom Mental Health Law: treatment is only justified against the patient's will if the treatment is beneficial or effective and also if the condition itself can in fact be treated.

Coercive treatment

Coercive treatment is not always explicit. Voluntary admissions to hospital or attendances at out-patient clinics, while far outnumbering those undertaken on an involuntary basis, may not be as voluntary as they seem. The patient concerned may attend, as happens in all branches of medicine, against their better judgement on, for instance, the insistence of their family or their general practitioner. They are often under implicit threat of becoming an involuntary patient if, say, they refuse treatment. This implies that there may be sufficient unstated threat to coerce them into complying with treatment on some occasions – thus, they effectively cease to be voluntary patients.

Autonomy requires that the patient is given information upon which to base decisions. Practitioners select the information which they convey to patients, thereby often compromising the patients' ability to make fully rational decisions regarding their own treatment. This is only justifiable if benefits outweigh harms and the other conditions for genuine paternalistic treatment are met. It will be apparent that the principles of beneficence and non-maleficence figure strongly in situations such as these.

Conclusion

We have explored some of the ethical considerations forming a daily part of forensic nursing practice and considered some of the justifications for genuine paternalism in it, hopefully making explicit the underlying highly value-laden and paternalistic nature of psychiatry, especially where this impacts on forensic nursing practice. We have explored justifications for this paternalism stemming from a true respect for autonomy and not a hollow concept of liberty. Throughout, we hope we have demonstrated that, while no imposition of treatment may be justified in the case of the fully autonomous patient save where it is legitimised to protect the autonomy of others, it would be inhumane for the moral practitioner not to act paternalistically in the case of patients who are incompetent by virtue of treatable mental disease.

RESPECT FOR PERSONS AND THE FORENSIC NURSING PROCESS

As a moral enterprise, forensic nursing throws up numerous dilemmas with which the forensic nurse must wrestle on a daily basis. We have already discussed at length some of the challenges which surround the maintenance of autonomy, and the complex ethical questions which serious reflection on autonomy throws up. In this section we will turn our attention to an issue which stands at the centre of all our ethical enterprises: *respect for persons and the form of personal relationships.*

Whilst there may be continuing debate over the precise role of the forensic nurse, there is a general consensus that at the heart of the forensic nursing task lies a desire to care for persons in all of their fullness and to enable them to attain and maintain the maximum possible quality of life (Thompson and Mathias 1994; Swinton, Chapter 9 of this volume). As such, issues of personhood and human relationships lie at the heart of authentic forensic nursing. Consequently, the ethical principle of 'respect for persons' is fundamental to the forensic nursing task, in that it suggests that forensic nurses should retain respect for mentally disordered offenders, irrespective of their capacities, social status, behaviour or values. It places each human being on an equal level and assigns them equivalent rights and responsibilities based on the assumption that as 'persons', they have a degree of worth which transcends that of other creatures and objects within the world. This principle calls upon forensic nurses at all times to ensure that their patients are treated as *persons* with relational, spiritual and material needs befitting of such a status.

Nevertheless, whilst respect for persons may be the ideal goal, the specific demands of the forensic context can make this one of the most difficult ethical principles to adhere to in any kind of meaningful way. Forensic nurses are caught in a dilemma. On the one hand, they are faced with the difficult reality of having to respect the personhood of individuals who show little respect for themselves or for others; who are frequently aggressive and violent, sometimes dishonest, often deceitful; and who may appear to have little or no remorse for the antisocial acts they may have perpetrated. On the other hand, their professional role means that it is not possible for them to offer any kind of meaningful nursing care if they do not or cannot respect the personhood of the other. It is therefore of the utmost importance that the forensic nurse is very clear as to what constitutes the status of 'person', and what it means to act towards another in a personal manner, i.e. in a way which acknowledges and seeks to nurture and maintain the personhood of the other.

Relational foundations: the meaning of 'person'

Before we can begin to understand what it means for forensic nurses to offer genuine respect to mentally disordered offenders, it is necessary to begin by delineating precisely what we mean when we use the term 'person'. Campbell (1972, pp.107–108) suggests that 'the term "person" functions as a description of the status we grant to human beings over against animals and inanimate objects'. He argues that to treat someone as a person is to assume an attitude towards them which confirms them in their humanity and reveals a level of meaning and a form of relationship that is not available to other creatures. Whilst most of us might intuitively agree with such an analysis, it still begs the question as to what basis we use to grant the status of 'person'. Is it available to all human beings, or is it dependent on the presence or absence of certain identifiable criteria?

Within moral philosophy, there has long been a tradition of identifying the defining factor that confirms the status of 'person' as *reason*. Some of the seminal ethical thinkers such as Aristotle, Descartes and Kant considered the capacity to reason from particular situations to general rules and being able to apply these rules consistently to oneself and others as being the mark of a rational being who has the freedom and the ability to choose between alternatives (Campbell 1972, p.108). However, reasonable as such an approach may appear to be, there are at least two serious difficulties with such a rationalistic definition of the person.

First, whilst post-enlightenment western society has become used to valuing human beings according to such things as intellectual achievement, rationality, productivity and social success, for the forensic nurse working with individuals whose lives are very often 'unproductive' in the socially accepted sense of the word, and whose behaviour is frequently 'unreasonable' because of psychosis, personality disorder or a disability in their cognitive faculties, a rational definition of personhood is extremely unhelpful and might in fact be potentially dangerous. If reason is held to be the criterion for personhood, those who are deemed 'unreasonable' can easily become viewed as 'non-persons', and as such vulnerable to attitudes and models of care which focus on depersonalised control and impersonal, 'faceless' block management strategies.

Persons-in-relation

Second, contemporary developments within moral philosophy and communitarian ethics (Macintyre 1996; Hauerwas 1981) and certain strands of feminist thought, particularly within the area of care ethics (Noddings 1986), have pointed towards the fundamental relationality of the human person. The Cartesian/Kantian idea that human beings are rationally defined isolated individuals upon which universal ethical principles can be worked out is rapidly losing credibility. More and more, it is being recognised that personhood is not an individual essence, but is in fact the culmination of the continuing process of human interaction. To be a person means to be in relationship with other persons. 'I exist as an individual only in personal relation to other individuals. Formally stated, "I" am one term in the relation "You and I" which constitutes my existence' (Macmurray 1991, p.28). *We become the persons we are not in isolation, but in relationship.* It is only as I relate to others that I discover who and what I am. I become a mother, father, brother, sister, friend and so forth only as I encounter others in community, and they enable me to discover the nature of my personhood. Whilst I may have a physical form, the various aspects which constitute me as a person cannot be discovered through a process of isolated introspection. In fact, they cannot even exist apart from my relational encounters!

I cannot be a person without the assistance of others. To be a person is to be in relationship with another person. To be deprived of the sources of relationality necessary for the maintenance of one's personhood is to become a 'non-person'.

Personal relationships

Human beings are therefore seen to be thoroughly relational beings. However, authentic human relationships that propel individuals towards a positive sense of what they are as persons are of a specific type and have a particular focus. *Authentic human relationships are always personal relationships* (Macmurray 1991; McFadyen 1990). For a relationship to be personal, it is necessary for one to treat the other as a person with whom one desires to *relate*, rather than as an object which one wishes to *use* or manipulate for one's own purposes. An example of an impersonal relationship would be a master and a slave. The master seeks to relate to the slave only as an object that he desires to use for his own ends. To use the terminology of Buber (1987), the master maintains an 'I–it' relationship with the slave, whereas a truly personal relationship is always based on an 'I–thou' encounter. Genuinely personal relationships adopt an 'I–thou' stance that sees the other as a person, and seeks to relate to them on that basis, irrespective of circumstances.

Understood in these terms, 'respect for persons' implies a relationship of involvement with other persons, such that our choices and intentions are governed by their aims and aspirations as well as our own. To respect another person means acknowledging their inherent relationality and doing all that one can to ensure that their personhood is sustained and nourished by the forms of personal relationship one enters into with them, and enables them to access from sources outside of oneself.

IMPLICATIONS FOR FORENSIC NURSING PRACTICE

The understanding of the nature of persons and the texture of personal relationships presented above has important implications for forensic nursing practice. In common with all members of the multidisciplinary team, forensic nurses are called to offer care that is personal and aimed at establishing and maintaining the personhood of mentally disordered offenders. Despite frequent encounters with violence, 'inhuman' behaviour and deviance, forensic nursing remains a fundamentally relational enterprise. It has to do with persons relating to other persons and, through that relationship, bringing some form of healing and/or relief from psychological or physical disorder. Certainly, the nature of its patient group means that the maintenance of relationships may be particularly difficult. Nevertheless, the basic principle of caring-through-relationship remains the same for forensic nurses. *Forensic nursing is a thoroughly relational form of human practice.*

Personality disorders

Nevertheless, in practice, many of the offenders encountered by forensic nurses manifest forms of illness and disorder that make it very difficult for the nurse to maintain the type of relational orientation which has been described. For example, we might consider how a forensic nurse envisions and treats someone with a serious psychopathic personality disorder. On the surface the person can often appear to be functioning at a 'sub-personal' level, in that his relationships are manipulative, exploitative and self-centred. He may show an absence of guilt for actions that have fundamentally violated the personhood of another human being. He often has a total disregard for societal norms and may show no desire for any kind of communal living or express any sense of fellow feeling for others. It might in fact be that he has a chronic inability to form lasting relationships (Rosenhan and Seligman 1984). Under such circumstances, it is very easy for the nurse to lose respect for the person and to develop forms of relationship and structures of management which reflect an impersonal 'I–it' mentality. Such impersonal care is embodied in practices and language which cease to see the 'person-as-a-person', and instead find their primary focus in the person-as-an-illness: 'psychopath', 'schizophrenic' and so forth (Estroff 1989; Strauss 1992). Under such circumstances, it is a person's diagnosed condition, rather the person-as-person, which determines the particular nature and form of relationship the nurse will enter into with the patient. Such a focus on pathology means that questions about personal relationships and their function within the therapeutic process may well not even be asked! The assumption may be that the mentally disordered offender's primary need is to be controlled in order to prevent the negative consequences of the worst aspects of his psychopathic condition. The thing to note at this point is that *the assumption underlying this approach is that the mentally disordered offender needs something done to him.*

However, if we assume that the mentally disordered offender as a person, in the sense that we have outlined previously, has a fundamental need for relational connection and support, we are enabled to ask different questions. Instead of asking what can we *do* for or to this person, perhaps a more appropriate question might be, what can we *be* for this person? Noak, in his paper 'Care of people with psychopathic disorder', observes: 'Many psychiatrists with experience of working in remedial establishments would agree that a sympathetic member of staff, capable of winning the individual's respect and able to be with him when day-to-day crises appear, is able to achieve more than a psychotherapist who sees the individual at stated times' (Noak 1995a). It is very often not those who have the most knowledge of therapeutic technique or psychopharmacology who are of most benefit to people with severe personality disorders. Rather, it is those members of the multidisciplinary team who have the time and the inclination to commit themselves to the individual and enter into truly personal relationships with them that are of most long-term therapeutic benefit. Understood in this way, it becomes apparent that the forensic nurse who is able to embody and contextualise the principle of respect for persons within her everyday practice has a fundamentally important and unique role within the multidisciplinary care of people with serious personality disorders. By being able to see through the diagnosis to the person behind the diagnosis, and by entering into meaningful personal relationships with mentally disordered offenders with personality disorders, forensic nurses are in a position to offer a form of personal care which no other discipline is capable of providing.

Respect for persons within the multidisciplinary team

There is also a wider dimension to respect for persons within the context of personality disorder. Thorley and Stern suggest: 'Personality disturbance involves some of an individual's most unique and intangible characteristics. For that reason, personality disorders produce some of the most frustrating work for psychiatrists' (in Noak 1995a). If this is the case for psychiatrists, how much more true must it be for nursing staff, who are involved with delivering care 24 hours a day! 'Heavy psychological and social pressures are placed on the nurse therapist and it is imperative that multidisciplinary staff work together and support each other, so that optimal effective care can be delivered' (Noak 1995b). Respect for persons must reach beyond the individual member of the multidisciplinary team offering respect for the individual mentally disordered offender. Respect for persons must become the fundamental ethical principle that lies at the heart of the multidisciplinary team's structures and goals. If the forensic nurse is not respected by colleagues and is not effectively supported by the team structure, their ability to offer personal care can be dangerously undermined. For the multidisciplinary team to take seriously the principle of respect for persons will mean ensuring such things as adequate staffing, effective person management, accessible staff support and counselling services and adequate resources to ensure that morale and practice remain personal and focused, not only on the mental health of the mentally disordered offender, but also on the mental health of the various members of the team.

The politics of personhood

Following directly on from the previous points is the observation that genuine respect for persons demands a strong public stance from forensic nurses as advocates for healing, justice and constructive institutional change. We have previously suggested that one of the marks of the professional status of forensic nursing is its social function whereby nurses can move beyond duties to specific clients and speak out on broad matters of public policy and justice. Genuine respect for persons means seriously addressing the structures, policies and attitudes which may cause care to become depersonalised. Strong (1997) suggests that 'special hospitals exist for those who require treatment under conditions of maximum security because of their "dangerous, violent or criminal propensities" ... But many special hospital users present no risk to anyone but themselves.' This type of patient mix, whilst perhaps 'economically necessary', is clearly inappropriate and can only be detrimental, particularly to the care of those weaker members of the institutional community who are often caught up within stringent and depersonalising regimes which focus primarily on control (Strong 1997, p.18). This, coupled with the fact that the large special hospitals are too big, means that serious problems regarding the balance between therapy and control are inevitable. As one forensic nurse starkly puts it: 'With so many patients you can only run them like prisons. Nursing goes out the window' (Strong 1997, p.18). Such an environment inevitably leads to depersonalised practice. If nursing is to 'come back in through the front door', it is critical that the forensic nurses' respect for persons takes on a critical dimension of socio-political awareness. Effective personal care can only be provided in an environment and within a political climate that lends itself to the possibility of respecting persons.

CONCLUSION

In this chapter we have tried to introduce forensic nurses to some of the complexities of developing ethical practices within a moral context which makes morality and moral decision-making extremely difficult. Whilst some might see ethical reflection as an activity which is secondary to nursing care, we have tried to show that in fact the two are inextricably interconnected. What we believe about the nature of such things as personhood and autonomy profoundly impacts upon the ways in which we act as forensic nurses. If practice does not include ethical reflection it opens itself up to the possibility of becoming abusive and depersonalised. Whilst this book has pointed towards many ways in which the forensic nurse has a unique role within the multidisciplinary team, perhaps it is at the level of ethics and morality that its greatest professional impact can be felt. Forensic nurses, with their constant and committed daily care of mentally disordered offenders, form the bedrock, the strong foundation, of the multidisciplinary team. They also provide the primary ethical context within which the practice of caring takes place. It is their responsibility to ensure that the multidisciplinary team functions in ways which are personal and life-affirming, and which focus on the development of therapeutic autonomy and authentic personhood. As such, the forensic nurses' role as a moral agent is the pivot upon which authentic person-centred multidisciplinary teams can be built and upon which compassionate nursing strategies can arise, be nurtured and sustained.

CHAPTER 11

The Role of the Forensic Nurse in Clinical Supervision

Mary A. Addo

INTRODUCTION

This chapter describes the role of the forensic nurse in clinical supervision for nurses working with mentally disordered offenders. The aim is to highlight some of the challenges that forensic nurses face: how clinical supervision can help them to maintain their emotional stability, and self-effectiveness in nursing practice. There is no finite model of clinical supervision and it is possible to move between different modes at any one time (Butterworth and Faugier 1992, 1993).

An attempt is made using Heron's (1986) 'six category intervention analysis' to illustrate the forensic nurse as clinical supervisor in secure settings. This framework differs from that of a mentor, preceptor or manager and worker relationship (Merriam 1983; Fristch and Strohlein 1988). It is an empowering, ongoing personal experience that is developed and redefined within the supervisory relationship (Chambers and Long 1995).

The scope of this topic is vast and cannot be dealt with within the limits of this chapter. From personal experience of clinical supervision as a supervisor and supervisee, I am aware of the immense personal and professional enrichment that occurs as a result of this process, provided it is sensitively and genuinely performed. Often, supervision in nursing is viewed negatively by nurses, but it should be perceived positively as a process that allows nurses to set time aside for reflective work, and wash off 'emotional grime' caused by the nature of their work within the supportive tenets of clinical supervision, thus enabling nurses to take care of themselves. Like most things in life you do not know the value until you have experienced it. It is hoped that nurses intending to work with mentally disordered offenders and their managers will find this chapter of value.

FORENSIC NURSING AND ROLE CHALLENGES

Taylor (1988) asserts that forensic psychiatry is charged with both the welfare of the individual person and the safety of the community at large. The majority of patients in forensic psychiatric environments come from diverse backgrounds such as the courts, the police and mainstream acute psychiatric wards. This includes:

- those who have committed offences and are awaiting trial;
- those fit to stand for trial but found to be mentally ill;
- those sentenced after trial and serving their sentence but who become mentally ill during this period;
- those of whom the court requires a psychiatric assessment report before deciding on appropriate disposal.

The past decade has seen a growing interest in the care and treatment of mentally disordered offenders. Gunn (1986) maintains that this interest is related to several factors such as social pressures, assessment of dangerousness, treatment methods, and the need to know what goes on in forensic environments; for example, the inquiry into the care and treatment of Christopher Clunis (Department of Health 1994).

Working with mentally disordered offenders is often complex, not because of their illness and criminal behaviour, but because of the environment, ongoing legal constraints, and no one professional group being equipped with all the necessary knowledge, skills and expertise to provide care and treatment, as the problems they present are often too complex, and demand specialist skills from a multidisciplinary and multi-agency approach. That means forensic nurses have to work in collaboration with other professional groups and agencies to deliver that care (UKCC (1992a) code of professional conduct, clause 6).

However, if members of multidisciplinary teams are not well organised and managed, then forensic nurses are bound to become frustrated and demoralised by the confusion that emerges with roles, rivalries and conflicts (Reed 1984; Milne 1993; Appleyard and Maden 1979; Guy 1986; Addo 1997). Traditionally, forensic psychiatric nursing has been viewed as a stressful area in which to work (Phillips 1983; Jones *et al.* 1987; Caplan 1993). A major challenge and source of stress for forensic nurses is role ambiguity, thus the need to provide a therapeutic environment and maintain security in a parallel fashion with a patient population who have the potential for violence. This makes forensic nurses perceive themselves as gatekeepers instead of therapists, a situation referred to as the 'dilemma of therapeutic custody' (Burrow 1991). At times this leads to forensic nurses being accused of putting more emphasis on custodial skills rather than therapeutic nursing care. Working in a secure setting with a population of dangerous patients requires that forensic nurses have awareness not only of their own safety, but also that of others in the environment, at all times. They also have to be cognisant of both the Mental Health Act and Criminal Procedures Act and constantly strive to develop effective and optimal therapeutic relationships with mentally disordered offenders, which at times is problematic (Gunn and Taylor 1983).

There is also the continuous observation and reporting of problems associated with this group of people with complex needs; the risk of hostage taking; absconding; escape attempts; the 'prison culture' which may occur due to the prison experience; nurses' dissatisfaction with perceived job role; and the effects of being confined to such secure environments. Jones *et al.* (1987), in their study of psychiatric nurses, found that nurses working in secure environments are faced with fear of assault and accusations of malpractice. Previous research (Phillips 1983; Numerof and Abrams 1984; Roth 1986; Harris 1989; Caplan 1993; Buchan 1995; Alexander 1997) asserts the potential stressful nature of nursing as an occupation. Confronted with the experience of role strain and other challenges forensic nurses face in working with mentally disordered offenders, it is argued that forensic nurses are exposed to particular stresses different from those of colleagues working in mainstream general psychiatry. This difference is attributed to the fact that forensic nursing brings nurses face to face with the individual labelled not only mentally disordered but what I call the four Ps (person–patient–prisoner–perpetrator) whom others will not welcome in their everyday social encounter with people. Despite the offence(s) committed, forensic nurses are expected to show empathy; be non-judgemental and give unconditional, positive regard (Rogers 1951) no matter how much abhorrence, resentment and anger they personally may feel towards the patient, the patient's denial of offence(s), and the lack of any remorse shown towards the victims of such offence(s).

This continual daily contact in the forensic nurse's routine work can at times turn traumatic: for example, when a detained patient committed into hospital care under the Criminal Procedures Act absconds from the confines of the secure setting; or a new nurse starting work for the first time in a secure setting is confronted with some patients who are skilled at inducing fear and anger in others, and at their happiest when creating fracas in the confines of the secure setting. In maintaining such a professional front some forensic nurses may suffer in silence the distress of this aspect of their work (Heron 1977). Not knowing what lies ahead is a major worry when you enter into a territory with no prior knowledge of its workings. The experience of the new nurse will be that of feeling vulnerable. However, how competently he or she handles the situation depends on the clinical supervision received as this will be the key to how therapeutically they behave towards the patient and others. The argument is that when nurses have to deal with the so-called 'patients from hell' they need clinical supervision to support them to deal with their vulnerability (Chambers and Long 1995).

According to Heron (1977), the primary relationship between human beings and their environment is that of vulnerability, and that in human distress the concept complementary to it is that of human catharsis, which he defines as a complex set of psychosomatic processes by which the human body is purged of an overload of distress due to cumulative frustration of basic needs. In this context catharsis as an intervention is about forensic nurses learning the art of taking care of themselves through setting time aside to wash off work-related 'emotional grime'.

In congruence with other authors, Heron (1977, p.35) asserts that in the course of the practitioner's work, their own level of distress rises accordingly, yet their very adoption of the 'expert' role maintains a defensive repression on this professionally induced stress. He argues that the result of this is unacknowledged intra-psychic tension among the helping professionals of all kinds, about which a collusive silence is maintained, but to which the suicide figures bear eloquent testimony. If forensic nurses are to provide care in a humane fashion for mentally disordered offenders amid the plethora of dilemmas they face, they need to be helped through facilitated clinical supervision to reflect, learn, bear and share their distress regarding their patients and their families, patient care and nursing interventions, colleagues and other members of the multidisciplinary team. This support can be provided on a one-to-one basis or in groups with clinical supervisors from the same speciality or other members of the multidisciplinary team.

THE NEED FOR CLINICAL SUPERVISION

A review of the literature demonstrates that adopting the process of clinical supervision will ultimately result in quality nursing care standards and good outcome for nurses, patients and the National Health Service (Clothier Report on the Allitt enquiry 1994; Delphi study by Butterworth 1994; *Working for Patients*, DoH 1989; DoH 1993a; Scottish Executive Directors of Nursing Group 1997; *Working in Partnership*, DoH Mental Health Review Team 1994; *Report of the Confidential Inquiry into Homicides and Suicides by Mentally Ill People*, RCP 1996; Storey and Dale 1998; UKCC 1986, 1992b, 1994).

A key issue also relates to the education and training of pre-registration nurses in forensic nursing (Gunn 1986; Lloyd 1995) and the lack of professional development following initial pre-registration (Myco 1980; Barnett 1981; Kershaw 1985; Hibbs 1989; Chiarella 1990; Friend 1991). In the light of technological changes, clinical governance and evidence-based practice indicate that clinical care cannot be managed without supporting staff delivering the service. To achieve this requires nurses who are innovative, flexible and knowledgeable lifelong learners committed to their professional development (UKCC 1986; WNB 1989; ENB 1990; Audit Commission 1991; Reed Report, DoH and HO 1992; Gunn 1986). According to Fowler (1996a), the introduction of the flattened hierarchies in the National Health Service took away the middle management, thereby removing the traditional professional support system that existed in nursing. The DoH (1993a) states that little evidence exists that confirms the clinical supervision impact on patient care, albeit information about its professional benefits exists.

Despite this absence of any explicit confirmation of the impact of clinical supervision on patient care, an intuitive and seemingly rational argument can be put forward for a process that supports the accountability and responsibility that are implicit in the 'new nursing' of the twenty-first century. As stated by Peplau (1991), a nurse cannot pay attention to the cues in the situation when her own needs are uppermost and require attention in the situation. Her observations are, unwittingly, focused upon the way in which her unrecognised needs are being met by a patient. Until the actual needs of the nurse are met, or identified, so that she is aware of what she is, and how she functions as a barrier to the patients' goals, she does not have control such as is required in carrying out the 'shoulds' and 'musts' indicated in nursing literature. Nurses can achieve this if they are offered opportunities to examine closely their role, their nursing actions and the clinical practice setting in which they work, if they are to reject mythical thinking and traditional solutions that have suppressed the advancement of nursing knowledge and practice.

Clinical supervision framework

The definition of clinical supervision used in this chapter is an intensive, interpersonally focused, professional, helping process in which one person who is skilled, knowledgeable and empathic is designated to facilitate another's clinical therapeutic competence (Critchley 1987). Heron's (1986) six-category intervention analysis in which equal value is placed on each of the intervention styles that can be used interchangeably, and in combination at any point in the supervision process, is advocated. These six categories are authoritative (namely prescriptive; informative; confronting), which take the form of 'I tell you ...'; and facilitative (namely cathartic; supportive; catalytic), which take the form of 'you tell me...'.

Using these specific styles enhances the creation of therapeutic ambience (Chambers and Long 1995). The clinical supervisor's role in this model is to support the supervisee to develop self-understanding, self-awareness and emotional growth, the emphasis being centred on the supervisee's cognition (Heron 1986). This allows nurses to develop self-awareness, by understanding what comes from without (from the patient) and what comes from within (the nurse's own perception), and prevents the creation of nurses who become 'undefused walking time bombs' waiting to explode. This view is supported by Proctor (1988), Carkhuff (1969) and Rogers (1993) who assert that restorative work via facilitative clinical supervision process is a way of responding to intimate interactions with the patients, in which nurses, by the very nature of nursing work, necessarily allow themselves to be affected by the patient's pain, distress and disability. Proctor (1988) further asserts that the emotional stress which nurses experience is due to the necessary empathy which the nurse–patient relationship requires, as well as the frequent need to face situations of loss. Hawkins and Shohet (1991) assert that not attending to these emotional issues leads ultimately to a workforce whose efficiency and ability to deal with concerns or critical incidents is very much reduced. In this situation they argue that nurses are more likely to over-identify with their patients, show co-dependency behaviours (Whitfield 1991), feelings of staleness, rigidity and defensiveness, and experience burn-out (Miller 1991; Maslach and Jackson 1982).

Pointing to the benefits of supervision in the helping professions, Hawkins and Shohet (1989, p.5) state:

> Our experience of supervision is that supervision can be an important part of taking care of oneself, staying open to new learning and an indispensable part of the helper's on-going professional development, self awareness and commitment to learning, as nursing is a profession which requires a great deal of emotional commitment from its members.

Practice experience can be a particularly rich source of learning for nurses, and reflecting on one's clinical work encourages peer review activity which is seen as the hallmark of professionalism (Schon 1987; Passos 1973). It is clear from this assertion that the crucial element is the need to make sense of professional activity, to ensure that all practice is based on sound judgement. This involves the nurse seeking meaning from experience and, more controversially, imposing meaning on events in practice, thereby creating new knowledge. This opportunity to identify, explore and challenge assumptions can be said to contribute to improving nurses' morale, job satisfaction and a workforce that is emotionally stable, competent, in control of themselves and the work environment and develop competence through critical reflection on their experiences (Hallberg and Norberg 1993; Addo 1997; Carr and Kemmis 1986; Schon 1983, 1987). The six categories of intervention have been presented separately, but in practice they are interdependent and can be used interchangeably. The appeal in Heron's (1986) framework is that it provides a core of interventions for introducing experiential and self-directed learning in nursing practice. The different categories can be used to create an endless variety of supervision processes, depending on the supervisor and supervisee; the way in which the relationship is developing; the emerging potential of the supervisee; and the creativity and insight of the supervisor. However, the effectiveness of this framework depends on the skills of the clinical supervisor and their own need for receiving supervision.

Forensic nurse/clinical supervisor role

The role of the clinical supervisor is a multi-faceted task which encompasses the functions of clinical expert and educator. As a facilitator, the clinical supervisor provides a supportive educational environment from which the supervisee can practise and learn from experience, apply theoretical knowledge, appropriate attitudes and the art of therapeutic communication for the treatment of patients. This is done primarily through the medium of the supervisory relationship. The supervisor and supervisee agree from the outset about the context and ground rules of the relationship, emphasising its facilitative and supportive nature. The key concepts necessary for the successful operation of this facilitative model of clinical supervision are empathy, valuation, congruence and commitment (Chambers and Long 1995) and credibility of the clinical supervisor (Fowler 1996b; Addo 1997).

Prescriptive role

The clinical supervisor establishes a safe learning environment and explicitly seeks to influence, guide and direct the supervisee's behaviour without encroaching on the self-determining abilities of the supervisee, since the supervisee may lack the 'know-how' of technical skills, awareness of policies, procedures and the 'dos' and 'don'ts' in forensic nursing work. It is about making the supervisee aware of the organisation's contracts. Good role modelling of the clinical supervisor enables the supervisee to achieve confidence in role via teaching and learning, ensuring that standards of care and work are what they should be. The degree of knowledge, competence, skill and level of awareness and other factors will determine how often the clinical supervisor is prescriptive. Despite its lack of appeal, the prescriptive role has its place in the supervision process in forensic nursing when concepts such as dangerousness, risk management, clinical governance and evidence-based care are prerequisites of forensic nurses. With skilful use, the supervisee is supported to develop personally and professionally, thereby safeguarding patient care and the supervisee.

Informative role

This role involves the clinical supervisor acting as an information resource for the supervisee, imparting relevant knowledge and information to the supervisee that is meaningful, therefore expanding the supervisee's knowledge. It is about sharing good practice; encouraging change in clinical practice; networking; and creating awareness of current forensic research work to promote evidence-based care (McFarlane 1984). It can be a source of inspiration for the supervisee, but if over-used can dull the motivation for self-directed learning in the supervisee; and, if undone, the supervisee can be left disempowered by ignorance, making the supervisee vulnerable to the professional and political struggles in the workplace.

Confronting role

This role enables the supervisee to identify and challenge personal and professional blocks that are stifling personal development and progress, with a view to promoting reflection in action and on action. It is about telling the supervisee an uncomfortable truth, but done with empathy and with no hidden aggressive or combat agendas. The clinical supervisor is up-front, gives clear, constructive, direct feedback, challenging myths, beliefs and attitudes that are creating barriers in the supervisee's clinical practice and function within the multidisciplinary team, and of which the supervisee is defensively unaware. The main aim is about being uncompromising (a standard prodder), no matter what the situation.

Cathartic role

This role facilitates the supervisee in discharging and dealing with painful and difficult undischarged distress that may be disabling and distorting the supervisee's behaviour and work. The clinical supervisor creates a safe haven, offering opportunity for the supervisee to discharge any painful feelings of anger in storming, sounds and movements; grief in tears, sobbing; talking about fears in trembling, shaking; and embarrassments in laughter. The clinical supervisor pitches cathartic intervention at a level of distress which the supervisee is ready to handle in a relatively undisruptive way. This enables verbalising of spontaneous generated insight and helps the supervisee to shift from analysis of experience to reflecting upon it. The supervisee is encouraged to express both negative and positive feelings. Allowing the supervisee the opportunity to explore and express personal distress, re-stimulation, transference and counter-transference issues related to work, dealt with in supervision, enables the supervisee to become more competent in dealing with his or her feelings and consequently those of others. When the clinical supervisor takes on the role of 'good enough supervisor' (Hawkins and Shohet 1989), a concept derived from the work of Winnicott's (1965) notion of 'good enough mother', it allows the supervisee to feel the strength of being held or contained in the supervisory relationship (Klein 1960). The catharsis-facilitating role of the clinical supervisor allows the supervisee to grow and develop as a person, to gain self-awareness into their own self strengths and weaknesses and ways of being which the supervisee is blind to or denigrates in self.

Support role

Being genuine, empathic, non-judgemental, an active listener, challenging, trusting, committed and caring are essential preconditions for all the other roles within this clinical supervision framework, allowing the supervisee to feel free to disclose aspects of their work without fear of reproach. The role is to affirm the worth of the supervisee as a person: their qualities, attitudes of mind, actions, artefacts and creations. It enables the supervisee to believe that what they do as professionals is self-actualising, credible, valuable, worthwhile and humane (Maslow 1987). This role includes approving, confirming and providing validation of the worth of the supervisee, sharing experiences as well as encouraging the supervisee to celebrate and value themselves. The outcome is that the supervisee is able to think and act more positively as he or she hears these assertions of their own worth.

Catalytic role

This involves enabling the supervisee to learn by self-direction, self-discovery, reflective work, learning and problem-solving within the context of the supervision process and beyond it. The supervisee is helped to become more responsible for who they are and for their learning. This involves eliciting from the supervisee the unconscious patterns in their behaviour in different situations, exploring theoretical knowledge as the basis for their practice, critical appraisal of care protocols and decisions made about patient care. The essence is the facilitation of change, and the clinical supervisor needs to be aware of any internal or external factors which may impinge on this process. By internal factors, I mean preoccupation with their own personal needs, feelings and negative thoughts (Peplau 1991) in order for the supervision session to be meaningful for the supervisee.

By using selective reflection, the clinical supervisor can summarise or paraphrase back to the supervisee content taken from the whole supervision session for deeper exploration: the implications for the supervisee as a person and as a nurse, for the supervisee's clinical practice and as a member of a multidisciplinary team. In checking for the supervisee's understanding, the supervisor presents the summary of points of view expressed by the supervisee and the orientation within the problem as put forward, and offers empathy by trying to see the world from the supervisee's perspective. Showing sensitivity to the areas of professional development in the supervisee's cognition, the clinical supervisor acts as a catalyst for change in helping the supervisee to learn about self. The important issue here is helping the supervisee to recognise blind and dumb spots in their thinking and work on them.

CONCLUSION

Forensic nursing is an emerging, challenging field which requires specialist knowledge, skills and competencies. Changes continue to take place in the treatment and care of mentally disordered offenders. In light of the demands and dilemmas faced by nurses working with the mentally disordered, forensic nurses need a supportive facilitative process of clinical supervision (such as described in this chapter) if they are to maintain their emotional and psychological health to function at an optimum level to provide quality care. Clinical supervision offers them the opportunity to reflect on their work situation, to take care of themselves and learn how best to care for those entrusted in their care through personal growth and professional development for practice.

CHAPTER 12

Staff Stress, Coping Skills and Job Satisfaction in Forensic Nursing

Kevin Gournay and Jerome Carson

INTRODUCTION AND BACKGROUND

Research into staff stress really expanded in the 1980s (Payne and Firth-Cozens 1987); however, its roots go back much further to the classic studies of Isabel Menzies (Menzies 1959). Published studies can be categorised into four groups. First, there are autobiographical accounts of so-called 'wounded healers'. These have become increasingly popular (Rippere and Williams 1985; Jamison 1996; Deegan 1996). These are personal accounts of how mental health workers have dealt with their own psychiatric problems. Second, there are descriptive accounts of stress, which often describe the basic stress models and several of which include tips on stress management (Thompson 1983; Farrington 1995). Many of these are summaries of information available in any number of general stress textbooks. Third, there are reviews of the literature (Jones 1987; Sullivan 1993a; Carson, Kuipers and Gournay 1999). These are review-published studies with an obvious focus on the empirical literature. Fourth are the empirical studies themselves, which can be subdivided into within-profession studies (Sullivan 1993b) and between-profession studies (Cushway, Tyler and Nolan 1996). We have recently reviewed the broader stress literature for all mental health professions (Gournay and Carson 1997), and in this chapter will confine our comments to studies on mental health nurses.

After reviewing the literature on stress in mental health nurses, we will then focus on some of the specific stressors facing forensic mental health nurses. Finally, we will then describe the Special Hospitals' Nursing Staff Stress Survey, and will present some preliminary findings from this research.

The issue of stress in mental health nurses holds a particular fascination for many researchers. Wheeler (1997a) states that not only is nursing a stressful profession, but that stress may be implicated in both the high turnover and the high suicide rates. Jones' (1987) early review could identify only six studies in the worldwide literature that focused specifically on mental health nurses. A later review (Sullivan 1993a) found few additional studies. The early studies that were conducted (Dawkins, Depp and Selzer 1985; McCarthy 1985; Trygstad 1986; Landeweerd and Boumans 1988; Handy 1990; Carson, Bartlett and Croucher 1991; Schafer 1992; Bamber 1992; Thompson and Page 1992; Sullivan 1993b; Fielding and Weaver 1994) can all be criticised as none had a sample of more than 100 nurses. All had small non-representative samples, which made it virtually impossible to generalise from their findings to the wider population of mental health nurses. It was not until the large Claybury CPN Stress Study was completed that it was possible to obtain a more accurate picture of stress and coping in mental health nursing (Fagin *et al.* 1995; Carson, Fagin and Ritter 1995a). This study surveyed 323 ward-based mental health nurses and 245 community mental health nurses. The authors found that CPNs were significantly more emotionally exhausted by their work, but had lower depersonalisation scores on the Maslach burn-out inventory (Maslach and Jackson 1986). Job satisfaction levels were significantly higher in CPNs for total and intrinsic satisfaction levels on the Minnesota scale (Weiss *et al.* 1967). Caseness rates on the general health questionnaire GHQ-28 were 41 per cent for CPNs and 28 per cent for ward-based nurses. The authors concluded that CPNs clearly faced greater occupational stress, but enjoyed their work more and had better therapeutic relationships with their patients. This study is important for two main reasons. First, because of the large sample involved, the findings are likely to be more easily generalised. Second, the authors used standardised measures of the stress process, whereas many previous workers had used scales developed by themselves with no information on their reliability or validity (Sullivan 1993b; McLeod 1997).

Wheeler (1997a, 1997b) criticises the methodology of a lot of the nursing stress research. Most of the research has used cross-sectional rather than longitudinal designs. Longitudinal studies are quite rare (Astrom *et al.* 1991; Melchior *et al.* 1996). It should be noted though that some experts argue that processes such as burn-out are so complex that simply using longitudinal designs is no guarantee that you can capture the process more adequately (Schaufeli and Enzmann 1998). Wheeler suggests that most workers focus on the frequency and determinants of stress, to the exclusion of factors such as coping skills. Indeed, there is only one published study on coping skills in mental health nurses (Kipping 1998). Few studies focus on the response to, and the effects of, stress on staff. Finally, he suggests that few studies are guided by any theoretical model. Hence, they often comprise ad hoc collections of measures without any clear theoretical underpinning. Reeves (1994) compares psychiatric and general nurses on a range of demographic variables and the GHQ-28, and while she provides the usual textbook models of stress, her selection of measures is no reflection of any specific model. Clearly, nursing stress research has to be more theoretically based if we are to try and understand this complex process.

Our own research suggests that there are three main elements to the stress process (Carson and Kuipers 1998). *External stressors* include specific occupational stressors, major life events and hassles and uplifts. *Stress outcomes* may be good in terms of staff having high job satisfaction, low burn-out and psychological well-being. Conversely, they may be poor with low job satisfaction, high levels of burn-out and psychological distress. These stress outcomes are moderated by a number of *mediating variables*. Staff are less likely to succumb to the effects of stress if they have high self-esteem, good social support, are resilient, have good physiological release mechanisms, have a sense of personal control and mastery and are emotionally stable. We suggest that there are at least seven of these mediating variables (Fagin *et al.* 1996). Measures selected in any investigation of stress in staff need to tap into each element of this stress process. Hence, they need to include a measure of stressors and mediating variables and to assess stress outcomes. It is obviously very difficult to capture the complexity of this process in any single investigation as this would entail three stressor measures, at least seven measures of mediating variables, and three separate stress outcome measures. Some 13 different scales in all, without even collecting demographic details! We do, however, at least need to conduct studies that enable us to test and develop theoretical models of the stress process.

STRESS IN SPECIAL HOSPITAL NURSES

It seems likely that nurses working in the special hospitals may be especially vulnerable to the effects of stress, given the nature of these environments. Tarbuck (1996) describes the post-inquiry atmosphere of Ashworth Hospital. The media scrutiny of these hospitals is a particular problem. Dealing with patient violence is a major problem in a forensic setting. Arnetz, Arnetz and Petterson (1996) surveyed 2600 Swedish nurses and found that 30 per cent had experienced violence at work. For psychiatric nurses, the lifetime prevalence of violence was 76.5 per cent. Flannery, in a major review, stated that '... in some cases rates of injuries to nursing personnel from patient assaults exceeds injuries for workers in construction, considered to be the most dangerous occupation' (Flannery 1996, p.63). Love and Hunter (1996) show the injury rate per 100 employees to be 8.3 for mining, 13.1 for manufacturing, 14.2 for heavy construction, 18.4 for forestry and 22.4 for nursing. Carmel and Hunter (1989) studied a one-year period in a large forensic hospital and found that 'battery' injuries (sustained through direct assault by patients) were 6.1/100 nurses and 9.9/100 for 'containment' injuries (those sustained while restraining patients). Larkin, Murtagh and Jones (1988) have estimated that there is one serious life-threatening assault per week in a special hospital. Chandley and Mason (1995) provide several case descriptions of the sorts of chronically assaultative patients that are nursed at Ashworth.

It is perhaps not surprising, given the large incidence of violence in nursing staff working in forensic settings, that staff stress is seen as a priority for research. Robinson (1994) conducted a survey of nursing research priorities. Stress was the number one priority for nurses at Ashworth and Broadmoor and was second after 'change' for nurses at Rampton. Despite this interest, the major textbook of forensic psychiatry (Gunn and Taylor 1993) does not address the issue of nursing staff stress. Nor indeed is there any mention of staff stress in a more recent text (Kaye and Franey 1998).

To date there have been two published accounts of stress in forensic nurses. The first of these is the study conducted by Jones *et al.* (1987) of nurses at Rampton Hospital. Of the 718 nurses working at the hospital, 349 completed questionnaires, a 49 per cent response rate. The researchers collected biographical data and administered the GHQ-12. They had a 30-item scale of job demands, a 37-item scale of job supports and constraints and finally a 15-item scale of job satisfaction. The researchers found that the main Lickert score for the total sample was 10.24, which is higher than levels of other occupational groups, but lower than for unemployed samples. Charge nurse grades had the highest GHQ-12 scores with nursing assistants the lowest. The main types of job demand were found to be administrative, patient supervision and aversive demands. For nursing officers, administrative demands were highest and for charge nurses, patient supervision was highest. Job satisfaction scores were again lower than for other occupational groups that the researchers had surveyed. In summary, the researchers found that nursing at Rampton Hospital was more stressful and also less satisfying than other professional occupations. But, if it is any consolation, it is better than being unemployed!

The second study was by Kirby and Pollock (1995). They surveyed 38 nurses working in a regional secure unit. They administered the Moos Ward Atmosphere Scale (Moos 1969) and the Occupational Stress Indicator (Cooper, Sloan and Williams 1988). The secure unit scored higher on staff control, anger, aggression and spontaneity than a comparable unit from America on the Moos scale. Comparing these forensic nurses with other mental health nurses showed that they scored higher only on three dimensions of the occupational stress indicator. These were 'broad view of satisfaction', 'broad view of control' and 'type A'. The sample was, however, quite small and the study suffered from not having a good measure of stress outcomes such as the Maslach Burnout Inventory or the General Health Questionnaire.

THE SPECIAL HOSPITALS' NURSING STAFF STRESS SURVEY

The Special Hospitals' Nursing Staff Stress Survey is the largest study yet conducted of stress in nurses working in the special hospitals. As has been highlighted above, nurses in these settings may be especially vulnerable to the effects of stress given that they are nursing some of the most disturbed patients in the entire National Health Service. Similarly, the adverse publicity that the hospitals have generated has probably further eroded staff morale. The only major study conducted previously (Jones *et al.* 1987) was conducted at Rampton Hospital in the mid-1980s. The present survey is a total population survey of nurses working at all four special hospitals.

The main aims of the survey are:

- to survey stress, coping and job satisfaction in the four special hospitals;
- to investigate demographic variables of interest to service managers such as support, sickness and alcohol consumption;
- to provide a 'benchmark' or baseline of current levels of stress;
- to develop stress management interventions based on the findings of the research;
- to examine if nursing staff caring for patients with personality disorders face additional stressors.

In designing the study, special attention was paid to the issue of confidentiality. Participants were given a 'study pack' with the study questionnaires, a consent form, information sheet and a stamped addressed envelope to return the questionnaires directly to the researchers. A printed response booklet contains the study questionnaires. These include:

- *A demographic questionnaire.* This has 52 items and was devised in close consultation with senior managers from all four hospitals. It covers a wide range of items from age, sex, nursing grade, experience, fitness to more attitudinal items.
- *The Perceived Stress Scale.* This is a ten-item scale developed by Cohen and colleagues for use in stress surveys (Cohen, Kamarck and Mermelstein 1983). It measures the individual's experience of stress in the last month. Scores range from 0–40, with higher scores reflecting higher levels of stress.
- *Rosenberg Self-Esteem Scale.* This is another ten-item scale that measures an individual's level of self-esteem. Originally developed by Rosenberg (1965), the current version is the modified four-response format of Wycherley (1987). In addition to a total self-esteem score, a categorical score can also be obtained.

- *The Psych-Nurses Methods of Coping Questionnaire.* This 35-item scale was developed by Stephen McElfatrick and Jerome Carson. Previous measures of coping skills are generic scales – this is the first scale to have been developed specifically for mental health nurses (McElfatrick *et al.* 1999). Strategies can be broken down into five broad factors:

  - *Factor 1 – Diverting one's attention away from work* (nine items)
    Sample items include: 'I deal with stress "by making plans for myself that have nothing to do with work" and "by having a stable home life that is kept separate from my work life."'

  - *Factor 2 – Self-regulation and self-attitude* (six items)
    This covers items like: 'I deal with stress "by having confidence in my own ability to do the job well" and "through being able to draw upon my own knowledge and experience when necessary."'

  - *Factor 3 – Social support at work* (six items)
    'I deal with stress by "having confidential one-to-one supervision" and "through having team supervision."'

  - *Factor 4 – Positive attitude towards one's role at work* (nine items)
    This focuses on issues such as: 'I deal with stress "by knowing there are those who hold me dear" and "by reminding myself that others have placed their trust in me."'

  - *Factor 5 – Emotional comfort* (five items)
    'I deal with stress "by discussing with colleagues problems as they arise at work" and "by knowing that should I ever need them, support and advice are available."'

- *General Health Questionnaire (GHQ-12).* This 12-item scale was used in the recent NHS Workforce Survey (Borrill *et al.* 1996; Wall *et al.* 1997). The GHQ is the most widely used psychiatric screening tool worldwide (Bowling 1995). In addition to a total score which is computed using either the GHQ or Lickert formats, a 'caseness' score is also obtained. Caseness is defined as a score of four or more (Goldberg and Williams 1988).

- *The Minnesota Job Satisfaction Scale.* This is a well-established measure of job satisfaction which was developed by Weiss and his colleagues at the University of Minnesota (Weiss *et al.* 1967). It has been used in several nursing research studies (Koelbel, Fuller and Misener 1991; Fagin and Bartlett 1995; Butterworth, Bishop and Carson 1996). This 20-item scale covers three dimensions: intrinsic, extrinsic and total job satisfaction. Intrinsic job satisfaction deals with factors such as responsibility, recognition and achievement. Extrinsic factors cover salary, image and job status. The total score comprises both plus an additional two items that do not load on either factor. The higher the score, the better the level of job satisfaction.

At the time of writing, two special hospitals have been surveyed. Response rates were around 30 per cent. To preserve the confidentiality of each hospital, they are referred to as Hospital 1 and Hospital 2. The combined sample reflects the responses of 318 nurses. In terms of the stress model described above (Carson and Kuipers 1998), stressors were assessed by the Perceived Stress Scale, mediating variables by the Rosenberg, Psych-Nurses Methods of Coping Questionnaire and by items from the demographic checklist, and stress outcomes by the Minnesota and GHQ-12 scales.

PRELIMINARY FINDINGS FROM THE SPECIAL HOSPITALS' NURSING STAFF STRESS SURVEY

Stress measures

A number of questions on the demographic questionnaire asked about stress levels. There were two quantitative scales that focused on 'stressors' (the perceived stress scale) and 'strain' (the general health questionnaire, GHQ-12). Staff were asked, 'Do you think that the hospital is a more stressful environment than it was five years ago?' In Hospital 1, 88 per cent of staff said 'yes' and in Hospital 2 the figure was 69 per cent. Staff were also asked to comment on whether they felt that stress was increasing in mental health nursing generally. In Hospital 1, 98 per cent of nurses felt there had either been moderate or massive increases in stress in recent years. The figure was identical for Hospital 2. One of the main stressors facing mental health nurses is being assaulted by patients. In Hospital 1, 43 per cent of the nurses had been assaulted by a patient in the last 12 months. The figure for Hospital 2 was 44 per cent. Special hospital nurses are more than twice as likely to be assaulted compared with their colleagues in other branches of mental health nursing.

Levels of alcohol and cigarette consumption are often regarded as indicators of staff stress. Respondents were asked to report how much they consumed from four options. Rates of heavy smoking (defined as more than 20 cigarettes per day) were 18 per cent for Hospital 1 and four per cent for Hospital 2. Comparable figures from normative samples are nine per cent for ward-based nurses, 5.6 per cent for CPNs (Brown and Leary 1995), and only one per cent for nurses in the clinical supervision evaluation project (Butterworth et al. 1997). Alcohol consumption was more of a problem. The percentage of staff drinking more than 21 units of alcohol a week was 16 per cent for both of the special hospitals surveyed. Comparable figures for ward-based mental health nurses were four per cent, for CPNs 2.4 per cent and two per cent for nurses from the clinical supervision project. Heavy drinking would therefore appear to be a significant problem for special hospital staff.

Finally, on the perceived stress scale the average total stress score for Hospital 1 was 17.87 (sd = 6.14) and for Hospital 2 = 18.14 (sd = 5.87). This compares with an average score on this measure of 16.10 (sd = 6.63) for nurses working in Inner London acute psychiatric wards (Brown 1997). The average score from normative samples is 13.02 (sd = 6.35) (Cohen and Williamson 1988). It suggests that special hospital nurses experienced higher levels of stressors than other mental health nursing staff and much more so than members of the general public. Despite this, caseness rates on the general health questionnaire were comparable to nurses in the wider NHS. The caseness rate was 29 per cent in both special hospitals, which is virtually identical to the rate for NHS nurses in general of 28.5 per cent (n = 4085) (Wall et al. 1997). As was mentioned earlier, additional scores are obtained from the GHQ. With respect to the 12-item form, Lickert scores are often reported, as total GHQ scores are often so low. For instance, the mean GHQ total score overall was only 2.83. The mean Lickert score for Hospital 1 was 12.87, and for Hospital 2 it was 13.25. This is higher than the average of 10.24 reported for Rampton in the mid-1980s (Jones et al. 1987), and suggests that levels of psychological distress are increasing. It is well above the average for other employed samples. Banks et al. (1980) report an average of 8.80 for 552 male employees in an engineering plant. Perceived stressors and stress outcomes are thus worse for special hospital nurses.

Coping skills

The main measure of coping skills employed in the present study was the Psych-Nurses Methods of Coping Questionnaire. The scores of special hospital nurses alongside comparative samples are given in Table 12.1. While total coping skills scores for both special hospital groups are quite similar with Hospital 1 averaging 124.52 and Hospital 2 averaging 123.10, this masks substantial sub-scale differences. On each factor there was a significant difference between the two hospitals. Nurses in Hospital 2 used significantly more diversion strategies (Factor 1) and had a more positive attitude towards work (Factor 4). In contrast, nurses in Hospital 1 used significantly more self-regulation (Factor 2), more social support (Factor 3) and more emotional comfort (Factor 5).

An overall comparison of total coping skills scores shows that mental health nurses in ward settings average 125.33 and in the community average 133.89 (McElfatrick 1997). The special hospital average of 124.11 is lower, suggesting that special hospital nurses may not be employing as many coping strategies as other mental health nurses. Given the importance of coping skills in moderating the effects of stress, this may be an important finding. The picture is somewhat more complex than this. For instance, on Factor 5, emotional comfort, nurses in

Hospital 1 had the highest scores of any group. Yet on Factor 4, positive attitude towards work, Hospital 1 had the lowest scores by far. Clearly, further more detailed analysis is required.

Table 12.1 Psychiatric Nurses Methods of Coping Questionnaire scores for special hospital nurses and other mental health nurses

	Hospital 1	Hospital 2	Mann-Whitney	Ward-based	CPNs
Factor 1 Diverting attention	25.41 (4.20)	34.76 (5.73)	p<0.01	35.27 (4.53)	36.29 (4.03)
Factor 2 Self-regulation	26.05 (4.37)	22.10 (4.17)	p<0.01	22.27 (3.26)	23.67 (2.80)
Factor 3 Social support	22.79 (4.29)	17.33 (5.00)	p<0.01	17.98 (3.88)	20.41 (4.23)
Factor 4 Positive attitude	24.46 (4.51)	30.33 (6.29)	p<0.01	31.21 (4.87)	33.44 (4.29)
Factor 5 Emotional comfort	25.75 (4.11)	17.99 (3.89)	p<0.01	18.60 (3.32)	20.07 (2.70)
Total coping skills score	124.52 (18.09)	123.10 (19.82)	p<0.01	125.33 (15.04)	133.89 (13.10)

(Standard deviations are in parentheses.)

In addition to quantitative items, staff were also asked: 'What helps you cope best with the pressures of your job?' This item not surprisingly generated a wide range of responses with the more conventional being: 'Looking forward to time off, holidays, relaxation at home, socialising in pubs, dancing, exercise, humour, discussions with colleagues.' The less conventional response was: 'Reminding myself that most people know better than me and when I believe that things are being dealt with wrongly I am either too old fashioned or intellectually limited to grasp the situation correctly!'

Attempting a broad categorisation of these responses for nurses from Hospital 2 shows that the best coping response is support from colleagues. Some 42 per cent of nurses report this. Amazingly, this is identical to the 42 per cent figure for CPNs (Carson *et al.* 1995b). Family support was reported by 20 per cent of respondents (this was 13% in the Clinical Supervision Project and 5% for CPNs). Hobbies and interests and sports were cited by 16 per cent of nurses. Interestingly, alcohol was cited by 11 per cent of staff, suggesting again that for a significant minority of special hospital nurses alcohol misuse is a problem. Finally, support from partner was reported by 8 per cent of nurses, contrasting with a figure of 5 per cent for CPNs.

Job satisfaction

Job satisfaction was assessed using both standardised measures and items in the demographic questionnaire. Given the importance of colleague support in coping with stress, noted above, it is notable that 90 per cent of nurses in Hospital 1 and 88 per cent of nurses in Hospital 2 stated that they felt supported by colleagues they worked with. Job security levels were 43 per cent in Hospital 1 and 52 per cent in Hospital 2. Yet these are higher than the 29 per cent figure reported by Leary and Brown (1995) for nurses working in traditional asylum settings. Nurses in Hospital 1 felt that the media undermined their morale more than nurses in Hospital 2 (70% versus 55%).

Table 12.2 presents the scores on the Minnesota Job Satisfaction Scale. This has three components: intrinsic, extrinsic, and total job satisfaction. The results are clearcut. Nurses in the special hospitals have the lowest levels of job satisfaction in comparison with mental health nurses working in both hospital and community settings and also with nurses from the Clinical Supervision Project. The average total satisfaction score for special hospital nursing staff was 60.13. The next figure is that for ward-based mental health nurses with 62.6, community mental health nurses at 66.1 and finally Clinical Supervision Project nurses with 68.9. Clearly, attention needs to be paid to the issue of how to bolster the job satisfaction of special hospital nurses.

Table 12.2 Minnesota Job Satisfaction scores for special hospital nurses and other mental health nurses

	Hospital 1	Hospital 2	Ward-based	CPNs	Clinical Supervision Project
Extrinsic satisfaction	15.8 (4.29)	14.91 (4.44)	16.5 (4.6)	16.4 (4.6)	17.9 (6.1)
Intrinsic satisfaction	38.35 (7.16)	39.32 (6.46)	40.1 (7.3)	44.1 (6.4)	44.4 (4.1)
Total job satisfaction	60.34 (11.16)	59.63 (11.31)	62.6 (11.7)	66.1 (10.2)	68.9 (9.1)

Additional analyses

Three additional analyses are presented. First, the relationship between GHQ caseness and the study dependent variables. Second, the effects of staff assaults. Third, a comparison between staff with high self-esteem and staff with low self-esteem.

GHQ caseness

The criterion used for determining caseness was a score of 4 or more. This is a strict criterion, but it was the one also used in the large NHS study (Wall *et al.* 1997). By this criterion, some 93 nurses were classified as cases. This left 224 nurses who were non-cases. Both these groups were then compared on the study dependent variables.

The two groups were similar in age: 38.43 (cases) vs 38.76 (non-cases). Cases had worked slightly longer in the hospital: 11.34 years compared with 10.94 years. In response to the question, 'How confident are you in yourself at the moment?' (rated on a scale 0–100), cases averaged 59.91, non-cases averaged 76.36 (p<0.01). Job satisfaction was significantly lower for cases. Extrinsic satisfaction was 13.92, intrinsic satisfaction was 35.39 and total job satisfaction was 54.57. Respective figures for non-cases were 16.22, 39.97 and 62.44 (all p<0.01). The average Perceived Stress Scale score was 23.76 for cases and 15.54 for non-cases (p<0.01). The total coping skills score for cases was 113.44 and for non-cases 128.56 (p<0.01). Cases took an average of 20.09 days off sick in the last year in comparison with 9.75 days for non-cases (p<0.01). These findings confirm the construct validity of the GHQ-12.

Staff assaults

Some 130 nurses out of the total sample had been assaulted in the last year. Some 170 answered that they had not been assaulted. (Clearly, not all nurses responded to this question.) Both groups were then compared on the study dependent variables.

Staff who were assaulted were significantly younger: 36.83 vs 39.99 (p<0.01). Job satisfaction levels were significantly lower in staff who had been assaulted: extrinsic 14.85 vs 16.06 (p<0.05); intrinsic 37.63 vs 39.12 (p<0.05); and total job satisfaction 58.35 vs 61.16 (p<0.05). Total coping skills were also lower in assaulted staff, 122.07 vs 125.86, but this was not a significant difference. The mean GHQ-12 score was 3.35 for assaulted staff vs 2.42 for non-assaulted staff (p<0.05). Perhaps the most striking difference was in the amount of sickness absence in both groups. Staff who had been assaulted took on average 19.19 days sickness absence in the last 12 months, in contrast to 8.14 for non-assaulted staff (p<0.01). Being assaulted, clearly, has a profound effect on staff.

Self-esteem

Low self-esteem, defined as scores of 20 to 40 on the Rosenberg Scale, was seen in 64 of the nurses surveyed. This group was then compared with a high self-esteem group, staff with scores of 10–13 on the scale, n = 107. Both these groups were then compared on the study dependent variables.

Staff with low self-esteem have lower extrinsic job satisfaction, 14.45 vs 16.08 (p<0.05); lower intrinsic job satisfaction, 35.61 vs 40.52 (p<0.01); and lower total job satisfaction, 55.50 vs 62.80 (p<0.01). Perceived Stress Scale scores were 22.64 for low self-esteem staff and 14.66 for high self-esteem staff. The mean GHQ score for low self-esteem staff was 5.12 vs 1.53 for high self-esteem staff (p<0.01). Low self-esteem staff averaged 110.68 for total coping skills, whereas high self-esteem staff averaged 132.94 (p<0.01). Low self-esteem staff took an average of 18 days off sick, in comparison with 7.2 days for high self-esteem staff (p<0.01).

These findings confirm the importance of self-esteem as a mediating variable (Carson *et al.* 1997; Thomsen *et al.* 1988).

CONCLUDING COMMENTS

There have been so few studies of stress in forensic psychiatric nursing that it is difficult to state with any precision whether the pressures of the job are increasing. The study conducted at Rampton in the mid-1980s (Jones *et al.* 1987) found the mean Lickert score to be 10.24. To date, from our own study the scores have been 12.87 at Hospital 1 and 13.25 at Hospital 2. This does tend to suggest that stress outcomes are slightly worse for forensic mental health nurses. This was also confirmed by nurses' opinions, with the majority saying that their hospital was more stressful than five years ago.

One of the main findings to emerge from the Special Hospitals' Nursing Stress Survey has been the high prevalence of assaults by patients on staff. Love and Hunter (1996) reported that the injury rate was 22.4 for nursing. Our own figures show that 43.5 per cent of all nursing staff have been attacked in the preceding year. This rate is more than twice as high as that for any other branch of mental health nursing. Staff who have been assaulted are then in turn more likely to have high rates of sickness absence, more than two times that of their non-assaulted colleagues, and have higher levels of psychological distress and lower rates of job satisfaction. Given the nature of the patient population nursed in special hospitals, it may not be possible to reduce the rate of staff assaults significantly, but, clearly, staff need to be provided with proper incident debriefing and support following such attacks.

Excessive alcohol consumption would appear to be a problem for a significant minority of special hospital staff. We estimate that 16 per cent of staff in both hospitals surveyed to date are drinking more than 21 units of alcohol per week. As worrying was the fact that 11 per cent of staff suggested that alcohol helped them cope best with the pressures of their jobs. Perhaps aware of the problem, some managers suggested to us in advance of the study that including this item on our demographic questionnaire might prove unpopular with some nurses, who might not then tell the truth. It seems likely that there may have been some under-reporting of alcohol consumption.

The issue of coping skills is one that requires further attention. We have found that nurses working in special hospitals not only use fewer coping strategies on average, but may use different strategies to manage their stress levels. In common with other mental health nurses, peer support is by far the most important coping strategy, being cited by 42 per cent of nurses. Family support would also appear to be very important for special hospital nurses.

Job satisfaction levels were lower for special hospital nurses than for other groups of mental health nurses and for nurses from the Clinical Supervision Project (Butterworth et al. 1997). Service managers have the difficult task of not only bolstering but improving levels of staff job satisfaction.

The Special Hospitals' Nursing Staff Stress Survey has helped us develop a better understanding of stress, coping and job satisfaction in forensic nurses. The challenge now is to use the knowledge we have acquired to help develop stress management interventions that might improve the health, well-being and job satisfaction of special hospital nurses.

ACKNOWLEDGEMENTS

We are especially grateful to Louise Batchelor who conducted the surveys of both special hospitals described here. The study has been funded by a bequest to the Section of Psychiatric Nursing from Dr Jim Birley. We are indebted to all the nurses and special hospital managers for their support with the survey.

CHAPTER 13

The Role of the Forensic Psychiatric Nurse in the Netherlands

Hans-Martin Don and Tom van Erven

INTRODUCTION

In this chapter the question will be addressed as to whether there is such a profession as a psychiatric nurse in the Netherlands. The major developments in psychiatry and psychiatric nursing will be described, and in addition the relationship between penal law and the so-called 'Ter Beschikking Stelling' (TBS) measure will be explained. Finally, a pilot study will be presented, in which the question of psychiatric nursing is investigated.

The main aim of this chapter is to highlight the major developments and issues in psychiatric nursing in the Netherlands. However, we acknowledge that the issues that will be discussed deserve more detail than is provided by this chapter.

Forensic psychiatry in the Netherlands is characterised by several major developments. On the one hand, these include an increase in in-patient as well as out-patient facilities. On the other hand, one can observe a change in focus of the authorities towards the implementation of cost-reducing mechanisms. One of these mechanisms is the linking of budgets to the duration and content of the treatment of specific groups of patients, which are subsequently called treatment modules. This last development has had major implications for the forensic psychiatric nurse, because they have to further distinguish their profession from other nursing professions.

PSYCHIATRY IN THE NETHERLANDS: A REVIEW

The history of psychiatry in the Netherlands

The onset of 'modern' psychiatry in the Netherlands can be traced back to the early nineteenth century (Vijselaar 1982). Within Europe this was approximately 30 years later than France, where in 1793 Pinel freed patients of the Bicêtre of their chains, or England where 'the Retreat' was founded. Schroeder van der Kolk played a major role in the development of modern psychiatry in the Netherlands, as he encouraged the process of reforming Dutch psychiatry in 1837 (Cahn 1970) and heavily influenced the first Mental Health Act of 1841.

Before 1800 there was no legislation concerning the mentally insane in the Netherlands. During the French occupation (1810–1813), the 'Code Civil' was enforced, stating legislation about patients who were considered permanently insane. In 1814 a Royal statement was added to this legislation, regarding patients who were considered temporarily insane. At the time the first Civil Act was passed by parliament (1838), the 'Code Civil' and the Royal statement of 1814 lost their legal basis. As mentioned before, in 1841 the first Mental Health Act was accepted, which was concerned with only those patients who were considered not permanently insane. The second Mental Health Act (1884) corrected this situation and was applicable to all mentally ill patients. In addition, this second legislation ensured the controlling position of the state. Not until 1992 was the third Mental Health Act (Wet Bijzondere Opneming Psychiatrische Ziekenhuizen (BOPZ)) passed by parliament, after more than 20 years of debate. This latest legislation is primarily concerned with the enforced admission of patients into psychiatric hospitals (van Erven 1992).

Until 1925, patients who were considered to be criminally insane were admitted into general psychiatric hospitals. An important example of these hospitals is the former State Psychiatric Hospital in Eindhoven (1918), which accommodated most of these patients. In 1925 the Psychopath Act was passed by parliament and following this the first psychopath asylums were founded in 1928. These asylums later became our TBS clinics. TBS stands for 'Ter Beschikking Stelling', which can be translated as 'disposal to be treated on behalf of the state'.

Penal law and forensic psychiatry

The Dutch penal code contains a special provision for offenders who have committed an offence for which they cannot be punished. A suspect can be found not guilty because the court considers there to be grounds for exemption; for example, when a patient cannot be held responsible for his actions (Roozendaal 1997), which in Dutch legal terms is called 'ontoerekeningsvatbaar'.

The concept of 'ontoerekeningsvatbaarheid' refers to the fact that a suspect cannot be held responsible for crimes or offences because he or she suffers from a specific developmental or psychiatric disorder. Hence, a psychiatric disorder can lead to the verdict 'ontoerekeningsvatbaarheid' (Table 13.1). It is important to notice that there are gradations the court can use in its verdict with regard to the concept of 'ontoerekeningsvatbaarheid' (Table 13.2).

In the case of 'ontoerekeningsvatbaarheid', the court will generally invoke a measure of compulsory psychiatric treatment, especially when an offender has committed a serious and violent act, with a high risk of recurrence. Important in these sorts of measures is that they are not meant to punish as such, but are meant to protect society and aim at curing, improving and educating the offender (Roozendaal 1997). In the following subsection the TBS measure will be discussed further.

Table 13.1 Axes-I and-II diagnoses (DSM)	
TBS population 1996	
Only Axes-I	16%
Only Axes-II	25%
Axes-I and Axes-II	59%
Total	100%
Absence of diagnosis	100
N (total)	752

(Dr. F.S. Meijers Instituut 1997)

Table 13.2 Verdict of responsibility	
TBS population 1996	
Responsible	1%
Slightly diminished	2%
Diminished	47%
Strongly diminished	31%
Not responsible	20%
Total	101%
N (not known)	289
N (total)	563

(Dr. F.S. Meijers Instituut 1997)

TBS

The TBS measure is primarily meant to protect. This protection is twofold: protection by detention in a secure clinic; and protection by means of (compulsory) psychiatric treatment in order to reduce the risk of re-offending. A TBS order is indeterminate, initially for two years but subsequently renewable by a court.

The Netherlands have founded special provisions for TBS patients (Table 13.3). First of all, there are seven TBS clinics which are part of the Department of Justice, and are therefore the responsibility of the Minister of Justice. Second, there are seven forensic psychiatric units (part of general psychiatric hospitals) and three forensic psychiatric clinics. Both units and clinics are part of the Dutch mental health care system and therefore the responsibility of the Minister of Health. Patients with a TBS admitted to the latter are also subjected to legal restrictions imposed by the Department of Justice concerning the amount of freedom they have outside the clinic.

In total, there are about 1000 beds available for the detention and treatment of forensic psychiatric patients (i.e. TBS patients).

Table 13.3 List of forensic facilities in the Netherlands
Clinics that are part of the Department of Justice (TBS clinics)
Dr. F.S. Meijers Instituut
Dr. S. van Mesdagkliniek
Rijksinrichting Veldzicht
Dr. H. van der Hoevenkliniek
Prof. Mr. W.P.J. Pompekliniek
Oldenkotte
De Kijvenlanden
Clinics that are part of the Department of Health
Hoeve Boschoord
Het Forensisch Psychiatrische Circuit van de GGZ Eindhoven
Forensisch Psychiatrische Kliniek APZ Drenthe

An important aspect of treatment within the clinics and units is the general care-giving. This care is given by a variety of health care professionals. Within the mental health care hospitals and units the most important group of professionals is the nursing specialist. Within the TBS clinics the group of professionals is more varied and tends to include more social workers and development workers.

The next section will describe in detail the work of the nursing profession providing care in forensic psychiatric settings.

THE DEVELOPMENT OF THE PSYCHIATRIC NURSING PROFESSION

A historical review

The first courses in psychiatric nursing date back to 1845. However, only in 1884 was a clear curriculum obtained, mainly as the result of changes that were made within the law. The first official degree in psychiatric nursing was gained in 1893. In general, one could say that the contents of the courses followed opinions and attitudes towards psychiatric care and psychiatric patients, and therefore occupational therapy formed an important part of the psychiatric care that was given. The courses were based on the concept of 'training on the job' and there was a strong connection between learning and working. Throughout the course a degree of loyalty and availability towards the institutions was expected from the students.

Although the initial steps to develop nursing courses were initially taken by private institutions, subsequent developments have always been carefully monitored and regulated by the government through the introduction of laws: as with most educational laws, they followed successful private initiatives (Goudswaard 1993). Legal protection of the nursing care professional was first established in 1942. The measures that were then introduced regulated the different courses within the health care system and therefore protected the professional. The degree in psychiatric nursing became an official degree and obtained a special logo, namely 'Het Zwarte Kruis' (translated: 'the black cross'). The nurses had to register themselves in an official registry. The law provided for the protection of the name of the psychiatric nurse, but not yet the protection of the profession itself.

After the Second World War some important developments took place within the psychiatric patients' care system. For example, the introduction of neuroleptic medication did not only affect the patients, but also psychiatric nursing care. From 1972 day-courses in psychiatric nursing were established, and subsequently a degree in Higher Education in Nursing Care was introduced. This higher education course aimed at training nurses within all aspects of health care. The degree from this course qualified a nurse to work in physical health care settings, psychiatric health care settings and in institutions for the learning disabled, and also as a community health care worker.

Finally, two important recent developments need to be mentioned: the implementation of a law for workers within health care settings, Beroepen Individuele Gezondheidszorg or BIG (BIG 1997) and the latest changes in the education system. The purpose of the law is to improve and control the quality of the professional work within health care settings and the protection of patients against malpractice. The law ascertains that nurses obtain a certain amount of expertise within their profession and that they are capable of independent care-giving and judgements. The fact that registration is for a limited period of time means that certain demands are being put upon the expertise of the professional in case they want to extend their registration.

The recently established law (BIG) is in a sense partly responsible for the changes that have taken place within the nursing education system. As explained before, the nursing profession has developed expertise on two different levels, and nursing courses focus on these levels. The differentiation within the courses has contributed to a better co-operation and co-ordination within the nursing education system, even though the essence of nursing education is still based on learning and working, like in the early days.

Psychiatric nurse versus forensic psychiatric nurse

The professional nursing profile is the basic element of nursing care in the Netherlands. The definition of nursing as described by the American Nursing Association (1980) has served as the starting point for the development of this profile. The association defines nursing as: 'the diagnosis and treatment of human responses to actual or potential health problems'.

Characteristic of subsequent developments of the nursing profession has been the distinction between two levels of nursing. The first level describes the nurse as a professional who is responsible for the diagnostic process, the planning of care and referring of patients. The second level describes the nurse as a professional who is responsible for the provision of care to the patients that are referred to him/her in an independent manner.

At the forensic psychiatric hospital (FPC) where both authors work, both levels of nursing are used within the care system. The treatment of a patient is based on treatment plans, which are reviewed at multidisciplinary meetings on a regular basis. The idea of the treatment plan stems from measures that were taken within laws concerning treatment contracts and compulsory psychiatric treatment. The main characteristic of the multidisciplinary treatment is that each professional is responsible for his or her contribution to the treatment plan and each contribution is considered equally valuable. The team consists of psychiatrists, psychologists, social workers and nurses. For legal reasons, the psychiatrist is considered responsible for all medically related procedures within a treatment plan. Nurses are primarily concerned with the individual care of patients and with the therapeutic processes that take place on the ward. By monitoring these processes, the nurse is able to put into operation an individual treatment plan. This results in a 24-hour-based programme that contributes to the therapeutic process. The means by which the operation of this 24-hour-based programme can take place is, first of all, the result of the psychiatric condition of the patient and, second, of the theoretical background of the clinic. In addition, it is important to realise that the offence the patient has committed and the compulsory character of the treatment, in relation to the overall aim of the treatment to reduce re-offending, contribute to the way the treatment and treatment plan is implemented. For example, at the FPC certain regulations concerning safety have been formulated which nurses have to obey in their day-to-day work with patients. In other words, the forensic aspects play a major role in the individual treatment of patients. An example of a therapeutic tool that can be used is the so-called 'delict-scenario' (translated: offence-script), through which the therapist and patient describe and adapt the offence and circumstances that have led to the offence, including a script to be used in crises.

Official courses for forensic psychiatric nursing are not available in the Netherlands: all nurses obtain a general nursing degree and many follow subsequent courses to specialise in different directions. However, it is important to notice that the number of forensic psychiatric nurses is small. As was mentioned before, there are about 1000 beds reserved for forensic psychiatric patients within the Dutch mental health care system and justice system. Based on this figure, one can assume that the number of forensic psychiatric nurses is about 500, which is a relatively small group for specialist courses.

The question is then how, if at all, can a nurse specialise as a forensic psychiatric nurse? One of the most important ways of specialising is the day-to-day practice of working in a forensic psychiatric setting and the day-to-day interaction with forensic psychiatric patients. Second, most institutions organise their own specialist courses. Within the FPC, each new member is offered a short course in forensic psychiatry, which deals with the following aspects: introduction to the forensic field, legal and penal regulations, specific psychopathology and interacting with disturbed patients.

The philosophy of the FPC is based on the assumption that each forensic psychiatric patient is primarily a psychiatric patient. This basic assumption is then linked to the specific way in which a patient is admitted and the compulsory character of the treatment. This combination has specific consequences for the care that can be given. The basic assumption also raises questions about the extent to which one can distinguish caring for forensic patients from caring for 'normal' psychiatric patients. A group of first-level nurses (responsible for the diagnostic process, the planning of care and referring of patients) have been questioned about this issue, and the results of this (pilot) study will be described in the next section.

A PILOT SURVEY

Introduction

Hardly anything has been published in the Netherlands, if anything at all, about the phenomenon of the 'forensic psychiatric nurse'. So the question arises: 'Is there such a person as a forensic psychiatric nurse?' In order to shed some light on this matter, we have conducted a small survey amongst the staff nurses (first level) of our own clinic. Because of a strict deadline, they had to respond within a limited period of time. Out of the group of 34 staff nurses (predominantly male: 85 per cent), 53 per cent responded on time. Nearly 80 per cent is aged between 36 and 45 years. On average, they have been working in a psychiatric setting for 15 years, and about 12 years in forensic psychiatry. We assume that the results presented provide the reader with a representative insight into the overall views of 'forensic psychiatric nurses' about their profession.

To compare our data with the data obtained by our UK colleagues (Kettles and Robinson, Chapter 2), we used the same eight questions they used in their study in England and Scotland. We also analysed the data by means of a qualitative thematic analysis using categorical descriptive accounts.

Results

In response to the first question 'Is there such a person as a forensic psychiatric nurse?', the majority (68 per cent) answered 'Yes'. Most of these answers are more or less of a Descartian-like format 'Je pense, donc je suis', 'I work in a forensic clinic, so I am a forensic psychiatric nurse'. Whether any special qualities are considered necessary, the answers seem to imply that there needs to be a certain affinity to, or preference for, the specific patient population, i.e. mentally disordered offenders. As well as that, such personality characteristics as flexibility, being stress resistant and being able to take a lot on were mentioned. As a person you have to have it in you to cope with these patients.

The remaining 32 per cent did not think that special qualities were needed to be a forensic psychiatric nurse. All psychiatric nurses could do the work and learn the specifics by doing the job.

The second question was: 'What makes a forensic nurse different from a mental health nurse?' There is no fundamental difference in core skills, but the nature of the patient population puts emphasis on specific skills. Patients are not just patients, but patients who have committed a serious crime. The primary goal is to prevent re-offending. Therefore, the environment is more controlled and there is always the possible discrepancy between treatment on the one hand and securing society on the other. A 'real' forensic psychiatric nurse considers the patient *behind* the criminal. You need a 'strong' personality and a lot of life-experience to cope with forensic patients.

Question three: 'What are the key characteristics of the forensic psychiatric nurse role for (a) qualified nurses and (b) nursing assistants?' The core duties of the qualified nurses are directed towards security and assessing dangerousness. Personal qualities such as calmness, maturity, independence, stress resistance, transparency and patience are seen as elementary for a qualified forensic psychiatric nurse.

In the Netherlands, nursing assistants are 'nurses in training', who are trained to become nurses. They are also considered to possess the above-mentioned personal qualities, and on top of that are in the process of learning and 'expanding' most of these qualities. In other words, they need a degree of eagerness to learn the 'specifics'. Some qualified nurses are of the opinion that a forensic clinic is not a good learning environment for nurses in training.

The answers to question four: 'What sort of training/preparation have you had that enables you to work with mentally disordered patients?', indicated that de facto there is no formal training or special preparation. Education, training and preparation that is considered necessary is done on the job and you learn as you go along. General or specialised, non-specific training courses and educational programmes are available, and staff nurses attended a wide variety of these, guided by their own preferences. Special training courses, such as on TDB (threatening and destructive behaviour), are available but not obligatory.

Question five: 'What sort of training is required?' In contrast with the UK findings, there was no considerable list generated. The TDB training was mentioned seven times. Most training needs were mentioned once or twice, but were not necessarily specific for a forensic situation. The training needs that were mentioned included, for example: courses in sociotherapy, systemtherapy (a form of psychotherapy where a system, family, small or large group is treated), communication training and all kinds of psychotherapy-related training courses and courses in forensic psychiatry in the Netherlands, in specific legal aspects, in crime scenario and in recidivism prevention.

'What are the dilemmas facing you when caring for and treating the mentally disordered offender?' was question six. The two most prominent dilemmas that were mentioned were the duality between 'patient versus criminal' and between 'treatment versus protection of society'. The limitations in ways of caring that are set upon by legal restraints and the lack of motivation for treatment because of forced admission were two other important dilemmas. Other dilemmas that were mentioned were difficulties coping with certain crimes, and the excessive amount of money invested in forensic patients compared with other groups of patients, such as the elderly or learning disabled. In contrast with this, an increasing dilemma seems to be the shortage of nursing staff because of an average 36-hour working week (instead of 40 hours). This reduction in working time has caused under-staffed shifts, and as a result poor communication with other professionals.

Question seven stated: 'How does the forensic psychiatric nurse differ from other disciplines?' The most prominent differences are of a general nursing nature: providing the 24-hour care for the patients; being the core of the team and providers of most basic information about the patients. Nurses create the basic environment; they are the 'engine' behind the clinic. They are the ones who have to endure all patients' emotions most prominently and they almost exclusively provide security for others as well as themselves.

The final question was: 'What do forensic psychiatric nurses contribute to the multi-professional team?' The most important contribution is to provide information about a number of aspects concerning the patients. They are up-to-date with the most relevant information concerning day-to-day behaviour and peculiarities of the patients. Being assigned to a specific patient, they are the core contributors to the cure and care. In other words, they know patients best. There is no specific mention about problems with regard to their recognition as an important, regarded and appreciated discipline.

We included an extra question, namely whether they knew of any official Dutch publications concerning forensic nursing or forensic psychiatric nurses. The answer was unanimous: 'No!' A computer search gave the same result – there were no books, chapters or articles found about forensic nursing or forensic psychiatric nurses in the Netherlands.

Discussion

A pilot of this size and format always suffers from methodological problems. For example, it is difficult to assess the extent to which the answers are representative of the group of forensic psychiatric nurses as a whole. Also, the opinions that were obtained are from a one-dimensional source, i.e. nurses only. However, the results are important because they give us some basic insight into the central issue at hand: 'Is there such a person as a forensic psychiatric nurse?'

The answer to that question was twofold. For some the answer was: 'No, because there is no formal forensic psychiatric nurses' training programme and there is no legislation recognising the "forensic psychiatric nurse".' A possible reason for this is that the number of nurses working in forensic psychiatric clinics and TBS clinics in the Netherlands is very small compared with the total number of nurses working in our country. Out of 180,000 nurses, there are some 14,000 psychiatric nurses of which approximately 500 (<0.3 per cent of all nurses) are 'forensic psychiatric nurses'. Another possible reason could be that the characteristics of forensic nursing are in essence of a non-nursing kind, i.e. providing security.

For others the answer was: 'Yes, because there are nurses working in forensic facilities learning the specifics of what is required by doing their job.'

The results have shown that, although the core of nursing activity is not different from what nurses do in general, there are a number of specific features to forensic nursing. The most prominent that were mentioned were:

- providing security for society;
- the pressure of working with a group of mentally ill patients who have committed serious crimes;
- the specific limitations in possibilities of care because of the strict legal procedures they need to obey.

Most 'forensic psychiatric nurses' considered themselves a special breed of nurses because of the personal qualities they regarded necessary to be able to cope successfully with the special demands of the patient population.

CONCLUSION

The overview of the developments in the psychiatric nursing profession make it clear that the process of becoming more and more professional is a slow one. Only after more than a hundred years is the nursing profession finally anchored in the law BIG. By that, not only did the title of nurse become a legal reality but also the contents of their job.

As far as the forensic psychiatric nurse is concerned, there is no clear separate specialism within the nursing profession. There is the question of whether or not such a specialism is desirable or necessary. On the one hand, there is a clear tendency of a growing self-consciousness of forensic nurses within the nursing profession. This is caused by the gradual increase in the number of forensic psychiatric hospital beds as well as by the continued process of increasing professionalism of nurses in general. On the other hand, the absolute number of nurses working in forensic psychiatric facilities always will remain limited and therefore too small to become a separate officially recognised specialism.

In essence, the above question is not the central issue at hand, and therefore of no real consequence. The central issue at hand is the question of what care patients and society need and what answers the forensic nursing professionals can give in this regard. These answers about the kind of 'forensic nursing care' that will be provided determine whether or not there will be such a person as a forensic psychiatric nurse. The majority of first-level staff nurses included in our pilot survey hold the clear opinion that working with forensic psychiatric patients requires specific personal qualities and skills.

The conclusion is that the formal answer to the question whether or not officially there is such a person as a forensic psychiatric nurse in the Netherlands is 'No'. Developments of the profession in relation to forensic demands will possibly give a different answer in the future.

CHAPTER 14

Forensic Mental Health Care in Australia

Colin Holmes

LEGISLATION AND SERVICES OFFERED IN AUSTRALIAN STATES AND TERRITORIES

In the general absence of Australian Federal or State policies, strategies or coordinated systems, services for mentally ill offenders (MIOs) have developed in a rather ad hoc fashion according to the history and circumstances peculiar to each State and Territory. In most cases, services remain split between the corrections and health care systems, and the latter include almost the only remaining 'stand-alone' psychiatric facilities receiving new funding. Since each State and Territory has its own criminal and mental health legislation, a brief discussion of these has been included in the following survey of services.

The Australian Capital Territory

In the Australian Capital Territory, in which lies the nation's capital, Canberra, mentally ill offenders are dealt with in criminal legislation under the Crimes Act (1900) and the Crimes (Amendment) Act (A.C.T.) (1994). The Act covers 'unfitness to plead' and provides for 'special hearings', and a verdict of 'not guilty by reason of mental illness' in appropriate cases. The conditions (Sec. 428N) represent a strict reading of M'Naghten, being confined to capacity for knowing what he or she was doing, or knowing that it was wrong. It is noteworthy that the relevant civil legislation, the Mental Health (Treatment and Care) Act (A.C.T.) (1994), concerns 'mentally dysfunctional offenders', meaning a person who has been ordered by a court to submit to the jurisdiction of the Mental Health Tribunal. Unusually, rather than defining 'mental illness', Section 4 of the Act defines 'mental dysfunction' and 'psychiatric disorder'. Mental dysfunction refers to:

a disturbance or defect, to a substantially disabling degree, of perceptual interpretation, comprehension, reasoning, learning, judgement, memory, motivation or emotion

whilst psychiatric illness refers to:

a condition that seriously impairs (either temporarily or permanently) the mental functioning of a person and is characterized by the presence in the person of any of the following symptoms: delusions, hallucinations, serious disorder of thought form, a severe disturbance of mood, sustained or repeated irrational behaviour indicating the presence of [these] symptoms.

There are no services for MIOs in the Australian Capital Territory's health system. The only corrections facility, Belconnen Remand Centre, provides a maximum security environment for up to 46 male and female inmates, and includes psychiatric consultation services but no designated beds for the mentally ill, who are therefore transferred to facilities in New South Wales.

New South Wales

The primary civil legislation controlling the care of MIOs in New South Wales is the Mental Health Act (1990) and the Mental Health (Criminal Procedure) Act (1990), together with the associated amendments. The former Act includes definitions of important terms, including 'mental illness' and 'mental disorder', which are distinguished in the legislation, and 'forensic patient' is defined by the Mental Health Act (NSW) (1990), in the 'Dictionary of Terms Used in the Act', as:

(a) a person who is detained in a hospital, prison or other place pursuant to an order under [the Mental Health (Criminal Procedure) Act 1990, or Section 7(4) of the Criminal Appeal Act 1912]; or

(b) a person who is detained in a hospital pending the person's committal for trial for an offence or pending the person's trial for an offence; or

(c) a person who has been transferred to a hospital while serving a sentence of imprisonment and who has not been classified by the Tribunal as a continued treatment patient. (Mental Health Act 1990, p.114)

Regarding services for MIOs, any expectation that because it was the first state New South Wales would be the most advanced is liable to be disappointed, despite a recently renewed sense of purpose and revitalised morale. The Corrective Services Department has catered for MIOs for many years by providing hospital services at its maximum secure facility at Long Bay Prison, south of Sydney. These services now form part of the general health care provided by the New South Wales Health Department's 'Corrections Health Service', presently administered by a Chief Executive Officer with a background in nursing administration.

Long Bay is one of Australia's largest prison complexes, housing up to 1400 inmates and individuals subject to periodic detention, in a mixture of ancient and modern buildings. The hospital has one general medical and three psychiatric wards, catering respectively for 30 acute, sub-acute and 'forensic' patients (i.e. 'not guilty by reason of mental illness'). It offers a wide range of therapeutic activities including group and individual art therapy, occupational therapy, social skills, anger management, and other groups, all of which involve nurses; indeed, the art therapy programme is led by a nurse specialist. Nurses also run leisure activities including music, literacy, cooking and pottery classes, t'ai chi and yoga. The nursing establishment includes roughly 21 Registered Nurses to each ward, and about half of these have a specialist psychiatric qualification. These nurse–patient ratios compare favourably to health system facilities, especially considering that a complement of Corrections Officers is also in constant attendance to oversee security and control disturbances.

This separation of functions, not possible in health service units, is regarded by many of the nurses as a useful protection of their therapeutic role. Clinical supervision is being introduced for nursing staff, with the assistance of the local Area Health Service, and role descriptions are based on the competencies and standards published by the Australia and New Zealand College of Mental Health Nurses. Some 75 per cent of the prison hospital's admissions are in respect of transient disturbances, the remaining 25 per cent involving a major psychotic illness. The hospital wards are cramped, stark, and anti-therapeutic in appearance, and although a few cells have recently been upgraded to look more homely, they have all the paraphernalia of a high security prison. The inadequacy of the physical facilities is widely acknowledged and there are plans for comprehensive renovation.

Mental health services at the new 900-bed Metropolitan Remand and Reception Centre (MRRC) at Silverwater in Western Sydney include a multidisciplinary 24-hour 'crisis intervention team' (CIT), involving four Registered Nurses. The team assesses all new arrivals with a history of self-harm or psychiatric disorder, supports inmates with a diagnosed psychosis, and provides rapid response to crisis situations, conducting assessments and arranging transfers to the Long Bay Prison Hospital where necessary. In the year 1997/98, CIT contacts at the MRRC amounted to 5276 (Corrections Health Service 1999, p.47), and it can be reasonably be said that this is a substantial workload for a team of four!

Also available across the State's corrective services are multidisciplinary 'risk intervention teams' (RITs), comprising a custodial officer, a psychologist and a nurse, which aim to provide an effective alternative to short-stay transfers to the Long Bay Hospital. This is particularly useful for facilities located at great distances from Long Bay. In the period 1996/97, the RITs made some 5678 appointments for inmates to see psychiatrists (Corrections Health Service 1998, p.51).

Mulawa Prison near Parramatta, west of Sydney, is Australia's largest women's prison, nominally catering for about 200 inmates but often having to cope with substantially more. Mulawa's grossly inadequate psychiatric observation unit has recently been decommissioned, and redesigned by the staff themselves: when rebuilding is finished it will provide for observation and assessment of up to 30 inmates, mostly with a substance abuse problem. The main mental health problems involve borderline personality disorder, and a recently opened therapeutic unit for up to 12 inmates offers a range of rehabilitation programmes, including anger management, sexual and gender-related therapies and social skills training; the unit is staffed by corrections officers and a psychologist. The CIT had 2943 contacts at Mulawa in the 1996/97 period (Corrections Health Service 1999, p.46) of which roughly one in three were related to self-harm or suicidal behaviour, and one in six resulted in referral to a psychiatrist. In the year 1997/98, this increased by 17 per cent to 3453 (Corrections Health Service 1999, p.47), which might be considered staggering for a 200-bed facility. The number of recorded suicide attempts and incidents of self-harm doubled between 1996/97 and 1997/98 (Corrections Health Service 1999, p.44).

Such increases are reflected across the whole corrections system, however, as a result of the introduction of mandatory reporting of all threats of, or actual, self-harm. Furthermore, the seriousness of the incidents at Mulawa, and the rate of successful suicides, has been substantially reduced in the last few years according to detailed unpublished data held by the Governor. The new Bunya medium secure unit, described below, is located nearby, at the Cumberland Centre in Parramatta, and arrangements for easy transfer and return of patients between the facilities has been negotiated, with the result that Mulawa transferred some 20 female prisoners with a serious mental illness to Bunya in the first six months of operation, i.e. the last six months of 1998 (Corrections Health Service 1999, p.36).

Services for MIOs in the corrections system in New South Wales have been the subject of repeated investigations and reports, notably by Bluglass (1997) and Barclay (1997). Some of Bluglass's criticisms were echoed in the much more positive, and openly available, Discussion Paper submitted by Barclay. This arose as the result of a forum held in April 1997 by the Corrections Health Service Board and the Centre for Mental Health, the psychiatric arm of the New South Wales Health Department. While Bluglass detected a fundamental failure to apply what he took to be good principles of forensic mental health care, and suggested that a revolution was needed, Barclay dealt more with internal processes and practices. He recommended gradual reform, cataloguing and assessing many suggestions made by individuals in the service, from the carpeting of areas of the wards in Long Bay Prison Hospital to the continuing education needs of nurses. Barclay recommended:

- transferring authority for the management of the Long Bay Prison Hospital from Corrective Services to the Corrections Health Service;

- separating services for mentally ill offenders from those for mentally disturbed offenders (such as those with a diagnosis of personality disorder or those in short-term situational crisis);

- appointing a non-medical Director of Corrections Mental Health Services; and

- pursuing the development of a State Forensic Mental Health policy.

Some of these suggestions have already been implemented, notably the transfer of authority for the management of the Prison Hospital from Corrective Services to the Corrections Health Service. There have been improvements in the physical facilities, plans are being considered for a low security 'halfway house', and a multidisciplinary committee has been convened to consider the creation of a State Forensic Mental Health Strategy.

Since these reports, the New South Wales Independent Commission Against Corruption (1998) has reported on inappropriate relationships between nurses and inmates, centring on two particular cases. The Corrections Health Service has accepted its recommendations and especially swift action has been taken to develop Professional and Ethical Guidelines. Advice and approval for these was sought from a variety of international agencies, and by November 1998 the third edition of the guidelines had been approved and circulated. This is an important development, incorporating many key principles and beliefs about the nature of the nurse–inmate relationship, advising on how to recognise and respond to inappropriate advances, manipulation and demands by inmates, and association with ex-inmates. These guidelines deal with sexual issues, as well as issues of confidentiality, the role of staff education and clinical supervision.

In addition to these services administered by the Corrections Health Board, two purpose-built forensic units are presently operating in the New South Wales public health system. These are the Kestrel Unit, located near Newcastle, some 200 km north of Sydney, and the Bunya Unit, located near Parramatta, on the western outskirts of Sydney.

The Kestrel Unit offers high security facilities for up to 28 men, but has been hampered in its usefulness by its geographical isolation from the agencies with which it must deal and from the families and friends of many of its patients. Originally described as a 'medium security unit', it has gradually come to be regarded as a high security facility, particularly in relation to the newly opened 'medium secure' Bunya Unit.

The Bunya Unit opened in July 1998 and is designated a 'medium secure forensic' facility for patients with a serious mental illness. Admission is mostly from Long Bay Prison Hospital, Mulawa Prison, and direct from the courts and only in exceptional circumstances are patients accepted from within the psychiatric sector. The emphasis is upon intensive programmes of activity, rehabilitation and therapeutic interpersonal relationships, and although it has a seclusion room this is rarely used. Nurses have been selected for the unit on the basis of their experience, good interpersonal skills and positive attitudes, rather than formal qualifications in forensic mental health. This reflects the fact that opportunities to obtain such qualifications have been limited in Australia to a single postgraduate course, offered by the University of Western Sydney Macarthur, designed specifically for nurses working in the corrections system. At the time of writing, women occupy over half of the Bunya Unit's 24 beds, and these represent the first and only designated beds for female MIOs in the State.

The Unit has a small associated research development group, funded by the Health Department via the Centre for Mental Health, which is developing the resources and policies for the conduct of future multidisciplinary research. Bunya is also a Clinical Development Unit, a multidisciplinary version of the Nursing Development Units described by the Kings Fund Centre in London (Turner-Shaw and Bosanquet 1993; Freeman 1996), and in this respect is part of a designated research group operating out of the local University of Western Sydney Nepean. The Unit encourages patient participation in care planning, has introduced formal patient assessment tools as part of its normal procedures, and is already the site of a number of research projects.

The State currently has only a single Court Liaison Nurse based in Newcastle, offering a locally initiated court diversion service. Central support for such schemes has been expressed by the New South Wales Attorney General in response to calls by magistrates for a more effective system than hospital referral. This nurse, employed as a Clinical Nurse Specialist, liaises with a variety of agencies, conducts assessments of mental status in relation to bail arrangements, fitness to appear, and so on. In the initial phases of the work he has received clinical supervision from senior staff based at the Kestrel Unit.

A major problem facing the development of forensic psychiatric services in New South Wales is the shortage of appropriately trained personnel. Nurses presently graduate from university-based comprehensive courses in which mental health plays only a small part and psychiatric care often very little. This creates a problem for managers of psychiatric services, who find it necessary to create schemes whereby new recruits undertake postgraduate psychiatric courses. Until they have undertaken additional education they are ill-equipped to work with the mentally ill, and yet most want to leave university behind and start practising as Registered Nurses, if only because of financial pressures. The prospect of further training is a major deterrent to those who might be interested in psychiatric nursing: psychiatric nursing is also viewed as falling outside what they have become used to seeing as mainstream nursing. It is, therefore, extremely difficult to recruit new nurses and even more difficult to get them to undertake postgraduate courses. The bedrock of psychiatric nursing expertise remains those staff who trained under the old system and have accumulated many years of experience and occasionally additional qualifications. The proportion of older staff is very high and increasing, and in many areas those over 50 years of age represent a majority of the workforce. It is within this context that forensic psychiatric care is developing.

Victoria

Victorian psychiatric services were among the last to be deinstitutionalised, and whereas New South Wales abandoned separate psychiatric nurse training in 1988, Victoria only followed suit in 1995. Nevertheless, in a number of respects, services for MIOs in Victoria are probably the best in Australia. The centralisation of a major part of the State's mental health administration, research and training facilities in Parkville, Melbourne, has proved a valuable strategy, providing an accessible, geographically central focus, within easy reach of major hospitals and universities. There are established forensic science institutions, including the Victorian Forensic Science Centre at McLeod, the Victorian Institute of Forensic Medicine at Monash University and the National Institute of Forensic Science at La Trobe University.

Additionally, a number of initiatives have sought to create centres of excellence, research and training in mental health, including the creation of the Mental Health Research Institute of Victoria at Parkville, and the Centre for Forensic Mental Health at Monash University.

The relevant civil legislation is the Mental Health Act (Victoria) (1986), of which Sections 15 and 16, comprising Division 3 of the Act, concern 'persons convicted of criminal offences or in a prison'. Section 15 allows courts to make a 'hospital order' rather than pass sentence in those cases where the defendant is found guilty but is considered to be suffering from a treatable mental illness and an authorised psychiatrist has agreed to accept admission. This may be for purposes of assessment and can lead either to continued detention in appropriate psychiatric facilities or the passing of sentence; in the latter case, the period spent in the hospital is deducted from any period of imprisonment. Section 16 concerns the transfer of mentally ill prisoners to in-patient psychiatric facilities, those prisoners, together with those detained according to Her Majesty's Pleasure under the Crimes Act (1958), being referred to as 'security patients'. Division 4 of the Mental Health Act regulates the appeals, leave, transfer and conditions for security patients, and specifies that any security patient serving a prison sentence must be discharged upon expiration of the sentence.

The Mental Health Act has recently been amended in accordance with the Crimes (Mental Impairment and Unfitness to be Tried) Act (1997), which defines the criteria for determining if a person is unfit to stand trial, replaces the defence of 'insanity' with that of 'mental impairment', and institutes new procedures relating to these circumstances. It defines a 'forensic patient' as a person remanded or committed to the custody of an approved mental health service under the Act, or a person transferred from prison to a residential service under Section 21A of the Intellectually Disabled Person's Services Act (1986). The provisions of the Act are similar to those applying in New South Wales. The definition of mental impairment (Section 20) constitutes a strict reading of the M'Naghten Rule, being based solely on the cognitive ability of the defendant to appreciate the quality and nature of their actions. Upon a finding of 'not guilty by reason of mental impairment', the court requires that the person be placed under either custodial or non-custodial supervision, nominally of a duration related to the sentence that they might have received had they been found guilty (Section 28). The Act allows for variation to be made between custodial and non-custodial orders, for emergency apprehension of those not in custody, and for the revocation of supervision orders as a court deems appropriate. It creates the 'Forensic Leave Panel', which adjudicates requests by forensic patients for leave of absence and, among its general provisions, abolishes the making of 'Governor's Pleasure' orders. The ultimate authority in all matters relating to the provisions is the Director of Public Prosecutions.

Throughout the Act, only registered psychologists or medical practitioners may report upon the person's mental state, and the word 'nurse' does not appear anywhere in the Act. This is widely regarded as unfortunate, since many forensic psychiatric nurses have completed comparable training and actually have expertise in making such assessments; some also hold postgraduate qualifications and have many years' experience of direct contact with MIOs. However, we should note that this only applies to the upper courts and that nurses are very active in the magistrates' courts, as described below.

The Victorian Institute of Forensic Mental Health (formerly the Forensic Psychiatry Service) was established by the Mental Health (Victorian Institute of Forensic Mental Health) Act (1997), effective from 1 July 1998. It is charged with the responsibility of providing, promoting and assisting in the provision and planning of the State's forensic mental health services, including related education and research, and operates under the auspices of a Council answerable to the State Minister for Health. The Institute serves three principal groups of people: prisoners with serious mental illness, prisoners referred from courts under sentence for treatment according to Section 93 of the Sentencing Act (1991), and people found Not Guilty by Reason of Insanity and detained at Her Majesty's Pleasure ('forensic patients'). Convicted persons who are mentally ill and not subject to a prison sentence are the responsibility of the Area Mental Health Services, who may seek no-cost advice from the Institute, which may also provide specialist in-patient services in more difficult cases. Although it has only recently become operational, detailed descriptions of the Institute's policies and programmes, including the legislative framework and research activities, are already in the public domain (Victorian Institute of Forensic Mental Health 1998).

Existing forensic psychiatric facilities are located at Rosanna (58 beds), but a new 120-bed unit, the Thomas Embling Hospital at Fairfield in Melbourne, will open in March 2000: this will subsume a dedicated Women's Unit of about 10 beds. The Institute also manages an acute assessment unit and after-hours crisis intervention at the government-run Metropolitan Assessment Prison in Melbourne. Referrals are initially made to a psychiatric nurse, to whom all prisoners from certain special groups, including Aborigines, young people, intellectually disabled and those with a history of mental illness, are automatically referred. The prison offers on-call crisis cover, and reception, acute assessment and out-patient services provided by a team presently including nine psychiatric nurses and a Clinical Nurse Specialist as well as psychiatrists and a welfare officer.

The Institute offers a court service, provided by a Court Liaison Nurse (there are presently two in Victoria and two more planned), a scheme first piloted in 1994 and which has proved a very successful part of the State diversion scheme. The Court Liaison Nurse assesses defendants as they arrive in custody prior to appearing in court, receives referrals from the police, the magistrates, and other legal experts, and sees all new arrivals with a history of mental illness. They undertake a Mental Status Examination, a suicide and general risk assessment and the nurse screens out individuals with transient reactions, drug-induced conditions and others who are not mentally ill. These are extremely busy positions and the nurse attached to the Melbourne Assessment Prison, for example, assessed 319 clients in the 12 months to May 1997, submitted 342 reports and attended 228 court hearings.

In addition to follow-up services and programmes aimed at monitoring and treating mentally ill offenders subject to community treatment orders, the community-based services managed by the Institute include a psychosexual treatment programme, involving a psychiatrist, clinical psychologist, psychiatric nurse and social worker. These kinds of community-based services are also expected to expand rapidly.

There has recently been extensive privatisation of the Victorian prison system, including the associated psychiatric services. There is a special psychiatric unit within Port Phillip Prison, for example, and one in the Deer Park women's prison. These involve two private health care providers, which do not come under the aegis of the Institute, but are monitored by the Prisoners' Health Care Monitoring Unit, which is part of the Victorian Department of Human Services. Many of the professionals involved in caring for MIOs regard this as an unhelpful fragmentation of the service, creating difficulties relating to authority and legitimacy, standard setting and resourcing, agency interfacing and continuity of care.

The other states

Only South Australia and the Australian Capital Territory have retained a separate psychiatric nurse training. The South Australian laws regarding the disposal of MIOs are quite different to those of New South Wales, being embodied entirely in criminal legislation and allowing for direct transfers between the courts, prisons and the health system. The State's only forensic psychiatric facility is James Nash House in Adelaide, and is administered by the State Forensic Mental Health Service which also provides visiting specialists to the prison system. Its patients are discharged to the nearby Glenside Hospital, which serves as a stepping stone to the community. Pressure on places is forcing a slight extension, which will add approximately another eight beds. The Department of Correctional Services has recently funded a Chair in Forensic Psychology at the University of South Australia, together with two joint appointments at lecturer level.

Turning to Western Australia, like most recent mental health legislation the Mental Health Act (Western Australia) (1996) is very specific as to terminology, treatment practices, and the penalties that arise when its provisions are contravened. It includes, for example, precise procedures for the referral, transfer and transportation of patients, and strict conditions for the exercise of seclusion and mechanical restraint. It specifies exactly who constitutes a 'mental health practitioner' for the purposes of the Act: this includes Registered Nurses with 'at least three years' experience in the management of persons who have mental illnesses'. The Act also involves an interesting crossover between legal and clinical terminology in relation to MIOs. Subject to the customary exclusions, it defines mental illness as 'a disturbance of thought, mood, volition, perception, orientation or memory that impairs judgement or behaviour to a significant extent'. However, Section 43 refers to 'mentally impaired defendants' as defined in the Criminal Law (Mentally Impaired Defendants) Act (Western Australia) (1996), that is as suffering from 'intellectual disability, mental illnesses, brain damage or senility' (Sec. 8). This Act defines the conditions under which a person may be found 'unfit to stand trial'. Persons found unfit may be 'acquitted on account of unsoundness of mind', released unconditionally or subject to a 'Conditional Release Order', 'Community Based Order' or 'Intensive Supervision

Order', or made subject to a custodial order (Sec. 22). Treatment and detention is regulated by the Mentally Impaired Defendants Review Board. The Frankland Centre, run by the State Health Department, is Western Australia's only forensic psychiatric unit in the health sector. It offers 30 short-stay beds, primarily for purposes of assessment, and takes both men and women.

In Queensland, the Mental Health Act (Queensland) (1974) has been the subject of numerous criticisms, especially concerning the power of doctors to institute involuntary detention, and the relation between types of treatment and consent, and is currently being reviewed (see, for example, the Queensland Association for Mental Health website). Part 4 of the Act deals with persons involved in criminal proceedings and found either 'unfit for trial', or of 'unsound mind' at the time of the offence. These persons are included in the category called 'restricted patients', whose release is regulated by the Patient Review Tribunal. A State policy for forensic mental health in Queensland has been gestating at least since early 1997 and has not yet received formal approval. Nevertheless, service development is clearly following principles adumbrated in the draft document circulated in August 1997, notably and uniquely in Australia, that services will be delivered as part of a comprehensive district mental health service, organised around special target groups, rather than via a specialised statewide service. Patients will be 'mainstreamed' as far as security and other considerations allow ('extended secure beds'), and 'forensic' specialists will provide a service extending beyond those who have, or are alleged to have, committed an offence. One anomaly that has already arisen as a result is that community forensic services are currently developing in a different district from those in which in-patient services have developed, and so the two are unable to operate in tandem. It is planned that existing services, based in Brisbane, will soon be supplemented by a new facility in Townsville, offering 10 high security and 20 extended secure beds.

Although the Queensland prison service does not include mental health beds, it does employ a small number of mental health nurses, and since July 1998 there has been a Court Liaison Nurse working in the lower courts in Brisbane. Some 60 per cent of the people assessed by the Court Liaison Nurse suffer from a serious mental illness and 20 per cent have a major substance abuse problem; associated psychiatric professionals regard the scheme as a great success and are gathering statistical evidence to support a case for further appointments.

In the Northern Territory, the relevant civil legislation is the Mental Health Act (Northern Territory) (1996), and once again it is Part 4 of the Act which concerns the treatment of MIOs, and Section 25 specifies conditions under which they may be subject to compulsory treatment. Perhaps in an ominous glance to practices of years gone by, the final sentence of that Section prohibits authorisation, by a court or magistrate, of the sterilisation of offenders for reasons of mental illness alone. Expert evidence in matters of assessment, transfer, authorisation of treatment and so forth is sought specifically from medical officers, and these are ultimately the responsibility of the Chief Medical Officer. Application for the review of orders may be made to the Supreme Court. The Northern Territory has a new forensic psychiatric unit in Darwin, on the campus of the Royal Darwin Hospital.

Tasmania became an intense but temporary focal point for forensic mental health issues on 28 April 1996, when a young man, Martin Bryant, shot dead 32 people and injured numerous others at the historic site of the convict settlement at Port Arthur. The reverberations from these terrible events are still being felt in communities across Australia. The small population, low crime rate and peaceful atmosphere have never suggested a need for elaborate legislation or services in respect of mentally ill offenders. Port Arthur has certainly changed that perception.

It has to be said that Tasmania lags behind in terms of its services to mentally ill people, and this is reflected in its continuing reliance on the 36-year-old Mental Health Act (Tasmania) (1963). This principally represents a revision of the Mental Hospitals Acts of 1858 and the Mental Deficiency Act of 1920. The framework remains substantially unchanged since 1963. Thus, for example, it concerns persons suffering from 'mental disorder', 'psychopathic disorder', 'subnormality' and 'severe subnormality', defined in the same way as in the English Mental Health Act of 1959. Part 4 relates to 'patients concerned in criminal and other proceedings', including persons subject to be detained during Her Majesty's Pleasure, according to Section 392 of the Criminal Code. Section 6 of the Act allows persons requiring care in conditions of special security to be detained in facilities for that purpose, and these may include a prison or special institution, in which case the controlling authority is the Director of Corrective Services. The legislation is currently being revised, and at the time of writing the new Criminal Justice (Mentally Disordered Offenders) (Tasmania) Act is going before Parliament.

Tasmania's only forensic psychiatric services are provided by the hospital in Risdon Prison on the outskirts of Hobart. Unlike the rest of the prison, the hospital is a modern facility, catering for a mixed group of general and psychiatric patients, both male and female, and security is maintained by corrections staff. Officers and nurses are employed by the Justice Department, but other health professionals are employed by the Health Department. Problematic issues include the strong focus on security, the mix of patients and the absence of adequate community liaison and support services. A new health-based forensic mental health unit is planned for the old Royal Derwent psychiatric hospital site, and this will provide eight beds. Despite the enormity of the events at Port Arthur, it must be remembered that Tasmania has a small population and a low crime rate and that the demand on services is correspondingly small. At present there is no Court

Liaison Nurse in Tasmania, but there are plans to have one attached to the new Remand Centre intended for Hobart.

ROLES, POLICIES AND THE FUTURE

Roles of forensic mental health workers

No disciplines have nationally approved statements, endorsed by their professional bodies, as to their role in forensic mental health. Organisations employing forensic mental health nurses sometimes have a locally developed 'Statement of Duties', and this may refer to the Code of Ethics and Code of Conduct produced by the Australian Nurses' Council, the 'Standards of Practice' listed by the Australian and New Zealand College of Mental Health Nurses (1995), and the 'Competencies for Registered Nurses' formulated by the Australian Nurse Registering Authority Conference (ANCI 1995). Role descriptions and actual roles sometimes appear not to match in practice, however, and key personnel spoke informally to the author of having worked out their role as they went along. In New South Wales, local Statements of Duties for forensic mental health nurses establish special roles and responsibilities over and above those working in general mental health contexts. In Queensland, on the other hand, since the two types of service are largely integrated, no special forensic role description has been developed.

Little consideration has been given to what types of skill mix a future service may need, who should provide what skills, and how this corresponds to educational needs and opportunities. The only project currently under way that I have identified as dealing with these issues is being conducted by Alicia Evans and David Wells of the Victorian Institute of Forensic Mental Health. Their study, funded by the Royal College of Nursing Australia, explores how the development of forensic services might involve an expansion of general and mental health nursing roles (Evans and Wells 1999).

Education issues

Education of the workforce will become a major issue as services overflow out of corrections and into the health system and the community. There are few opportunities for formal training in forensic psychiatry, although a number of universities offer postgraduate courses in forensic psychology. At the time of writing, only one course in Australia is directed specifically at forensic nursing care: this has been offered for a number of years by the University of Western Sydney Macarthur and is aimed specifically at nurses working in the prison system, but it is not confined to mental health. The University of Adelaide in South Australia is planning a similar course for offer in 1999. The University of Western Sydney Nepean, in partnership with the New South Wales Institute of

Psychiatry, is intending to offer a multidisciplinary, multi-agency course in forensic mental health, with exit points at Graduate Certificate, Graduate Diploma and Master's level.

There are several Professors of Forensic Psychiatry in Australian universities, and the Forensic Psychiatry Section of the Australia and New Zealand Royal College of Psychiatrists was the second specialist section to be formed, in 1968. It has allowed non-psychiatrists to participate in some of its activities (Rubinstein and Rubinstein 1996, p.36), and has helped the College to produce a number of relevant position statements, including one on violent offenders. Similarly, the Australian Psychological Association has a forensic psychology section, and forensic psychology courses are available in several Australian universities, including Melbourne University, the University of South Australia, and the University of Western Sydney Macarthur.

For those nurses working in forensic settings, there is an informal association run by staff from the Victorian Institute of Forensic Mental Health, and this publishes an occasional newsletter. Some nurses in forensic settings join the multidisciplinary Australia and New Zealand Association for Psychology, Psychiatry and the Law (ANZAPPL), which accommodates a diverse range of individuals from professional, clinical and academic fields with a loose interest in the psychology/law interface, rather than simply those who work with MIOs.

There is presently no academic journal based in Australia that is dedicated to forensic psychiatry or forensic issues generally, and so relevant items appear in discipline-based journals. The only way to maintain a forensic journal in Australia, given the small numbers of professionals involved, would be to make it cross-disciplinary. Indeed, Australian health services are very slowly working toward an integrative approach in which the traditional boundaries between the disciplines are being recognised as permeable and dynamic. Most disciplines find this a daunting prospect and have engaged a number of self-protective strategies aimed at strengthening their distinctive identity and mapping out clearly delineated domains of legitimacy. This is evidenced in a number of exclusionary outcomes, such as the opposition by medicine to the concept of the Nurse Practitioner, and the inclusion of registered psychologists and exclusion of nurses as expert witnesses in the Victorian legislation.

Nevertheless, it seems inevitable that the current interdisciplinarity, in which each group brings its own distinctive set of skills and expertise to a problem, will gradually yield to a post-disciplinarity in which individuals simply contribute whatever they can without being regarded as trespassers on the domain of other disciplines. It is becoming patently clear that knowledge and skills are never the property of any particular group and that in an increasingly complex world they cut across traditional professional and epistemological boundaries. This is particularly obvious in relation to forensic mental health, where skills and insights concern a complex, dynamic set of characteristics operating in concert, involving multiple agencies and systems including the individual client, the community, and the health and corrections services.

National mental health policy statements and some of the State legislation refer to 'mental health professionals' rather than specific disciplines, and there is good evidence to suggest that Australian forensic mental health will lead the way in directing attention away from interdisciplinary border disputes and toward the creative synthesis of expertise in pursuit of the goals of a quality forensic mental health service.

TOWARDS STATE AND FEDERAL STRATEGIES

Victoria is the only state which already has a forensic mental health policy, but policies for New South Wales and Queensland are being developed, and nurses are involved directly in that task. Although the Second National Mental Health Plan for Australia, published in July 1998, reaffirmed the principles contained in the National Mental Health Strategy of 1992, and did not comment specifically upon services for mentally ill offenders except where they may be indigenous Australians, tentative moves toward a national forensic mental health policy have been made. A report was prepared for the Australian Health Ministers' Advisory Committee National Mental Health Working Group by the Victorian Institute of Forensic Mental Health, following a workshop held in August 1996. Unfortunately, the draft report was distributed for comment as this chapter was being written and a consideration of its contents could not be included.

Formulation of Federal or State policies has been difficult for a number of reasons: first, each state has very different legislative and service frameworks already in place; second, it is susceptible to unhelpful interest shown by some social activists and media organisations; third, just as in other countries, forensic mental health is complicated by overlapping and sometimes competing professional discourses, notably of medicine and law; and, lastly, prospective development inherits a legacy of keenly contested legitimacy and authority, dating back to the dawn not only of Australian psychiatry but of Australia as a European colony. It is not clear how, in the face of this problematic context, a national forensic mental health strategy could have enough specificity to help establish evidence-based practice, effective quality care, or appropriate inter-sectoral partnerships. Nevertheless, a national policy involving a statement of principles and goals is necessary and long overdue.

WEB PAGES TO CONSULT

Australian mental health and criminal legislation
http://www.austlii.edu.au/databases.html

Australian and New Zealand Association of Psychiatry, Psychology and Law Inc.
http://psychmed.mmcc.monash.edu.au/anzappl

Australian National Mental Strategies via the Federal Department of Health and Aged Care
http://www.health.gov.au/hsdd/mentalhe/index.htm

Australian Nursing Council Inc. site for the Code of Conduct and Code of Ethics
http://www.anci.org.au/publications.htm

Corrections Health Services (New South Wales)
http://www.chs.health.nsw.gov.au

Mental Health Act (Tasmania) (1963)
http://www.thelaw.tas.gov.au:5760

Mental Health (Victorian Institute of Forensic Mental Health) Act (1997)
http://www.dms.dpc.vic.gov.au/sb/1997_Act/A00460.html

Queensland Association for Mental Health
http://www.powerup.com.au/~qamh/IMI.html

ACKNOWLEDGEMENTS

The author is grateful to Roger Orr, Director of Nursing, Corrections Health Services, New South Wales, Mark O'Connor of the Kestrel Unit, and many others involved in the care of mentally ill offenders in Australia who freely gave me whatever information I requested and more besides, and donated their precious time and energy to my efforts. Any errors of fact are entirely my own.

CHAPTER 15

The Role of the Forensic Nurse in Canada

An Evolving Speciality

Cindy Peternelj-Taylor

INTRODUCTION

The problems surrounding the care and control of the socially undesirable – the criminal, the dangerous and the mentally ill – have historically plagued Canadian society. As early as the nineteenth century, 'lunatic asylums' for mentally ill criminals emerged in Canada. Regrettably, both the criminal and the non-criminal mentally ill were frequently incarcerated (Green, Menzies and Naismith 1991).

Unfortunately, these problems continue to haunt contemporary Canadian society, and the criminalisation of the mentally ill remains a sad, but true, reality. Canadians who are mentally ill and are believed to have committed a crime, or those who have committed a crime and are believed to be mentally ill, are caught in a 'revolving door syndrome' that includes prisons, correctional facilities, jails and the mental health care delivery system (Canadian Nurses' Association (CNA) 1991; Health Canada 1995; Peternelj-Taylor 1998a).

Forensic psychiatric nursing is emerging as a fairly new and unique speciality area of nursing practice; however, unlike many other nursing specialities in Canada, there is little understanding of what forensic nursing represents. Through the examination of factors affecting current Canadian developments in forensic psychiatric nursing, the evolution of the role of the forensic nurse in Canada will be considered in this chapter.

In an attempt to illustrate a truly Canadian perspective, only Canadian writers and literature are referred to. However, it is recognised that writers from other countries, predominantly from both the United States and the United Kingdom, may have influenced the writers cited. The information featured in this chapter is a synthesis of the author's knowledge and experience, combined with the insights and reflections gleaned from ten forensic psychiatric nurse experts from across the country.

FACTORS AFFECTING FORENSIC PSYCHIATRIC NURSING IN CANADA

There are many factors that affect the implementation of the nursing role with a forensic population. Among two of the most commonly cited are the criminalisation of the mentally ill and the nature of the treatment setting in which nursing practice occurs. These contextual factors are significant to understanding the evolution of the forensic nursing role in Canada.

Criminalisation of the mentally ill

Criminalisation of the mentally ill has been frequently attributed in Canada and abroad to the de-institutionalisation movement of the 1960s and 1970s, and more recently to an increased desire for retribution against criminals in general (CNA 1991; Health Canada 1995; Peternelj-Taylor and Hufft 1997; Peternelj-Taylor and Johnson 1993, 1995). The philosophical goals of de-institutionalisation were admirable; however, community services have consistently failed to reach consumers who have difficulty navigating the system. Many end up 'falling through the cracks', and find themselves reluctantly seeking treatment within a correctional facility (CNA 1991; Kent-Wilkinson 1993).

In a 1991 Canadian Nurses' Association discussion paper on mental health care, individuals incarcerated in the criminal justice system were identified as a disadvantaged group – a shortfall of the current mental health care delivery system. Canada-wide data on the prevalence of individuals with mental disorder who become involved in the criminal justice system is not available. However, it is estimated that 10 per cent to 15 per cent of all incarcerated individuals have a mental disorder and require services usually associated with severe or chronic mental illness (Davis 1992; Health Canada 1995; Peternelj-Taylor and Johnson 1993).

In addition to those with mental disorder, many offenders present with mental health problems associated with a criminalised lifestyle: substance abuse and violence and aggression (manifested in domestic and sexual violence) are among the most common.

Treatment setting

In Canada, a true national system for the care of the forensic client is non-existent. Challenges in providing mental health services for this population are very real, and enduring contradictions regarding how best to meet the needs of the forensic population prevail (CNA 1991; Conacher 1993, 1996; Health Canada 1995). Great variation exists not only from coast to coast, and from province to province, but also within provinces. There is no doubt that the care and management of mentally disordered offenders, or those offenders with mental health problems, poses a major challenge to the criminal justice system and the mental health system alike (Conacher 1996; Health Canada 1995). Unlike the forensic services offered in the United Kingdom, a separate parallel forensic system is non-existent in Canada.

Following many years of unresolved debate regarding the care and treatment of the mentally ill in the Canadian correctional system, the Chalke Report (1972) recommended that the federal correctional system develop a unified psychiatric service sensitive to meet the needs of the forensic population and comparable to the community standard. Specialised psychiatric mental health services are available in each of the five penitentiary regions of Canada. To date, these services, operated by the Correctional Service of Canada, are the only services that come close to resembling a national system for the practice of forensic psychiatry (Chalke, Roberts and Turner 1995; Conacher 1993, 1996; Green *et al.* 1991; Smale 1983).

Nurses working with forensic clients may be employees of highly specialised secure mental health facilities operated by health care systems or, more commonly, they are employees of correctional systems that provide their own mental health services. Forensic psychiatric nursing in Canada is practised across a broad spectrum of settings, including the community, provincial psychiatric hospitals, secure units within general hospitals, and more custodial settings such as young offender institutions, prisons, jails and other correctional facilities (Kent-Wilkinson 1993; Peternelj-Taylor and Hufft 1997; Peternelj-Taylor and Johnson 1993, 1995).

NATURE AND SCOPE OF FORENSIC NURSING IN CANADA

Nurses have been working with forensic clients or mentally disordered offenders for many years, and although the terminology used to describe nursing with this population has varied, nurses working in this speciality area have not consistently been referred to as forensic nurses. Many terms have been used to describe nursing with forensic populations, and generally are linked to the setting in which the nurse is employed (Peternelj-Taylor and Hufft 1997). More commonly, the term prison nurse or correctional nurse is used (Norens 1971; Day 1983; Lehman 1983; Smale 1983).

Interview vignette. In the late 1970s I worked on a locked ward in a large provincial psychiatric hospital. At that time I conducted pre-trial assessments for individuals remanded from the courts, as well as provided treatment and programming for individuals who were found not guilty by reason of insanity, and who were being held indefinitely. I never considered myself a forensic psychiatric nurse, nor was the unit referred to as a forensic unit. It was not until a few years later when I applied for a job at a new maximum-security forensic psychiatric institution that I was really exposed to the term 'forensic'.

Specialised practice versus practice in a special environment

Nurses working within the forensic milieu have frequently been referred to as pioneers (Fraser 1994; Kent-Wilkinson 1993; Lehman 1983). Influenced in part by the growing awareness of the overlap between the criminal justice system and the mental health system, forensic psychiatric nursing has been described as one of the most rapidly expanding fields of nursing practice (Kent-Wilkinson 1993; Peternelj-Taylor and Hufft 1997). A nurse with many years' experience working with offenders was left wondering if defining a nurse as a forensic nurse met a social need, stating: 'It is complex; perhaps by using the term forensic it is assumed that clients are getting specialised treatment for specialised problems.'

Are nurses who work with mentally disordered offenders specialists? Or are they simply working in special environments? Is there such a person as a forensic nurse? If so, is this person different from a general mental health nurse? When the term 'forensic' became popular in Canada is difficult to trace, and very few nurses have attempted to define what forensic nursing means. Petryshen (1981) was the first to go on record and simply defined forensic nursing as the 'application of psychiatric knowledge to the provision of mental health care to the mentally disordered offender' (p.26). Even in Niskala's (1986, 1987) landmark study that addressed the competencies and skills required by nurses working in forensic settings, no definition of forensic nursing was presented. In an attempt to develop a working definition of forensic psychiatric nursing, Peternelj-Taylor and Hufft (1997) define the speciality as 'the integration of mental health nursing philosophy and practice, within a socio-cultural context that includes the criminal justice system, to provide comprehensive care to individual clients, their families, and their communities' (p.772).

Although nurses interviewed varied in their responses to the question 'Is there such a person as a forensic nurse?', the majority concluded that such a speciality exists, and all but one replied that they saw themselves as forensic nurses.

> *Interview vignette*: I know I generally refer to myself as a correctional nurse. I guess I use correctional nursing because people know what it is I do when I say that. When I say forensic nursing nobody knows what I mean; at least with correctional nursing, they have an idea of where I work and what I do. However, I do not think correctional describes it either – it tends to focus more on the custodial side of things and I do not see myself there – I see myself as being therapeutic. What would I call myself? A nurse working in corrections.

In Canada, correctional nursing and forensic nursing are often used interchangeably, particularly if the 'correctional nurse' is practising psychiatric mental health nursing in a correctional setting. Canadian nurses working with mentally ill offenders or those with mental health problems grapple not only with clarifying their role as a forensic nurse versus a mental health nurse, but also as a forensic nurse versus a correctional nurse.

Interview vignette: The debate between whether forensic psychiatric nursing is a specialty or simply psychiatric nursing in a special environment sure has entered my thoughts. I am not entirely sure of the answer to this debate. Yet the debate is great as it gets us thinking about what we practise and how we practise.

For some nurses, however, the designation of forensic nursing as a speciality is very clear, as is evident in the following vignette.

Interview vignette: I believe forensic psychiatric nursing is a distinct speciality of nursing practice. If 'speciality practice' is determined by the need for a distinct body of knowledge, an identified population base, and specific roles that distinguish it from other areas of nursing – then I perceive forensic psychiatric nurses to have all of these.

How the role of the nurse is defined may restrict or enlarge the nurse's image and potential influence within the forensic setting and the community at large. The similarities and differences between forensic psychiatric nurses and general mental health nurses, as expressed by the nurses interviewed, are summarised in Table 15.1.

Table 15.1 Similarities and differences between forensic psychiatric nurses and general mental health nurses

Similarities	Differences
The custodial role is increasing in both areas	Practice directly interfaces with the law, and requires knowledge that is directly outside of the general knowledge of mental health nursing
Importance of the therapeutic nurse–client relationship in working with clients	
Importance of boundary maintenance	Utilise confrontation more
Use of therapeutic counselling skills	The client is an individual who has come into conflict with the law and is either sentenced or awaiting trial
Mental status examination skills and other psychosocial assessment skills	
Ability to collect a comprehensive health history	The client is a mentally ill offender, or an individual accused of a crime, with a question of fitness to stand trial or mental competency
Ability to look at family of origin issues	The need to deal with legal issues concerning patients, and thus clarify the role of providing custody and caring
Non-judgemental attitudes	
Look at behaviour and its causes	The need to deal with individuals' loss of freedom and the intrusiveness of society into their lives as a result of the loss of freedom
Individualised programming to meet the needs of the client	
	The practice environment is unique or different, generally a secure/controlled facility
	There is no assurance of confidentiality for the client

Professional identity

Psychiatric mental health nursing has not always been seen as a desirable career choice for nurses, and many nurses experience stigma at a professional level, as prestige and rewards are attached to more glamorous areas of health care. When the nurse practises forensic psychiatric nursing and works with mentally disordered offenders, the nurse is often doubly stigmatised. Role development for this group is confounded by the myth that nurses who work with forensic clients are 'second class' and unable to secure employment elsewhere (Peternelj-Taylor and Johnson 1993, 1995). This stigma is experienced as a dilemma for many nurses, one that threatens their professional identity. Unfortunately, 'Colleagues and other health care providers do not understand or appreciate how one can work with these patients, and that these patients require care as well.'

It is disconcerting to note that nurses working in forensic environments do not always identify with the nursing profession. This may be a reflection of the way mental health care is delivered in Canada, or the way positions are advertised. Rather than hiring a specific discipline, employers often look for 'multi-skilled' generic workers, who have a background in any number of the mental health disciplines (Gallop 1996; VanDeVelde-Coke 1998). Currently, the Correctional Service of Canada hires 'Programme Officers' to supplement treatment delivery to the mentally ill offender. Individuals hired into these positions may be nurses, but are more commonly occupational therapists, recreational therapists or behavioural science technicians (a new category of mental health worker who is not responsible to any regulatory body). It can be argued that theoretical knowledge and skill takes precedence over discipline. However, as Gallop (1996) points out, nurses belong to a discipline where therapeutic skills – group therapy, counselling and programming – are 'largely acquired by osmosis or experience and not by credentials' (p.5).

> *Interview vignette.* For a while I did not even use the term nurse. I did not identify with nursing. I guess I was disillusioned with nursing, based on nurses' failure to be committed to what is therapeutic. For a long time I identified with other professionals because I saw that they were doing a better job (in my opinion) than nursing was. I am, however, committed to nursing, but as a rule I think other professions are better at what they do, because they are better prepared.

Forensic psychiatric nurses are often overheard referring to themselves as mental health workers, or therapists, as if they are embarrassed to identify their discipline-specific expertise. Has the nursing profession failed nurses in staking their professional claim as nurses?

> *Interview vignette.* I tend not to think of myself as a nurse. Nurses are not given credibility in the system we are working in. I can write a report that is far superior to any psychologist's, but when 'nurse' is behind someone's name, it is

discounted. There is still that interpretation: nurse – hospital – what do they know about forensics? So I tend not to play it up. I am a therapist or a team member, and I downplay the nurse part.

Education and preparation

In Canada, registered nurses and registered psychiatric nurses (only in the western provinces) are employed in the majority of forensic settings. In a limited number of settings in some provinces (primarily in provincial psychiatric hospitals), auxiliary nursing personnel (registered or licensed practical nurses) are also employed. No national standards regarding the preparation of nurses working in forensic settings exist. The Correctional Service of Canada is moving toward baccalaureate preparation for all new nurses hired by the service by the autumn of 1999. Although an admirable goal, the nursing shortage in Canada has left many employers wondering where they will find baccalaureate-prepared nurses to fill vacant positions.

Studies conducted in the 1980s concluded that nurses working with forensic clients wanted additional specific formal education in forensic nursing (Niskala 1986, 1987; Phillips 1983). Niskala (1986, 1987) concluded that the additional training and skills may not relate specifically to forensic nursing *per se*, but, rather, nurses would benefit more from updating their skills in managing specific behaviours or conditions.

> *Interview vignette.* I would say that the diploma programmes in nursing do not prepare nurses to work in this setting, and I am not even convinced that the baccalaureate programmes do, to tell you the honest truth. I think it requires specialised training in the mode of treatment that has been identified as most effective; for example, cognitive behavioural therapy. Probably the best educational preparation would be some form of postgraduate work, not necessarily a Master's degree but some certification programme that focuses on the therapeutic modalities most commonly used in the forensic setting.

Very few opportunities exist for specific certificates and/or degrees in forensic psychiatric nursing in Canada. More commonly, forensic nursing content is being integrated into existing nursing curricula. In these programmes, students are provided with opportunities to care for the mentally disordered offender, generally as part of their psychiatric mental health clinical practicum. The relationship between the College of Nursing, University of Saskatchewan and the Regional Psychiatric Centre – Prairies, Correctional Service of Canada has successfully facilitated student placements in the basic baccalaureate programme, the post-registration programme and the graduate programme. Nurse educators considering forensic placements for students need to emphasise theory, practice and research as complementary sources of growth and development (Peternelj-Taylor and Johnson 1996).

Although few opportunities exist for specific education in forensic nursing in Canada, two programmes warrant mention. Since 1995, nursing students at the University of Calgary can take an elective course entitled 'Nursing and health care in forensic populations'. This course, taught in the classroom, is designed to explore the many roles of the forensic nurse, and features guest lecturers from the many sub-specialities of forensic nursing (e.g. clinical forensic nurses, medical examiners, sexual assault examiners, forensic psychiatric nurses and so forth). Nurses wishing to pursue a certificate in forensic health studies have the opportunity to enrol in a comprehensive multidisciplinary Internet programme offered through Mount Royal College's Centre of Health Studies, in Calgary, Alberta. Two courses have already been developed and are currently available:

1. Introduction to theories, concepts and issues in forensic populations.
2. Health care in forensic psychiatric and correctional populations.

Continuing education and professional development

As a profession, nurses must ensure that nursing practice is guided by theories, concepts and goals that are realistic to the practice setting (Goering 1993). Recognising that the learning needs of forensic nurses differed from nurses in general, the first national conference focusing on nurses working in the forensic milieu was hosted by the College of Nursing, University of Saskatchewan and the Regional Psychiatric Centre – Prairies, Correctional Service of Canada in 1989, and has been held biennially since then. Due to the overwhelming success of the national conferences, in 1997 the decision was made to switch the conference from a national event to an international one. Since its inception, 'Custody and Caring: The Nurse's Role in the Criminal Justice System' has focused on work-life issues and clinical issues unique to nurses working within the criminal justice system.

Those who were interviewed indicated that nurses needed to take responsibility for their own professional development.

Interview vignette: Nurses have not always been committed to their own professional development, and are often threatened by the achievements of those that are. I guess some would argue that this is oppressive group behaviour. Nursing has experienced oppression, but I am not ready to accept that for an excuse for what we are doing. We need to be committed to our own professional development and rather than being threatened by others' achievements we need to embrace them, celebrate them, and see them as role models.

Multidisciplinary practice

The practice of forensic psychiatric nursing is collaborative and multidisciplinary by its very nature. This is necessitated by the complexity, diversity and dissimilarity of the forensic clientele in terms of their presenting problems, life experiences and mental health care needs. Teamwork is essential to working in a forensic environment. A cohesive multidisciplinary team is critical to safe and professional practice, and can guard against manipulation, splitting and therapeutic boundary violations (Peternelj-Taylor 1998b; Peternelj-Taylor and Johnson 1995; Schafer 1997).

In the forensic environment, boundary blurring and overlap between disciplines is common. The degree of overlap forensic nurses experience between themselves and the other mental health professionals or between themselves and the correctional staff is dependent on the setting in which they work, the mission of the facility, the modality of treatment, and the strength of the multidisciplinary team. Nurses who work in correctional facilities quickly learn that the priorities of the correctional system centre around confinement and security, and these principles will always take precedence over nursing care. Even those who work in accredited mental health facilities operated by the Correctional Service of Canada realise that the correctional mandate always comes first. One interviewee clearly addressed this point and stated: 'Although a hospital, the rules and policies that impact on a regular correctional facility also impact on us!' This can be problematic as role blurring can engender role confusion for nurses unless they have developed a core set of nursing values and a strong professional identity before entering the role-blurring situation. (Miller 1984; Peternelj-Taylor and Johnson 1995). Unfortunately, Gallop (1996) concludes, 'sifting out what we do [action] from how we do it [process] from how we understand it [theory] is difficult' (p.7). As one nurse observed: 'This is a real difficult place for nurses to find themselves; because of the lack of understanding of so many people, the role is not clearly defined.'

Over the years, nurses have worked effectively with psychiatrists, social workers, psychologists, occupational therapists and recreational therapists – at times collaboratively, and at other times competitively. Additions to the multidisciplinary team, such as the behavioural science technician, are often at the expense of nursing positions, and many settings are experiencing the loss of nursing positions to other disciplines. All nurses interviewed could see the erosion of nursing positions within their institutions.

> *Interview vignette.* It has often been said that we are our own worst enemies. By not being flexible we have lost nursing positions to other disciplines. We assumed because of our large numbers we were safe, and that no one else would want our job.

Programme management

In recent years, the Canadian health care scene has witnessed many changes, among the most novel being the abandonment of functional matrix management in favour of programme management. Programme management is increasingly being embraced by facilities providing forensic services. Traditionally, multidisciplinary teams consisted of several professional departments who provided service to clients; although committed to the success of the programme, matrix management saw the distribution of accountability and financial resources across many departments, and individual team members frequently experienced a dual-reporting function. Not only is this costly, but it is also confusing with the lines of responsibility poorly understood, thereby further confounding accountability (Chiasson 1997; VanDeVelde-Coke 1998).

Under programme management, departments are either eliminated or altered to de-emphasise professional autonomy and to stress the importance of a multidisciplinary team approach (Chiasson 1997; VanDeVelde-Coke 1998). 'Professionals may view the loss of their department as the loss of identity for their profession within the institution' (VanDeVelde-Coke 1998, p.143). The loss of a formalised nursing department can be particularly difficult for forensic nurses who often struggle with their professional identity (Peternelj-Taylor and Johnson 1995).

Many nurses view programme management as threatening, and worry about the monitoring of clinical practice standards (VanDeVelde-Coke 1998), while others welcome the opportunity to work and learn from other disciplines.

Interview vignette: I believe that nursing has benefited from programme management. It forced all the disciplines to work in close proximity; it challenged us all to be the best that we could be, and as a result the clients also benefited. Some would argue that you lose touch with your professional standards, but I am not sure that I need my supervisor to be a nurse to ensure that my practice is in keeping with my professional standards – that is something that I carry with me – it is not dependent on having a nurse manager.

Issues surrounding professional territoriality can be of concern when adopting programme management, and team building is often time-consuming, frustrating and potentially explosive (VanDeVelde-Coke 1998). Furthermore, how programme management is implemented can be an extremely sensitive issue for nurses, especially when combined with concurrent loss of nursing positions and the perceived demise of the role of the nurse in the forensic setting.

Interview vignette: Nurses in some settings are undergoing tremendous turmoil, seeing themselves replaced, by and large, with social workers, with one nurse always being kept on staff, though to give out medications and to monitor their effects. However, the nurses are just as skilled in cognitive-behavioural counselling and group dynamics as other staff members.

The issues surrounding multidisciplinary practice in Canada are often enmeshed with programme management, job security and territoriality. What will nurses be known for? Is medication management the only contribution that nurses make to the multidisciplinary team? Will nurses sit back and idly watch their role being absorbed by other disciplines? The whole concept of role clarification is not unique to forensic settings, as one experienced nurse who had just returned to forensic nursing after a 10-year hiatus observed: 'All nurses in our health care system have had to answer the question, "Just exactly what does a nurse do?" I believe that the same process may have to occur in forensic psychiatric nursing.'

Nature and scope of practice

Caring has frequently been described as the essence of psychiatric mental health nursing. The profession's obligation to this conviction is not altered by the fact that the individuals being cared for are mentally disordered offenders in non-traditional practice settings. Forensic nurses must be knowledgeable, skilled practitioners, who are capable of providing the offender with a level of care comparable to the community standard (Fraser 1994; Peternelj-Taylor and Johnson 1993, 1995).

Characteristics of the forensic nurse

Canadian literature suggests that nurses working in forensic environments must have good communication skills, be able to work independently as well as within a team structure, and possess physical and psychological assessment skills. Essential attributes have been described as professionalism, confidence, decisiveness and the ability to work in a secure environment. Personal characteristics as stability, integrity, assertiveness and maturity are also seen as desirable (Day 1983; Niskala 1986, 1987; Petryshen 1981; Peternelj-Taylor and Johnson 1993).

> *Interview vignette.* Role modelling, that's it! Role modelling is probably more significant than the other skills. I work in the client's living area, therefore he has access to me in the therapeutic relationship, and he watches my interactions with other staff and with other clients. So I think role modelling is a key skill. They watch us and evaluate us. As one client put it, he determined who he could benefit from therapeutically based on his observations of staff members' ability to 'walk their talk'!

Responses of the nurses interviewed supported the conclusions drawn from the literature and are summarised in Table 15.2. Apart from being able to balance the demands of custody and caring in a secure environment, the characteristics and attributes identified in the literature and by the nurses interviewed are equally relevant to psychiatric mental health nurses in general, and are not exclusive to forensic nursing.

Table 15.2 Characteristics of the forensic nurse

○ Respect and dignity for another human being, no matter how horrific the crime

○ Role modelling by teaching pro-social values

○ Excellent listening and assessment skills

○ Being flexible and being able to adapt therapy to the individual

○ Believing people can change

○ Self-awareness of own values and belief systems

○ Confidence in one's own abilities

○ Enriched understanding of sub-cultures

○ Excellent report-writing skills

○ Being able to recognise one's limitations

○ Ability to motivate change

○ Assertiveness

○ Non-judgemental attitude

○ Maturity

○ Life experiences

Forensic nursing's unique contribution to the multidisciplinary team

The roles and responsibilities assumed by the forensic nurse may not vary much from the other disciplines and differentiating the unique contribution of the nurse to the multidisciplinary team is not always easy. This is an issue that psychiatric mental health nurses in particular have frequently struggled with. Of those interviewed, three themes emerged: 24-hour responsibility, medication management and the provision of holistic care. General contributions to the team are summarised in Table 15.3.

Table 15.3 Contributions to the multidisciplinary team

General contributions

- Psychosocial evaluation and assessment
- Individual therapy
- Crisis intervention
- Short-term supportive therapy
- Group therapy
- Advocacy
- Case management
- Liaison with community and other agencies

Unique contributions

- Management of the therapeutic milieu
- Medication management
- Provision of holistic care

Twenty-four hour responsibility

In most forensic institutions, nurses still make up the largest single group of professionals, and are the only health professionals invariably present 24 hours a day, seven days a week (it is recognised that in many institutions correctional staff are also present 24 hours per day). It is rare to find other health care professionals working in the evenings or weekends. Even in facilities that have adopted programme management, it is nurses who are consistently available to the client. Does treatment only occur Monday to Friday during the traditional day shift when all team members are present? Do professionals other than nurses work evening shifts or night shifts? Do these hours only represent custodial care? Or is this also time for treatment?

> *Interview vignette.* The 24-hour observation is most useful in the recording of the traits of the personality disordered offender, specifically to determine the risk of re-offending or dangerousness to society. In the example of the male offender charged with spousal abuse or homicide – the observation of their attitude towards women in general and women in authority positions is consequential. Also, observations of attempts to split staff, tendencies of attempts to control the unit, the absence of expression of remorse or guilt, and their rationale as to why the crime was committed, are all critical observations.

Experienced nurses are very cognisant of the fact that clients, in particular personality disordered clients, are very skilled at saying and doing the right things during the interview hour or while in group therapy. How treatment goals are internalised and how the client interacts with others over the course of the day is critical to ongoing assessment and evaluation. Management of the therapeutic milieu has always been, and will continue to be, a powerful intervention strategy for nurses. Even under programme management, other disciplines assigned to a particular unit or programme come and go throughout the day, and may retreat to their offices when not directly involved with counselling. It is a rare event to see other disciplines on duty during the evenings or weekends.

Recently, a nurse guiltily discussed her concerns about losing patience with a very difficult borderline personality disordered client and concluded that she wished she had the same level of tolerance seen in the unit psychologist. However, the psychologist was not on the unit throughout the day when the client constantly tested unit rules and regulations and badgered the nurse in an attempt to have her needs met.

The assessment of the client over a 24-hour period is critical. Nurses assess activities of daily living, coping skills, interaction with others, response to therapy and response to prescription medication.

Medication management

All nurses interviewed indicated the importance of the role of the nurse in medication management, from administration through to monitoring and evaluating therapeutic efficacy. The importance of educating clients regarding mechanism of action, side-effects and self-care strategies were also identified. Issues surrounding compliance are often embroiled in the meaning that a client attaches to taking medication, and working closely with clients is critical to successful outcomes. Although this is a critical role that no other discipline can fulfil, nurses expressed concern that this is not the only thing that they want to be known for. In response to the question 'What does the nurse contribute to the multidisciplinary team?', one nurse responded flippantly: 'We give medication!' Although true, the playful banter may have covered up some anxiety over the difficulty that nurses often experience describing what it is they do.

Provision of holistic care

Nurses have traditionally been known for the holistic approach inherent to the provision of care. The holistic underpinnings of nursing practice enable the nurse to view clients in their totality, and embrace holism in their assessments, interventions and evaluations. However, as one nurse cautioned, other disciplines are also embracing holistic principles as part of their domain of practice.

Interview vignette. I do not think we can say we have the corner on a holistic approach. This is just as much a part of social work or occupational therapy as it is of nursing. Nurses may be more knowledgeable regarding the medical aspects of care, but a social worker probably has more knowledge about family and systems theory, and an occupational therapist is more knowledgeable about cognitive assessments. We each contribute something kind of unique, but I do not know if anyone has the corner on the holistic approach.

Dilemmas facing forensic nurses

The dilemmas facing the forensic nurse in Canadian settings centre around the conflicting responsibilities of providing mental health care to clients in secure environments. Nurses charged with caring for forensic clients must find a balance between the security limitations of the milieu and the health care needs of the forensic population. This contradiction, often referred to as 'custody and caring', can be immobilising; as employees, nurses frequently walk the line between the requirements of security, health care and client advocacy (Fraser 1994; Peternelj-Taylor and Johnson 1993, 1995).

Conflicting convictions: custody and caring

Nurses interviewed identified the conflicting convictions of custody and caring as the number one issue in the care and treatment of the mentally disordered offender. This paradox, that requires special attention and discernment, is probably the single factor that differentiates the forensic nurse from the general mental health nurse. The contradictions surrounding this paradox permeate every aspect of a nurse's work. Kent-Wilkinson (1993) states that 'the humanistic values of the mental health system constantly clash with the control and security goals of the criminal justice system' (p.476). However, a dichotomy between the two responsibilities need not be.

> *Interview vignette:* It is certainly a lot different from regular nursing, I guess more or less because of the security aspect. You are always taught that safety is a priority – so in this case, unless your environment is secure and you are feeling safe in your environment, you cannot really go forward and provide the type of treatment that the client needs. Unfortunately, no matter what you do, you still have to be security conscious when you interact with the clients – everyone is a potential threat – yet at the same time, you have to develop a trusting relationship. It is a bit of a conflict, but somehow we manage to squeak through it.

Regardless of the size and type of institution, every forensic nurse, like all other forensic employees, is responsible for the protection of society through responsible management of the offenders in their charge.

> *Interview vignette:* Clients see us somewhat as an authority figure but not totally, they get confused too. On the one hand, we do therapy with them, but on the other hand, if they do something wrong, we are also expected to charge them. So here we are, this caring group of professionals, but we are involved in security functions that really are not nursing functions. So is there a way to do that in a

caring way? I think it is a struggle, you know – some manage to do it and others don't.

Frequently, the custody and caring debate is framed within the context of doing what is therapeutic for the client versus what is safe for the community. Although nurses recognise the limitations that are frequently placed upon them because of these dual responsibilities, they also believe that these can be complementary, as illustrated in the following vignette.

> *Interview vignette.* For me, the two are not that separate. I believe what is therapeutic for the client is also healthy for the community, and I do not see them as that separate. I do not want to take an unrealistic risk on an offender and recommend a release that will be detrimental to him or to the community. I believe it is only an issue if you choose to make it an issue.

Other nurses talked about their role in tertiary prevention, and felt if they did their jobs well, they had a contribution to make in preventing the client from re-offending. Thus, while working in a mental health context, reducing an offender's risk and dealing with criminogenic factors remains the foundation of this speciality area of nursing practice.

Management of the nurse–client relationship

The ability to establish a therapeutic relationship with a forensic client is one of the most important competencies required by nurses working in forensic settings. The nurse–client relationship affects every aspect of the nursing process, and ultimately the provision of quality care (Peternelj-Taylor 1998a, 1998b). However, developing a therapeutic nurse–client relationship can be difficult, particularly when the client has committed a heinous crime.

> *Interview vignette.* I do not know how you get beyond the crime. I know I have been able to do that over the years, but I am not quite sure how you do that. I think there has to be a degree of forgiveness of that person, your own forgiveness of them, whatever that might be, whether it is conscious or subconscious, I do not know. You still have to see the individual as a person and that goes back to respect, you still need to respect them as a person, and I do not know if everybody can do that, that everyone can build that trust relationship and go beyond the crime.

Nurses interviewed also commented on how restricted they felt at times with not being able to practise in a way that they would like to. One nurse stated 'We are taught to heal with our hands, but this is not allowed in our setting.' Others anguished over doing what they felt was best for their clients, because of the security limitations of the setting, as illustrated in the following vignette.

> *Interview vignette.* Giving a client a hug or showing some sort of human caring is frowned upon in the correctional setting, and in fact if you were to step out on a

limb and do that you would probably be suspected of crossing a professional boundary, or that you were somehow too involved with your client.

Unfortunately, some nurses have 'crossed the line' by overstepping their professional boundaries and have become intimately involved with clients. All relationships have the potential for boundary violations; however, it is the intensity of the forensic environment that contributes to the immediate risk of complicated relationships. Forensic institutions are considered 'hotbeds' for potential problems (Gallop 1993; Peternelj-Taylor 1998b; Schafer 1997).

Nurses have been socialised to be caring and concerned for their clients; this is often at the expense of being able to manage their therapeutic boundaries. Self-reflection needs to be nurtured as a lifelong process for nurses working in forensic settings. As such, Schafer (1997) warns that social activities – for example, playing a game of cards – can be confusing for the client, and nurses need to weigh the therapeutic value against the potential risk of blurring professional boundaries.

Interview vignette: I am committed to a therapeutic role with my patients. I guess that is about boundary maintenance in my mind. I think when we forget about the therapeutic role there is boundary blurring and clouding. As nurses we engage in dual roles with our clients, or social roles – in that they need to learn social skills. But I am convinced that this creates some kind of role blurring for clients. So when we do engage in these activities we need to do so with a goal and purpose in mind.

Much work needs to be done in the whole area of management of therapeutic boundaries. Strategies need to be developed within forensic nursing practice that deal with issues surrounding boundary violations before, during and after they arise (Peternelj-Taylor 1998b; Schafer 1997).

Public opinions of crime, criminality and the mentally ill

Forensic institutions are controversial. They arouse strong convictions from various sectors who debate over their proper function and place in society – the need to provide a humane level of care as defined by society and subject to changing convictions regarding the forensic client's worthiness (Peternelj-Taylor and Johnson 1995).

Interview vignette: I am worried that the role of the nurse in forensic psychiatry is becoming one defined around custodial care of psychiatric patients within the legal and mental health systems. Many forensic psychiatric nurses have found that their roles have changed and their skills are under-used as funding cuts have been implemented and roles have had to be realigned.

Unfortunately, the current attitude of public animosity toward offenders in general precludes the allotment of more than the absolute minimum to forensic institutions. The whole notion of warehousing of the mentally ill offender is ever-present, and rehabilitation into the public arena is a formidable problem due to the public and political antipathy toward offenders. One nurse observed: 'There is still a considerable portion of our population who believe that someone who is mentally ill and incarcerated really has no hope at all of ever becoming a productive, law-abiding citizen.' Frequently, a 'lock the door and throw away the key' mentality prevails.

> *Interview vignette.* Many people in society today are much more vocal and demonstrative about opposing the offender's release back into the community. It becomes very hard as a forensic nurse trying to prepare someone to go back to the community as a law-abiding individual. They are tainted, there is no forgiving, there is no giving up of what they have done. Not only is this hard for 'Joe Public' but it is hard for the individual to give that up, they know what they have to go and face. So how do you prepare him to go out and meet the public like that? I do not know, it is one of the harder parts of our job. The dilemma between the public's right to know versus the offender's individual rights even to recover, to change or to improve is constantly challenged.

As public sector institutions, forensic facilities are accountable to society, as is clearly illustrated in the public outcry that occurs when a mentally disordered offender is released only to re-offend. In cases like this the system has failed the victim, society and the offender (Peternelj-Taylor and Johnson 1995). The many factors affecting the care of the mentally disordered offender can never be comprehensively addressed using a narrow or fragmented approach, and both specialists and specialised agencies working alone cannot hope to meet the needs of the forensic population. A fundamental shift in thinking is required to embrace the notion of teamwork 'without walls'. Multi-sectoral co-operation is seen as an avenue to truly meet the needs of the forensic population, and includes not only justice and health, but also the social and economic sectors (Health and Welfare Canada 1988; Health Canada 1995). Nurses are ideally situated to be key players in not only multidisciplinary treatment, but also multi-sectoral collaboration.

FUTURE CHALLENGES

Professional role development for forensic psychiatric nurses in Canada is enmeshed with issues surrounding professional identity, job security and territoriality. The unfortunate reality of nursing practice in forensic environments is that no nursing position is secure. Forensic nurses need to become a visible force in mainstream nursing in Canada, and perhaps more importantly, prove themselves as a vibrant force, capable of significant contributions to the multidisciplinary team. Goering (1993) concludes that to truly influence the context of care 'we must educate nurses to be willing to take risks, to be persistent, and to be politically astute' (p.9). Two ways of achieving this end are through research and the development of standards for forensic nursing practice.

Research

The ongoing evolution of forensic nursing as a speciality is dependent on the establishment of a nursing culture that supports and nurtures the development of nursing research. Although nurses in Canada have been writing about nursing in the forensic milieu for many years, the literature remains largely anecdotal. It is safe to assert that research in forensic nursing is largely underdeveloped, even though a gold mine of opportunities exists. This is a direct reflection of the development of the speciality at this point in time. Forensic psychiatric nurses must first become consumers of research; it is hoped that then they might be in a position to explore problems from a qualitative and quantitative perspective. A pursuit of an active research agenda is fundamental to keeping the speciality alive and well in Canada. One nurse in particular was adamant that forensic nurses need to value research in their practice.

> *Interview vignette.* Behind the commitment to be therapeutic, [nurses] have to be willing to accept research – look at it critically, evaluate it and build upon it. Nurses need to base their practice on research, rather than on myths such as 'they don't get better' or 'only low-risk or first-time offenders benefit from treatment'. Instead of basing their practice on research, nurses tend to discount research and remember the cases that validate their beliefs in the myths rather than those that dispute them. Ultimately, nurses need to be committed to evidence or research-based practice.

Standards for forensic nursing practice

To date, there are no provincial or national organisations that address the idiosyncratic needs of nurses working with forensic clients. However, the author learned of a new National Education Committee of the Correctional Service of Canada that is working collaboratively with the Canadian Nurses' Association in an attempt to become a special interest group in forensic nursing. Establishment of a special interest group is dependent on the development of Standards of Nursing Practice that identify unique knowledge within the field, define the population under care, specify recurrent core phenomena, as well as the specific techniques and measures to be implemented (CNA 1986; Austin *et al.* 1996).

Becoming a special interest group of the Canadian Nurses' Association would certainly be a tremendous step forward for forensic nurses, and would align this group with mainstream nursing. Although the work of this committee is very much in its infancy, this is a very exciting development for forensic nursing in Canada. The group will no doubt be faced with many challenges. To meet CNA's mandate, standards of practice must be applicable to any setting in which forensic psychiatric nursing occurs, regardless of whether the nurse practises as part of the mental health care system or under the jurisdiction of the criminal justice system. Likewise, not all nurses who work in forensic settings are practising mental health nursing; many are generalists that are employed in health care centres of prisons and other correctional facilities. Thus, standards would have to be written in a manner that embraces both of these groups of nurses. Some might argue that the standards of practice developed by the Canadian Federation of Mental Health Nurses (1998) are both pertinent and relevant to the practice of forensic psychiatric nursing. Therefore, forensic nurses may not be able to demonstrate ways in which forensic nursing differs from psychiatric and mental health nursing. Many of the questions addressed in this chapter will be revisited as the goal of developing standards for practice for forensic nursing is pursued.

Traditionally, CNA special interest groups that have sought speciality status have followed up with certification examinations. Certification for nursing specialities promotes excellence in nursing and demonstrates that those certified have met a National Standard (CNA 1986, 1995). Currently, there are nine special interest groups of the CNA; psychiatric and mental health nursing and occupational nursing are among this group. If and when forensic nursing is added to this list is dependent on forensic nurses' abilities to meet the criteria for specialisation – only time will tell.

CONCLUSION

The care and management of the mentally disordered offender poses a major challenge to criminal justice systems and the mental health system alike. Attending to the context of care is essential, and influences the nature and scope of forensic nursing practice. The debate surrounding forensic psychiatric nursing as a speciality area of nursing, versus general mental health nursing, was explored in this chapter. Although many similarities were noted between the two groups, nurses interviewed generally believed forensic nursing to be a distinct speciality area of nursing practice. Goering (1993) states that 'valuing the nurse–patient relationship should be the common ground uniting psychiatric nurses no matter where, how, or when they practice' (p.3). Following this simple declaration, perhaps forensic psychiatric nursing is not truly a distinct speciality within nursing. However, it is the 'where', the 'how' and the 'when' that forensic nurses might take issue with. The context of care directly impacts on a nurse's ability to provide mental health services to the mentally ill offender.

As forensic nurses brace themselves for the next millennium, 'change, challenge, and competency' (CNA 1997, p.30) will likely be the guideposts. How nurses cope with this transition will in part be determined by how they define their role, the knowledge and skills that are required, and, most importantly, their unique contribution to the multidisciplinary team. The visibility of forensic nursing needs to be raised to expose the exciting and rewarding contributions that are made by nurses in forensic settings. Forensic nurses, like all other nurses, will need 'formal credentials to justify and regulate [their] practice and to be able to say this is what nurses do' (Gallop 1996, p.10).

CHAPTER 16

The Role of the Forensic Nurse in the USA

Anita G. Hufft

INTRODUCTION

The current practice of forensic psychiatric nursing is viewed as an evolving nursing speciality from which new nursing theory and models of health care delivery will emerge. The reader is invited to imagine those futures with us and build on the foundations presented in this text.

CONTEXT FOR PRACTICE

Although aspects of forensic psychiatric nursing have been documented in the literature for over a decade, this speciality in nursing has only recently been recognised in the United States (Peternelj-Taylor and Hufft 1997). Forensic psychiatric nursing serves to bridge the gap between the criminal justice system and the mental health system, and is a nursing speciality where practice is integrated with knowledge of forensic science. While nurses comprise the largest group of health care professionals in the correctional system in the United States, there are relatively few nurses working in correctional or forensic settings with certification or advanced degrees in psychiatric nursing. As Moritz (1982) reported nearly twenty years ago, there is still little detailed information about the nurses who practise in forensic settings in the United States.

HISTORICAL BACKGROUND

It has only been within the last twenty years that the right to mental health services was established for prison inmates. In 1976, the United States Supreme Court in *Estelle vs Gamble* established a right to treatment for prison inmates. In 1977, in the *Bowring vs Godwin* decision, psychiatric and psychological services were given equal importance with other medical services for physical ailments (Dvoskin and Steadman 1989; Sanders and DuPlessis 1985). The modern era of forensic psychiatric practice was formally initiated with this action as the need for interdisciplinary collaboration and individualised treatment planning emphasised the nursing role in forensic settings.

FEDERAL VERSUS STATE SYSTEMS

The United States separates the custody of the criminal offender into state and federal jurisdictions. Each state has its own laws and policies, and nurses practising from state to state experience a wide variety of roles, expectations, physical resources and boundaries dictating clinical and professional alternates. Prisons (long-term facilities) are run by federal or state authorities usually for those with sentences greater than one year. There are currently more than 3300 jails (short-term facilities) in the United States and most of those in custody are in jails (Laben and Blum 1997).

Psychiatric care in federal facilities includes out-patient and in-patient care, completion of individual evaluations and forensic studies for the federal courts, and performance of pre-admission evaluations (Conroy 1990). All nurses working in the federal prison system are employees of the US Department of Justice (Hufft and Fawkes 1994).

Organisation of health care within correctional settings differs from state to state and there is no national health care policy or plan which dictates consistent care of the mentally disordered offender.

PROFESSIONAL STANDARDS

The practice of forensic psychiatric nursing is guided by professional standards of nursing, the state or jurisdictional laws and policies governing the location in which the nurse practises, and universal standards for the accreditation of correctional health care facilities. Lynch (1995a) clearly identifies the concept of *mutual responsibility*, in which nurses share responsibility with the legal system in addressing the needs and care of victims of crime, victims with liability-related injuries and perpetrators or suspects of crime.

For the American nurse, the definition of forensic nursing is presented in the document, *Scope and Standards of Forensic Nursing Practice* (ANA and the IAFN 1997). The role places forensic nursing in the 'medical-legal investigation of injury and/or death of victims of violence, criminal activity and traumatic accidents'. Forensic nursing is cited as being a 'significant resource in forensic psychiatric practice'.

The treatment of incarcerated patients is viewed as a distinct role within the umbrella of forensic nursing roles. The ANA standard identifies forensic psychiatric nursing care in terms of crisis intervention, interaction with grieving families, analysis of psychiatric records for legal proceedings and expert witness testimony (p.4). The theoretical foundations for the definition of forensic nursing in the standard is based on an understanding of 'arena of the law' which includes any practice setting where health care services intersect with the criminal justice system.

The *Scope and Standards of Nursing Practice in Correctional Facilities* (ANA 1995) identifies guidelines based on the setting for practice, and is used by all nurses working in prisons (which are state or federally mandated), jails (which come under local jurisdiction) or other custody locations. This document highlights two distinct nursing roles: correctional nurse and forensic nurse. Standards for correctional practice are intended to be used in conjunction with other standards for clinical practice, and the forensic psychiatric nurse practising in a correctional or other secure setting would refer to the correctional standards and the psychiatric mental health standards described previously. Nurses working in correctional facilities are expected to provide heath care services, as distinct from evaluation or testimony, as their sole responsibility, and, therefore, matters of nursing judgement are their responsibility (ANA 1995). The basic philosophy is that the health care provided in those facilities is equivalent to that which is provided in the community in which the facility is located and subject to the same regulations. The fact that the incarcerated individual is totally dependent on correctional resources for health care gives nurses an increased responsibility to advocate for appropriate care. Forensic psychiatric nurses with master's degree preparation or beyond would be expected to carry out direct advanced psychiatric nursing practice, incorporate scientific knowledge and research into the development of practice protocols, and evaluate health care in those settings.

DESCRIPTION OF MENTALLY ILL OFFENDER POPULATIONS

The incarceration rate in the United States has almost doubled from 744,208 in 1985 to 1,630,940 (Bernardoni 1997; Bureau of Statistics 1999) in 1996. Currently, correctional facilities in the United States house more mentally ill individuals than do hospitals and mental institutions: 210,000 severely mentally ill individuals are in jails and prisons, while approximately 70,000 are being treated in public psychiatric facilities. Of those in the public facilities, almost 30 per cent are forensic patients (Vitucci 1999). In-patient beds in correctional prison facilities run 97 to 99 per cent full (Bernardoni 1997). Other statistics bring the problem of mental health treatment into focus, emphasising the rates of presenting mental disorders among inmates, ranging from one to seven per cent for people with severe mental illness to 20 per cent for people with non-psychotic and personality disorders (Metzner 1997; Laben and Blum 1997). This situation has created an environment in which there is increasing emphasis on responding to prison management problems rather than individual patient need (Dvoskin and Steadman 1989; Dvoskin and Broaddus 1993).

In general, inmates in the United States are poor and uneducated. Inmates generally come from chaotic lifestyles, disrupted family and social support systems, and are likely to have a history of violence, abuse and lack of access to health care. Because of a significant prevalence of substance abuse, inmates have rates of infection for human immunodeficiency virus (HIV), tuberculosis, hepatitis B and sexually transmitted diseases that far exceed other populations (Crawford 1994; Jordan *et al.* 1996; Applegate, Cullen and Fisher 1997; Harrell, Cook and Carver 1998; Laben and Blum 1997).

Compared with inmates in England and Wales, the US prison population receives longer sentences for comparable offences, are more likely to have spent their childhood living with only one parent, are older, more likely to be divorced, and more likely to have been employed prior to incarceration (Lynch *et al.* 1994). It is interesting to note that general statistics on prison and jail populations in the United States, including those in the National Criminal Justice Reference Service, do not maintain consistent data on medical or health problems of inmates or of mental health categories of offenders. It is difficult to measure the impact of mental health disorder on the prison population or to assess the distribution of mental health services in prisons and jails. In one state, a correctional psychiatric centre has only eight beds for women. It is unclear what happens to mentally disordered female offenders when those eight beds are full, but one nurse interviewed for this text commented, 'I guess this state can only have eight women at a time with mental illness needing hospitalisation; that's our rate' (Personal communication 1998). Indeed, in a New York State decision regarding allocation of state funding, it was suggested that 'since the mentally ill in prison were already "institutionalised", there was little need for specialised mental health services' (Dvoskin and Steadman 1989). While this attitude is not currently driving policy, many individual prison and jail staff dealing with scarce resources and increasing workload respond to inmates as if it were.

Freudenberg *et al.* (1998) report that 10 per cent of women in prison self-report a history of mental illness. The Substance Abuse and Mental Health Services Administration (SAMHSA) reported in 1993 that six per cent of the total jail population suffers from severe mental illness and the incidence among women is as high as 25 per cent. A study by the National Institute of Mental Health (Goodman, Pensinger and Shine 1993) indicated that only one-third of individuals with severe psychosis or a major mood disorder were treated within a week of jail intake.

SPECIAL POPULATIONS
Women

In every year since 1981, the rate of growth in numbers of female prisoners in the USA has exceeded that of males. In 1996 the total population of women in prison was 73,607, which accounted for 6.3 per cent of all incarcerated nationwide. This rise in incarcerations has followed a rise in non-violent and petty offences in the United States. These facts support the observation that women have been disproportionately affected by current sentencing practices (Belknapp 1996). Women are more likely to receive severe sentences as compared with men with the same offence, particularly if substance abuse is involved. Questions of child custody and mandated treatment for substance abuse are increased in women, as well as the likelihood that women will have mental health consequences upon incarceration.

The number of women incarcerated in California prisons increased by 450 per cent between 1980 and 1993 (Berkowitz *et al.* 1996). Over one-third of the women incarcerated in the United States are serving sentences for drug-related offences, and rates of addiction are high. Substance abuse often continues while in prison, and drug dealing has been observed to be a profit-making venture within the prison system. A study by Jordan *et al.* (1996) concluded that female inmates were found to have higher rates of antisocial and borderline personality disorder, in addition to higher rates of substance abuse, as compared with women in community epidemiological studies. This situation highlights the mental health vulnerability of this population. Couple this risk with the fact that most prison systems in the United States are modelled on male characteristics and needs, then the ability to provide mental health and psychiatric care to women is a difficult challenge for any forensic psychiatric nurse.

The negative impact of imprisonment for women is complicated by the complex roles women play in families and society. Since they are usually the predominant provider of child care, separation from children is especially hard on women. They tend to have lower visitation rates than males and suffer isolation and role alterations, which negatively impact on their self-esteem and ability to adapt. Symptoms of depression are higher among women, along with physical complaints related to somatic origin (Belknapp 1996).

Approximately 80 per cent of women entering state prisons are mothers, 85 per cent of whom have custody of their children. Two-thirds have children under 18 years of age (Nadelson 1998). Separation from children and the mothering role is a major life event characterised by loss, grieving and mood alteration. For those women who lack coping skills and a social support system, risk of depression is increased.

Juveniles

Despite evidence that aggregate rates of crime have been static or declining for the past two decades, there has been a significant change in violent crime committed by young people in the United States. A major turning point occurred around 1985 when the rate of homicides committed by young people, the number of homicides they committed with guns and the arrest rate of non-white juveniles for drug offences all doubled (Blumstein 1995). This trend accompanied the increased drug trafficking of the mid-1980s and currently reflects the emphasis on juvenile crime, development of juvenile resources and growing frustration over prevention of violence, abuse and mental illness among juveniles. Increasing numbers of nurses are focusing their clinical practice on adolescent psychiatric nursing among juvenile offenders, adolescents with mental illness who intersect with the criminal justice system and adolescents involved in gangs (McKay 1998).

The most frequent mental disorders presenting in the juvenile populations in custody in the United States include adjustment disorder with depressed mood, other types of adjustment disorders, depressive mood disorders, bipolar disorders and psychotic disorder. Kemph, Braley and Ciotola (1997) found the typical youthful offender with mental disorder to be a white male, 19 years old, of average intelligence, with a sporadic work record and poor academic performance who quits high school in his senior year. Current treatment considered to be successful in this population usually includes psychotropic medication.

Ethnic and racial minorities

As in other countries, the ethnic and racial minorities are over-represented in US prisons and jails (Metzner 1997; National Institute of Justice 1996). Black, non-Latinos represent 44 per cent of the total jail population in the United States, with 14 per cent Latino. The jail incarceration rate among African-Americans is six times that of whites. It is interesting to note that rates of mental disorder are higher among whites than among African-American women (Jordan *et al.* 1996). However, given the high rates of incarceration and the lack of understanding of the meaning of mental illness and effective treatment, African-Americans, Native Americans and Latinos remain a vulnerable population in prisons.

Elderly

The mean age of inmates in the prisons of the United States is increasing. The elimination of parole under a new federal law requiring determinate sentencing will only intensify this trend, and prison and jail populations will continue to mirror the aging US population. Among incarcerated elderly, psychiatric disorders are a growing concern, with up to 54 per cent of older male inmates reported as meeting criteria for psychiatric disorder (Koenig *et al.* 1995). Only a small number of studies in any prison setting have examined rates of psychiatric disorders by age, and most have found higher rates at older ages. Similar to rates found in Great Britain, Koenig *et al.* (1995) found major depression was 50 times that in the community; more than one-third of the inmates fulfilled criteria for a depressive disorder.

FORENSIC PSYCHIATRIC NURSES: PREPARATION AND CREDENTIALS

Lynch (1991) has reported that forensic science is relevant to nursing curricula, and there is emerging evidence to support its inclusion in nursing education, as well as programmes in advanced practice nursing. There are a growing number of schools within the United States which integrate forensic nursing into existing nursing courses or offer nursing electives in forensic psychiatric nursing (Hufft and Peternelj-Taylor, in press). Indiana University Southeast, for example, offers clinical electives in forensic psychiatric nursing at both undergraduate and graduate level. In addition, current curriculum strategies include the integration of forensic nursing into general education across baccalaureate nursing programmes.

While forensic psychiatric nursing is experiencing a rapid growth of role development in the United States and there is renewed emphasis on professional certification across all nursing specialities, most nurses working in forensic psychiatric settings report 'no special preparation for their roles and see themselves as general nurses working in a special setting' (Personal communication 1998). Many health care professionals come into corrections unintentionally and without specific preparation.

The movement to educate and credit nurses in clinical forensic practice is moving quite fast in the United States. However, the speciality of forensic psychiatric nursing is evolving primarily as advanced practice psychiatric nursing in forensic settings. The challenge for forensic psychiatric nurses is to develop research agendas which will produce that body of nursing knowledge unique to forensic psychiatric nursing.

LIVED EXPERIENCE OF NURSES WORKING WITH MENTALLY DISORDERED OFFENDERS IN THE USA

One Michigan nurse reports being an adult psychiatric nurse working in the Bureau of Forensic Mental Health Services as exciting and having advantages (Kassof 1995). Her worksite is an 850-bed female prison, which houses a mental health unit with a 40-bed capacity. One advantage that this nurse identifies is the absence of the influence of managed care: '...the insurance industry does not control our length of stay and we are able to maintain clients in treatment based on need rather than economics' (p.13). She describes an environment in which, along with conflicting goals of the Departments of Corrections and Mental Health, exists a system where clients are 'surrounded by a closed prison perimeter and stigmatised as "bugs" by some prisoners who reside in the general population' (p.13). The majority of clients with whom the nurse works are dually diagnosed, and recognised as having behaviours consistent with untreated post-traumatic stress disorder (from sexual and/or physical abuse) and maladaptation to incarceration. Therapeutic regimes include individual therapy one to three times per week, focusing on encouragement and support of the expression of previous traumas and resulting anger. Group activity focuses on improvement of self-esteem, building life skills, symptom management, medication management and art/music therapy.

For the purposes of this text, conversations with nurses working with mentally disordered offenders in a variety of settings were conducted. A set of interview questions were posed, which invited these nurses to describe their practice, including their observations and perceptions about forensic psychiatric nursing. Their responses revealed a general lack of academic preparation for psychiatric nursing practice or forensic nursing. There were 142 respondents of which 67 per cent were either Licensed Practical Nurses or Associate Degree Nurses. Twelve per cent had Baccalaureate Degrees in Nursing and only two of the respondents were Master's Degree prepared.

Most health care providers working with mentally disordered offenders are willing to speak with others about their work. They are enthusiastic to share their ideas about forensic psychiatric nursing, and admitted a sense of isolation, frustration and concern about their ability to impact on the health of mentally disordered offenders. And yet, even though most nurses in the interviews used for this text had not been provided with continuing education or staff development in forensic psychiatric nursing and experienced limitations in their nursing intervention options, their stories reveal a passion for the work, dedication to their work and the feeling that they were quite capable in their work.

Reflections on the professional role

Interviews with nurses working with mentally disordered offenders reveal a diverse and complex set of role expectations held by nurses working in a variety of settings. In the United States there is no single, clear definition of forensic psychiatric nursing. When asked the question 'Have you ever heard of the term forensic nursing', responses from nurses fall into three major categories.

Nurses who primarily work in areas of death investigation, sexual assault nurse examination or victim services acknowledge the term with the understanding that forensic nursing is about:

1. Nurses who primarily evaluate patients to determine their ability to understand responsibility for their behaviour. This role is primarily associated with the process of determining fitness to stand trial or competency for trial or execution.

Nurses working with mentally disordered offenders generally define forensic nursing either as:

2. Application of nursing to populations of clients who have problems with the law or the criminal justice system; or

3. Nurses who practise psychiatric nursing in correctional or secure settings.

Nurses in practice readily identify specific aspects of forensic psychiatric nursing they feel differentiate them from other mental health nurses. Key aspects of the role are knowledge of the legal system and applying that knowledge to the care of patients. Nurses working in forensic psychiatric settings acknowledge an intense environment with more security concerns. Interestingly, dangerousness of patients and rights of patients are *not* considered significantly different or vital to the nursing mission by most nurses working with mentally ill offenders. This is contrasted by the assumption held by other nurses who predominantly work with victims, who feel that assessing dangerousness, knowing the criminal offence for which the patient is incarcerated or accused, and limited rights of the patient are crucial to implementing the role.

Nurses working with mentally disordered offenders are vocal about the need to be non-judgemental and the need for increased confidentiality between patients and nurses. Assessment of mentally disordered offenders is viewed as complex and ongoing, and most nurses feel that an understanding of the aetiology of violence and issues related to victimisation are important bases of knowledge to which the forensic psychiatric nurse must apply expected competencies in general psycho-bio-social assessment, therapeutic communication and control and development of a safe and healing milieu.

Other health care providers, such as occupational therapists and psychologists, describe their work with the mentally disordered offender as specific and well defined. They describe evaluation of patient status and functional abilities as the primary focus of their work. They feel their work is never ordinary or predictable though, and cite many opportunities for exploring innovations in therapeutic approaches outside of the evaluation components of their work. Physician assistants and some psychologists report that they do not see their role as different from the nurses – they just get to go home at 5 o'clock! This statement focuses on a primary difference, perceived by almost all of the health care professionals interviewed, which identifies the continuous, comprehensive nature of nursing responsibility for the status and care of the mentally disordered offender, as opposed to the scheduled and controlled interactions expected of other professionals.

Sources of role strain

Not unlike colleagues around the world, a principal source of role conflict is the dilemma of whether to help the client, to further the system, or to serve what is perceived to be the best interests of society (Hilkey 1988). If the correctional environment is unsafe or perceived to be unsafe by inmates, they often resort to inappropriate or aggressive behaviour to protect themselves. Isolation from peers or creation of a 'prison family', both of which can hold aspects of adaptation and maladaptation, are challenges to the nurse to assess and intervene. There is a continuous struggle to identify what are truly disordered behaviours. Assessment strategies for other groups of clients may not be appropriate, and forensic psychiatric nurses in the USA face the challenge of defining behaviour, assessment of risk for violence and development of interpersonal skills within a population whose survival often depends on secrecy, lying, coercion, manipulation and mistrust (Johnson and Hoover 1988; Jemelka *et al.* 1989; Personal communications 1998).

Primary treatment modalities often centre on environmental safety and prevention of manipulation by inmates. Frustrations among forensic psychiatric nurses are mirrored in the rest of the mental health care team, and often staff may mimic behaviours similar to those witnessed in the inmates (Hilkey 1988).

Providing therapy in prison is a professional challenge. Disciplinary actions often interfere with treatment or may be used as a resistance to treatment. Significant numbers of inmates with mental disorders display the unmet need for affiliation and a history of failed interpersonal relationships. The group treatments that may be effective in assisting these individuals to resocialise (or socialise for the first time) are often not available. Treatment facilities in the United States often have policies which segregate mentally disordered offenders from each other, do not allow nursing intervention without correctional staff involvement, and discourage group treatment for security purposes (Hilkey 1988; Johnson and Hoover 1988).

Nurses working with mentally disordered offenders report a general lack of preparation for the role. They consistently acknowledge that education and experience are critical to successful role mastery, but are frustrated at the scarce opportunities to acquire skills specific to the role. Nurses report that they feel ill-prepared in terms of knowledge about violent and persistent manipulation, forensic assessments, documentation skills and de-escalating impending violence. Control issues are always predominant as areas of conflict and stress. Often, nurses are concerned about what the scope of their role is and where the boundaries are. In some settings, usually due to under-staffing, correctional officers are given medical duties such as observation and assessment of patients when in seclusion, placing patients in seclusion, and administering medications. This is troubling to many nurses, and they are frustrated that, often, their role is reduced to maintaining the nurses' station, administering medications and providing written documentation.

The ethical–legal issue of medical restraints (use of medication to sedate or control patient behaviour, usually against the patient's will) and the use of forced medical treatment, either to establish competency or control behaviour, is an issue over which nurses in practice are clearly divided. About half of the nurses interviewed reported frustration at the unavailability of court orders to force medications to convicted felons under their care. Usually, the practice is ordered only if the patient is a danger to self or other, and only for a limited time. These nurses desire the option to continue treatment, and feel a loss of control and a certain 'uselessness' in their attempts to provide care to patients without such orders.

Other nurses are clearly uncomfortable with the lack of confidentiality of patient records and patient treatment (in some facilities all correctional officers have complete access to any patient record). Nurses report frustration, protecting what they feel is the patient's right to confidentiality and a certain amount of autonomy over their treatment. Nurses report a certain disregard for informed consent, options for treatment and advocacy for a patient's right to refuse treatment.

Nurses in practice report that constant vigilance is needed to protect against patient manipulation and staff counter-transference. Under-staffing, lack of time and scarcity of expert clinicians limits opportunity for critical incident stress management. Nurses and other staff are left to their personal resources for coping with day-to-day experiences and this often proves inadequate to prevent burn-out and role strain.

There is considerable concern among nurses that there is not enough preparation for the role. Nurses feel that many new nurses and other health care providers do not have a working knowledge of the offender, and that this lack of understanding of characteristics and needs results in many personnel who are unable to be empathic, are uncaring, are judgemental, and contribute to poor care management.

There is a feeling among many nurses who work with mentally disordered offenders that those nurses or other health care providers who are most concerned with knowing a particular inmate's offence (with the exception of those doing pre-trial or pre-sentencing evaluations) are essentially those, with the weakest clinical skills. Nurses with the most longevity in correctional psychiatric settings report an increasing trend to identify new personnel who not only have background in psychiatric nursing, but also display professional and personal maturity and also communicate an understanding of the population with whom they will be interacting. They see this as a positive trend, one that will elevate the practice of forensic psychiatric nursing in the United States.

Concurrent with recruiting better-qualified health care professionals, nurses in practice observe the need for increased professional development within the professional role. They desire staff education in their places of work which focuses on specific issues identified in that setting, as well as the increased opportunity to meet with other nurses and health care professionals who work with mentally disordered offenders in other sites. The work of nurses in the United States tends to be isolated and controlled by regional practices. Nurses feel that a significant amount of role stress could be alleviated by interacting and learning from those outside their particular setting and region, thus decreasing feelings of isolation and increasing their repertoire of clinical options and strategies.

Self-concept of the nurse working with mentally disordered offenders

The ANA *Standards of Nursing Practice in Correctional Facilities* (1995) clearly delineates the role of the nurse within the scope of health care and separates the conduct of nursing from the establishment of custody. The self-concept of the nurse practising in these settings is far from clear. Given the underlying role strain described above, it is evident that there are critical issues related to self-concept for the nurse working with offender populations. Occasionally, a nurse may work with offender and victim populations, especially if he or she is a clinical nurse specialist with advanced nursing credentials. These nurses may review court records and other documents for adherence to standards of practice for legal action. They may provide direct counselling and therapy, and work with others to establish public policy, influence legislation or educate others. When a nurse works with both populations of offenders and victims there is a risk of conflict over the issue of: 'To whom is my obligation?'

The public perception of recidivism and psychiatric rehabilitation among the mentally disordered offender is influenced by the media, which often exploits treatment failures or misrepresents individual cases to increase circulation or viewer ratings (Berlin and Malin 1991). The mental health practitioner, due to professional ethics and the duty to provide patient confidentiality, cannot systematically refute this 'news'. Those making policy seem to think the public wants a 'get tough' approach which emphasises punishment while most of the American public prefers to emphasise treatment and rehabilitation. Nurses who advocate the mental health care of the incarcerated are often in conflict with the expectations of the facility in which they work. The public expectation promoted by media and advocacy groups of the 'tougher treatment of criminals' emphasises victim rights over offender care. It is problematic to nurses working in the field who feel that both groups deserve quality nursing care. The tendency to polarise the response to the growth of both offender and victim populations in the United

States has also divided the concept of forensic applications in nursing. Most individuals who come to prison are eventually released and, without appropriate mental health treatment, will likely relapse. There is a distinct need for those working in forensic psychiatric nursing to develop a self-concept consistent with ANA Standards and to take a greater advocacy role for victims and perpetrators, in institutional and community settings, consistent with advanced practice roles emerging at this time.

THE FUTURE OF FORENSIC PSYCHIATRIC NURSING PRACTICE IN THE USA

Current trends in the United States are calling for increased access to mental health services, more emphasis on prevention, and community partnerships. Milwaukee's community support programme is an example of a community-based model which attempts to overcome the limitations of the 'jailing–parole–jailing' cycle that so many with mental disorders experience (McDonald and Teitelbaum 1994). This programme adopts a 'carrot and stick' approach to managing mentally ill offenders in the community along with prevention programming for those who have not yet entered the criminal justice system. Emphasis on compliance with medical and therapeutic services, money management, housing and other support services, and close monitoring provides a unique and compelling environment for forensic psychiatric nursing.

The 1990s saw the emergence of the managed health care model and the transfer of this approach to health care delivery to mental health care. Managed mental or behavioural health care has as its goal control of costs of care. As implemented in the United States, quality measures which identify 'best practices' and fair access to care have been major components of successful managed care (Wheeler 1996). Often seen as a deterrent to quality nursing care in the traditional sense, managed care has been accompanied by characteristics which provide opportunities for nurses. An increase in the variety of settings in which health care is delivered, emphasising alternatives to hospitalisation, legitimises any interventions appropriate for nursing. An enlargement in the scope of practice which advantages the emergence of the advanced practice role of nurses provides an environment for the development of a forensic psychiatric nursing speciality. Emphasis on collaborative practice reinforces the model by which most correctional and forensic settings operate, and emphasis on case management, a skill embedded within nursing roles, further values the nursing role. The dependence on quality standards which drives the focus of patient care on patient outcomes and, in the case of the mentally disordered offender, on appropriate social functioning becomes a useful tool in advancing nursing research in forensic psychiatric nursing.

It is noteworthy that most managed care programmes do not cover psychiatric or substance abuse therapy on court order, psychological testing, lifestyle management, stress management or experimental treatment (Wheeler 1996). It is ironic that the mentally ill offender may actually be advantaged in terms of access to treatment since their care is not currently budgeted through managed care insurance. It will be interesting to see what trends the future holds!

In August 1998, nurses working in forensic settings from different regions of the United States met in Indianapolis, Indiana, at the Sigma Theta Tau International Headquarters to discuss the development of the core curriculum for forensic psychiatric nursing preparation in the USA. It is uncertain, at this time, how the essential content of forensic nursing knowledge will be identified for basic competency. Many questions have yet to be answered about what *all* forensic nurses should know. Central to the task is the development of nursing knowledge specific to forensic psychiatric nursing. The domain concepts of nursing must be defined to reflect the unique characteristics of environment as legal/criminal justice context; the human being as victim and/or perpetrator of crime; health in terms of specified adaptations to trauma; and nursing as a set of roles and responses with clinical intent and outcomes particular to this population. This is the work of the next decade.

CHAPTER 17

The Role of Forensic Nurses in Norway

Roger Almvik, Trond Hatling and Phil Woods

INTRODUCTION

Within this chapter some insight is provided into the role of the nurse who chooses to work within forensic mental health services in Norway. A point which has to be made clear at the outset is that no specific forensic nursing title or speciality exists in Norway. Indeed, although it would be preferred, there are no specific guidelines to ensure that nurses have undergone post-basic mental health training. In Norway, all nurses on qualification are generic nurses, whose training has given equal weight to medicine, surgery and psychiatry. Thus, when reference is made to the forensic nurse here it means a nurse who has chosen to work within the forensic services in Norway.

First, an overview is provided of the characteristics of Norwegian forensic care. Second, the role of forensic nurses is discussed. The majority of forensic nurses work within the regional and county secure units. However, there are nurses working within the prison system. Moreover, there is now one of the regional secure units which has created a nursing post called an *extra-mural nurse*. Translated into English, this means 'outside the walls nurse'. Finally, the post-basic mental health training that is available is discussed. Highlighted are differences between generic and forensic roles; multidisciplinary working; and the deficits in past and future mental health training.

CHARACTERISTICS OF NORWEGIAN FORENSIC CARE

Until the early 1980s, all forensic nurses in Norway worked at the main service provider of mental health services for mentally disordered offenders – the Reitgjerdet Hospital. This was a central institution covering all health care regions, and in many ways was comparable to what, in British terms, would have been characterised as a special hospital. However, as a consequence of inquiries and media attention that highlighted professional misconduct, unsatisfactory conditions and discharge policy, the Reitgjerdet hospital was closed in 1987. Prior to the closure, Norwegian psychiatry had already begun the process of decentralising its forensic services. Also, a number of health policy decisions improved mental health care offered to prisoners.

Today, there are four established regional secure units in Norway – two in Oslo (Gaustad Hospital and Dikemark Hospital), though from 1998 under the administration of Aker Hospital; one in Bergen (Sandviken Psychiatric Hospital); and one in Trondheim (Tröndelag Psychiatric Hospital, regional secure unit Brøset). These are now the forensic hospitals, and although they are geographically placed within mainstream psychiatric institutions, in practical terms they are independent units with a very different patient population and organisational structure.

These units provide secure services for five different health regions and a population of 4.3 million. Together, they provide care and services, at any one time, for approximately 50 patients. Only one of the units (in Trondheim) has a traditional affiliation to the university system – the Norwegian University of Science and Technology. In addition to these regional secure units, most counties have established their own services. Presently, there are 11 institutions run by county councils, altogether providing 100 beds (Linaker et al. 1993).

Single rooms (some with en-suite facilities), spacious wards and private facilities characterise the physical environment of the regional units. For example the Brøset hospital in Trondheim was designed for up to 250 patients. It now provides care for a maximum of 18, still using many of the same building facilities such as the very spacious occupational therapy department which includes a full-size sports ground, swimming pool, library and a gym/assembly hall.

Most of the regional secure units are limited to between five and eight beds per ward, including seclusion areas (see below) for acutely disturbed and aggressive patients. The number of wards per unit varies between two and four. All the units have access to physical training areas, while outdoor facilities vary from unit to unit. This emphasis on small (in relation to the number of patients) units appears to be linked to the view that this enables close individual attention combined with high staffing levels. This ensures a good security level despite a high level of activities outside the hospital area.

Generally, secure forensic care is provided under high staffing conditions in Norway – county council secure units have an average staff-to-patient ratio of three staff to every patient (range 2.3–5.5). The regional secure units have an average of five staff to every one patient (range 4.7–5.7). This is qualified nursing cover and there are additional nursing assistants on duty (Skaug, Bjarnar and Föyn 1992). The average staff-to-patient ratio for all secure units was 4.4:1 in 1997.

Although the regional secure units are often described as providing 'high security' care, their level of security would equate to medium security in British terms. There are also a number of even more locally based county secure units to support the regional secure units. The county council units would be the equivalent of low to medium security (intensive care) wards. Altogether, there are 150 beds in Norway specifically for handling dangerous patients. Therefore, nowadays these units are where the forensic nurses predominately work; with a few others within the prison system.

THE FORENSIC PATIENT POPULATION

There is a considerable variation in the period for which patients are admitted to the regional secure units. Every patient is assessed by both a psychiatrist and a tribunal every six months to determine if their stay needs to continue. Some patients might stay in the units for several years, although the number of these patients are decreasing due to the capacity and ability to take care of forensic patients in general psychiatric hospitals. The average length of stay in 1997 was six months. At the Brøset hospital specifically, observation and short-term care is an integrated part of its function. Compared with the other three regional secure units, it has a shorter average period of admission.

In a survey undertaken by Linaker et al. (1993), information was provided on 91 patients, including 45 from the regional secure units. Eighty-six per cent of the patients were detained under the strictest section in the Norwegian Mental Health Act (Norwegian Parliament 1961), 22 per cent were sentenced to preventative detention and 15 per cent were serving a sentence.

In terms of diagnosis, approximately two-thirds were assessed as having schizophrenia, up to 67 per cent were also assessed as having a personality disorder and less than 50 per cent diagnosed as substance abusers. Up to 20 per cent of the patients showed suicidal behaviour.

Most of the units indicated that one fundamental criterion prior to admission was the dangerousness of the individual – hence, 75 per cent of the patients were regarded as dangerous both inside the unit and outside in society (Kleive 1996). Moreover, approximately 10 patients out of the 91 were regarded as not dangerous and were not serving a sentence; were not on preventative detention; nor were suicidal. It is our belief that this group are the patients waiting to be taken care of at a lower security level and thus can be regarded as having undergone necessary treatment.

What we can observe from the above is that the role of the forensic nurse in these secure units is to provide the daily care for a detained patient population which has schizophrenia and a high co-morbidity of personality disorders. They are classed as highly dangerous, many are suicidal and have a history of substance abuse. All in all, it could be concluded that they are a difficult group for forensic nurses to care for.

FORENSIC NURSING IN REGIONAL SECURE AND COUNTY COUNCIL UNITS

Within this section we shall now discuss some of the key issues that face forensic nurses working in the regional secure and county council units. Forensic nursing care is delivered within Norway from a multidisciplinary base. Indeed, a survey by Linaker *et al.* (1993) showed that most units prefer delivering care from a key-worker-based system. Each patient is referred to an individual therapist (usually a doctor, psychiatrist or psychologist). The ward-based key-worker, usually the psychiatric nurse or an auxiliary nurse, then carries out the daily therapies and care. The individual therapist liaises between once and three times a week with the nurses. Moreover, reports of individual patient progress are fed back by all disciplines involved in the care at multidisciplinary weekly ward rounds. Furthermore, all units reported that they offered organised multi-disciplinary or, in most cases for nurses only, group supervision for all qualified nursing staff – usually on a bi-weekly session.

Although the approach to care is multidisciplinary, the autonomy that nurses have in the care process can be limited. Some of this autonomy is dependent on which of the two diverse leadership strategies are in place. The first is where the leadership is shared between psychiatry, psychology and nursing (Kleive 1996). The second is where a psychiatrist will be the leader for all three disciplines. Generally, though on major organisational issues nurses have limited autonomy, at ward level they have relative freedom to develop care plans, put interventions in practice and evaluate care. All major manager roles at ward level are held by nurses and are positions filled by psychiatric nurses.

Strategies for management of violent incidents are, in general, based on policies and management strategies specific to each separate psychiatric hospital. There is no national strategy for this area of care. However, all strategies are based on the Mental Health Act (1961), although a new law is currently being considered.

There are no specific regulations in the Mental Health Act considering strategies. Moreover, Section 2 of the Mental Health Act only states 'The King can lay down rules on the admission to use coercive medical treatment.' Coercion is in the regulations (revised in 1988) defined as seclusion and mechanical restraints, but it is also permitted to use pharmacological means in this respect. The indication for this use is 'if the conditions make it unavoidably necessary to prevent the patient/client from harming himself or others, and only when more gentle means have shown to be obviously in vain or inadequate'. It is not permitted to use ECT treatment, unless it is a question of emergency or necessity in legal terms. These means can be used with both voluntary and involuntary patients.

Use of restraints and seclusion

As we will see in this section, the use of seclusion and restraint is a major issue and undoubtedly within the role of the forensic nurse in Norway. Indeed, it is usually a nurse that will deliver these interventions before the ensuing arrival of a doctor.

Under Section 3 of the Norwegian Mental Health Act provisions (Ministry of Health and Social Welfare 1977), the following legal mechanical restraints can be used in Norwegian psychiatric hospitals:

- belts (in general);
- belts for bed purpose, usually 5-point belts;
- hand and foot-belts;
- straitjacket.

Although belts in general, for bed purpose and for hands or feet, are used in the management of the violent patient, the straitjacket is not in use in today's hospitals. Mechanical restraints are allowed in hospital settings only, and a doctor shall prescribe all use of them. However, as with most violence it is the nurse who is first on the scene. Therefore, they can initiate the use of restraint in such an emergency situation and then immediately report this to the doctor on duty. As a general rule, the use of any restraint should last for as short a time as is reasonably possible; and never for more than eight hours without attempting to release the patient.

The first author's personal experience is that, usually, mechanical restraints are used for emergency and for short-time use only. This opinion is confirmed by recent studies on the usage of restraints in Norway (Hatling and Krogen 1998). In 1994, 17 out of 20 hospitals used mechanical restraints 1564 times to 360 patients with an average of four hours per time. Compare this with 1997 figures, where 18 out of 21 hospitals used mechanical restraints 1896 times to 409 patients with an average of 10.3 hours per time. As these figures show, there are significant variations between institutions and years. Moreover, to some this figure may seem particularly high; however, it should be borne in mind that in Norway seclusion is rarely used as an alternative. The number of patients for which mechanical restraints have been used have remained fairly stable for the last two decades; however, the hours spent in mechanical restraints by each patient have been reduced by two-thirds from 137 in 1980 to 48 per year in 1997 (Hatling and Krogen 1998).

When patients are under mechanical restraint they should always have at least one member of staff nearby and, of course, should never be left alone without any supervision whatsoever. This, of course, lies within the role of the forensic nurse.

In practice, this means that on acute and forensic/secure units there is a room designed for mechanical restraint usage and that at least one of the staff has physical contact with the restrained patient or will be situated at the bedside.

In stark contrast to restraint, seclusion is rarely used in Norway. In a recent study, Hatling and Krogen (1998) found that in 1994 3 out of 20 hospitals reported that they used isolation for 26 patients for a total of 500 hours (one institution accounted for 15 of them). In 1997, 7 out of 21 used isolation for 35 patients for a total of 890 hours (one institution accounted for 16 of them). The highest figures for the last two decades were in 1981 when 116 patients were isolated for a total of 11,400 hours.

Open area seclusion

Although seclusion rooms are normally not used in Norway, what is often in use is what is termed 'open area seclusion' (Bjorkly 1995). In Norway this is an important component of the milieu treatment for violent patients, and it is a major role of the forensic nurse to deliver this. Some form of open area seclusion facility is present in most hospitals, or at least those including an acute/admission ward and/or secure units.

The behavioural indications usually indicative of the implementation of open area seclusion are:

- aggressive behaviour to others;
- self-mutilation and/or suicidal behaviour;
- self-initiated seclusion (rarely);
- disruptive and/or psychotic behaviour that do not represent any danger to self or others. (For example, continuous boisterous behaviour, lack of impulse control and other behaviour that represents a serious threat to the ward atmosphere.)

Open area seclusion means that the patient is placed in a separate lockable area together with two or more staff, usually forensic nurses. The patient is never isolated alone in a single, locked seclusion room. The seclusion area usually consists of several rooms and is best described as a miniature ward rather than a simple seclusion or isolation room.

Høyer and Drange (1994) obtained information about the use of open area seclusion from 80 out of 143 psychiatric wards. They found that in 1989/90 1517 patients were placed in open area seclusion for a total of 14,800 days. For most institutions they found that the use of seclusion fell when the use of open area seclusion increased.

Moreover, the period of seclusion in an area like the one described above is used therapeutically to help the patient improve interpersonal communication and problem-solving skills. Hence, the patient is not brought to the seclusion area solely for de-stimulation and calming down but also to assist in achieving reality orientation and improving social skills. In short, the goal of this concept is to help the patient realistically view the situation and their own behaviour, and to help them establish an alternative and more positive coping behaviour.

Risk management

Perhaps not surprisingly, risk management has for more than a decade now been a main topic for discussion among Norwegian forensic nurses. Despite the need for a high competence of risk management, the training in how to handle violent and risky situations has never been formalised or national guidelines been provided. This has led to a growing number of private firms offering hospitals an education package. Additionally, some hospitals have established guidelines and education programmes themselves both for internal and external use. This section cannot describe the full variety of courses offered within the Norwegian forensic health system, but gives an insight into some of the key issues.

There are no standards or guidelines for how long courses on risk management should be. Generally, they vary from one to three days, with most courses for one day combining both theoretical and practical issues. It is strongly advised that hospitals/wards/units follow up the practical training by arranging refresher courses of their own. For example, at the Brøset hospital a minimum of two hours weekly training is obligatory for all nursing staff.

Most courses focus on the relation between anxiety and aggression as well as establishing a confidence among staff. The aim is to make them feel safer in potentially dangerous situations, leading to a more relaxed atmosphere and, thus, making the staff better prepared for dealing with risky situations. A major factor underpinning these courses is that aggression itself is not dangerous, but how the outcomes of aggressive feelings are experienced or how nurses meet the patients in aggressive situations are. The debriefing after violent incidents is also a major concern in these courses, focusing on how the staff can learn from previous episodes.

The first author has some experience with debriefing systems, providing the staff with a daily 20-minute debriefing as a part of the regular ward routine. Furthermore, most hospitals have their own debriefing groups with staff specially trained on debriefing. These groups are initiated following a major violent incident, which includes an emergency meeting as well as long-term follow-up of the staff involved.

FORENSIC NURSING IN OTHER SETTINGS

Although most forensic nurses in Norway work in the regional secure units and their role has been discussed, we previously identified some other areas in which they work.

There is one forensic nursing position in Norway with the title *extra-mural nurse*. Translated into English, this means 'outside the walls nurse' or, perhaps more appropriately, forensic community nurse. This forensic nurse works in the regional secure unit in Oslo, the Dikemark Hospital. There are several functions to this role:

- to provide a liaison service between the hospital and the prison health services;
- to follow up patients, through direct patient contact, after discharge from the hospital to the prison;
- to supervise the health personnel within the prison (usually nurses);
- to provide treatment sessions for inmates;
- to assess patients that are referred to the hospital from the prison.

As will probably be immediately noted, these can be viewed as not very dissimilar to the role of forensic community mental health nurses in the United Kingdom that are discussed in Chapter 5 in this text (Woods, Brooker and White). The role of this nurse has been more and more valued during the last few years and the three other regional secure units are considering introducing it too.

Also within Oslo, there is one team of forensic nurses (all qualified psychiatric nurses) that are employed by the regional secure units to work within one of the prisons. This is unlike the rest of the health workers in the prisons, who are employed by the local health authorities without any requirement that they are psychiatric nurses.

As mentioned above, prison nurses are employed by the community health services, and the prisons then in turn pay for the services given. Generally, there are few nurses in Norwegian prisons and even fewer who are psychiatric nurses. For example, in Trondheim there are two full-time forensic nurses providing care for 150 inmates. However, staffing is slightly better in more recently established prisons. The majority of the inmates are struggling with different psychiatric disorders and substance abuse, and therefore these forensic nurses have a very high workload. More specifically, their role does not include providing any form of therapy – mostly, they are handing out medication and trying to meet the basic medical needs of inmates.

DIFFERENCES BETWEEN THE FORENSIC
NURSE AND PSYCHIATRIC NURSE ROLE

As highlighted earlier in this chapter, there are no specific nurses in Norway called forensic nurses. However, psychiatric nurses working specifically with mentally disordered offenders function and work differently from other psychiatric nurses. Although most secure units are integrated as a part of larger general psychiatric hospitals, there are a few characteristics on the secure units which differ from the general ones.

First, most patients are long-stay patients even though the secure units to some extent also provide services to patients from other units or wards which cannot be handled within the ordinary system. These latter patients might be short-stay patients where certain treatment programmes (therapeutic or medical) are initiated, after which the patient will be returned to the ordinary ward or hospital. Except for Brøset, the other regional secure units are typical long-stay units with a very low turnover within the patient population; this is due to treatment culture or difficulties transferring the patients because general psychiatric hospitals refuse to take them back.

Second, ward-based security is paramount to these nurses' roles, even though the ward culture compared to ordinary wards and hospitals is not that different (Krøvel, Bjørn and Rør 1997).

Third, due to the high staff/patient ratio, it is, as described elsewhere in this chapter, possible to have a variety of activities both on and outside the ward. No studies have so far been undertaken to examine these two nurse roles in detail. We assume that such studies will show that heterogeneous forensic nursing roles have emerged from settings as varied as county and regional forensic units.

NURSE EDUCATION IN NORWAY

Probably not dissimilar to other European countries, the nurse education system in Norway has no specific qualification of forensic nurse. Many nurses who choose to work in forensic care have all qualified as psychiatric nurses under the continuing education system. Indeed, this is the preferred qualification which a forensic nurse should have.

Mental health care has been traditionally regarded as a discipline of medicine. Therapy and treatment given to acute and seriously mentally ill people was usually within the hospital system and additionally in private care. With the advancements in chemotherapy available for treating mental disorders and more sophisticated methods of therapy, there is an ever-growing number of patients receiving community-based therapy. Further, individuals suffering from severe mental illness are today, if properly planned and organised, offered advanced therapy outside the hospital walls.

This has been followed by a significant decrease in the number of hospital beds, and the need for a multidisciplinary approach to these people's needs has become more obvious. Mental health nursing in Norway, traditionally, has been through postgraduate education within the field of mental health. By initiating a new education programme – mental health worker – health professionals from several other disciplines are also, together with nurses, now offered a new programme of education.

Psychiatric nursing as a continuing education

Until recently, the continuing education leading to the title 'psychiatric nurse' was based on a one-year programme. Students entering the programme had completed three years of basic nursing education and had practised for at least one year within the field of nursing. Most of the applicants come from psychiatric hospital units, psychiatric nursing homes, community health care agencies, or even somatic institutions.

The programme's objectives were to allow the students to acquire an understanding for and develop attitudes that make them able to meet the community's needs for psychiatric nursing. Guidelines for the educational programme have been provided by the Ministry of Education, Research and Church Affairs. The philosophy of the programme was in many ways built on the same principles and ideology as generic nursing education. One central underlying principle is the idea of 'holism', indicating that man functions as an integrated being, where physical, mental, spiritual and environmental forces exist in continuous interaction. Moreover, these four dimensions will dominate the person's needs in different ways according to the stress put on each particular area. The concern of nursing will be the patient's ability to meet his particular needs. Nursing interventions are based on patient needs that for some reason fail to be met.

Another important issue was the belief that a human being, basically, is able to be active and responsible in solving his own health-related problems. This belief leads to a relationship between patient and nurse which is based on collaboration and equality. According to the guidelines from the Department of Education, the patient's subjective experiences and the nurse's scientifically based knowledge and objective observation will together make up the foundation on which the attitudes and interventions of psychiatric nursing are being made. Describing the essence of psychiatric nursing in this way is, however, continuously a subject for discussion among psychiatric nurses in Norway. There are many who claim that nursing is based on scientific knowledge and at the same time, according to hermeneutic theory, you can never be objective in your observations.

Psychiatric nursing is thus based on the very same principles that guide general nursing education and practice, generating a desire to care for the individual in a way that shows respect for the personal values and qualities of each person. The characteristic of psychiatric nursing foremost is a result of the methods used. The Norwegian psychiatric nursing programme defines that mental illnesses, to a great extent, lead to disturbed interpersonal relationships. The most important methods used in psychiatric nursing therefore are of an interpersonal character.

Depending on the patient's particular problem and needs, the nursing methods can be identified as supportive/comforting, or aimed at personal insight and development. Two-thirds of the programme, therefore, consisted of courses termed 'psychiatric nursing'. The rest was made up of subjects such as psychology, psychiatry and sociology.

The nursing subjects were divided into three blocks:

- Through Part I the students were introduced to the ideologies underpinning psychiatric nursing. In general, the courses consisted of theories within the areas of philosophy, ethics and nursing science.

- During Part II the aim was to look at psychiatric nursing in the light of theories on which the social sciences are built. Preventive health care as offered to healthy and high-risk groups within the population was the focus of this area of psychiatric nursing. The students were introduced to scientific methodology of investigation.

- Part III focused on integrated knowledge in psychiatric nursing as offered to individuals found to have significant deficits in their ego-functions. The students were asked to make use of scientific approaches in collecting data, making assessment, and implementing selected methods of nursing care.

The teaching methods used in the programme differed according to participants' needs. They alternated between lectures, student group activities and independent studies. Student participation was strongly encouraged. Exercises improving communication skills and developing personal growth were integrated in most course content. These important aspects were also enhanced through counselling of individuals or groups of students throughout the year of the study. Selected problems were focused on through the use of role-play, video and communicative techniques. The collaboration with the practice area was regarded as valuable and important, and an area of future investment.

Mental health worker

This above postgraduate psychiatric nurse education system has now been phased out and a new education programme – mental health worker – is now offered to health professionals from several disciplines, as well as nurses. It aims to allow health and social workers who work with people suffering from a variety of psychiatric disorders to improve their abilities to care through using their own resources. It involves an interplay with the service users, relatives and other health services. Emphasised is the need for multidisciplinary co-operation. The students qualify to work with patients/clients/users in both community and hospital-based settings. Furthermore, they are provided with insight into other health professions' roles.

The entrance requirement is that students will have completed the three-year education within nursing, social work, physiotherapy or occupational therapy and have at least two years' work experience as a professional. The education programme is divided into two sections:

1. A shared common introduction including the human being, psychiatric disorders and the social environment, organisation of the psychiatric services, communications interplay and conflict-solving strategies.

2. An in-depth study on aspects of psychiatric nursing, physiotherapy, psychosocial work and occupational therapy. The study on psychiatric nursing mainly corresponds to the former postgraduate education described above.

Interestingly, and perhaps more importantly within this new training approach of mental health worker, no specific developments for the forensic nurses' role is mentioned. Moreover, this can only highlight a major challenge and goal for the future. A goal that even might be achieved as this new mental health worker programme is likely to undergo several changes and corrections after this year's 'debut'. It is up to forensic nurses to develop their own identity.

Therefore, this new mental health worker education leads to less focus on nursing theories and more contributions from other health care disciplines. There is increased attention to multidisciplinary understanding and work, with less focus on institutional care and more on care in the community. The fact that this education is now given to disciplines with little or no tradition of compulsory care or treatment will probably have impact on the future roles of forensic nurses and might lead to recruitment problems in the forensic field. In real terms, this could indeed lead to widening the gap between theory and practice in forensic nursing.

DISCUSSION

In a way probably not dissimilar to other European countries, nurses in Norway receive no specific training for working in forensic psychiatric care. Moreover, some of the dilemmas that they face are not specific to their country. With services provided by different agencies, there is a need for co-ordination of services.

Secure forensic psychiatric care is provided by four small regional secure units with support from more locally provided units. In all, the service totals no more than 150 beds. The regional secure units provide a maximum of 50 of these beds and are at the sharp end of Norwegian forensic care, and equate to medium secure provision in the United Kingdom. Care is provided in spacious accommodation with high staffing levels for intensive therapy provision.

The nurse who chooses to work in these units must nurse volatile and dangerous individuals where nothing is left to chance. If more nurses are needed to care, they are simply provided. Some of the dilemmas that they face are specific to their country as legislation in Norway allows mechanical restraint to be used.

A major venue for meeting other forensic nurses in Norway is the annual multidisciplinary forensic psychiatry conference. Here, issues of interest such as legislation, new research and treatment programmes are discussed. This conference is arranged locally by the secure units, but is under the influence and supervision of the Norwegian Professional Forum for Forensic Psychiatry (FFsN) – a multidisciplinary professional forum highly influenced by nurses.

Extensive changes are ensuing, including nurse training where nurse-continuing education is being encapsulated within a multidisciplinary framework. The chosen approach is one of holism where the individual undergoing treatment is helped to grow and develop towards better social functioning.

CONCLUSION

No specific training or qualification exists in Norway for forensic nursing. Generally, the country's forensic psychiatric provision is small compared with other European countries. However, the dilemmas and patients cared for are no different from those of forensic nurses in other countries. Moreover, multidisciplinary working is seen as an integral part of any service, and high value is placed on research and development in the service.

CHAPTER 18

The Role of the Forensic Nurse in Germany

Alison Kuppen and Uwe Dönisch-Seidel

INTRODUCTION

In this chapter we will explain the development and details of forensic nursing care in Germany by the example of an especially secure ward of the Rheinische Kliniken Bedburg-Hau, one of the largest psychiatric hospitals in North-Rhine-Westphalia, located close to the border with the Netherlands. This psychiatric hospital was built in 1911 on an area similar to a park, and comprises approximately 50 stately buildings in art nouveau style. Even at that time, a specially secured house was constructed in the centre, not similar to a hospital, but like a prison, with long corridors, cells and high walls around the building. From the beginning this house was meant for very seriously mentally disordered patients, and also for violent cases.

Furthermore, the whole clinic, constructed for approximately 2000 patients, had at its disposal four farms and housekeeping facilities and was therefore in a position to supply itself independently. Due to its size and location in a rural region, it was built to offer accommodation for chronically psychiatric patients from the whole Rhineland. At that time, ideas about care did not comprise treatment with the objective of an early discharge – the aim was to create a home where sick and disabled people could find good relationships and a good atmosphere for a long-term stay by taking into consideration humanitarian factors. Only a few psychiatrists were available, so that almost exclusively the nursing staff took care of the patients.

POSTWAR TRENDS IN FORENSIC CARE IN GERMANY

The assumption of power by the National Socialists and the Second World War had disastrous effects for psychiatry and in particular for forensic care in Germany. Thousands of psychiatric forensic patients were marked as 'not worthy of life' and died through the machinery of horror.

After the war, psychiatry in Germany developed very slowly. It took until the 1970s before society turned towards the pushed aside and deposited patients. Treatments with the goal of discharge, priority of ambulant and part-time patient treatment as well as extensive programmes of dehospitalisation were developed. Psychiatry should no longer take place in large hospitals, on the fringes of society, but close to the community. The patients should be treated in the place where they have lived, in known surroundings and, if possible, where they became sick. For a while this did not affect forensic care at all. The priority of care still remained in the hands of the nursing staff. Only a few doctors or therapists were working in forensic care. Personnel were chosen because of physical measurements, i.e. their size, weight and stature, and in many cases they were transferred to forensic care for disciplinary reasons.

Treatment plans were almost non-existent. In forensic wards restlessness and acts of violence were not unusual. Again and again, patients tried to escape by sawing through the grills or by attempting to scratch stones out of the walls, and numerous aggressive acts against the nursing staff occurred. The reason was not only the lack of treatment plans and the slowly developing possibilities for medical treatment but, above all, the way of accommodating the patients, who were placed in halls of more than 10 people. In addition, the nursing staff were not allowed to have contact with the patients, for instance, through conversation. Furthermore, only male staff were working on the wards.

Before the therapeutic concept of forensic care arrived, the nursing staff tried, by numerous activities, to change the working conditions as well as the accommodation conditions for the patients. Still nobody strove for discharges or thought they might be possible, but they tried to structure the weekday, and to change it. Therefore, together with the patients, leisure activities and holiday trips were organised, leisure amenities, sport activities and parties were organised, and a widely spread programme of work therapy and occupational therapy was offered. Many nurses, before starting their job in the clinic, had learnt a skilled trade, and used these previous experiences in work and occupational therapy. This resulted in the first considerable improvements of the atmosphere in forensic care and allowed the lifting of the senseless prohibition of contact. Subsequently, the necessity was recognised to reduce the number of patients per ward, to open the doors within the wards at least during daytime, and to lead the patients to a normal life by giving them the opportunity to read newspapers, to watch television and to furnish their rooms according to their individual needs. Except in special cases, extreme safety conditions did not have to be considered.

NEW LAW FOR FORENSIC PATIENTS

In 1984 a special law for accommodation of forensic patients was enacted. This law had very clear directives about the treatment of the patients and aiming at rehabilitation (Volckart 1997). The main points of the law are: the checking of treatment of forensic patients every half year; checking the necessity for further accommodation once a year by a magistrate; and every three years a neutral expert giving his view regarding further necessity for treatment and accommodation. This law valued the need for therapy more importantly than the need for protection, of course without disregarding the latter. Additional therapy rooms were built, and the structure of the staff was changed. On the one hand, more and more nurses were employed on forensic wards. On the other hand, many new professional groups joined in order to fulfil the therapeutic requirements.

The implementation of this law, with all its consequences for the different professional groups – especially for the nursing staff – is still not complete. At present, a negative trend can be noticed, because, as a result of various violent sexual crimes in Germany and Europe, the population views forensic care and its patients in a very suspicious and disparaging manner. Again, the demand for safety is higher than for therapy, discussions about 'untreatables' arise and the public would like to accommodate violent sex offenders in closed facilities for the rest of their lives. Not least, because financial funds are lacking, there is also no willingness to provide the money necessary for the law to be fully implemented.

EXAMPLE OF A FORENSIC WARD

The following describes the example of the forensic ward 29.2 in the Rheinische Kliniken Bedburg-Hau and the attempt to achieve the aim of specific forensic treatment plans, especially from the point of view of the nursing staff.

Description

At present, the ward has 20 places for treatment, but is permanently over-subscribed by up to 20 per cent. The structure of the patients is very mixed. On one ward there are schizophrenic patients as well as patients with personality disorders and lightly handicapped patients. One-fifth of the patients are female. The majority of the patients are accommodated following an offence of killing or severe sexual crime, with some because of arson and other sorts of civic and physical offences. Since this ward is a specially secure one, there are long-stay patients as well as patients being moved due to some crisis and newly accommodated patients who first have to undergo the diagnostic process. This extreme mix of patients creates big problems for a homogeneous treatment conception. This reflects the situation of forensic care in Germany, though there are some hospitals that have built up specialist wards for particular diagnoses within the institution.

The nursing staff work eight-hour shifts. Four nurses are present during early and afternoon shifts; on the night shift two nurses are present; and one nurse is also responsible for other wards. Sixty-eight per cent of the nursing staff are men,

32 per cent are women. This corresponds more or less with the total number of men and women in forensic care in the clinic. Half of the nursing staff have worked in forensic care for 10 years or more. Two nurses have attended a nursing-management course and are working as head nurses, one nurse attended professional training on forensic care and 12 nurses attended a governmental nursing education course for three years. In addition, five qualified people received a two-year in-house education and three nurses work as untrained nurses. The other therapeutic staff consist of two psychotherapists, one doctor, one part-time social worker, one part-time sports therapist and two work therapists, as well as teachers and creative therapists for dance, arts, music and drama, each working with the patients on the ward for some hours.

Comparing the variety of working groups and the various qualifications with the situation existing approximately 10 years ago, when the nursing staff took care of the patients almost alone, one can easily imagine the massive difficulties of change and orientation. During the past 15 years, the nursing service has been an insecure profession, with nurses having fully justified fears about their livelihood. A feeling of being pushed aside, out of the qualified fields of activity, developed, along with insecurity about the question of how many jobs should be available for nurses in future. The problems were compounded by lack of help in working towards higher qualifications for the nursing staff and the disadvantage of shift-work compared with other working groups. New working groups took over more and more areas of responsibility previously performed by nurses. The remaining activities to be carried out by the nurses tended to be only those activities close to the responsibility of a 'security corps', except at those times when the new working groups were not on duty, i.e. after work and at the weekend.

As a result of the employment of specialist therapists, the nursing staff lost all activities they regarded as meaningful. A feeling of personal uselessness arose. They complained about decisions taken in isolation by other responsible persons, they felt excluded from important decision-making processes and were not sufficiently informed about the outcomes.

Multidisciplinary approaches

On the other hand, it is obvious that no employee, no matter in which area they were working, could be endowed with the necessary knowledge and experience to meet the complex and complicated demands of modern forensic care, with its forensic-psychiatric, psychotherapeutic, group-dynamic and background therapeutic responsibilities. The result is not only the recognition of the need for further training and continuous education, but also the understanding that these complicated tasks can neither be fulfilled by one single person nor, purely additively, by all of them. Therefore, a new form of teamwork for all working groups had to be found, which would enable them to think again about sharing tasks, responsibilities, control and many other relevant issues.

During recent months in particular, the pressure of public opinion has increased the psychological pressure on the staff. This, together with the structure of these strongly closed wards, and the knowledge of the crimes committed by the patients, easily favour a depreciatory attitude, the transmission of destructive, aggressive feelings and the repetition of rigid family structures. In order to fight against this trend, and to create a caring, therapeutic atmosphere which is permanent, special effort from all team members, and above all from the leading persons, is necessary (Urban 1998).

The therapeutic milieu

The therapeutic milieu is often not sufficiently integrated into the care of patients. The disregard of the importance of a therapeutic milieu often corresponds with a lack of a mutually agreed and binding educational plan. In this situation, the alignment of his behaviour to more or less conscious standards and criteria is entirely up to the individual employee. Consequently, patient care is more controlled by duty rosters, by the doctors on duty, by the specific interests of the ward leaders, or even by the fear of possible complaints, than by a therapeutically and pedagogically reflected plan. Nevertheless, the therapeutic and pedagogic plan has to be compatible with the nursing plan.

So far, a nursing plan still dominates on ward 29.2, in which each nurse carries out every activity for every patient, i.e. in general the nursing work is activity orientated. Due to this fact, the nursing work is schematised, so that patients are not individually nursed and looked after according to their psychiatric and physical demands. On the contrary, they have to adjust themselves to the flow of work in the service; and, of course, this adjustment, with its associated subordination of the patients, corresponds to some extent to the tendency towards punishment which emerges over and over again in the employees of forensic care. The sources of this tendency are the prejudices and personal values and attitudes towards the crimes of the patients. Consequently, the distances between employee and patient increase, and power structures and hierarchies are manifested. Since patients proved by their crimes their incapability to adjust to conventional social rules, they fail to conform in a ward's daily routine, and will be regulated by an independent system of sanctions without a good reason.

Therefore, laying down general basic principles, or guiding principles, becomes important. For example, there needs to be a basic psychological view and psychologically orientated treatment, observance of humanistic principles, protection of human dignity and respect for the person, despite the necessary restrictions of the right of self-determination. Treatment has to help the patient and be oriented towards self-help. It should enable increased autonomy and a sense of responsibility, including the capability to ask for help during crises. Furthermore, clear psychotherapeutic targets should be included, especially improvement of faith in oneself and one's intention to recover, development of understanding of the disease, organisation of an intrinsic therapy motivation, and the ability to cope with emotional conflicts.

In view of those targets, it is very important to recognise that any development requires a willingness on the part of each employee to work towards change. Lack of knowledge, and 'not-yet-being-able-to', should not be seen as failure and therefore a source of shame and censure.

Job satisfaction

A research of job satisfaction for forensic care employees at the university of Essen found results that proved very helpful in this context (Schalast 1998). The study investigated several forensic wards. Employees working on those stations with worked-out treatment plans in the form of pilot projects and with integration of all working groups described an extremely high job satisfaction, as did employees on wards with intensive further education for the employees; for instance, a social-therapeutic additional education. Furthermore, the study very clearly showed the connection between the support received from superior officers and the experience of stress, and especially the connection with job satisfaction. It seems that having a good relationship with superiors makes it easier for the employees to cope with stress. Furthermore, this study proved that the employment of women affects the atmosphere on the ward in a positive way. Therefore, there is a positive connection between the number of women in a team and the climate on the ward.

Consequently, during the last few years, on ward 29.2 of the forensic department of the Rheinische Kliniken Bedburg-Hau several areas considered new approaches and then, in working groups, developed and implemented them to projects and plans.

Co-operation and communication

The exchange of information is important for consistency of care according to mutual aims. Therefore, at each change of day shift, the nursing section has a one-hour overlap, in order to ensure continuity.

Every morning from 8am to 9am, the nurses of the early shift meet with the therapists and the social workers for a morning meeting and plan the day together. On Mondays, a team meeting takes place during the overlap of early and evening shift, attended, if possible, by all therapeutic employees and the members of both day shifts. Every Wednesday, they work on petitions and requests from the patients in a three-hour morning meeting, where also petitions from individual patients will be heard. According to the instructions of the law for treatment of forensic patients, every half-year a treatment-plan conference is held for each patient, attended by all employees working with the patient. An external experienced psychotherapist comes once a month to help as an independent specialist in reflecting on the work, problems and other matters of the whole ward team. Every Friday morning, all patients and the on-duty nurses and therapists meet in a ward meeting.

Primary nursing model

For quite some time a working group has been dealing with the implementation of the model of primary nursing (Kellnhausen 1994). In this model, one nurse is responsible for one patient, and is the contact person for the patient, for the family, and for the members of the therapeutic teams.

In the beginning they tried to implement group nursing on the ward. Four nurses were made responsible for four patients, with a mix within the nursing group of male and female, young and old, experienced and inexperienced colleagues. The basic idea of the application of the principle of group nursing was to enable the nursing staff, whose creativity, independence and self-responsibility so far had not been given a strong special emphasis, to actively work within the team. In addition, nursing staff who had previously borne too much responsibility and had been taking on too great a work-load should be in a position to ease the burden by having smaller spheres of responsibilities. However, experience proved that very active and involved nurses continued to do most of the work, and reluctant, inactive nurses still remained in the background. Therefore, this experiment was quickly abandoned and the primary nursing model introduced. Nevertheless, there are still great anxieties about too close human contact and too great a responsibility for single employees.

Further training and education of the nursing staff

The considerable changes to the style of nursing work, as described above, are not possible without intensive further training and education. So far, in Germany, there is little further training and education, especially for nursing staff in forensic care. The Landschaftsverband Rheinland, responsible for the Rheinischen Kliniken, allows a very restricted number of persons to attend special education as forensic nurses in Solingen, and some nurses from ward 29.2 have done this. They receive lessons in subject areas such as: protection against and dealing with aggression and violence; understanding of roles and professional identity; legal bases; treatment of specific psychiatric obstructions; dealing with sexuality.

Support of the resources of the nursing staff

The nursing staff on the ward have many different interests, including sports, music, handicrafts, gardening work and games. The relationship with the patient provides long-term support of the healthy parts of the patient and is facilitated by mutual interests of employees and patients with corresponding interests, hobbies and contents. Therefore, the nursing staff are motivated to contribute their own interests to the work on ward 29.2 (Peerenboom 1996).

International co-operation

For more than 10 years, the forensic department of the Rheinischen Kliniken has maintained a partnership contract with the forensic clinic in Eindhoven, the Netherlands. The result is an improvement of the treatment plan and professional qualification through exchange of staff. Mutual discussions of affairs are still held at regular intervals. In addition, ward 29.2 decided to test the German version of the Behavioural Status Index (Reed *et al.* 1996) and the hospital has since established it in Germany in collaboration with many other forensic clinics.

Integration of new therapy methods

In recent years, ward 29.2, while accommodating a high proportion of severely mentally disordered people who have committed serious offences, has made strenuous efforts to integrate new therapy methods, especially in the field of sexual offenders, by use of non-verbal body-centred therapies like dance, arts, drama and music (Dönisch-Seidel 1998b). In the early stages, workshops were offered to the employees in order to learn about the new therapy methods.

Relapse prevention

The pressure on the forensic care system has increased considerably in recent years in Germany and Europe, due particularly to sexual crimes, and more intensive development of criteria for relapse prevention has become necessary. The employees of ward 29.2 work out opportunities, not only by collaboration in the BSI-project, which enables therapy evaluation and, in the long run, the provision of prognosis, but also by concrete development of important criteria for the provision of prognosis (Dönisch-Seidel 1998a).

CONCLUSION

Ward 29.2 still has a long way to go before it completes the change from a safe-keeping facility for chronically sick lawbreakers to a modern forensic treatment ward. Major obstacles are the present pressure from the public and the implementation of massive economic cutbacks. More positively, the international exchange offers the opportunity to pursue the targets of job satisfaction of the employees as well as the best possible treatment opportunities for the patients in the future.

CHAPTER 19

A Global Perspective in Forensic Nursing

Challenges for the 21st Century

Virginia A. Lynch and Zug G. Standing Bear

FORENSIC SCIENCE IN HEALTH CARE

Although the oldest known legal code, that of Babylon's King Hammurabi, contained legislation on the practice of medicine some 4200 years ago (Camp's 1976), the normalisation of scientific specialities in what we now know as forensic science is largely a product of our twentieth century. Forensic science, the application of science to the field of law, had developed slowly and almost uniformly in the field of medicine for centuries with only occasional deference to other disciplines. In one such early departure, it is noted that court testimony concerning sexual assault and proof of pregnancy in France prior to the Revolution was limited to nurse–midwives (Camp's 1976). Prescient, perhaps, of a forensic specialist in nursing.

The explosion of technology in the twentieth century gave impetus to a number of developments that have created specialities in forensic science in numerous fields not heretofore considered within areas of legal specialisation. These developments include:

1. The growth and refinement of scientific instrumentation and measurement in a number of fields has created forensic science applications to the extent that forensic laboratory divisions and forensic consulting firms have been created solely to carry out and develop these techniques in a forensic setting. Some examples include: the invention of the comparison microscope and the creation of the discipline of firearm and toolmark identification; print and impression detection, comparison and measurement; radiologic detection of child abuse in the examination of bone fractures, thus giving rise to the field of forensic radiology; and the development of powerful computers and computer programs that have

aided in the expansion of such fields as forensic engineering. The development of instrumentation such as the gas chromatograph/mass spectrometer and atomic absorption spectrometry as well as the various non-instrumental chromatographic techniques have found important and far-reaching forensic applications in the field of chemistry. Forensic applications in the use of the colposcope has been expanded uniquely within the field of forensic nursing in the area of adult sexual assault examination.

2. There have been astonishing advances in the field of communications: radio, telephone, television, computerisation of communications (the Internet and the World Wide Web), satellite relays. With communications so rapid and pervasive, a forensic scientist in Switzerland with a question may receive an instantaneous answer on an electronic mail list server from a colleague in New Zealand. As the world becomes smaller via instantaneous communications, forensic science is becoming aware that our discrete disciplines are not independent entities that are isolated from other fields. Quite the contrary, we are linked in one vast scenario of interaction and cannot solve the problems of crime, violence, neglect and environmental degradation in isolation. And so, out of this technological revolution comes the realisation that in order to create a better world we must share knowledge, recognise the skills of others and work together in interdisciplinary harmony.

3. The development of technology, science and communications has also spawned new growth in the merging of forensic scientists to form professional associations where information may be shared, compared and disseminated. The resulting conferences, exchanges, educational programmes and publications have assisted forensic scientists not only in advancing their own fields, but have encouraged and facilitated the integration of colleagues from numerous disciplines for the improvement of forensic science in general, and an appreciation for the capabilities of colleagues in allied fields. Presently, numerous international, national, regional and discipline-specific forensic science professional associations abound, from the relatively small International Association of Blood Pattern Analysts to the oldest of these professional associations, the American Academy of Forensic Sciences (AAFS), which has recently celebrated its 50th anniversary. The International Association of Forensic Nurses (IAFN), founded with 72 members in 1992, now numbers over 2000 members and has sponsored exceptional Annual Scientific Assemblies each year since 1993.

FORENSIC CHALLENGES IN THE ART
AND SCIENCE OF NURSING

Any new field is bound to behold those who question its relevance, importance and/or viability. Forensic nursing is no exception. Forensic nurses welcome these criticisms, for they bring about reflection and examination, and out of discourse comes resolution and strengthening of the basis upon which the discipline is formed. Key criticisms of the viability of forensic nursing as a discrete speciality of nursing were raised succinctly by Whyte (1997). Whyte's main contention is that forensic nursing as a distinctive branch of nursing does not exist because what is called forensic nursing is nothing more than mental health nursing (an already existing nursing branch) with some forensic aspects. Second, Whyte implies that because the emphasis on the development of forensic nursing in the United States is victim-centred, versus the United Kingdom which is perpetrator-centred, and because there are differences in the way in which typologies of forensic nursing practitioners are described, there are grounds to question the concept or existence of forensic nursing itself. These critiques must be addressed, as any discussion of the future must resolve questions about the present and past.

To relegate the discrete discipline of forensic nursing to only a dimension of mental health nursing (or clinical forensic nursing to simply a dimension of emergency care, etc.) is to miss the point of the broader field of forensic specialisation in nursing and diminishes its significance. Progress is the product of divergent views of reality: conversing and becoming a new reality as evidenced by continual changes in concepts of forensic science and nursing. Further, the importance of interdisciplinary co-operation and co-ordination would be lost. If the concept of forensic activity in nursing is merely an adjunct dimension or possibility of other nursing practice, then the notable strides made over the past decade in the name of forensic nursing as a singular entity have been futile and should be dismantled. Among other actions, this would include disbanding the 2000-member IAFN and its constituent subdiscipline councils, reversing the decision of the American Nurses Association (ANA) Congress of Nursing Practice in their designation of forensic nursing as a clinical speciality and terminating the membership criteria for Forensic Nursing as speciality practice recognised by the American Academy of Forensic Sciences. Conversely, these organisational formations and recognitions are clear evidence of a need for the continued development of the field.

The field of forensic nursing becomes stronger and more viable by the variety of its practitioners within forensic nursing, as well as outside in the wider forensic science environment. A mental health nurse may be at the same time a psychiatric nurse and a forensic nurse, a fact which is common in many fields. A forensic scientist may also be a criminologist; a forensic engineer may also be a civil engineer. The forensic speciality permits the nurse to become immersed in the forensic science community in both nursing and beyond, for discussion, advice and the exchange of research and information. Nurses that minister to incarcerated mental health patients cannot properly care for and ensure the security of the patient, themselves and others in a vacuum. Many incarcerated convicted criminal mental health patients were victims of crimes themselves. Forensic psychiatric nurses may benefit greatly by studying the research of sexual assault nurse examiners, forensic clinical nurse specialists, death investigators, legal nurse consultants and nurse attorneys. Where else can this be done except in the context of the discipline of forensic nursing? Moreover, a psychiatric nurse predominantly working with forensic patients also benefits from studying the work of other forensic specialists in such diverse fields as psychiatry, jurisprudence, pathology and biology, and criminalistics.

The fact that forensic nursing may take differing aims and perspectives in different geographic areas is simply a reflection of a combination of the newness of the discipline and/or the tradition of practice in a particular locale. In some states of the USA, forensic nurses hold the elected office of county coroner, whereas in some Canadian provinces the office of coroner is restricted to physicians or solicitors (lawyers). Traditional and legal differences are naturally going to colour the way in which a discipline is viewed and practised. Also, because there are differing views of operational definitions (for example, the typologies of forensic nurses), these differences are typical in any discipline. Even in more established disciplines, such as criminology, there are differences in offender typologies and theoretical categorisations (Siegel 1998).

In almost all of its applications, forensic nursing as a discipline speaks to violence, most often human violence, whether it is violence against one's self, other humans and/or the environment; this remains the common ground that links the various elements of forensic nursing together.

THE ROLE AND RELEVANCE OF FORENSIC NURSING

Violence is a pervasive force that impacts health care worldwide (Standhope and Lancaster 1996; Reiss and Roth 1993). The growing interest in developing a forensic subspeciality in psychiatric nursing is a reflection of the results of increasing global violence. The consequences of human violence involve not only victims of physical and psychological trauma, but also those who have committed criminal acts, or pose a threat of violence to themselves, thus bringing nursing into the arena of the law. The need for clinical specialists and standardised protocol specifically responsible for the care and treatment of forensic patients has been identified (Lynch 1991; Neff and Kidd 1993).

To date, a co-ordinated effort to ensure that these categories of forensic patients receive comprehensive medical attention, evidentiary examinations, emotional support and referral has been addressed through the evolution of forensic specialists in nursing as a consequence of work-place role development

(Lynch 1995a). Additionally, when the patient has been accused of a crime, the focus of the forensic nurse is on the psychiatric nursing assessment, evaluation and treatment of the defendant prior to a criminal hearing or trial.

The evolution of forensic nursing emanated from the earliest times as the role of nurses required them to provide procedures with legal implications. Considering that the term 'forensic' defines the discourse between science and the law, any subdiscipline of science that practises its speciality within the arena of the law is practising the principle of forensic science. In the field of health care, this connotation refers to both medicine and nursing (Lynch 1995b).

FORENSIC MEDICINE IN MENTAL HEALTH

Although the origins of the unique aspects of medical practice originated in ancient times, contemporary forensic medicine evolved from the changing needs of society in the United Kingdom. From the inception of the practice of forensic medicine several clearly distinct subspecialties are recognised with individual roles, target populations and individual practice sites which are mirrored by their counterparts in forensic nursing (see Figure 19.1).

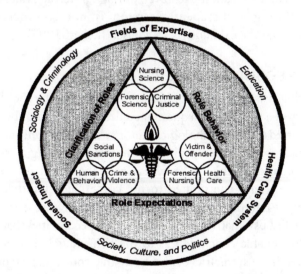

Figure 19.1 Comparative Practice Model

Among the subspecialities of forensic medicine, forensic psychiatry represents the medical counterpart of forensic psychiatric nursing. Forensic psychiatry is the medical speciality practised by physicians who deal with various aspects of human behaviour, with specific emphasis on problems related to courtroom testimony in the prosecution of a criminal case and the evaluation of a defendant whose competence to handle personal affairs or to execute legal documents may be in question (Eckert 1997). This speciality of the forensic medical sciences was initiated in England with the application of the M'Naughten Rule (Quen 1968) in which an insane person was found not guilty by virtue of insanity (Ray 1838). Credentials for this specialist include being licensed to practise medicine with additional training for specialisation in the field of psychiatry. In the United States, certification by the American Board of Psychiatry follows a psychiatric residency or fellowship under the direction of an assigned psychiatrist. Beyond this point, the forensic speciality is implemented by further knowledge and skills pertaining to the investigation, examination and study of criminals, and recommendations for the commitment of psychiatric patients, prior to Board Certification in Forensic Psychiatry (Eckert 1997).

Although the commonality of a medical speciality training in psychiatry is the foundation for practice, the forensic specialisation is the juncture for differentiation. One unique difference is the population of clients and environment in which the forensic physician practises, as well as the goals. General psychiatrists have no formal role in criminal investigation and no legal or ethical obligation to use their skill to elicit confessions from criminal suspects. Also at a juxtaposition is the issue of confidentiality. A general psychiatrist is ethically bound to strict confidentiality and privileged communication. However, during a forensic evaluation, information shared during a therapeutic session is not considered privileged communication and the examiner is so advised (Eckert 1997).

FORENSIC TECHNIQUE IN PSYCHIATRY

Forensic psychiatrists provide a significant evaluation of the social, medical and cultural history of a decedent in a questioned death suspected to be a suicide. This technique, referred to as a 'psychological autopsy', helps to confirm or rule out the manner of death as an accident, suicide or homicide. During a criminal investigation, the forensic psychiatrist may evaluate the psychiatric nature of the assailant that may have contributed to the crime. Such information can offer important insight into the perpetrator's behaviour. The case is reviewed for the type of personality, psychiatric problems and other peculiarities that are displayed, leading to a reasonable conclusion as to the behavioural characteristics of the unknown offender. Psychiatric evidence in the courtroom is preceded by a thorough evaluation of the suspect's mental status to determine their state of mind at the time of the offence. The forensic psychiatrist determines the competency of the accused and their ability to stand trial. Psychiatric testimony, for the prosecution or defence, may also counter opposition witnesses involving a psychiatric problem, presenting contrasting opinions related to insanity and competency (Eckert 1997).

As forensic psychiatry originated in the annals of English jurisprudence, the role of the forensic psychiatric nurse evolved from those who provided nursing care for the same patient population served by forensic psychiatrists. The mentally disordered offender and the environment in which they practised their nursing skills indicate the uniqueness to forensic nursing practice within forensic psychiatry, the criminal justice system and the nursing profession.

FORENSIC PSYCHIATRIC NURSING

Forensic psychiatric nursing is a designated subspeciality of the discipline of forensic nursing, recognised by the American Nurses Congress of Nursing Practice (McHugh 1997). Although the development of a nursing speciality is not dependent on a corresponding medical speciality, the contemporary forensic psychiatric nurse provides a complementary, associate role to the forensic psychiatrist and the field of behavioural sciences. As nurses have related a desire for an increased role in forensic psychiatric care, the opportunity for advanced education, specialisation and independent practice has evolved, particularly in the area of forensic assessment. In the United States, advanced education, increased responsibilities and professional development have brought forensic psychiatric nursing into the mainstream of nursing practice. Acceptance of forensic nursing as a scientific discipline by the American Academy of Forensic Sciences in 1991 has contributed significantly to the acceleration of this speciality practice.

A significant percentage of the work of forensic psychiatry deals with the area of the evaluation, diagnosis and treatment of criminal psychopathology. In many respects, forensic psychiatry and its related fields can be characterised as the study of human behaviour and the law. The forensic psychiatric nurse has an important and expanding role in providing the behavioural evaluations of criminals and non-criminals, psychiatric patients, and persons involved in crimes and disasters. This specialist's expertise is a primary supporting component of the forensic sciences in general and the forensic behavioural sciences specifically. According to Coram (1993), the psychiatric forensic nurse appropriately serves alongside the traditional disciplines of forensic psychiatry and forensic psychology. The forensic psychiatric nurse may provide a greater dynamic of anatomical and physiological evidence since psychologists do not have the physiological background related to natural diseases, congenital anomalies or pharmacology necessary to identify critical issues in diagnosis. Although a psychiatrist is knowledgeable of medical issues, a nurse provides a more comprehensive, holistic evaluation.

Nursing responsibilities in this role include but are not limited to court-ordered evaluations on felony defendants concerning legal sanity or competency issues related to the current criminal charges, and are the primary focus of this nurse–client relationship. The forensic focus of the evaluation is the defendant's state of mind and motivation immediately prior to or during the commission of the crime. This nursing role may also include therapy for those clients deemed incompetent and returned to treatment for the purpose of regaining competency prior to a hearing or trial (Coram 1993).

FORENSIC TECHNIQUE IN PSYCHIATRIC NURSING

Specific to the United States, role behaviours that differentiate the forensic psychiatric nursing specialist from the general mental health nurse are the expectation of court testimony, consultation with attorneys, and criminal justice agencies. The forensic psychiatric nurse is often requested to provide expert testimony to superior or district courts. Credibility in a court of law is based on education, experience and professionalism. In the United States, a forensic nurse with appropriate credentials is accepted as an expert in the area of forensic mental health and may testify opposite a psychiatrist. The need for objectivity is critical to the role of expert witness, whose opinion must remain above reproach. Another differentiating aspect of the forensic psychiatric nurse unique to the United States is the ability to 'educate' the court or jury on a specific issue.

Primary differences related to the nurse–client relationship are predicated upon the possibility that a crime has been committed (Coram 1993). Significant distinction in patient population is also noteworthy where the client of the clinical forensic nurse is generally the victim, either living or dead, and the client of the forensic psychiatric nurse may be the accused or the perpetrator.

In a similar context, nurses who rely on corresponding skills in forensic psychiatric nursing are those identified as correctional nurses in forensic facilities. Kent-Wilkinson (1995) defines the speciality practice of forensic correctional nursing as the provision of bio-psychosocial nursing care to individuals who have been charged or convicted of a crime. Practice settings in North America may include remand centres, state or provincial hospitals, correctional institutions, penitentiaries and half-way houses. Because of the vast expansion of prisons and other institutions of incarceration, the urgency for medical and nursing professionals to provide mandated health care is one of the most immediate concerns in managing the criminal justice system.

Although both correctional and forensic psychiatric nurses interact with the offender, the nature of the relationship and the timing differentiate their roles (Coram 1993). Facilities for the evaluation and treatment of mentally ill offenders also separate forensic nurses from the traditional clinical environment. Generally, these treatment facilities are administered by the department of corrections or mental health services, with registered nurses increasingly providing a crucial role in the delivery of forensic assessment services. In the development of new roles and new responsibilities, professionals differ in perspective regarding legitimacy, entitlement and dominion related to individual titles, position descriptions and terminology. It will be incumbent upon each subspeciality of forensic nursing to delineate and clarify their individual identities as they establish their professional presence.

Although forensic nursing has a single nucleus pertaining to judicial procedure, it has clearly divided into unique subspecialities with new patterns of primary care services and service delivery based on the intricate relationship between health care and the law. As new subspecialities evolve, the boundaries between professions and within professions will merge, as implementation of policy and practice, or lack thereof, are defined and defined again. This text has examined a myriad of definitions, roles, policies and practices from various countries pertaining to forensic psychiatric nursing as a unique speciality. The issues under discussion related to the care of forensic patients by mental health nurses have changed and will continue to change, as will the need to reconceptualise traditional visions of the care-giver and the services. Although there is a certain congruity of role common among many of the authors, clear and distinct differences will remain constant. These differences reflect diversity of culture, societal needs and professional role definition existing in their sphere.

The foundation of forensic nursing practice that distinguishes role expectations and role behaviours from the traditional perception of nursing involves an integrated practice model integrating nursing science, forensic science and criminal justice (see Figure 19.2). As clearly as there are unique specialities in

Figure 19.2 Integrated practice model of the theoretical framework for the development of the forensic nurse role. The three points of the triangle represent the areas from which the knowledge base is drawn: nursing science, forensic science and criminal justice (Lynch 1990)

forensic medicine, there exist forensic specialities in nursing that serve in a collaborative alliance with the forensic physician in each specific category of forensic practice. The need to provide a nursing specialist skilled in the aspects of clinical forensic medicine, forensic psychiatry and forensic pathology, as well as in jurisprudence, has been received.

DEFINING FORENSIC NURSING PRACTICE AND ITS COMPONENTS

The genesis of a new speciality in nursing is emerging in response to the increase in legal issues surrounding patient care as we move into the twenty-first century. In the United States, forensic nursing has been recognised as one of the four major areas for nursing development in the next millennium by the American Nurses Association (Maurillo 1996). As a speciality practice, forensic nursing unites health care and the law in a mutual concern for social justice. Forensic nursing is multidimensional in definition, addressing the legal, civil and human rights of patients in custody, victims or perpetrators of criminal violence, both living and deceased. In the clinical environs this *forensic role* is defined as 'the application of clinical and scientific knowledge to questions of law and the civil and criminal investigation of survivors of traumatic injury and patient treatment involving court-related issues. It is further defined as the application of the nursing process to public or legal proceedings: the application of the forensic aspects of health care to science and the law' (Lynch 1996a). The *forensic nurse* is defined as a nurse specialising in the application of clinical or community-based nursing practice involving victims or those accused or convicted of intentional or non-intentional injury or other criminal acts (Lynch 1996b). Therefore, a registered nurse qualified by education and experience in the specialised treatment of victims of violent crime, suspects or perpetrators of criminal acts, or patients with liability-related injuries, and whose primary focus during assessment is on the evaluation of mental status or competency, the investigation of trauma whether physical or psychological, at the crime scene or in the clinical environs, or through review of medical records, and involving evidence or assessment data for use in a court of law, is practising forensic nursing – whether the patient is living or dead (Lynch 1996b).

THE ROLE AND RELEVANCE OF THE FORENSIC NURSE

As the art and science of medicine differs in scope and practice unique to given cultural, social and legal implications, forensic nursing also differs from nation to nation. In the United States, the forensic nursing specialist serves a vital role in the investigation, evaluation and care of forensic patients involving both the health and justice systems. Role specificity of the forensic psychiatric nurse and other primary roles include the following:

- *Forensic Psychiatric Nurse.* Specialises in the care and treatment of patients in legal custody who have been accused of a crime or have been court mandated for psychiatric evaluation while awaiting trial. Assesses, evaluates and provides therapy for criminal defendants, may also assist staff members who have witnessed assaults or experienced patient suicide.

- *Clinical Forensic Nurse.* Provides care for the survivors of crime-related injury, both victim and suspect, or patients in legal custody, as well as deaths that occur within the health care institution. This specialist has a duty to defend the patient's legal rights through the proper collection and documentation of evidence that represents access to social justice.

- *Forensic Nurse Investigator.* Employed in a medical examiner or coroner's jurisdiction, protects the decedent's legal rights through a scientific investigation of the scene and circumstances of death, including notification of death to next-of-kin. May also be employed by nursing homes, insurance agencies and private or public agencies to verify information and document evidence pertaining to abuse, neglect or fraud on the health care system.

- *Forensic Nurse Examiner.* Provides an incisive examination and evaluation of trauma related to sexual assault and other types of interpersonal violence. Serves as a liaison between the health care institution, legal agencies and court of law. May be appointed as officiator of death in jurisdictions where no forensic physician is available to fulfil the statutes of law regarding death.

- *Forensic Correctional Nurse.* Specialises in the care and treatment of large institutionalised populations in jails, prisons or other correctional facilities. Must be cognisant of the legal and custody requirements of their patients involving sexual assault, homicide, recovery of contraband and prediction of violent behaviour. Documents and reports problems common to patients confined in close quarters.

- *Legal Nurse Consultant.* Provides consultation and education to judicial, criminal justice, and health care professionals; investigates medical records; evaluates accuracy in documentation of legal issues related to health care such as personal injury, product liability, and malpractice, among other legal issues.

- *Nurse Attorney.* A registered nurse who attains a juris doctorate in Law and becomes a practising attorney. Nurse attorneys constitute nursing jurisprudence, the equivalent of medical jurisprudence which is comprised of physicians who practise both medicine and law. Nurse attorneys provide a valuable resource to health care institutions, patients, physicians and nurses who are involved in medical malpractice, neglect or other liability-related issues.

Although forensic nurses share numerous common interests and role behaviours, the primary difference among them is their goals and the specific patient population with which they work. There is a firm belief that the bonds of trust and understanding between nursing professionals and their clients is built on a deep commitment to promote the best interest of public health. Forensic nurses represent health care's response to anti-violence strategies and protection of individual human rights (Lynch 1995a).

THE FUTURE OF FORENSIC NURSING

The introduction and expansion of new roles in forensic nursing are bringing about constructive changes in management, education and practice. These new roles may overlap existing roles, which often provided only fragmented or ineffective treatment to patient care with legal implications. With formal and informal education in the aspects of nursing practice involving court-related issues, more expert clinicians are available to provide services to the forensic patient population.

Through the years, the working partnership between nursing and science has spawned a vast and virtual reality of the forensic specialist in nursing. The modernisation of society has created the need for this role. Entire networks of forensic nursing responsibilities have begun to evolve and to augment the boundaries of nursing practice in response to the needs of society. Vast categories of role behaviours are identified as belonging to this speciality alone. Hospitals, community programmes, private agencies and military treatment facilities are among those who are establishing positions for the forensic nurse as a clinical investigator. Recent evidence of the impact of this new field is indicated by the recognition of forensic nursing as a clinical speciality by the United States Air Force Nurse Corps, which has launched an initiative to ensure that there will be a forensic nurse in every USAF medical treatment facility worldwide. Through the *Total Nurse Force Strategic Plan and Trifold Summary of Goals and Objectives* that spearheads patient-driven services, this mandate will reach globally to indoctrinate designated nursing professionals in the basic principles and techniques of clinical forensic nursing between October 1998 and October 1999. As the spectrum of forensic nursing continues to expand into a viable design for proactive health care policies, the many subspecialities of forensic nursing will continue to evolve where nursing and patient care interfaces with the law (Lynch 1996a).

Forensic science is particularly relevant to current nursing education. Previously, the concept of clinical forensic practice has been omitted in traditional nursing curricula. It has been conspicuous by its absence, and a recent trend among forensic medical practitioners has emphasised the benefits of a sound forensic education among clinical nursing professionals (Smock, Nichols and

Fuller 1993). Academic programmes that identify the need and demand for education and practice in this field have escalated in recent years. We must continue to work toward establishing entry-level academic criteria, national and international certification, and standards of practice, for this will establish the credibility of forensic nursing. As we monitor advances in science and medicine, it is essential for nursing education to keep pace by providing curricula for both generalists and specialists to fill positions which will become available for forensic nurses in the future. As new employment opportunities evolve, our peers in the forensic and nursing sciences will set the pace and expectations of the forensic nurse. For those who expect to become leaders in the field of forensic nursing, preparation must include advanced nursing education. Those who are prepared to operate the increasingly intricate technological equipment, to develop instructional design via digital technology, who understand genetics and appreciate its impact on the health and justice systems, who can relate the epidemiology of crime to nursing practice, are the forensic nurses who will lead us into the next century (Lynch 1996a).

Advanced nursing practice

Speciality practice requires exceptional quality preparation for roles that have not previously existed or have evolved from a combination of roles within the existing discipline. Nurses who choose to practise in an area that combines elements from physiological, psychiatric and correctional nursing with the criminal and judicial systems must prepare to meet the standards of a wide range of experts in the forensic sciences.

Although any profession will remain unequally divided among the generalists and specialists, the need for advanced practice in forensic psychiatric nursing has been identified. Yet, in the USA, the majority of patients are cared for by nurses without college degrees. Luther Christman, one of America's pioneers in nursing, stated: 'Imagine how poor the quality of physician care, dental care, and that of clinical psychologists and other specialties would be if there were as many layers of personnel and as much diverse training as exists in nursing' (Christman 1995). As we continue to confront the disparity in education between the majority of nurses with that of the medical and legal professionals in the forensic arena, it is incumbent upon nurses themselves to raise the image and profile of forensic nursing as a scientific discipline.

The future of the forensic nurse practitioner and forensic clinical nurse specialists is being defined. Since 1996, in a precedent-setting move, Beth El College of Nursing and Health Sciences at the University of Colorado in Colorado Springs (UCCS) has offered a graduate programme in nursing preparing clinical nurse specialists in forensic nursing. This course of study provides a foundation for general forensic nursing practice. Currently, a new programme has been designed for the Forensic Nurse Practitioners in Correctional Nursing. It is reasonable to expect that specialists with advanced nursing preparation in other subspecialities within forensic nursing will evolve from this foundation. It is predicted that the next academic endeavour in forensic nursing at UCCS will incorporate an advanced degree in forensic psychiatric nursing.

Speciality practice is determined by the need for a distinct body of knowledge not readily available in general nursing practice. Because forensic practice environs have distinct boundaries, limitations and demands which differ from traditional nursing settings, specialised knowledge is required. The health consequences of violence represent an epidemic of forensic patients with unique needs that requires specific preparation of nurses in scientific curricula. The need has been identified, the patient population exists, and the practitioners who will fill these roles in forensic health care are evolving. Thus, being forensically competent is not an option for nurses who practise in contemporary health care, it is an obligation.

The nature and importance of the problem

As evidenced by recent headlines worldwide, the application of forensic science to health care related to social justice systems has become an increasingly common occurrence. With the escalating demand for a greater number of specialists, enhanced expertise, and availability of forensic education, the forensic nurse now plays a far more prominent role in the investigation and adjudication of civil and criminal litigation.

Because forensic nursing is continuing to evolve as a speciality practice, many role functions overlap between clinical medicine, psychiatry, pathology, criminal justice and nursing. Definitions of mental illness, mental health and criminal behaviour are based on the current philosophy and value system of society – a society that is constantly changing (Kent-Wilkinson 1993, p.24). However, certain commonalties remain constant among the subspecialities of forensic nursing. Social stigmas related to the nature of forensic science generally are also related to forensic nursing practices due to the impact of human cruelty involved in cases of child abuse, sexual violence, mass murder or infanticide. Whether practising in the field of death investigation, sexual assault or forensic psychiatric nursing, feelings of revulsion and fear towards those who work within the scope of the forensic sciences are often expressed. Forensic professionals are frequently denigrated as professionals and demeaned for their willingness to be involved in a perceived negative role. Despairing remarks are not uncommon regarding the forensic pathologist by other medical professionals, such as: 'They can't take care of living patients.' Or the nurse death investigator who was asked, 'Couldn't you pass your Boards?' The psychiatric nurse caring for the criminal offender who has committed the most heinous crimes of human depravity may be asked, 'How can you stand your work?' The sexual assault nurse examiner is often told not to discuss their job at a family function if someone inquires about what they do.

Yet, failing to recognise the importance of the forensic genre is to fail to recognise the unique courage, specialised knowledge and skills required to practise in a role that is little understood by social norms. Society as a whole fails to recognise the crucial extent of the forensic specialist's responsibilities that ultimately help to ensure public health and safety. The foundation of health care lies essentially within the questioned issues pertaining to injury, illness and death. Without a scientific investigation of the mechanism of injury, the aetiology of disease or the cause of death, we cannot begin to provide solutions to the ravages of human life. The shared philosophical bonds of the forensic professionals remain the strength that motivates them beyond the boundaries of tradition. Forensic nurses stand among those who do not shy away from the indignities of life or death involving horrific cases of violence, of rape and of the psychopathology that others often still choose to ignore.

Scope of forensic nursing practice

A comprehensive and enlightened forensic community health programme will provide four major components of care: prevention of social violence; forensic intervention at the time of injury or death; post-traumatic incident care for the victims; and an evaluative assessment and rehabilitation for the offender (Lynch 1995a). Forensic nurses provide an innovative resource for the health and justice system when addressing these issues.

Nurses whose professional endeavours bring them into contact with the legal system must appreciate the significance of their work and the extent of their responsibilities in dealing with prosecutors, law enforcement officials and the judicial system. Training, experience and acquired expertise alone are no longer sufficient for the forensic nurse. It is also essential that the forensic specialists in nursing be aware of evidentiary rules, appreciate the significance of written documentation, and be adept in the preparation of trial testimony. Because nurses are often expected to provide care for forensic patients without any special education pertaining to this patient population, it is critical to establish clearly defined standards in forensic nursing practice. Such standards have been addressed in a comprehensive overview of forensic nursing generally; however, specific standards in forensic mental health remain to be clarified and will require the involvement of the forensic psychiatric nursing community. Without a clear charter to address health care and human needs in a world of violence, forensic nursing will be unable to achieve the tenets of their mission.

An international paradigm

In the twenty-first century, forensic nursing will become a significant force in policy and programme development aimed at determining the manner in which victims and perpetrators of human rights abuses, interpersonal violence and political torture will be managed on a global scale. The theoretical framework of forensic nursing holds implications and applications for forensic nursing in any health care system from basic to advanced practice. An integral part of nursing in any country involves the application of the nursing process in assessment, intervention and evaluation. These concepts also provide a systematic approach to the investigation, examination, evaluation and intervention of cases with forensic implications. Considering that 78 countries in the world continue to practise torture and summary executions, embrace rape as a spoil of war, and have established laws to control and dominate women and children through physical and religious indignities, much remains undone in the alleviation of human suffering. Yet, forensic physicians who are trained to evaluate and document physical and psychological defilement are limited in number and accessibility. Forensic nurses can aid in providing professional expertise in the clinical forensic evaluations of victims in proactive roles through public education and service. Restructuring of forensic services in the Republic of South Africa has produced a model programme preparing nurses to fill essential roles in death investigations, sexual assaults, domestic violence and critical incident stress debriefing. The Northern Cape Institute for Forensic Studies in Nursing was established in Kimberley in 1998 and has now expanded its curriculum to include forensic health science for police, fire personnel and emergency services (Lynch 1999). This is a prototype for role development in forensic specialisation that can be replicated worldwide. As South Africa struggles in transition to a democracy, forensic nurses are in the forefront of their history. Glenda Wildschut, forensic psychiatric nurse, a recognised human rights advocate, served as the only nurse on South Africa's Truth and Reconciliation Committee (Weaver and Lynch 1998). She has contributed significantly in the evaluation and assessment of war criminals, and provided crucial emotional support to victims as they prepared to testify to the atrocities of Apartheid. Recent expansion in forensic nursing roles and education have influenced medicolegal policies in Australia, Canada, Central America, Japan, New Zealand, Singapore and Turkey. Through the application of forensic nursing standards and scope of practice in industrialised and third world countries, specific initiatives will emerge to challenge societies throughout the world to eliminate unacceptable political, cultural and social practices that remain a constant threat to freedom and human rights.

Forensic psychiatric nursing is not unique to any geographical location. Issues related to the psychiatric care of patients who have been court mandated for evaluation and treatment present a unique and formidable task for the mental health profession. Nurses have long been considered an integral part of the assessment and treatment process. Let it be certain, however, that in the United States the nurse who assists in the judicial process by assessing the mental status of alleged offenders at the time of the offence and/or subsequent to their arrest is recognised as a forensic psychiatric nurse.

CONCLUSION

Clearly, forensic nursing is poised to enter the twenty-first century with exceptional quality professionals and with great energy, coupled with an attitude of unbridled enthusiasm. It is with this optimism that we look forward to a new century of close co-operation and solid partnership with the forensic medical community and the various forensic sciences. Education founded on sound clinical evidence and research is essential to the future of forensic nursing.

Among the challenges of the new millennium there exist unlimited opportunities. As advanced education establishes expertise and credentials, forensic psychiatric nurses will excel in role functions not previously considered within their purview. Consider for example the need for consultation to other forensic disciplines where knowledge of behavioural science is lacking, contributions to research in criminology and the epidemiology of violence, as well as providing greater responsibilities in evaluation of abnormal psycho-pathology. Forensic nurses are now employed in areas beyond the traditional nursing domain, such as the US Federal Bureau of Investigation and US Offices of States Attorneys General. Interesting and innovative education programmes that offer intellectually stimulating content provide potential for new and exciting career opportunities within realistic achievement.

"Radical changes are occurring in education and technology at a time that has also come for a global trend and interest in the forensic behavioural sciences. Online courses implicitly go beyond the issues of distance to honour the interactive, communal character of learning and the emerging capabilities of the World Wide Net" (Kent-Wilkinson 1999). Advances such as these are providing access to quality education in forensic nursing universally in industrialized and developing countries where no formal education programs in this emergency field yet exist. "Since 1994, related Internet resources have become an increasing viable component in higher education pedagogy. This has led to significant interest in the implementation of Internet-based virtual teaching" (Kent-Wilkinson 1999).

Although several academic institutions have established limited curricular options, the rapid growth and development of forensic nursing has provided an impetus for other universities and colleges to include forensic nursing in their strategic plans. Since the escalation of crime and violence is the primary variable in forensic health care, we must commit the human and fiscal resources of our academic institutions to specific initiatives aimed at understanding, managing and preventing this trend. Graduates of these programmes will be uniquely qualified to serve in a variety of forensic roles in both private and public agencies and will be prepared to enhance the current level of forensic nursing practice.

The demand for services of nurses with forensic expertise is great and will become even greater in the decades to come. Occupational opportunities in criminal justice agencies and government systems offer challenging roles for nurses with forensic knowledge and skills. Considering the institutions of forensic science that indicate the need for an alternative approach to recruitment and retention of personnel, quality forensic services and an expansion of the role of forensic specialists, forensic nursing can make a substantial difference in the character of how our society responds to the victims and perpetrators of human violence.

CHAPTER 20

From a Reactive Past into the Proactive New Millennium

Alyson M. Kettles and David K. Robinson

In this book we have offered national and international accounts of the forensic nurse and discussed some of their unique role and contribution to the multi-professional care and treatment of the mentally disordered offender. Such insights, we hope, have given a basis on which to develop ideas and thinking around this unique role. Most of all, we hope the content has stimulated people entering mental health nursing and those who have either not thought about entering this field of nursing or those with a thirst for knowledge who wish to find out more.

We have sought the views of many individuals, and authors of the chapters have either used examples of their own research or used empirical approaches in seeking these views. Below, we tease out some key issues, before discussing some contemporary issues linked to discussions held following contributions at the 1999 International Forensic Mental Health Conference, Melbourne, Australia.

Thirty nurses attended a three-hour workshop examining the role and vision of forensic nursing. This followed a keynote address on the role of the forensic nurse (Robinson 1999), drawing upon the study of Kettles and Robinson (1998). In addition, there were two other papers presented supporting the role of the forensic nurse given in parallel sessions: The Role of the Australian Forensic Nurse: Scope of Practice Issues (Evans 1999, personal communication) and Nursing in Secure Environments Project (UKCC project) (Storey 1999, personal communication).

FORENSIC NURSING: AN UNCLEAR ROLE

Maybe it is at this point that it would be useful to answer some of the questions posed by Whyte in Chapter 1. He set out to ask whether or not a clear and unambiguous definition of forensic nursing exists. From what has been presented by the chapter authors, we have seen that there are numerous definitions of forensic and forensic nursing presented throughout this book. The clarity and unambiguous nature of each relates to its use for each component of the role and area of specialist practice. In this age of learning, there are so many definitions for everything and forensic care is no different in that people want to define what it is that they do.

Second, Whyte asks about the extent to which forensic nursing can differentiate itself from mainstream nursing. There is no doubt that so many of the authors have been able to make clear differentiation. This takes the form of either differentiating the client group from other client groups or it takes the form of differentiating the roles, responsibilities, tasks and interventions from those of mental health nurses working in other areas. For example, Collins (Chapter 3) sets out the security issues and their differentiation from other areas of mental health. He argues that nurses new to the MDO have specific dilemmas and skills deficits, often finding the transition extremely difficult. Another example is that of Hufft (Chapter 16), who sets out the very different role issues in the USA, such as the role of the forensic nurse in executions.

Whyte's third issue examines the extent to which 'forensic nursing' can be deemed to be nursing in its traditionally understood sense. Peternelj-Taylor (Chapter 15) gives excellent examples of why forensic nursing is nursing despite the problems faced by those working in this area. The lack of recognition as a distinct entity actually makes it harder for nurses to argue their case. If they are nurses like any other nurse then why do they need something extra or different to be able to do the job? If they are something different to nurses then should money, resources and personnel come from a different source rather than a nursing budget? Forensic nurses now have their own International Association as well as National Groups. These have yet to clearly define their aims and objectives for the MDO. However, such groups have developed expertise for staff to support each other and who understand the nature of the role they perform. They can do as so many other subspecialities of nursing have done before by working together to create the understanding needed and to fight for what is needed for their client group.

LACK OF EDUCATION

One of the most striking aspects of this book is that most authors make the point that there is a lack of education available specifically for the nurse working in the forensic field. There are courses available in some of the countries such as the USA and the UK but they are few and they are most likely only to offer 'top-up' education. For example, many of the courses are refreshers for such subjects as Managing Aggression and Violence, or Control and Restraint.

Often, staff are sent on courses with a particular therapeutic topic as the core, such as Cognitive Behaviour Therapy or Stress Management, and they are individually expected to apply it to their area of work during the research component of the course or afterwards when they return to practice. The central topic area is presented generically, and there may be staff from a variety of areas on the course. So, each person takes back to his or her workplace what he or she believes to be relevant from the material presented and then they attempt to apply it. A good example of this is the THORN programme in England, which presents psychosocial skills as its core material, and staff are selected from a variety of areas, particularly acute and community. Each person studies the applicability of psychosocial skills to their own clinical area. Like so many courses, there is little in the way of specialist application to the particular difficulties of forensic areas. As such, the nurse does not study nursing the mentally disordered offender (MDO) in secure/community settings as a uni-disciplinary area of study. Many courses are multidisciplinary in nature, although this is useful in itself as it provides staff with a view of each other's roles, a broad knowledge base of the whole subject area and the feeling of contributing to a whole picture.

The THORN programme is a good example of how initiatives for mental health care delivery have been adapted to the forensic population, thus indicating the advanced and specialised needs of practitioners and patients. Nurses need to see themselves as professionals within this context and to have the education to work as autonomous professionals within the team. They need to be able to see their part, their role, so that this enables them to take their place within the team without feeling that they 'have the least status as well as less autonomy' (Robinson and Kettles 1998, p.217).

The absence of a specific pathway into forensic nursing leads to role conflict, confusion in a dilemma situation and the problem whereby people who may be unsuitable for forensic care can enter this field of practice.

Given the advances being made in all areas of care for the MDO in both research and audit knowledge (some of which have been presented here), there is surely more than enough to begin educating nurses who work with MDOs in forensic nursing courses which are specifically designed for them. Alternatively, courses can be designed where there is discipline-specific material/modules and multidisciplinary material/modules where mixed groups of staff are involved.

The issue of pre-registration is even greater, with few student nurses experiencing forensic care as part of their first three years. The lack of forensic module options at pre-registration level is surprising. The few electives that exist tend not to encourage nurses to try forensic as an option. This results in nurses entering the profession often by default rather than by a specialised option.

The real problem of this issue has begun to be recognised in some countries, notably the USA and the UK, where the beginnings of such courses are slowly developing. However, in other countries the issue has not been recognised because of the legal and political issues, professional fragmentation or the small populations of nurses involved in such care.

MULTI-PROFESSIONAL RECOGNITION

In terms of multidisciplinary working, there is possibly nowhere else where the role of the nurse is as recognised by other members of the team as in the forensic field. Community psychiatric nurses and others might disagree with this statement, but the verbal reports from forensic nurses indicate that they believe that teamwork is very good overall despite the medical model of care and having to live with the decisions of other professionals.

What is clear from this text is that multidisciplinary working needs to be fostered and moved away from the medical model. Multidisciplinary working has already begun to happen around the globe, and everyone is clear that this needs not only to continue but also to be extended into every area of forensic practice. Regarding moving away from the medical model, the recognition of a forensic nursing profession with specialised education and career opportunities will further a strong nursing presence as an equal clinical team member.

The lack of multi-professional collaboration can be evident in the Prison Service, an area which is so often understaffed. Therefore, nurses are unable to participate as fully as they would like in teams which are either external to the prison in which they work or cross the boundary between prison and community. They cannot even leave the prison to participate in local forensic research or interest groups, which attempt to address the problem Accident and Emergency or Casualty Units have with certain groups of patients also cannot because of the staffing difficulties they face.

The Prison Service has a considerable number of nurses working within it. However, the culture and subcultures within this kind of secure environment make this an even more difficult place in which to nurse patients. Cohen (1993) argues that a complete overhaul of prison medical services is urgently required. There is also growing concern that women are diagnosed differently from men, but what remains to be seen is whether or not they are nursed differently as a result. As Mason and Woods state: 'The whole area of service provision for mentally disordered offenders is fraught with political, economic and ideological difficulties' (1998, p.482).

INTERNATIONAL CONFUSION

The forensic population is growing. Maybe more by society's pressures, need and circumstances than by the development of a strategy to deal with these problems, the forensic nurse has begun to emerge. In the USA there are now clear roles for nurses working within the forensic area; this includes the correctional nurse as described by Lynch and Standing Bear (Chapter 19). There are no clear forensic-specific roles in Australia, other than being a generic mental health nurse as expressed in Chapter 14 (Holmes); however, Evans (1999, personal communication) is already challenging this view.

There is a very real, clear dichotomy here between those countries which recognise the developing forensic nurse and those which do not. It is interesting to note that whilst there may be no formal recognition, there are clearly nurses calling themselves forensic nurses, and this is acknowledged by other disciplines. Clearly, some accept that the forensic nurse exists, such as the USA, whereas others do not; for example, the Netherlands. What is not clear, given that legislation is different and statistics are not kept, is whether or not those nurses classed as forensic nurses and those generic mental health nurses working in roughly equivalent areas are doing the same job with comparable results or not.

There is also the ideological divergence between those who believe that forensic nurses should develop into a clearly defined subgroup of mainstream nursing, in the same way that health visitors and community nurses have done, and those who do not. Whyte (Chapter 1) presents a very objective argument as to why there is no such thing as a forensic nurse yet; despite no formal recognition of such a title, what we see throughout the book is the numbers of staff who believe themselves to be just that.

This would be a valuable area for study of current and advanced practice, standards, competence and fitness for purpose. The move towards advanced and specialist practitioners in each part of nursing has clearly begun to infiltrate forensic nursing with the advent of specialist courses and advanced degrees, however rare they may be. The discussion of role expansion also exists with the idea that forensic nurses enter into care of the victim as well as the perpetrator. However, expansion cannot occur if the role has not been identified in the first place.

ROLE SUPPORT

Clinical supervision is relevant in any role but is essential for forensic nurses, given the evidence presented here about the stress levels suffered by nurses working in secure environments, the intensity endured, the levels of responsibility, the types and the need for autonomy.

If, as we have seen here, stress levels are higher for those working in secure environments then role definition may help staff towards employing particular coping skills in particular roles. This also applies to the fact that the media are perceived as undermining the morale of the nurses who work in secure environments. Role definition also helps staff to feel that they belong; that they are supported and that professional status helps to provide some level of self-esteem.

Clinical supervision within the secure environment and the implementation of stress management groups with external facilitators may help staff to extend their coping skills. The prevalence of assaults is probably an accepted fact of life for most staff working with this group of patients, but it must never be taken for granted, and efforts must continue to try to reduce these high levels. Clearly, the higher stress levels indicate a more challenging patient group, thus reinforcing further the forensic nursing differentiation of role.

The nature of the client group adds to the stress levels and the awareness of such difficult, demanding patients who have committed such heinous crimes is ever present. Clinical supervision to help staff deal with this group or even a particular patient is vital.

The high levels of family support reported by the nurses involved in Gournay and Carson's study (Chapter 12) may be influenced by the fact that so many of these secure facilities are still physically isolated from major towns and cities. Not only is there this kind of isolation, but there is also a prevalent psychological isolation for staff given the lack of courses or access to courses, the lack of consistent contact with the outside world and the lack of positive interest from the wider community. It is no surprise that the family members are who they turn to for support. There is also the fact that in some places many members of the family all work within the secure environment and so understand the nature of the work.

MEDIA ATTENTION

Even the development of the forensic nurse thus far has occurred partly as a response or reaction to the numerous reports of serious incidents within secure facilities. From this point on, the development of training and education for staff working in the forensic field must become part of a clearly thought-out strategy for the millennium. Proactive work can begin with the millennium and take us through to the end of the next century.

The media, as we know, tends to report only the bad news about personality disordered and high secure schizophrenic patients and the heinous nature of their crimes. Maybe what is needed is a concerted effort to educate the media and then through them to educate the public. Also, the attention the media give to staff because they can be open to allegations by manipulative, personality disordered patients means that public scrutiny is often at a high level.

Mental health has made great strides in the latter half of the twentieth century in educating the public. This job is not complete, but mental illness is generally no longer the terrifying thing it used to be. Where are the leaflets, the community workers and the lay texts to help the general public in understanding what is known in the forensic field? The public relations job which has been instituted in mental health now needs to be extended to forensic care.

Forensic care is a political and economic issue. Governments take a political stance on, and set up committees to deal with, forensic issues. Money is ring-fenced and allocated according to the policies of those governments. Forensic decisions and care are now high profile, with both political parties and the media intensely interested. Forensic nurses can play a large part in the urgent education required by both these groups.

Some of the government-controlled bodies that oversee high secure environments have as part of their remit the commissioning of relevant research; for example, the High Security Psychiatric Services Commissioning Board in England are becoming more aware of research requirements. This is relatively rare on a global scale but is very useful in informing decisions and educating the party in power. It is also noticeable that those who do commission such research include nursing research within the remit. Again, this is part of the dichotomy, where those who do not recognise forensic nursing as an entity tend not to commission any kind of research other than the occasional report, such as the Bluglass (1997) and Barclay (1997) Reports from Australia (Chapter 14).

The need for evidence, such as has been presented within the pages of this text, is a growing imperative within the forensic nursing field. Evidence-based practice is necessary now in every field of health care, but within the high and medium secure environments there is an even greater imperative to stamp out practices which have been part of the system since its inception. With the demanding, difficult client groups who have committed abhorrent crimes it is all too easy to not have to worry about their care as long as they are locked up. However, the complexity and difficulty of society now match the complexity and difficulty of the MDO. We become ever more complex ourselves and it is no longer enough to sit by and say that asylum is enough. Our practice must aim to do its utmost for people who become our patients, and for that we need evidence that what we do is good enough.

TOWARDS THE FUTURE
The challenge of the service

In summarising the key points from our contributors, it is clearly demonstrated that, informal or not, there is a worldwide recognition that the forensic nurse exists, even if there is some confusion over recognition, professional status and even the term 'forensic nurse' itself. It is here the perhaps confusing issue of not whether there is such a person but whether or not the title truly reflects the work and acknowledges the specialism in its own right. The wide variety of roles, particularly within the USA, does perhaps little to define and recognise those working with what is often the most difficult and challenging group of patients – the mentally disordered offender.

Not only does this group of patients suffer from many forms of mental illness, personality disorder and learning disability, but also their illnesses are often extreme. Quite often, we see new syndromes emerging, such as Munchausen's by proxy. Furthermore, they often overlap with many forms of dual diagnoses, which only serve to make care and treatment more difficult, but yet more challenging and thus more specialised. Coupled with this is the social deprivation, family history and sexual or behavioural abuse which often make the patient a former victim themselves. These issues, when taken with offences, which are often horrendous, make challenging behaviours and the deemed 'dangerous patient' not only demanding but also in need of specialised services. Such services to treat these patients have emerged over many years, particularly with special hospitals, but more recently with the ever-growing number of less secure facilities.

The current rate at which forensic beds are expanding is testament to the continuing need for services and the fact that there are increasing numbers of mental illness-related crimes. In the late 1980s and early 1990s, when regional forensic facilities were being built to provide secure local accommodation, issues such as bed limits and keeping units small were an emphasis. Today, there are few, if any, of these units that have not increased the numbers of beds, sometimes as much as twofold, and in parallel the number of nursing and related disciplines to care for and treat the patients.

A lack of direction

Education and career pathways have unfortunately not increased at the same rate and clearly not kept up with the demand for and increase in staff. This, as we have touched on elsewhere, has resulted in inadequately trained staff, mass staff shortages, a lack of recognition for the extremely important work and a speciality without a vision. A general nursing vision (Department of Health 1993a) which has done little to enhance any part of the mental health profession, let alone forensic services, has consumed mental health. Such so-called visionary approaches have only served to provide confusion and to apply models and approaches to patient care which are inadequate (Kettles and Robinson 1998). This has often resulted in purchasers purchasing care which is far from what could be, given the promotion of models directly related to the needs of the patient and staff it is meant for. A blanket approach can no longer be accepted as appropriate.

In a more recent vision of services which is slightly more relevant to the MDO needs (Department of Health Mental Health Review Team 1994), only a few words relate to forensic nursing and these patients. Whilst we agree that mental health competencies are extremely important and indeed are the backbone of skills, this book identifies many issues and challenges which demand recognition of additional skills and competencies in which to meet the needs of this challenging group.

So how has forensic nursing survived? Or, perhaps, how have forensic services survived? Well, it is certainly not through any clear vision or mission for the service. We have seen forensic services within the UK and Europe particularly grow over the last decade, but there is still no coming together of services in a common direction. There is considerable expertise, much of which we have not captured in this book. The journal literature and research communities are full of exciting programmes which report considerable improvements and services for patients. So, why, we ask, are forensic services steered by catastrophes rather than being informed by good practice and expertise in the field?

Since the 1970s, forensic services have been steered by various inquiries. These are not just within high secure facilities but across the field. The Fallon investigation, current at the time of writing, at Ashworth Hospital will yet again send the service into a spiral direction without any clear vision of what it is trying to achieve. A contrast in so-called expertise and political climates will not help move forward the real issues of giving direction and vision which professionals and especially nurses at the brunt of care can develop and aim towards. In short, we believe that good vision is reflective of a recognised and growing profession.

A common vision for direction

Every forensic unit and service has its own mission and direction which, in turn, is often fed by a nursing vision. These are often, perhaps, misguided by national documents mentioned earlier, but given the reflection of good local practice should form the basis of national strategies. In reviewing such innovations, this will provide the expertise and a climate to encourage sharing, thus feeding and fostering national direction, sharing, collaboration and common themes relevant to the dynamic future continuation of services.

Such a vision of developing services for the mentally disordered offender is extremely important to the recognition of the role of the forensic nurse. It is this fundamental starting point which will not only drive the service with common goals and aims but assist in the future growth and avoid catastrophes and inquiries. There has been too much reliance on so-called leaders who are perceived to be experts in the field. In addition, because there is multi-professional representation on groups which attempt to decide direction, there is the misguided assumption that it is representative of the needs and direction of the profession. Similarly, we have the same representatives who continue to offer narrow, personal views which do little to either recognise the contribution of others or the profession itself, or represent the valuable work and expertise which exists within the field.

It is our view that forensic nurses and, indeed, other disciplines working with the MDO have become experts in their own right at differing levels of competence, from research-based to good clinical practice and experience. It is this level of expertise which is not effectively being tapped into by so-called leaders deciding the direction of any service. There needs to be considerable and fundamental change here, which ensures that this clinical level influences service direction, and experts in the field or appropriate clinicians need to collate these views. Once these issues are addressed, we will be going some way to professional growth and recognition.

In bringing together some of the key issues to inform forensic care, the acknowledgement of practising clinicians in this development should be the key feature in informing the strategic direction of services. The importance of forensic nurses here as the most significant workforce working with mentally disordered offenders is crucial to the service and role development. Forensic nurses should not wait for representation but should ensure their voice is heard in developing their future. Although multi-professional views are important, there is no substitute for utilising and developing the knowledge and skills of those most directly working with the MDO patient. Whilst research and development is growing at a steady rate, much needs to be done in terms of tapping into, documenting and describing this vast wealth of experience. This should be the cornerstone of future role recognition and development.

Recognition of forensic nursing

The wide and varied role of the forensic nurse across the world is confusing at best, and the term 'forensic' has become a catch-all phrase for all those even remotely working within the criminal justice system. We therefore wish to separate out and suggest that the term forensic is perhaps misleading and put forward consideration of the role in relation to the patient group which it cares for, treats and has evolved around. Whilst most in the service agree that there is such a person, it is unclear at what level it should be represented or recognised.

If there is no clear definition, it is not possible to clearly define the role. If there is no clear role, there can be no professional status and little development. In fact, this is probably one of the many reasons why forensic services have been crisis-led rather than aiming for any true vision. In addition, it has probably also been the reason why there has been little professional recognition of the role.

Registered Nurse for the Mentally Disordered Offender?

Currently, forensic nurses are functioning within an advanced practitioner role rather than within a specialism in its own right. Much needs to be done to move forward the role into that of a specialised practitioner and there are some important considerations and developments required first. Among many issues in relation to those discussed are a clearly defined role and a clear recognition, including a specialised body which does not just represent the forensic nurse but actively develops its professional status.

In defining the 'forensic nurse', we would not wish to offer a definitive solution but suggest that since it is beyond doubt that there is such a person working with MDOs we start by giving thought to the ultimate vision of a Registered Nurse for the Mentally Disordered Offender (RNMDO). Such a speciality would have clear boundaries and competencies, which would build upon the valuable mental health skills and competencies. In addition, it would express a clear role definition and enhance a specialised component of nursing.

This would also enable the development of models of care specific to the mentally disordered offender. These are much needed, as care is currently based on models of mental health care which reflect the ideas of individuality rather than communitarianism and of mental health and illness rather than of personality disorder. What has been consistently shown over time is that those MDOs who are sent to high or medium secure environments are there for considerable periods of time in closed communities. Many cannot be rehabilitated using traditional mental health methods and so new ones have developed or are developing. Nursing must also develop new ways to work with MDOs, and appropriate models of care are necessary. A balanced model of care which reflects individual worth within community is required (Melia, Moran and Mason 1999).

Education, as we have discussed elsewhere, is particularly problematic, with little at pre-registration and only just developing at post-qualification. The latter in itself recognises that there are additional skills and competencies that are more specialised and advanced than those currently on offer within mental health training programmes. In offering suggestions of the RNMDO, we do not push aside the valuable work of those already working with the MDO but, rather, acknowledge the skills they have developed and turn these into a new professional recognition, status and development.

Nurse training into the future

The British nursing leadership over the last two decades has been obsessed with importing models of care and training and education programmes that have either been discarded elsewhere or were outdated. The small élite who travel the globe bringing back such imports have failed to recognise the needs of the British nursing culture and the unique needs of their patients. Whilst we acknowledge some similarities, the expertise developed in the UK has been largely forgotten or ignored. Thus, we need a new generation of leadership which does not rely on being briefed by so-called experts but by those possessing expertise in the clinical field. Those who work on a day-to-day basis face the real challenges. Linked to research and development, there could be considerable influence.

Nurse training needs to be more flexible in responding to the demands of different patient groups and should no longer labour on with outdated training which follows common foundation for excessive periods and only offers branch programmes when it is either too late or students are unaware of specialist areas. Nurse training in the field of mental health should therefore examine the flexibility of commencing training with a common foundation of mental health, and branch and specialist training should cover all speciality areas with branch options for specialising in a particular field such as the mentally disordered offender. Mentally disordered offender programmes would then offer a wide range of specialised areas such as: community; criminal justice system; prison; court diversion; high, medium and low security settings.

There are also the 'hidden horrors' which must also be part of education processes. The issues of normal expectations and attitudes towards the MDO need to be addressed. The normal or public opinion belief in us may wish to see patients who have committed horrendous crimes incarcerated for life. However, the nursing and caring component requires us to assist in preparation towards discharge and optimum well-being. Coping with index offences is an issue which receives no attention in nurse training, and can result in the stressful conditions outlined earlier. It is here that a fine line is drawn towards the optimum balance between security and therapy.

Allegations, no matter how trivial, have been one source of stress. Coupled with media exposure, it now appears to many that patient rights have gone too far, resulting in fewer rights for staff. The move towards empowering of patient rights is a major factor in complaints and in the perceived staff disempowerment which have played an important role with personality disordered patients in Fallon's Ashworth Hospital enquiry. So how do we prepare for these and other issues such as the continuing threat of danger, victim reprisal, survival skills and moral dilemmas? Well, the answer is short, we do not. We have developed coping mechanisms and experience, but much remains to be done in teasing out these subtle components that make nursing the MDO a considerable advance from traditional mental health nursing.

DEVELOPING A SPECIALIST BODY

The representation of a specialism in nursing, such as a Registered Nurse for the Mentally Disordered Offender, requires the support of a specialist organisation to support and promote it. Whilst there are subgroups and specialist groups at, for example, the Royal College of Nursing and Forensic Psychiatric Nurses Association, these have had little impact on role recognition and development. Although there is a proliferation of seminars, conferences and courses, little has been done to recognise the speciality in its own right. A specialist body needs to encompass and expand its membership with clear identities and establishing appropriate credentials. Such bodies should pay less attention to the political agendas, ensuring a representative contribution to the future direction. These should not limit themselves nationally but should liaise closely with international developments.

Such bodies, whilst specialising in role identification and future development, need to ensure that role recognition is achieved not only within the nursing profession but also with the media and public. The lack of prestige and the frequent humiliation which working with MDOs brings through allegations and inquiries needs careful publicity which ensures forensic services are recognised for the demanding role they play. The hidden horrors associated with public perceptions of nurses working with MDOs often goes little way towards recognising the difficult yet largely unrecognised role they fulfil ensuring the patient's health is maintained and promoted whilst ensuring public safety is not compromised.

ACKNOWLEDGEMENTS

The authors would like to acknowledge the participants of the forensic nursing workshop held at the 1999 International Forensic Mental Health Conference, Melbourne, Australia.

Patients' Charter for the State Hospital

COMING INTO THE STATE HOSPITAL

If you need the special facilities of the State Hospital you will be admitted promptly – within one week of our team seeing you.

When you are admitted:

- A doctor will carry out a full medical examination within 24 hours.
- You will be allocated a trained nurse to have special responsibility for you.
- Your nurse will explain the State Hospital's facilities to you.
- You will undergo a detailed assessment of your illness. This will usually take place within 10 weeks of your arrival.
- The results of this will be explained to you.
- If you wish, you can have a relative or a friend with you while this is done.
- If you wish, we will also inform any close relation or friends you specify who will receive written information about the Hospital and your rights.

YOUR CARE IN THE STATE HOSPITAL

During your stay in the State Hospital:

- You will be treated as an individual with respect and dignity.
- You will be involved in planning your treatment.
- You will be given choices whenever possible.
- You will be given clear, understandable explanations.
- You will have the right of access to your personal health records (within certain safeguards in exceptional circumstances).
- All the details of your illness will be kept confidential.
- You can take part in a wide range of activities around the hospital.
- You will have access to an advocacy service.
- We will guarantee privacy for all patients with:

    – private bedrooms;
    – private toilet facilities;
    – private washing facilities.

PLANNING YOUR TREATMENT

To plan for your illness and the problems it causes:

- You will be allocated a consultant psychiatrist who will direct your treatment.
- You will be allocated a care team of support professionals – nurses, psychologists, social workers and other therapists.
- They will produce a treatment plan for you.
- Your care and treatment plan will be reviewed by your care team at least every six months.
- The treatment plan and its review will be discussed with you.
- If you wish, you can have a relative or friend with you while this is done.
- If you wish, any close relation or friend will be informed.
- Your care will be reviewed annually by the independent medical subcommittee.

SECURITY

Because of your illness, you need treatment in secure surroundings. The level of security which applies aims to:

- Protect you from other patients.
- Ensure you do not harm yourself or others.

You can, of course, have personal effects but:

- Some everyday items may be kept from you to avoid injury.
- It may be necessary to search your room.
- It may be necessary for you to be searched.

Although we have high security facilities, we aim to provide:

- A clean, warm and relaxing environment.
- A friendly, welcoming staff.

LEAVING THE STATE HOSPITAL

You will not remain as a patient in the State Hospital any longer than necessary. Most of our patients go on to a local hospital when they leave here. When you no longer need our special security:

- The hospital managers will approve your transfer without delay.
- Where necessary we seek the Secretary of State's approval for your transfer.
- We will arrange your transfer to a more suitable hospital or form of care.
- This will be as near as possible to your home care.
- The transfer will be as smooth as possible.
- We will not do anything to delay the transfer.

VISITORS

Like any other hospital you may have people come to visit:

- Because of your illness the team in charge of your care has to approve who can visit you, but:
    - the team will not refuse any visits unless absolutely necessary; and
    - if they do, the reason will be explained to you.
- Visiting times are 2 pm to 4 pm every day.
- Because people come to visit from all over Scotland and Northern Ireland we can arrange other times to suit on request (a phone call will do).
- We can provide help with transport.
- We can help with overnight accommodation.
- We can help with costs.
- Ask your social worker for details.

References

Addo, M. (1997) *Clinical Supervision: 'We don't want to stand alone'. Views from the front-line.* Unpublished MEd. Thesis. Available at the Queen Mother Library, University of Aberdeen.

Aggleton, P. and Chalmers, H. (1986) *Nursing Models and the Nursing Process.* Basingstoke: Macmillan Education.

Alexander, D.A. (1997) *Health in the Workplace Survey.* Grampian Healthcare NHS Trust: Department of Mental Health, University of Aberdeen.

Allan, G. (1989) *Friendship: Developing a Sociological Perspective.* Hertfordshire: Harvester Wheatsheaf.

American Nurses Association (ANA) (1980) *A Social Policy Statement.* Kansas City: ANA.

American Nurses Association (ANA) (1994) *A Statement on Psychiatric-Mental Health Clinical Practice and Standards of Psychiatric-Mental Health Clinical Nursing Practice.* Washington, DC: AMA.

American Nurses Association (ANA) (1995) *Scope and Standards of Nursing Practice in Correctional Facilities.* Washington, DC: ANA.

American Nurses Association (ANA) and the International Association of Forensic Nurses (IAFN) (1997) *Scope and Standards of Forensic Nursing Practice.* Washington, DC: ANA.

ANCI (1995) *ANRAC National Competency Standards for the Registered Nurse (2nd ed.)* Dickson, ACT: Australian Nursing Council Inc.

Andrews, D.A., Bonta, J. and Hoge, R.D. (1990) Classification for effective rehabilitation. *Criminal Justice and Behaviour 17*, 19–52.

Anonymous (1988) The nursing role in multiple personality disorder. *Professional Nurse 4*, 2, 58, 60, Nov.

Applegate, B.K., Cullen, F.T. and Fisher, B.S. (1997) Public support for correctional treatment: the continuing appeal of the rehabilitative ideal. *Prison Journal 77*, 3, 237–258.

Appleyard, J. and Maden, J.G. (1979) Multi-disciplinary teams. *British Medical Journal 2*, 6200, 1305–1307.

Arnetz, J., Arnetz, B. and Petterson, I. (1996) Violence in the nursing profession: occupational and lifestyle risk factors in Swedish nurses. *Work and Stress 10*, 2, 119–127.

Asher, R. (1972) The dangers of going to bed. In F. Avery Jones (ed.) *Richard Asher Talking Sense.* London: Pitman Medical.

Astrom, S., Nilsson, M., Norberg, A., Sandman, P. and Winblad, B. (1991) Staff burnout in dementia care: relations to empathy and attitudes. *International Journal of Nursing Studies 28*, 1, 65–75.

Atkinson, J. (1991) Autonomy and mental health. In P. Barker and S. Baldwin (eds) *Ethical Issues in Mental Health.* London: Churchill Livingstone.

Audit Commission (1991) *The Virtue of the Patient: Making the Best Use of Ward Nursing Resources.* London: HMSO.

Austin, W., Gallop, R., Harris, D. and Spencer, E. (1996) A 'domains of practice' approach to the standards of psychiatric and mental health nursing. *Journal of Psychiatric and Mental Health Nursing 3*, 111–115.

Australian and New Zealand College of Mental Health Nurses (1995) *Standards of Practice for Mental Health Nursing in Australia.* Greenacres, NSW: ANZCMHN.

Backer-Holst, T. (1994) A new window of opportunity: the implications of the Reed report for psychiatric care. *Psychiatric Care 1*, 1, 15–18.

Badger, D., Nursten, J., Williams, P. and Woodward, M. (1998) *Systematic Review of the International Literature of the Epidemiology of Mentally Disordered Offenders: Interim Report.* Reading: University of Reading Department of Community Studies.

Bailey, D. (1996) Services for mentally disordered offenders: a literature review. *Social Services Research 3,* 31–57.

Bamber, M. (1992) Reasons for leaving among psychiatric nurses: a two year prospective survey. *Nursing Practice 4,* 4, 9–11.

Banerjee, S., Exworthy, T., O'Neill-Byrne, K. and Parrott, J. (1992) An integrated service for mentally disordered offenders. *Psychiatric Bulletin 16,* 773–775.

Banks, M., Clegg, C., Jackson, P., Kemp, N., Stafford, E. and Wall, T. (1980) The use of the General Health Questionnaire as an indicator of mental health in occupational studies. *Journal of Occupational Psychology 53,* 187–194.

Barclay, W. (1997) *Discussion Paper: A Study of Corrections Mental Health Services in New South Wales.* Sydney: Corrections Health Service.

Barham, P. and Hayward, R. (1995) *Relocating Madness: From Mental Patient to the Person.* London: Free Association Books.

Barnett, D.E. (1981) Do nurses read? Nurse managers and nursing research report. *Nursing Times 77,* 50, 2131–2134.

Barton, S. (1995) Investigating forensic nursing. *The Kansas Nurse 70,* 34.

Beauchamp, T.L. and Childress, J.F. (1994) *Principles of Biomedical Ethics.* New York: Oxford University Press.

Belknapp, J. (1996) *The Invisible Woman: Gender, Crime and Justice.* Belmont, CA: Wadsworth.

Benner, P. (1984) *From Novice to Expert: Excellence and Power in Clinical Nursing Practice.* California: Addison Wesley.

Berkely, M. (1995) *People with Mental Health Problems Arrested in Oxford: A Review of Needs for Services.* Oxford: The Elmore Committee.

Berkowitz, G., Brindis, C., Clayson, Z. and Peterson, S. (1996) Options for recovery: promoting success among women mandated to treatment. *Journal of Psychoactive Drugs 28,* 1, 31–38.

Berlin, F.S. and Malin, H.M. (1991) Media distortion of the public's perception of recidivism and psychiatric rehabilitation. *American Journal of Psychiatry 148,* 11, 1572–1576.

Bernardoni, M.M. (1997) Academic partnerships prepare health care professionals for correctional careers. *CorrectCare 11,* 1, 1–8.

Bion, W. (1970) Container and Contained. In W. Bion (ed.) *Attention and Interpretation.* London: Maresfield Reprints.

Bjorkly, S. (1995) Open-area seclusion in the long-term treatment of aggressive and disruptive psychotic patients, an introduction to a ward procedure. *Psychological Reports 76,* 147–157.

Blackburn, R. (1993) *Psychology and Criminal Conduct.* Chichester: Wiley.

Blackburn, R. (1995) Personal communication.

Blackburn, R. (1996) Mentally disordered offenders. In C.R. Hollins (ed.) *Working With Offenders.* Chichester: Wiley.

Blackburn, R., Crellin, M.C., Morgan, E.M. and Tulloch, R.M.B. (1990) Prevalence of personality disorders in a special hospital population. *Journal of Forensic Psychiatry 1,* 43–52.

Blom-Cooper, L. (1995) The criminal lunatic asylum system before and after Broadmoor. *Clio Medica 34,* 151–162.

Bluglass, R. (1997) *Review of Forensic Mental Health Services, New South Wales.* Matraville, NSW: Corrections Health Service.

Blumstein, A. (1995) 'Youth, violence, guns and the illicit gun industry.' *Journal of Criminal Law and Criminology 86,* 1, 222–232.

Borrill, C., Wall, T., West, M., Hardy, G., Shapiro, D., Carter, A., Golya, D. and Haynes, C. (1996) *Mental Health of the Workforce in NHS Trusts.* Sheffield: Institute of Work Psychology, University of Sheffield.

Bowling, A. (1995) *Measuring Disease.* Buckingham: Open University Press.

Brewin, C.R., Wing, J.K., Mangen, S.P., Brugha, T.S. and MacCarthy, B. (1987) Principles and practice of measuring needs in the long-term mentally ill: the MRC Needs for Care Assessment. *Psychological Medicine 17*, 971–982.

Brooker, C. and White, E. (1997) *The Fourth Quinquennial National Community Mental Health Nursing Census of England and Wales: Final Report.* London: Department of Health.

Brooking, J., Ritter, S.A. and Thomas, B.L. (1992) *A Textbook of Psychiatric and Mental Health Nursing.* Edinburgh: Churchill Livingstone.

Brown, D. (1997) *Stress, Coping and Burnout in Nurses Working in Inner London Acute Psychiatric Wards.* Unpublished D.Clin.Psych Thesis, Institute of Psychiatry, King's College, London.

Brown, D. and Leary, J. (1995) Findings from the Claybury Study for community psychiatric nurses. In J. Carson, L. Fagin and S. Ritter (eds) *Stress and Coping in Mental Health Nursing.* London: Chapman and Hall.

Buber, M. (1987) *I and Thou.* Edinburgh: T. and T. Clark.

Buchan, J. (1995) Counting the cost of stress in nursing. *Nursing Standard 9*, 16, 30.

Bureau of Statistics (1999) Federal Justice Statistics Programme 1996. CD-ROM (document No. NCJ174436). Rockville, MD: NCJRS.

Burrow, S. (1991) The special hospital nurse and the dilemma of therapeutic custody. *Journal of Advances in Nursing and Health Care 1*, 3, 21–38.

Burrow S. (1993a) An outline of the forensic nursing role. *The British Journal of Nursing 2*, 18, 899–904.

Burrow, S. (1993b) The role conflict of the forensic nurse ... facilitating the health-management of the mentally abnormal offender. *Senior Nurse 13*, 5, 20–25.

Butterworth, C.A. (1994) *A Delphi Survey of Optimum Practice in Nursing, Midwifery and Health Visiting.* Manchester: Manchester University.

Butterworth, C.A. and Faugier, J. (1992) The supervisory relationship. In C.A. Butterworth and T.J. Butterworth (eds) *Clinical Supervision and Mentorship in Nursing.* London: Chapman and Hall.

Butterworth, C.A. and Faugier, J. (1993) *Clinical Supervision and Mentorship in Nursing.* London: Chapman and Hall.

Butterworth, T., Bishop, V. and Carson, J. (1996) First steps towards evaluating clinical supervision in nursing and health visiting. Part one: Theory, policy and practice development. A review. *Journal of Clinical Nursing 5*, 1, 25–35.

Butterworth, T., Carson, J., White, E., Jeacock, J., Clements, A. and Bishop, V. (1997) *It is Good to Talk: An Evaluation of Clinical Supervision and Mentorship in England and Scotland.* Manchester: University of Manchester.

Byrne, C., Kirkpatrick, H., Woodside, H., Landeen, J., Bernardo, A. and Pawlick, J. (1994) The importance of relationships in fostering hope. *Journal of Psychosocial Nursing and Mental Health Service 32*, 9, 31–34, September.

Cahn, L.A. (1970) *MEDEMBLIK een episode uit de Nederlandse psychiatrie 1884–1967.* Meijer Wormerveer n.v.

Camp, F. (1976) *Gradwold's Legal Medicine (3rd ed).* Chicago: Year Book Medical Publications.

Campbell, A.V. (1972) *Moral Dilemmas in Medicine: A Coursebook in Ethics for Doctors and Nurses.* Edinburgh: Churchill Livingstone.

Canadian Federation of Mental Health Nurses (1998) *Canadian Standards of Psychiatric and Mental Health Nursing Practice (2nd ed).* Ottawa: Canadian Federation of Mental Health Nurses.

Canadian Nurses' Association (CNA) (1986) *CNA's Certification Programme: An Information Booklet.* Ottawa: Canadian Nurses' Association.

Canadian Nurses' Association (CNA) (1991) *Mental Health Care Reform: A Priority for Nurses.* Ottawa: Canadian Nurses' Association.

Canadian Nurses' Association (CNA) (1995) *Certification Programme Candidate Information: Psychiatric/Mental Health Nursing.* Ottawa: Canadian Nurses' Association.

Canadian Nurses' Association (CNA) (1997) *National Nursing Competency Project, Final Report.* Ottawa: Canadian Nurses' Association.

Caplan, C. (1993) Nursing staff and patient perception of the ward atmosphere in a maximum security setting. *Archives of Psychiatric Nursing 7*, 23–29.

Carkhuff, R.R. (1969) *Helping and Human Relations: Primer for Lay and Professional Helpers.* Vol. 2. New York: Holt, Rinehart and Winston.

Carlise, C., Kirk, S. and Luker, K.A. (1996) The changes in the role for the nurse teacher following the formation of links with higher education. *Journal of Advanced Nursing 24*, 4, 762–770.

Carmel, H. and Hunter, M. (1989) Staff injuries from inpatient violence. *Hospital and Community Psychiatry 40*, 41–45.

Carr, W. and Kemmis, S. (1986) *Becoming Critical: Education, Knowledge and Action Research.* London: Palmer.

Carson, J., Bartlett, H. and Croucher, P. (1991) Stress in community psychiatric nurses: a preliminary investigation. *Community Psychiatric Nursing Journal 11*, 2, 8–12.

Carson, J., Fagin, L. and Ritter, S. (eds) (1995a) *Stress and Coping in Mental Health Nursing.* London: Chapman and Hall.

Carson, J., Bartlett, H., Brown, D. and Hopkinson, P. (1995b) Findings from the qualitative measures for CPNs. In J. Carson, L. Fagin and S. Ritter (eds) *Stress and Coping in Mental Health Nursing.* London: Chapman and Hall.

Carson, J., Fagin, L., Brown, D., Leary, J. and Bartlett, H. (1997) Self-esteem in mental health nurses: its relationship to stress, coping and burnout. *NT Research 2*, 5, 1–9.

Carson, J. and Kuipers, E. (1998) Stress management interventions. In S. Hardy, J. Carson and B. Thomas (eds) *Occupational Stress: Personal and Professional Approaches.* Cheltenham: Stanley Thornes.

Carson, J., Kuipers, E. and Gournay, K. (1999) Stress in mental health nurses: an updated review. *Psychiatric Care* (in press).

Carter, T.M. (1998) The effects of spiritual practices on recovery from substance abuse. *Journal of Psychiatric and Mental Health Nursing 5*, 409–413.

Chalke, F.R.C., Roberts, C.A. and Turner, R.E. (1995) Forensic psychiatry in Canada, 1945 to 1980. *Canadian Journal of Psychiatry 40*, 3, 120–124.

Chalke, R. (1972) *The General Program for the Development of Psychiatric Services in Federal Correctional Services in Canada.* Ottawa: Solicitor General of Canada.

Chambers, M. and Long, A. (1995) Supportive clinical supervision: a crucible for personal and professional change. *Journal of Psychiatric and Mental Health Nursing 2*, 311–316.

Chan, P. (1998) Paternalistic interventions in mental health care. *Nursing Times 94*, 36, 52–53.

Chandley, M. and Mason, T. (1995) Nursing chronically dangerous patients: ethical issues of behaviour management and patient health. *Psychiatric Care 2*, 1, 20–23.

Chiarella, M. (1990) Developing the credibility of continuing education. *Nurse Today 10*, 70–73.

Chiasson, M. (1997) The Regional Psychiatric Centre's transition to programme management. *Let's Talk 22*, 5, 15–17.

Chiswick, D. (1993) Forensic psychiatry. In R.E. Kendall and A.K. Zealley (eds) *Companion to Psychiatric Studies.* Edinburgh: Churchill Livingstone.

Christman, L. (1995) Science as the predictor of professional recognition and success. In A. Omery, C.E. Kasper and G.G. Page (eds) *In Search of Nursing Science.* Thousand Oaks, CA: Sage.

Clare, A. (1980) *Psychiatry in Dissent.* London: Routledge.

Clarke, L. (1996) Participant observation in a secure unit: care, conflict and control. *Nursing Times Research 1*, 6, 431–441.

Clothier, C., MacDonald, C.A. and Shaw, D.A. (1994) *The Allitt Enquiry.* London: HMSO.

Cohen, P. (1993) Safe inside. *Nursing Times 89*, 19.

Cohen, S., Kamarck, T. and Mermelstein, R. (1983) The Perceived Stress Scale. *Journal of Health and Social Behaviour 24*, 385–396.

Cohen, S. and Williamson, G. (1988) Perceived stress in a probability sample of the United States. In S. Spacapan and S. Oskamp (eds) *The Social Psychology of Health.* Newbury Park, California: Sage.

Conacher, G.N. (1993) Issues in psychiatric care within a prison service. *Canada's Mental Health 3*, 11–14.

Conacher, G.N. (1996) *Management of the Mentally Disordered Offender in Prisons.* Montreal and Kingston: McGill-Queens University Press.

Conroy, M.A. (1990) Mental health treatment in the federal prison system: an outcome study. *Federal Probation 54*, 44–47.

Cook, I. (1991) Spraining the trap. *Nursing Times 87*, 16–17.

Cooper, C., Sloan, S. and Williams, S. (1988) *Occupational Stress Indicator Management Guide.* Windsor: NFER-Nelson.

Coram, J. (1993) Forensic nurse specialists: working with perpetrators and hostage negotiation teams. *Journal of Psychosocial Nursing and Mental Health 31*, 11, 26–30.

Cordess, C. (1996) The multidisciplinary team – (1) Introduction, (2) The psychiatrist. In C. Cordess and M. Cox (eds) *Forensic Psychotherapy: Crime, Psychodynamics and the Offender Patient.* London: Jessica Kingsley Publishers.

Cordess, C. (1998) The offender. In D. Tantam (ed.) *Clinical Topics in Psychotherapy.* London: Gaskell.

Corrections Health Service (1998) *Corrections Health Service, New South Wales: Annual Report 1996/97.* Sydney: Focus Press.

Corrections Health Service (1999) *Corrections Health Service, New South Wales: Annual Report 1997/98.* Sydney: Corrections Health Service.

Cox, M. (1996) Postscript to 'The impact of the first forensic encounter – a trainee's view' by Ann Stanley. In C. Cordess and M. Cox (eds) *Forensic Psychotherapy: Crime, Psychodynamics and the Offender Patient.* London: Jessica Kingsley Publishers.

Crabbe, G. (1988) Care or control. *Nursing Times 84*, 28, 19.

Crawford, C.A. (1994) Health care needs in corrections: NIJ responds. *National Institute of Justice Journal 228*, 31–38.

Critchley, D.L. (1987) Clinical supervision as a learning tool for the therapist in milieu settings. *Journal of Psychosocial Nursing 25*, 8, 18–21.

Cunningham, D. (1990) Needs assessment. In E.J. Beck and S.A. Adams (eds) *The White Paper and Beyond.* Oxford: Oxford University Press.

Cushway, D., Tyler, P. and Nolan, P. (1996) Development of a stress scale for mental health professionals. *British Journal of Clinical Psychology 35*, 2, 279–295.

Dale, C. (1995) Changing the nursing culture in special hospitals. *Nursing Times 91*, 30, 33–35.

Davis, S. (1992) Assessing the 'criminalisation' of the mentally ill in Canada. *Canadian Journal of Psychiatry 37*, 532–538.

Dawkins, J., Depp, F. and Selzer, N. (1985) Stress and the psychiatric nurse. *Journal of Psychosocial Nursing 23*, 11, 9–15.

Day, R. (1983) The challenge: health care versus security. *The Canadian Nurse 79*, 7, 34–36.

Deegan, P. (1996) Recovery as a journey of the heart. *Psychiatric Rehabilitation Journal 19*, 3, 91–97.

Department of Health (DoH) (1989) *Working for Patients.* London: HMSO.

Department of Health (DoH) (1993a) *A Vision for the Future: The Nursing, Midwifery and Health Visiting Contributions to Health and Health Care.* London: National Health Services Management Executive/HMSO.

Department of Health (DoH) (1993b) *The Discharge of Mentally Disordered People and Their Continuing Care in the Community.* London: HMSO.

Department of Health (DoH) (1994) *The Report of the Inquiry into the Care and Treatment of Christopher Clunis.* London: HMSO.

Department of Health (DoH) (1997) *White Paper – The New NHS.* London: HMSO.

Department of Health (DoH) (1998) *Modernising Mental Health Services.* London: HMSO.

Department of Health ((1999) *The Report of the Committee of the Inquiry into the Personality Disorder Unit (PDU), Ashworth Inquiry.* London: Stationery Office.

Department of Health (DoH) and Home Office (HO) (1991) *Review of Health and Social Services for Mentally Disordered Offenders and Others Requiring Similar Services.* London: HMSO.

Department of Health (DoH) and Home Office (HO) (1992) *Review of Health and Social Services for Mentally Disordered Offenders and Others requiring Similar Services, Final Summary Report Cm 2088.* London: HMSO.

Department of Health (DoH) Mental Health Review Team (1994) *Working in Partnership: A Collaborative Approach to Care.* London: HMSO.

Derlega, V.J. and Winstead, B.A. (1984) *Friendship and Social Interaction.* New York: Springer-Verlag.

Dhondea, R. (1995) An ethnographic study of nursing in a forensic psychiatric setting. *Australian and New Zealand Journal of Mental Health Nursing 4,* 77–82.

Dolan, B. and Coid, J. (1993) *Psychopathic and Antisocial Personality Disorders. Treatment and Research Issues.* London: Gaskell.

Dönisch-Seidel, U. (1998a) Prognosen im Maßregelvollzug. In Th. Fabian *et al.* (eds) *Rechtspychologie kontrovers.* Bonn: Deutscher Psychologen Verlag GmbH.

Dönisch-Seidel, U. (1998b) Integration neuer Methoden in die Behandlung von Sexualdelinquenten. *Forensische Psychiatrie und Psychotherapie-Werkstattschriften 5,* 1, 203–208.

Downie, R.S. (1990) Professions and professionalism. *Journal of the Philosophy of Education 24,* 2, 147–159.

Downie, R.S. and Calman, K.C. (1994) *Healthy Respect: Ethics in Health Care.* Oxford: Oxford University Press.

Doyle, M. (1996) Assessing risk of violence from clients. *Mental Health Nursing 16,* 3, 20–23.

Dvoskin, J.A. and Broaddus, R. (1993) Creating a mental health care model. *Corrections Today 55,* 7, 114–119.

Dvoskin, J.A. and Steadman, H.J. (1989) Chronically mentally ill inmates: the wrong concept for the right services. *International Journal of Law and Psychiatry 12,* 203–210.

Dyson, J., Cobb, M. and Forman, D. (1997) The meaning of spirituality: a literature review. *Journal of Advanced Nursing 26,* 1183–1188.

Eckert, W.G. (1997) *Introduction to Forensic Sciences (2nd ed).* New York: CRC Press. 4, 237.

Emblen, J.D. and Halstead, L. (1993) Spiritual needs and interventions: comparing the views of patients, nurses and chaplains. *Clinical Nurse Specialist 7,* 175–182.

Engel, C. (1994) A functional anatomy of team work. In A. Leathard (ed.) *Going Inter-Professional.* London: Routledge.

English National Board (ENB) (1994) *Life-Long Learners: Partnership for Care.* London: ENB.

Erven, A.C.J.M. van (1992) *SGA-PATIËNTEN. De psychiatrie van een dilemma.* Utrecht: Proefschrift Rijksuniversiteit Utrecht.

Estroff, S.E. (1989) Self, identity, and subjective experiences of schizophrenia: in search of the subject. *Schizophrenia Bulletin 15,* 2, 189–196.

Evans, C.S. (1979) *Preserving the Person: A Look at the Human Sciences.* Illinois: Inter Varsity Press.

Evans, A. and Wells, D. (1999) *An Exploration of the Role of the Australian Forensic Nurse.* Report presented to the Royal College of Nursing, Australia, June.

Fagin, L. and Bartlett, H. (1995) The Claybury CPN Stress Survey: background and methodology. In J. Carson, L. Fagin and S. Ritter (eds) *Stress and Coping in Mental Health Nursing.* London: Chapman and Hall.

Fagin, L., Brown, D., Bartlett, H., Leary, J. and Carson, J. (1995) The Claybury CPN Stress Study: is it more stressful to work in hospital or the community? *Journal of Advanced Nursing 22,* 1–12.

Fagin, L., Carson, J., Leary, J., DeVilliers, N., Bartlett, H., O'Malley, P., West, M., McElfatrick, S. and Brown, D. (1996) Stress, coping and burnout in mental health nurses: findings from three research studies. *The International Journal of Nursing Studies 42,* 2, 102–111.

Fallon, P., Blueglass, R., Edwards, B. and Daniels, G. (1999) *The Report of the Committee of Inquiry into The Personality Disorder Unit, Ashworth Special Hospital.* Cm 4194–11. London: The Stationery Office.

Farrington, A. (1995) Stress and nursing. *British Journal of Nursing 4,* 10, 574–578.

Fawcett, J. (1989) *Analysis and Evaluation of Conceptual Models of Nursing (2nd ed)*. Philadelphia: F.A. Davis.

Fielding, J. and Weaver, S. (1994) A comparison of hospital and community based mental health nurses: perceptions of their work environment and psychological health. *Journal of Advanced Nursing 19*, 1196–1204.

Fisher, R. (1995) The ethical problems encountered in psychiatric nursing practice with dangerous mentally ill patients. *Scholarly Inquiry for Nursing Practice 9*, 2, 193–208.

Fitchett, G., Burton, L.A. and Sivan, A.B. (1997) The religious needs and resources of psychiatric inpatients. *The Journal of Nervous and Mental Disease 185*, 5, 320–326.

Flannery, R. (1996) Violence in the workplace 1970–1995: a review of the literature. *Aggression and Violent Behaviour 1*, 1, 57–68.

Fowler, J. (1995) Nurses' perception of the elements of good supervision. *Nursing Times 91*, 22, 33–37.

Fowler, J. (1996a) Education and debate. Clinical supervision: what to do after saying hello? *British Journal of Nursing 5*, 6, 382–385.

Fowler, J. (1996b) The organisation of clinical supervision within the nursing profession within the UK. *Journal of Advanced Nursing 23*, 471–478.

Frankl, V.E. (1964) *Man's Search for Meaning: From Death Camp to Existentialism*. Boston: Beacon Press.

Fraser, L. (1994) Correctional service of Canada nurses: a special breed. *Let's talk 8*, 6, 20–21.

Freeman, R. (1996) *How to Become a Nursing Development Unit: A Guide*. London: Kings Fund.

Freudenberg, N., Wilets, I., Greene, M.B. and Richie, B.E. (1998) Linking women in jail to community services: factors associated with re-arrest and retention of drug-using women following release from jail. *Journal of the American Medical Women's Association 53*, 2, 89–93.

Freudenberger, H.J. (1974) Staff burnout. *Journal of Social Issues 30*, 159–165.

Friedman, L.N. (1994) Adopting the health care model to prevent victimization. *National Institute of Justice Journal 228*, 16–19.

Friend, B. (1991) View from the top. *Nursing Times 8*, 87, 24–25.

Fristch, H. and Strohlein, G. (1988) Mentor support and academic achievement. *Open Learning*, June, 27–32.

Frith, C.D. (1992) *The Cognitive Neuropsychology of Schizophrenia*. Hillsdale NJ: Lawrence Erlbaum.

Gallop, R. (1993) Sexual contact between nurses and patients. *The Canadian Nurse 89*, 2, 28–31.

Gallop, R. (1996) Vision 2001: innovation and collaboration. *Canadian Federation of Mental Health Nurses Newsletter 18*, 4–12.

Gartner, J., Larson, D.B. and Allen, G.D. (1991) Religious commitment and mental health: a review of the empirical literature. *Journal of Psychology and Theology 19*, 1, 6–25.

Gilligan, C. (1982) *In a Different Voice: Psychological Theory and Women's Development*. Cambridge, MA: Harvard University Press.

Gillon, R. (1986) *Philosophical Medical Ethics*. Chichester: Wiley.

Glen, S. (1996) *Views of Nursing: Stages of Professional Competence*. Unpublished paper presented at University of Brighton Conference, October 7–8, 'Advancing Nursing Practice Through Knowledge and Beliefs'.

Goering, P. (1993) Psychiatric nursing and the context of care. In L. Chafetz (ed.) *A Nursing Perspective on Severe Mental Illness*. San Francisco: Jossey Bass Publishers.

Goffman, E. (1961) *Asylums*. London: Penguin.

Goffman, E. (1991) *Asylums*. London: Penguin.

Goldberg, D. and Williams, S. (1988) *A User's Guide to the General Health Questionnaire*. Windsor: NFER-Nelson.

Goodman, D., Pensinger, T. and Shine, B. (1993) Agencies improve mental health services in jails. *SAMHSA News 1*, 2, 1–3.

Goudswaard, N.B. (1994) *Inleidung tot de Geschiedenis van de Verpleegkunst*. Rotterdam: Erasmus Publishing.

Gournay, K. and Carson, J. (1997) *Stress in Mental Health Professionals and Its Implications for Staff Working with Forensic Populations: Review, Critique and Suggestions for Future Research.* London: Section of Psychiatric Nursing, Institute of Psychiatry, King's College, London.

Green, C.M., Menzies, R.P.D. and Naismith, L.J. (1991) Psychiatry in the Canadian correctional service. *Canadian Journal of Psychiatry 36*, 290–295.

Greenhalgh, T. and Hurwitz, B. (1999) Why narrative? *British Medical Journal 318*, 48–50.

Grounds, A. (1996) Forensic psychiatry for the millennium. *The Journal of Forensic Psychiatry 7*, 2, 221–227.

Gunn, J. (1986) Education and forensic psychiatry. *Canadian Journal of Psychiatry 31*, 273–281.

Gunn, J. and Taylor, P. (1983) Rehabilitation of the Mentally Abnormal Offender. In F. Watts and D. Bennet (eds) *Theory and Practice of Psychiatric Rehabilitation.* Chichester: Wiley.

Gunn, J. and Taylor, P. (eds) (1993) *Forensic Psychiatry: Clinical, Legal and Ethical Issues.* Oxford: Butterworth-Heinemann.

Gurdin, B.J. (1986) The therapy of friendship. *Small Group Behaviour 19*, 4, November, 444–457.

Guy, M.E. (1986) Interdisciplinary conflict and organisational complexity. *Hospital Health Service Administration 31*, 1, 111–121.

Hallberg, I. and Norberg, A. (1993) Strain among nurses and their emotional reactions during one year of systematic clinical supervision combined with the implementation of individualised care in dementia nursing. *Journal of Advanced Nursing 18*, 1860–1875.

Handy, C. (1995) *The Empty Raincoat – Making Sense of the Future.* London: Arrow Business Books.

Handy, J. (1990) *Occupational Stress in a Caring Profession: The Social Context of Psychiatric Nursing.* Aldershot: Avebury.

Harrell, A., Cook, F. and Carver, J. (1998) Breaking the cycle of drug abuse in Birmingham. *National Institute of Justice Journal 236*, 9–13.

Harrington, A. (1995) Spiritual care: what does it mean to RNs? *Australian Journal of Advanced Nursing 12*, 4, 5–14.

Harris, P.E. (1989) The nurse stress index. *Work and Stress 3*, 4, 335–346.

Hatling, T. and Krogen, T. (1998) *The Use of Forced Treatment in Norwegian Psychiatry – An Empirical Thoroughfare, Report STF78 F98506.* Norway: SINTEF Norwegian Institute of Hospital Research.

Hauerwas, S. (1981) *A Community of Character.* Indiana: University of Notre Dame Press.

Hawkins, P. and Shohet, R. (1989) *Supervision in the Helping Professions.* Milton Keynes: Open University Press.

Hawkins, P. and Shohet, R. (1991) *Supervision in the Helping Professions.* Milton Keynes: Open University Press.

Hawkins, P. and Shohet, R. (1993) *Supervision in the Helping Professions.* Milton Keynes: Open University Press.

Health and Welfare Canada (1988) *Mental Health for Canadians: Striking a Balance.* Ottawa: Minister of Supply and Services.

Health Canada (1995) *The Mentally Ill and the Criminal Justice System: Innovative Community-Based Programmes 1995.* Ottawa: Minister of Supply and Services.

Hearn, J. (1982) Notes on patriarchy, professionalism and semi-professionalism. *Sociology 16*, 2, 184–202.

Heron, J. (1977) *Catharsis in Human Development. Human Potential Research Project.* Surrey: Department of Adult Education, University of Surrey.

Heron, J. (1986) *Six Category Intervention Analysis. Human Potential Research Project (2nd ed).* Surrey: University of Surrey.

Hibbs, P. (1989) Targets for practice. *Nursing Standard 4*, 3, 24–25.

Hilkey, J.H. (1988) A theoretical model for assessment of delivery of mental health services in the correctional facility. *Psychiatric Annals 18*, 12, 676–679.

Hillis, G. (1993) Diverting tactics. *Nursing Times 89*, 1, 24–27.

Hinshelwood, R.D. (1996) Changing prisons. The unconscious dimension. In C. Cordess and M. Cox (eds) *Forensic Psychotherapy: Crime, Psychodynamics and the Offender Patient*. London: Jessica Kingsley Publishers.

Hinshelwood, R.D. (1999) The difficult patient. The role of 'scientific psychiatry' in understanding patients with chronic schizophrenia or severe personality disorder. *British Journal of Psychiatry 174*, 187–190.

Hopkins, N.J., Willett, K., Hayes, G. and Chelliah, A. (1997) *Matching Up to Good Practice in Risk Assessment*. Unpublished Audit Report, Wathwood Hospital RSU.

Hopkins, N.J., Willett, K., Hayes, G. and Chelliah, A. (1998) *Good Practice in Risk Assessment: Second Time Around*. Unpublished Audit Report, Wathwood Hospital RSU.

Høyer, G. and Drange, H. (1994) The evolution of using forced treatment in Norwegian psychiatric institutions. *Norwegian Journal of Medicine 111*, 1707–1713.

Hufft, A.G. and Fawkes, L.S. (1994) Federal inmates: A unique psychiatric nursing challenge. *Nursing Clinics of North America 29*, 1, 35–42.

Haffr, A.G. and Peternelj-Taylor, C. (in press) Forensic nursing. In J.T. Catalana (ed.) *Contemporary Professional Nursing*. Philadelphia: Davis.

Hunt, G.M. and Azrin, N.H. (1973) A community reinforcement approach to alcoholism. *Journal of Behaviour Research 2*, 91–104.

Hunt, M. (1983) Possibilities and problems of inter-disciplinary teamwork. In J. Clark and J. Henderson (eds) *Community Health*. London: Churchill Livingstone.

Hunter, R.J. (1986) *Dictionary of Pastoral Care and Counselling*. Nashville: Abingdon Press.

Hurst, K., Whyte, L. and Robinson, D. (1998) *Analysis of Nursing Activity within a High Secure Hospital*. Unpublished Report, Nuffield Institute for Health, University of Leeds.

Illich, I. (1985) *Limits to Medicine, Medical Nemesis: The Expropriation of Health*. London: Penguin.

Jackson, M. and Cawley, R. (1992) Psychodynamics and psychotherapy on an acute psychiatric ward: the story of an experimental unit. *British Journal of Psychiatry 160*, 41–50.

Jamelka, R., Trapin, E. and Chiles, J. (1989) The mentally ill in prisons: A review. *Hospital and Community Psychiatry 40*, 5, 481–491.

James, A. (1996) *Life on the Edge: Diversion and the Mentally Disordered Offender. Policy Report, Vol. 1.* London: The Mental Health Foundation.

Jamison, K.R. (1996) *An Unquiet Mind: A Memoir of Moods and Madness*. London: Picador.

Jaques, E. (1955) Social systems as a defense against persecutory and depressive anxiety. In M. Klein, P. Acimann and R.E. Money-Kyle (eds) *New Directions in Psychoanalysis*. London: Tavistock.

Jenkins, A. (1998) Invitations to responsibility. In Marshall, W.L. *et al.* (eds) *Sourcebook of Treatment Programmes for Sexual Offenders*. New York: Plenum Press.

Johnson, S.C. and Hoover, J.O. (1988) Mental health services within the federal bureau of prisons. *Psychiatric Annals 18*, 12, 673–674.

Jones, J. (1987) Stress in psychiatric nursing. In R. Payne and J. Firth-Cozens (eds) *Stress in Health Professionals*. Chichester: Wiley.

Jones, J.G., Janman, K., Payne, R.L. and Rick, J.T. (1987) Some determinants of stress in psychiatric nurses. *International Journal of Nursing Studies 24*, 2, 129–144.

Jones, M. (1952) *Social Psychiatry*. London: Tavistock.

Jordan, K., Schlenger, W.E., Fairbank, J.A. and Caddell, J.M. (1996) Prevalence of psychiatric disorders among incarcerated women. *Archives of General Psychiatry 53*, 513–519.

Jung, C. (1933) *Modern Man in Search of a Soul*. San Diego: Harcourt Brace.

Kassof, M. (1995) Prison mental health programme makes a difference. *Michigan Nurse 68*, 11, 13.

Kaye, C. and Franey, A. (eds) (1998) *Managing High Security Psychiatric Care*. London: Jessica Kingsley Publishers.

Kellnhausen, E. (1994) Primary nursing – Ein neues Pflegemodell. *Die Schwester/Der Pfleger 9*, 747–752.

Kelly, G. (1955) *The Psychology of Personal Constructs*. New York: Norton.

Kemph, J.P., Braley, R.O. and Ciotola, P.V. (1997) Description of an outpatient psychiatric population in a youthful offender's prison. *Journal of the American Academy of Psychiatry and the Law 25*, 2, 149–159.

Kennedy, N.M. and Ward, M. (1992) Training aspects of the Birmingham court diversion scheme. *Psychiatric Bulletin 16*, 630–631.

Kent-Wilkinson, A. (1993) After the crime, before the trial. *The Canadian Nurse 89*, 11, 23–26.

Kent-Wilkinson, A. (1996) Spouse abuse/homicide: a current issue in health risk management. *Journal of Psychosocial Nursing and Mental Health Services 34*, 10, 12–15.

Kent-Wilkinson, A. (1999) Forensic nursing issues: an international perspective through on-line education. Presentation at the World Police Medical Officers Association Meeting. Vancouver, BC.

Kershaw, B. (1985) Licence to practice. *Nursing Times 81*, 6, 46–47.

Kettles, A.M. and Robinson, D.K. (1998) The lost vision of nursing. *Psychiatric Care 5*, 4, 126–129.

Killian, M. and Clark, N. (1996) The multidisciplinary team – the nurse. In C. Cordess and M. Cox (eds) *Forensic Psychotherapy: Crime, Psychodynamics and the Offender Patient*. London: Jessica Kingsley Publishers.

King, I. (1971) *Towards a Theory of Nursing*. New York: Wiley.

Kinsella, C. and Chaloner, C. (1995) Attitudes to treatment and direction of interest in forensic mental health nurses: a comparison with nurses working in other specialities. *Journal of Psychiatric and Mental Health Nursing 2*, 351–357.

Kipping, C. (1998) Mental health nurses' strategies for coping with stress. *Mental Health Nursing 18*, 3, 18–22.

Kirby, S. and McGuire, N. (1997) Forensic psychiatric nursing. In B. Thomas, S. Hardy and P. Cutting (eds) *Stuart and Sundeen's Mental Health Nursing, Principles and Practice*. London: Mosby.

Kirby, S. and Pollock, P. (1995) The relationship between a medium secure environment and occupational stress in forensic psychiatric nurses. *Journal of Advanced Nursing 22*, 862–867.

Kirkpatrick, H., Landeen, J., Byrne, C., Woodside, H., Pawlick, J. and Bernardo, A. (1995) Hope and schizophrenia: clinicians identify hope-instilling strategies. *Journal of Psychosocial Nursing and Mental Health Service 33*, 15–19.

Kitchener, N. (1995) How effective is the new scheme for offenders? *Nursing Times 91*, 25, 11–12.

Kitchener, N. (1996) Forensic community mental health nurses and court diversion schemes. *Psychiatric Care 3*, 2, 65–69.

Kitchener, N. and Kidd, R. (1996) Nursing skills in the care of offenders. *Nursing Times 92*, 12, 13–14.

Kitchener, N. and Rogers, P. (1992) Gearing up to work in a secure unit. *Nursing Times 88*, 10 June, 24, 51.

Kitchener, N., Topping-Morris, B., Burnard, P. and Morrison, P. (1992a) The role of the forensic psychiatric nurse. *Nursing Times 88*, 8, 56.

Kitchener, N., Wright, I. and Topping-Morris, B. (1992b) The role of the forensic psychiatric nurse. *Nursing Times 91*, 25, 11–12.

Klein, M. (1960) *Self and Others: Object Relations Theory and Practice*. London: Tavistock and Routledge.

Kleive, L. (1996) Forensic psychiatric services in Norway. *The Journal of Forensic Psychiatry 1*, 170–176.

Koelbel, P., Fuller, F. and Misener, T. (1991) Job satisfaction of nurse practitioners: an analysis using Herzberg's theory. *Nurse Practitioner 16*, 4, 43–46.

Koenig, H.G., Johnson, S., Bellard, J., Denker, M. and Fenlon, R. (1995) *Journal of the American Psychiatric Association 46*, 4, 399–401.

Kroll, J. (1995) Religion and psychiatry. *Current Opinion in Psychiatry 8*, 335–339.

Krøvel, B., Bjørn, R.R. and Rør, E. (1997) *Violence and Psychiatry – About Understanding and Therapy*. Oslo: Tano Aschehoug.

Laben, J.K. and Blum, J. (1997) Persons with mental illness in jail. In N.K. Worley (ed.) *Mental Health Nursing in the Community*. St. Louis: Mosby.

Lally, J. (1993) Staff issue; training, support and management. In I. Fleming and B.S. Kroese (eds) *People with Learning Disability and Severe Challenging Behaviour*. Manchester: Manchester University Press.

Landeweerd, J. and Boumans, N. (1988) Nurses' work satisfaction and feelings of health and stress in three psychiatric departments. *International Journal of Nursing Studies 25*, 3, 225–234.

Landis, B.J. (1996) Uncertainty, spiritual well-being, and psychosocial adjustment to chronic illness. *Issues in Mental Health Nursing 17*, 217–231.

Larkin, E., Murtagh, S. and Jones, S. (1988) A preliminary study of violent incidents in a Special Hospital (Rampton). *British Journal of Psychiatry 153*, 226–231.

Lartey, E.Y. (1997) *In Living Colour: An Intercultural Approach to Pastoral Care and Counselling*. London: Cassell.

Leary, J. and Brown, D. (1995) Findings from the Claybury Study for ward based psychiatric nurses and comparisons with community psychiatric nurses. In J. Carson, L. Fagin and S. Ritter (eds) *Stress and Coping in Mental Health Nursing*. London: Chapman and Hall.

Lehman, A. (1984) Nursing's last frontier: Our Canadian prisons. *The Canadian Nurse 79*, 7, 37–39.

Lehman, M.K. (1993) Substance abuse treatment helps women in prison. *SAMHSA News 1*, 2, 4–5.

Leiba, T. (1994) Inter-professional approaches to mental health care. In A. Leathard (ed.) *Going Inter-Professional*. London: Routledge.

Linaker, O.M., Jacobsen, D., Refsnes, V. and Thoresen, R. (1993) Professional forum for secure units in Norway: report on the investigations Autumn 1991 and Spring 1993. *FSN-Nytt 3*, 1–4.

Lloyd, C. (1995) *Forensic Psychiatry for Health Professionals. Therapy in Practice, 46*. London: Chapman and Hall.

Love, C. and Hunter, M. (1996) Violence in public sector psychiatric hospitals: benchmarking nursing staff injury rates. *Journal of Psychosocial Nursing 34*, 5, 30–34.

Lynch, J., Smith, S.K., Graziadei, H.A. and Pittayathiakhun, T. (1994) Profile of inmates in the United States and in England and Wales 1991 (NCJ-145863). Washington, DC: US Department of Justice. Available electronically: http: //www.ncjrs.org/txtfiles/ walesus.txt

Lynch, V. (1990) *Clinical Forensic Nursing: A Descriptive Study in Role Development*. Master's Thesis, University of Texas at Arlington.

Lynch, V. (1991) Forensic nursing in the emergency department: a new role for the 1990's. *Critical Care Nursing Quarterly 14*, 3, 69–86.

Lynch, V. (1993) Forensic nursing – diversity in education and practice. *Journal of Psychosocial Nursing and Mental Health Services 31*, 11, 7–14.

Lynch, V. (1995a) Clinical forensic nursing: a new perspective in the management of crime victims from trauma to trial. *Critical Care Nursing Clinics of North America 7*, 3, 489–507.

Lynch, V. (1995b) Forensic nursing: an essential element in managing society's violence and its victims. *Standardization News*. April, 38–41.

Lynch, V. (1996a) Advances in forensic nursing: new dimensions for the 21st century. *Journal of Psychosocial Nursing and Mental Health Services 34*, 10, 6–7.

Lynch, V. (1996b) Dimensions of a forensic nurse. *On the Edge*. Fall, 2, 3.

Lynch, V. (1999) Forensic nursing: Crime prevention strategy in South Africa. Presentation at the Annual Meeting of the American Academy of Forensic Sciences. Orlando, FL.

Macintyre, A. (1996) *After Virtue: A Study in Moral Theory*. London: Duckworth.

Macmurray, J. (1991) *Persons in Relation: Volume II of The Form of the Personal*. London: Faber and Faber.

Marchant, C. (1992) Crime and treatment. *Community Care 8*, 948.

Marks, I.M., Hallam, K.S., Connolly, J. and Philpott, R. (1977) *Nursing in Behavioural Psychotherapy*. London: Royal College of Nursing of the United Kingdom.

Marshall, M. (1999) Modernising mental health services: time to define the boundaries of psychiatric care. Editorial, *British Medical Journal 318*, 3–4.

Martslof, D.S. and Mickey, (1998) The concept of spirituality in nursing theories: differing world-views and extent of focus. *Journal of Advanced Nursing 27*, 294–303.

Maslach, C. and Jackson, S.E. (1982) The measurement of experienced burnout. *Journal of Occupational Behaviour 2*, 99–113.

Maslach, C. and Jackson, S.E. (1986) *Maslach Burnout Inventory Manual*. Palo Alto, California: Consulting Psychologists Press.

Maslow, A.H. (1970) *Motivation and Personality*. New York: Harper and Row.

Maslow, A.H. (1987) *Motivation and Personality*. New York: Harper and Row.

Mason, J.K. and McCall Smith, R.A. (1994) *Law and Medical Ethics*. London: Butterworths.

Mason, T. and Mercer, D. (1996) Nursing: visions of social control. *Australian and New Zealand Journal of Mental Health Nursing 5*, 4, 153–162, December.

Mason, T. and Woods, P. (1998) Admission trends to a special hospital: court diversion and prison transfers. *Journal of Psychiatric and Mental Heatlh Nursing 5*, 6, 479–488.

Maurillo, G. (1996) Keynote Address. Annual Scientific Assembly of the International Association of Forensic Nurses. Kansas City, month

McAleer, J. and Hamill, C. (1997) *The Assessment of Higher Order Competence Development in Nurse Education*. National Board for Northern Ireland for Nursing, Midwifery and Health Visiting.

McCarthy, P. (1985) Burnout in psychiatric nursing. *Journal of Advanced Nursing 10*, 304–310.

McDonald, D.C. and Teitelbaum, M. (1994) Managing mentally ill offenders in the community: Milwaukee's community support programme. *National Institute of Justice Programme Focus*. Washington, DC: US Department of Justice.

McDougall, T. (1997) Patient empowerment: fact or fiction? *Mental Health Nursing 17*, 10, 4–5.

McElfatrick, S. (1997) *Stress and Coping in Mental Health Nurses*. Unpublished thesis, Psychology Department, University of Ulster, Jordanstown.

McElfatrick, S., Carson, J., Annett, J., Cooper, C., Holloway, F. and Kuipers, E. (1999) Assessing coping skills in mental health nurses: is an occupation specific measure better than a generic coping skills scale? Submitted for publication.

McFadyen, A.I. (1990) *The Call to Personhood*. Cambridge: Cambridge University Press.

McFarlane, J. (1984) Foreword. In D.F.S. Cormack (ed.) *Research Process in Nursing*. Oxford: Blackwell.

McHugh, J. (1997) Standards of forensic nursing practice. *On the Edge*. Spring, 3, 1.

McKay, M. (1998) *An Investigation of the Decision-Making Process and Self-Esteem in Adolescent Gang Membership*. Doctoral dissertation, Spalding University, 1998. UMI Dissertation Abstracts, 9824721.

McKie, A. and Swinton, J. (1998) *Community, Culture and Character: The Place of Virtue Ethics in Psychiatric Nursing*. Unpublished paper.

McLeod, T. (1997) Work stress among community psychiatric nurses. *British Journal of Nursing 6*, 10, 569–574.

McSherry, W. and Draper, P. (1998) The debate emerging from the literature surrounding the concept of spirituality as applied to nursing. *Journal of Advanced Nursing 27*, 683–691.

Melchior, M., Philipsen, H., Abu-Saad, H., Halfens, R., Van de Berg, A. and Gassman, P. (1996) The effectiveness of primary nursing on burnout among psychiatric nurses in long stay settings. *Journal of Advanced Nursing 24*, 694–702.

Meleis, A.I. (1991) *Theoretical Nursing: Developments and Progress (2nd ed)*. Philadelphia: Lippincott.

Melia, P., Moran, T. and Mason, T. (1999) Triumviat nursing for personality disordered patients: crossing the boundaries safely. *Journal of Psychiatric and Mental Health Nursing 6*, 15–20.

Mental Health Act 1983. London: HMSO.

Mental Welfare Commission for Scotland (1997) *Annual Report 1996–97*. London: Stationery Office.

Menzies Lyth, I. (1960) A case study in the functioning of social systems as a defence against anxiety. *Human Relations 13*, 95–121.

Menzies Lyth, I. (1988a) *Containing Anxiety in Institutions. Selected Essays, Volume 1*. London: Free Association Books.

Menzies, Lyth, I. (1988b) A psychoanalytic perspective on social institutions. In *Melanie Klein Today, Volume 2. Mainly Practice*. London: Routledge.

Merriam, S. (1983) Mentors and protégés: a critical review of the literature. *Adult Education Quarterly 33*, 3, 161–173.

Metzner, J.L. (1997) Analysis and commentary: an introduction to correctional psychiatry: Part 1. *Journal of the American Academy of Psychiatry and the Law 25*, 3, 375–380.

Mickley, J.R., Carson, V. and Soeken, K.L. (1995) Religion and adult mental health: state of the science in nursing. *Issues in Mental Health Nursing 16*, 4, 345–360, Jul–Aug.

Middleman, R. and Rhodes, G. (1985) *Competent Supervision: Making Imaginative Judgements.* New Jersey: Prentice Hall.

Miller, D. (1991) Occupational morbidity and burnout: lessons and warnings for HIV/AIDS carers. *International Review of Psychiatry 3*, 439–449.

Miller, W. (1984) The evolution of professional and interpersonal roles in psychiatric mental health nursing. *Proceedings of the First National Conference on Psychiatric Nursing, Ottawa, Canada*, 95–102.

Milne, D. (1993) *Psychology and Mental Health Nursing.* London: Macmillan.

Ministry of Health and Social Welfare (1977) *Norwegian Mental Health Act Provisions: Royal Resolution on Limited Access to the Use of Compulsory Treatment within Psychiatric Services in Norway.* Norway: Ministry of Health and Social Welfare.

Moltmann, J. (1985) *God in Creation: An Ecological Doctrine of Creation.* London: SCM Press.

Moos, R. (1969) *Ward Atmosphere Scale Preliminary Manual.* California: Social Ecology Laboratory, Stanford University.

Moran, T. and Mason, T. (1996) Revisiting the nursing management of the psychopath. *Journal of Psychiatric and Mental Health Nursing 3*, 3, 89–94, June.

Moritz, P. (1982) Health care in correctional facilities: a nursing challenge. *Nursing Outlook 30*, 4, 253–259.

Morris, L.E.H. (1996) A spiritual well-being model: use with older women who experience depression. *Issues in Mental Health Nursing 17*, 5, 439–455, Sept–Oct.

Muir Gray, J.A. (1997) *Evidence-Based Health Care: How to Make Health Policy and Management Decisions.* London: Churchill Livingstone.

Myco, F. (1980) Nursing research information: are nurse educators and practitioners seeking out? *Journal of Advanced Nursing 5*, 637–646.

NACRO (1993) *Community Care and Mentally Disordered Offenders. Mental Health Advisory Committee Policy Paper 1.* London: NACRO.

Nadelson, C.C. (1998) Gender and health policy. *Harvard Review of Psychiatry 5*, 6, 340–343.

National Board for Nursing, Midwifery and Health Visiting for Scotland (1998) *Project 2000 in Scotland. Employers' Needs and the Skills of Newly Qualified Project 2000 Staff Nurses.* Edinburgh: Department of Nursing, Queen Margaret College.

National Institute of Justice

NHS and Community Care Act 1990. London: HMSO.

Neff, J. and Kidd, P. (1993) *Trauma Nursing: The Art and Science.* St. Louis, Mo: Mosby Year Book.

Nelson, H.E. (1997) *Cognitive Behavioural Therapy with Schizophrenia.* London: Stanley Thorne.

New South Wales Independent Commission Against Corrucption (1998) *Investigation into the Department of Corrective Services – Second Report: Inappropriate Relationships with Inmates in the Delivery of Health Services.* Sydney: Australian Institute of Criminology.

Niskala, H. (1986) Competencies and skills required by nurses working in forensic areas. *Western Journal of Nursing Research 8*, 4, 178–181.

Niskala, H. (1987) Conflicting convictions: nurses in forensic settings. *Canadian Journal of Psychiatric Nursing 28*, 2, 10–14.

Noak, J.A. (1995a) Care of people with psychopathic disorder. *Nursing Standard 9*, 34, 30–32, May 17–23.

Noak, J.A (1995b) Partnership in Broadmoor. *Nursing Standard 9*, 17, 22–23, Jan 18–24.

Noddings, N. (1986) *Caring: A Feminine Approach to Ethics and Moral Education.* London: University of California Press.

Nolan, P. and Crawford, P. (1997) Towards a rhetoric of spirituality in mental health care. *Journal of Advanced Nursing 26*, 2, 289–294, August.

Norens, G. (1971) Nurses in prison. *Canadian Nurse 67*, 5, 37–39.

Norwegian Parliament (1961) *Mental Health Act*. Norway: Norwegian Parliament.

Numerof, R.E. and Abrams, M.N. (1984) Sources of stress amongst nurses: an empirical study. *Journal of Human Stress 10*, 2, 88–100.

Offer, D. and Sabshin, M. (1966) *Normality: Theoretical and Clinical Concepts of Mental Health*. New York: Basic Books.

Oldnall, A. (1996) A critical analysis of nursing: meeting the spiritual needs of patients. *Journal of Advanced Nursing 23*, 138–144.

Onions, T. (ed.) (1977) *Oxford Shorter Dictionary*. Oxford: Oxford University Press.

Ousley, L. (1998) *The Perception of Risk: Some Differences between Disciplines*. Unpublished Master's Study, University of Birmingham.

Parry, J. (1991) Community care for mentally ill offenders. *Nursing Standard 5*, 23, 29–33.

Parsons, T. (1951) *The Social System*. Glencoe: Free Press.

Passos, J.A. (1973) Accountability: myth or mandate? *Journal of Nursing Administration 3*, 3, 17–22.

Patterson, B.R. and Bettini, M.L. (1993) Age, depression and friendship: development of a general friendship inventory. *Communication Research Reports 10*, 2, 161–170, December.

Payne, R. and Firth-Cozens, J. (1987) *Stress in Health Professionals*. Chichester: Wiley.

Peay, J. (1996) Mentally disordered offenders. In M. Maguire, R. Morgan and R. Reiner (eds) *The Oxford Handbook of Criminology (2nd ed)*. Oxford: Clarendon Press.

Pedersen, P. (1988) The role of community psychiatric nurses in forensic psychiatry. *Community Psychiatric Nursing Journal 8*, 3, 12–17.

Peerenboom, P. (1996) Stationspflegekonzept. XIV. *Weiterbildungslehrgang zur Krankenpflege in der Psychiatrie im Landschaftsverband Rheinland*. Bedburg-Hau/Solingen.

Pensinger, T. (1993) Programme helps homeless individuals with severe mental illnesses. *SAMHSA News 1*, 2, 12–13.

Peplau, H.E. (1952) Interpersonal relationships. In H.E. Peplan (1952) *Nursing*. New York: G.P. Putnam Press.

Peplau, H.E. (1991) *Interpersonal Relations in Nursing: A Conceptual Frame of Reference for Psychodynamic Nursing*. New York: Springer.

Peternelj-Taylor, C.A. (1998a) Care of individuals in correctional facilities. In C.A. Glod (ed.) *Contemporary Psychiatric-Mental Health Nursing*. Philadelphia: F.A. Davis.

Peternelj-Taylor, C.A. (1998b) Forbidden love: sexual exploitation in the forensic milieu. *Journal of Psychosocial Nursing and Mental Health Services 36*, 6, 17–23.

Peternelj-Taylor, C.A. and Hufft, A.G. (1997) Forensic psychiatric nursing. In B.S. Johnson (ed.) *Psychiatric-Mental Health Nursing: Adaptation and Growth*. Philadelphia: Lippincott.

Peternelj-Taylor, C.A. and Johnson, R.L. (producers) and Bulk, F. (director) (1993) *Custody and Caring: A Challenge for Nursing* [video]. Saskatoon: University of Saskatchewan.

Peternelj-Taylor, C.A. and Johnson, R.L. (1995) Serving time: psychiatric mental health nursing in corrections. *Journal of Psychosocial Nursing and Mental Health Services 33*, 8, 12–19.

Peternelj-Taylor, C.A. and Johnson, R.L. (1996) Custody and caring: clinical placement of students in a forensic setting. *Perspectives in Psychiatric Care 32*, 4, 23–29.

Petryshen, P. (1981) Nursing the mentally disordered offender. *The Canadian Nurse 77*, 6, 26–28.

Phillips, M.S. (1983) Forensic psychiatry: nurses' attitudes revealed. *Dimensions in Health Service 60*, 9, 41–43.

Phipps, A.J. (1994) The Reed report: mentally disordered offenders. *Prison Service Journal 95*, 50–52.

Pietroni, P. (1994) Inter-professional teamwork, its history and development in hospitals, general practice and community care (UK). In A. Leathard (ed.) *Going Inter-Professional*. London: Routledge.

Pollack, S. (1980) Psychiatry and the Administration of Justice. In W.J. Curan, A.L. McGarry and C.S. Petty (eds) *Modern Legal Medicine, Psychiatry and Forensic Service*. Philadelphia: T.A. David.

Proctor, B. (1988) Supervision: a co-operative exercise in accountability. In M. Marken and M. Rayne (eds) *Enabling and Ensuring: Supervision and Practice*. Leicester: National Youth Bureau.

Pullen, L., Tuck, I. and Mix, K. (1996) Mental health nurses' spiritual perspectives. *Journal of Holistic Nursing 14*, 2, 85–97, June.

Quen, J. (1974) Historical reflections on American legal psychiatry. *American Academy of Psychiatry and Law 2*, 4, 237–241.

Raleigh, K., Hopkins, N.J., Shah, D.D., Middleton, H.C. and Millard, G. (1997) *Meeting Psychiatric Need in the Community*. Unpublished Audit Report, Rotherham Priority Health Trust.

Ray, I. (1838) An historical view of the M'Naghten case. In *Bulletin of the History of Medicine*. Boston.

Reed, J. (1992) *Review of Health and Social Services for Mentally Disordered Offenders and Others Requiring Similar Services*. London: HMSO.

Reed, J. (1994) *Report of the Working Group on High Security and Related Psychiatric Provision (The Reed Review)*. London: Department of Health.

Reed, S. (1984) Occupational therapists in the interdisciplinary team setting. In F. Cromwell (ed.) *The Changing Roles of Occupational Therapists in the 1980s*. New York: The Plenum Press.

Reed, V., Robinson, D., Woods, P. and Henderson, S. (1996) *Behavioural Status Index: Named Nurse Assessment Manual for the Assessment of Dangerousness and Risk*. Unpublished.

Reeder, D. (1991) Conceptualizing psychosocial nursing in the jail setting. *Journal of Psychosocial Nursing 29*, 8, 40–45.

Reeves, J. (1994) A comparison of the effects of stress in psychiatric and medical nurses. *International Journal of Psychiatric Nursing Research 1*, 1, 21–29.

Reiss, A.J. and Roth, J.A. (1993) (eds) *Understanding and Preventing Violence*. Washington, DC: National Academy Press.

Reynolds, W. and Cormack, D. (eds) (1990) *Psychiatric and Mental Health Nursing Theory and Practice*. London: Chapman and Hall.

Reznek, L. (1991) *The Philosophical Defence of Psychiatry*. London: Routledge.

Richards, P.S. and Bergin, A.E. (1997) *A Spiritual Strategy for Counselling and Psychotherapy*. Washington: American Psychological Association.

Rippere, V. and Williams, R. (eds) (1985) *Wounded Healers: Mental Health Workers' Experience of Depression*. Chichester: Wiley.

Robinson, D. (1994) A chance to bridge the gap: a strategy for research and development in the Special Hospitals. *Psychiatric Care 1*, 3, 97–101.

Robinson, D. (1999) Forensic Nursing: Developments and International Opportunities. Paper given at the 1999 International Forensic Mental Health Conference, Sofitel, Melbourne, Australia. Forensicare, Victorian Institute of Forensic Mental Health.

Robinson, D. and Kettles, A.M. (1998) The emerging profession of forensic nursing: myth or reality? *Psychiatric Care 5*, 6, 214–218.

Robinson, D., Whyte, L. and Fidler, I. (1997) Quality of life measures in a high security environment. *Nursing Standard 11*, 49, 34–37.

Rogers, C. (1951) *Client Centred Therapy*. London: Constable.

Rogers, C. (1961) *On Becoming a Person*. Boston: Houghton Mifflin.

Rogers, C. (1993) *On Becoming a Person*. London: Constable.

Roozendaal, M. (1997) *Forensische Psychiatrie, Jurisdische Hoofdlingen*. Eindhoven: GGZE.

Roper, N., Logan, W. and Tiernay, A. (1996) *The Elements of Nursing – A Model for Nursing Based on a Model of Living (4th ed)*. London: Churchill Livingstone.

Rosenberg, M. (1965) *Society and the Adolescent Self-Image*. Princeton: Princeton University Press.

Rosenhan, D.L. and Seligman, M.E.P. (1984) *Abnormal Psychology*. New York: Norton.

Ross, L.A. (1994) Spiritual aspects of nursing. *Journal of Advanced Nursing 19*, 439–447.

Roth, L. (1986) Correctional psychiatry. In W. Curran, A. McGarry and S. Shah (eds) *Forensic Psychiatry and Psychology: Perspectives and Standards for Interdisciplinary Practice*. Philadelphia: F.A. Davis.

Rowlands, R., Inch, H., Rodger, W. and Soliman, A. (1996) Diverted to where? What happens to the diverted mentally disordered offender. *The Journal of Forensic Psychiatry 7*, 2, 284–296.

Royal College of Nursing (RCN) (1997) *Buying Forensic Mental Health Nursing: An RCN Guide for Purchasers.* London: Royal College of Nursing.

Royal College of Psychiatrists (RCP) (1996) *The Report of the Confidential Inquiry into Homicides and Suicides by Mentally Ill People.* London: RCP.

Rubinstein, W.D. and Rubinstein, H. (1996) *Menders of the Mind: A History of the Royal Australian & New Zealand College of Psychiatrists, 1946–96.* Melbourne: Oxford University Press.

Runciman, P. (1990) *Competence-Based Education and the Assessment and Accreditation of Work-Based Learning in the Context of Project 2000: A Literature Review.* National Board for Nursing, Midwifery and Health Visiting for Scotland.

Ryan, D. (1997) Ambiguity in nursing: the person and the organisation as contrasting sources of meaning. In S. Tilley (ed.) *The Mental Health Nurse: Views of Practice and Education.* Oxford: Blackwell Science.

Rynerson, B.C. (1989) Counselling issues with prison inmate substance abusers. *Journal of Psychosocial Nursing 27*, 2, 12–17.

Sainsbury Centre for Mental Health (1997) *Pulling Together: The Future Roles and Training of Mental Health Staff.* London: Sainsbury Centre for Mental Health.

Sanders, J.B. and DuPlessis, D. (1985) An historical view of right to treatment. *Journal of Psychosocial Nursing and Mental Health Services 23*, 9, 12–17.

Sandler, J. and Sandler, A.M. (1984) The past unconscious, the present unconscious, and interpretation of the transference. *Psychoanalytic Inquiry 4*, 367–399.

Scales, C.J., Mitchell, J.L. and Smith, R.D. (1993) Survey report on forensic nursing. *Journal of Psychosocial Nursing 31*, 11, 39–44.

Schafer, P. (1997) When a client develops an attraction: successful resolution versus boundary violation. *Journal of Psychiatric and Mental Health Nursing 4*, 203–211.

Schafer, T. (1992) CPN stress and organisational change: a study. *Community Psychiatric Nursing Journal 12*, 1, 16–24.

Schalast, N. (1998) Die Erfolgserwartung der Mitarbeiter. *Forensische Psychiatrie und Psychotherapie-Werkstattschriften 5*, 1, 175–191.

Schaufeli, W. and Enzmann, D. (1998) *The Burnout Companion to Study and Practice: A Critical Analysis.* London: Taylor and Francis.

Schon, D. (1983) *The Reflective Practitioner.* New York: Basic Books.

Schon, D. (1987) *Educating the Reflective Practitioner.* San Francisco: Jossey-Bass.

Scottish Executive Directors of Nursing Group (1997) *Clinical Supervision: Report of the Executive Directors of Nursing Working Group.* Edinburgh: SEDNG.

Scottish Office (1999) *Health and Social Work Related Services for Mentally Disordered Offenders in Scotland. A Consultation Paper.* Edinburgh: The Scottish Office Department of Health.

Searles, H.F. (1979) *Countertransference.* New York: International Universities Press.

Sharp, K.J., Wilcock, S.E., Sharp, D. and Macdonald, H. (1995) *Literature Review on Competence to Practice.* Edinburgh: National Board for Nursing, Midwifery and Health Visiting for Scotland.

Shenson, D., Dubler, N. and Michaels, D. (1990) Jails and prisons: the new asylums? *American Journal of Public Health 80*, 6, 655–656.

SHSA (1995) *Service Strategies for Secure Care.* London: Special Hospitals Service Authority.

Shuler, P.A., Gelberg, L. and Brown, M. (1994) The effects of spiritual/religious practices on psychological well-being among inner city homeless women. *Nurse Practitioner Forum 5*, 2, 106–113, June.

Sims, A. (1994) 'Psyche' – spirit as well as mind. *British Journal of Psychiatry 165*, 441–446.

Skaug, T.H., Bjarnar, E. and Föyn, P. (1992) *Functions, Areas of Responsibility and Capacity of Norwegian Regional Secure Units.* Norway: Department of Social Affairs.

Smale, S.L. (1983) Nursing behind bars: a decade of change. *The Canadian Nurse 79*, 7, 31–33.

Smith, L.D. (1989) Medication refusal and the rehospitalized mentally ill inmate. *Hospital and Community Psychiatry 40*, 5, 491–496.

Smock, W., Nichols, G. and Fuller, P. (1993) Development and implementation of the first clinical forensic medicine training program. *Journal of Clinical Forensic Medicine 38*, 4.

Smucker, C. (1996) A phenomenological description of the experience of spiritual distress. *Nursing Diagnosis 7*, 2, 81–91, Apr–June.

Snow, M. and Thurber, S. (1997) Cognitive imbalance and antisocial personality characteristics. *Journal of Clinical Psychology 53*, 4, 351–354.

Staite, C. (1994) Diversion from custody for mentally disordered offenders. *Prison Service Journal 95*, 42–45.

Standhope, M. and Lancaster, J. (1996) *Community Health Nursing: Promoting Health of Aggregates, Families, and Individuals (4th ed)*. St. Louis: Mosby.

Stanton, A.H. and Schwartz, M.S. (1954) *The Mental Hospital: A Study of Institutional Participation in Psychiatric Illness and Treatment*. New York: Basic Books.

Stark, R. (1971) Psychopathology and religious commitment. *Review of Religious Research 12*, 3, 165–176.

Steinaker, N. and Bell, R. (1979) *The Experiential Taxonomy: A New Approach to Teaching and Learning*. New York: Academic Press.

Storey, L. and Dale, C. (1998) Nursing in secure environments. *Psychiatric Care Editorial 5*, 4, 122.

Strauss, J.S. (1992) The person – key to understanding mental illness: towards a new dynamic psychiatry, III. *British Journal of Psychiatry 161*, Supplement 18, 19–26.

Strong, S. (1997) Out of mind. *Community Care*, 20–26 March, 18–19.

Street, A. (1995) *Nursing Replay Researching Nursing Culture Together*. Melbourne: Churchill Livingstone.

Sullivan, P. (1993a) Stress and burnout in psychiatric nursing. *Nursing Standard 8*, 2, 36–39.

Sullivan, P. (1993b) Occupational stress in mental health nursing. *Journal of Advanced Nursing 18*, 591–601.

Swinton, J. (1999) *From Bedlam to Shalom: Towards a Practical Theology of Human Nature, Friendship and Mental Health Care*. New York: Peter Lang Press.

Swinton, J. and Kettles, A.M. (1997) Resurrecting the person: redefining mental illness – a spiritual perspective. *Psychiatric Care 4*, 3, 1–4.

Sykes, J.B. (1988) *The Concise Oxford Dictionary of Current English*. Oxford: Clarendon Press.

Symington, N. (1980) The response aroused by the psychopath. *International Review of Psychoanalysis 7*, 291–298.

Szasz, T. and Hollander, E.D. (1956) A Contribution to the Philosophy of Medicine, *American Medical Association Archives of Internal Medicine*, XCVII, 585–592.

Tarbuck, P. (1994a) The therapeutic use of security: a model for forensic nursing. In T. Thompson and P. Mathias (eds) *Lyttle's Mental Health and Disorder (2nd ed)*. London: Bailliere Tindall.

Tarbuck, P. (1994b) *Buying Forensic Mental Health Nursing: A Guide for Purchasers*. London: Royal College of Nursing.

Tarbuck, P. (1996) Rolling back the years: developing the practice of nursing after a public enquiry. In T. Sandford and K. Gournay (eds) *Perspectives in Mental Health Nursing*. London: Bailliere Tindall.

Taylor, E.J., Amenta, M. and Highfield, M. (1995) Spiritual care practices of oncology nurses. *ONF 22*, 1, 31–39.

Taylor, P. (1985) Motives for offending amongst violent and psychotic men. *British Journal of Psychiatry 147*, 491–498.

Taylor, P. (1988) Forensic psychiatry overview. *Current Opinions in Psychiatry 1*, 1–11.

Taylor, S. (1998) Helping with enquiries. *Mental Health Nursing 18*, 1, 26–27.

Thomas, B. (1994) Teamwork. In C. Hume and I. Pullen (eds) *Rehabilitation for Mental Health Problems: An Introductory Handbook*. Edinburgh: Churchill Livingstone.

Thomas, B., Hardy, S. and Cutting, P. (eds) (1997) *Stuart and Sundeen's Mental Health Nursing: Principles and Practice*. London: Mosby.

Thompson, J. (1983) Call sister – stress in the A and E department. *Nursing Times 79*, 31, 23–27.

Thompson, M. and Page, S. (1992) Psychological determinants of occupational burnout. *Stress Medicine 8*, 151–159.

Thompson, T. and Mathias, P. (1994) *Lyttle's Mental Health and Disorder*. London: Bailliere Tindall.

Thomsen, S., Dallender, J., Soares, J., Nolan, P. and Arnetz, B. (1988) Predictors for a healthy workforce for English and Swedish psychiatrists. *British Journal of Psychiatry 173*, 80–84.

Topping-Morris, B. (1992) An historical and personal view of forensic nursing services. In P. Morrison and P. Burnard (eds) *Aspects of Forensic Psychiatry*. Aldershot: Avebury Press.

Trygstad, L. (1986) Stress and coping in psychiatric nursing. *Journal of Psychosocial Nursing 24*, 10, 23–27.

Tudor, K. (1997) *Mental Health Promotion: Paradigms and Practice*. London: Routledge.

Turner-Shaw, J. and Bosanquet, N. (1993) *Nursing Development Units: A Way to Develop Nurses and Nursing*. London: Kings Fund.

Twibell, R.S., Wolski, A.W., Marine, M. and Schoger, J. (1996) Spiritual coping needs of critically ill patients: validation of nursing diagnoses. *Dimensions of Critical Care Nursing 15*, 5, 245–253, September.

United Kingdom Central Council (UKCC) for Nursing, Midwifery and Health Visiting (1986) *Project 2000 – A New Preparation for Practice*. London: UKCC.

United Kingdom Central Council (UKCC) for Nursing, Midwifery and Health Visiting (1992a) *Code of Conduct for the Nurse, Midwife and Health Visitor*. London: UKCC.

United Kingdom Central Council (UKCC) for Nursing, Midwifery and Health Visiting (1992b) *Scope of Professional Practice*. London: UKCC.

United Kingdom Central Council (UKCC) for Nursing, Midwifery and Health Visiting (1994) *Future for Professional Practice*. London: UKCC.

United Kingdom Central Council (UKCC) for Nursing, Midwifery and Health Visiting (1995) *Initial Position Statement on Clinical Supervision*. London: UKCC.

Urban, M. (1998) Paradigmenwechsel in der Psychiatriereform? *Report Psychologie 23*, 8, 626.

Vanderwall, C. (1997) The role of the community forensic mental health nurse: initiatives for cross-agency work. *Psychiatric Care 4*, 6, 283–286.

VanDeVelde-Coke, S. (1998) Restructuring health agencies: from hierarchies to programmes. In J.M. Hibberd and D.L. Smith (eds) *Nursing Management in Canada*. London and New York: W.B. Saunders, Co.

Vaughan, P.J. and Badger, D. (1995) *Working with the Mentally Disordered Offender in the Community*. London: Chapman and Hall.

Victorian Institute of Forensic Mental Health (1998) *Interim Policy and Program Manual*. Melbourne: Victorian Institute of Forensic Mental Health.

Vijselaar, J. (1982) *Krankzinnigen gesticht. Psychiatrische inrichtingen in Nederland 1880–1910*. Haarlem: Fibula-Van Dishoeck.

Vitucci, N. (1999) Corrections challenged with treating mentally ill inmates. *CorrectCare 13*, 3, 1; 14; 17–18.

Volckart, B. (1997) *Maßregelvollzug*. Neuwied: Luchterhand Verlag GmbH.

Wall, T., Bolden, R., Borrill, C., Carter, A., Golya, D., Hardy, G., Haynes, C., Rick, J., Shapiro, D. and West, M. (1997) Minor psychiatric disorder in NHS Trust staff: occupational and gender differences. *British Journal of Psychiatry 171*, 519–523.

Watson, A.S. (1992) The evolution of legal methods for dealing with mind-state in crimes. *Bulletin of the American Academy of Psychiatry and the Law 20*, 2, 211–221.

Watts, F. and Bennett, D. (1993) Introduction: The concept of rehabilitation. In F.N. Watts and D.H. Bennett (eds) *Theory and Practice of Psychiatric Rehabilitation*. Chichester: Wiley.

Weaver, J. and Lynch, V. (1998) Forensic nursing: unique contribution to international law. *Journal of Nursing Law 5*, 4.

Weeks, R. and Widom, C.S. (1998) Early childhood victimisation among incarcerated adult male felons. *Research Preview (FS000204)*. US Department of Justice, National Institute of Justice. Rockville, MD: National Institute of Justice.

Weiss, D., Dawis, R., England, G. and Lofquist, L. (1967) *Manual for the Minnesota Satisfaction Questionnaire*. Minnesota: Industrial Relations Centre, University of Minnesota.

Welsh National Board (WNB) (1989) *The Development of Professional Practice*. Cardiff: WNB.

West, A. (1996) The risks of burnout. In C. Cordess and M. Cox (eds) *Forensic Psychotherapy: Crime, Psychodynamics and the Offender Patient*. London: Jessica Kingsley Publishers.

Wheeler, H. (1997a) A review of occupational stress research: 1. *British Journal of Nursing 6*, 11, 642–645.

Wheeler, H. (1997b) Nurse occupational stress research: 2. Definition and conceptualisation. *British Journal of Nursing 6*, 12, 710–713.

Wheeler, L.M. (1996) Managed mental health care. In H.S. Wilson and C.R. Kneisl (eds) *Psychiatric Nursing (5th ed)*. Menlo Park, CA: Addison Wesley.

Whitfield, C.L. (1991) *Co-Dependence: Healing the Human Condition*. Deerfield Beach, FL: Health Communications.

Whyte, L. (1985) Safe as houses? ... Custodial care or therapeutic interventions. *Nursing Mirror 81*, 23, 48.

Whyte, L. (1997) Forensic nursing: a review of concepts and definitions. *Nursing Standard 11*, 23, 46–47.

Wicks, R.J., Parsons, R.D. and Capps, D. (1985) *Clinical Handbook of Pastoral Counseling Volume 1 (Expanded Edition)*. New York: Paulist Press.

Wilkinson, L. (1998) Liaison service provides safety network. *Nursing Times 94*, 37, 37.

Williams, A.H. (1983) Rischi nel lavoro congli adolescenti disturbati. Chapter in *Nevrosi e delinquenza. Uno studio psicoanalitico dell'omicidio e di aldri crimini*. Edizione Borla.

Wilson, S. (1998) *The Personal Characteristics of Effective Nurses*. Unpublished Bachelor's Project, University of York.

Wing, J.K. and Brown, G.W. (1970) *Institutionalism and Schizophrenia*. London: Cambridge University Press.

Winnicott, D.W. (1949) Hate in the countertransference. *International Journal of Psycho-Analysis 30*, 69–74.

Winnicott, D.W. (1960) The theory of the parent–infant relationship. In D.W. Winnicott (ed.) *The Maturational Processes and the Facilitating Environment*. London: Hogarth Press.

Winnicott, D.W. (1965) *The Family and Individual Development*. London: Tavistock.

World Health Organisation (1987) *Mental Health Services: A Pilot Study*. Copenhagen: Regional World Health Office for Europe Publishers.

Wulff, H.R. and Pedersen, S.A. *et al.* (1990) *Philosophy of Medicine: An Introduction*. Oxford: Blackwell Scientific Publications.

Wycherley, B. (1987) *The Living Skills Pack*. Bexhill: South East Thames Regional Health Authority.

Young, J.E. (1994) *Cognitive Therapy for Personality Disorders*. Sarasota, Florida: Professional Resource Press.

Zerwekh, J. (1993) Transcending life: the practice wisdom of nursing hospice experts. *The American Journal of Hospice and Palliative Care*, September/October, 26–31.

Zubin, J. and Spring, B. (1977) Vulnerability: a new view of schizophrenia. *Journal of Abnormal Psychology 86*, 260–266.

FURTHER READING

Bluglass, R. and Bowden, P. (1990) *Principles and Practices of Forensic Psychiatry*. Edinburgh: Churchill Livingstone.

Mason, T. and Mercer, D. (1998) *Critical Perspectives in Forensic Care. Inside Out*. Basingstoke: Macmillan.

The Contributors

Mary Addo trained as an enrolled nurse in 1979–81 at the then Foresterhill College of Nursing in Aberdeen and worked in Woodend Hospital before training to become a registered nurse in mental health in 1982–85. She has held a number of posts including that of section coordinator overlooking the nursing and operational needs of two acute wards, three long-stay wards and was also a lecturer practitioner for two years working between Foresterhill College and Royal Cornhill Hospital. She is on the 'Expert Register' of the National Board of Scotland.

Roger Almvik is a research fellow, who holds a joint post between at the Norwegian University of Science and Technology, Institute of Psychiatry and the Brøset Regional Secure Unit in Trondheim, Norway. He is also a visiting researcher at the University of Tromsö, Psychiatric Department Aasgaard, Norway. He has many years experience working in forensic care as a clinical team leader.

John Boyd practised as a registered mental nurse before graduating with a medical degree from Aberdeen University in 1988. He has worked as psychiatrist in acute care prior to becoming a consultant forensic psychiatrist in 1998. Currently he is studying law and ethics in medicine at Glasgow University.

Charles Brooker is currently a professor of mental health nursing in the School of Nursing, University of Manchester where he leads the mental health research programme area. He is currently investigating multidisciplinary team-working in secure environments. This research will help to provide the underpinning rationale for the design of post-qualifying, multidisciplinary training in the forensic field. He is also one of the founder members of the Virtual Institute for Personality Disorder.

Jerome Carson is a senior lecturer in clinical psychology at the Institute of Psychiatry, King's College London. He also has an honorary consultant clinical psychologist contract with the South London and Maudsley NHS Trust. He works in a busy community mental health team. His main research interests are the assessment and alleviation of nursing staff stress and the evaluation of community care services.

Christopher Cordess is a professor of forensic psychiatric at the University of Sheffield, and Honorary Consultant Forensic Psychiatric and Director of Research at Rampton Hospital. He is an associate member of the British Psychoanalytic Society. Christopher Cordess is co-editor with Dr Murray Cox of *Forensic Psychotherapy: Crime, Psychodynamics and the Offender Patient* published in 1996 by Jessica Kingsley Publishers.

Hans Martin Don works as a care manager in the Forensic Psychiatric Circuit of the Foundation for Mental Health Services in Eindhoven (The Netherlands). He has worked in forensic psychiatry for over 10 years. At the moment he is participating in the development of formal training for forensic workers.

Uwe Dönisch-Siedel worked at the Rheinische Kliniken, Bedburg-Hau for over 20 years. He is now responsible for the development of standards in forensic treatment and security at the Ministry for Women, Youth, Family and Health, North-Rhine-Westfalia, Düsseldorf.

Karen Elliott qualified 16 years ago from Sheffield University and has worked at Rampton Hospital for the last 12 years in the development and management of the speech and language therapy service whilst providing clinical input to patients with mental illness, learning disabilities and personality disorders. She has been Regional Advisor in Psychiatry for the RBSLT for 3 years and is active in the Special Interest Group in Mental Health, having been on the committee for the last 5 years. She lectures to students at Sheffield University on communication problems in psychiatry.

Tom van Erven is a clinical psychologist and psychotherapist. He works as a behaviour psychotherapist for psychiatrists in training and is the head of the research department of the Forensic Psychiatric Circuit of the Foundation for Mental Health Services in Eindhoven (The Netherlands). He is coordinating the Dutch part of the international multi-centre Behavioural Status Index (BSI) study. He has translated the BSI into a Dutch version.

Kevin Gournay is a chartered psychologist and a registered nurse. He is Deputy Head of the Department of Health Service Research at the Institute of Psychiatry which employs 130 staff and which runs numerous national and international studies. Kevin has the largest portfolio of Psychiatric Nursing Research projects in the world. He is also responsible for 7 evidence based multidisciplinary training programmes and directs 4 forensic research grants.

Trond Hatling qualified as a Registered Nurse in 1982. He worked for five years as a nurse at the Reitgjerdet hospital: a state asylum for the male criminally mentally ill. He is currently a researcher at the Norwegian Institute of Hospital Research in Trodheim, where the focus of his work is on psychiatric health services research. In particular he has been engaged in projects related to the 1997 Government White Paper on services to people with mental illness; coercion in Norwegian psychiatry; and setting standards for patient based information. His most recent project is on practice and productivity in psychiatric clinics.

Colin Holmes trained as a psychiatric nurse in the United Kingdom in 1972, and has since specialised in working in secure environments. He became a post-basic nurse tutor for West Berkshire Health Authority in 1985, took up a position as lecturer-clinician at Deakin University in Geelong, Victoria at the end of 1989, and as senior lecturer shortly afterwards. He was appointed Foundation Professor of Nursing (Mental Health) in February 1997, a position jointly funded by the University of Western Sydney Nepean, and the Western Sydney Area Mental Health Service. The Service is the site of a new medium secure forensic facility, the 'Bunya Unit'.

Nigel Hopkins qualified in 1971 and has in the main concentrated on working with an adult out-patient population. He has a committment to the development of psychotherapeutic interventions. Work since 1987 with older adults and people requiring continuing care was a preparation for work that had strong institutional characteristics, but it was only in 1996 that he took up a post as a clinical psychologist in a regional secure unit, moving to Rampton High Security Hospital in 1998. The work has been far more rewarding than he ever expected it to be.

Rachel Humpston graduated in 1994 from Derby University with a Bsc (Hons) in occupational therapy. She worked at Rampton Hospital with people with learning disabilities for three years. She worked within a community learning disability team in Nottingham for a year but has since returned to Rampton where she currently works with people with moderate to severe learning disabilities.

Anita G. Hufft is the Dean and the Associate Professor of Nursing at Indiana University Southeast, New Albany, Indiana. Her work includes consultancies with the Kentucky

Correctional Institute for Women; the Jefferson Alcohol and Drug Treatment Center and the Women's Division, Federal Medical Center, FCI, Lexington, Kentucky. Anita is also a member of the international Association of Forensic Nurses and her Particular interests include the care of women in correctional settings and the develpoment of parenting programmes for inmates.

Jean Jones is a senior social worker at Rampton Hospital with special interests and experience in multidisciplinary working, sex offender treatment programmes and risk management with people with learning disabilities.

Alyson M. Kettles is currently Research and Development Officer for Mental Health within Grampian Primary Care NHS Trust, Aberdeen, Scotland. Her recent research work includes Forensic risk assessment; the role of the Forensic nurse within Forensic teams and Nursing care planning research in all mental health areas. Her work as both a registered mental nurse and a health psychologist ensures that she deals with issues that are clinically relevant. In its final stages, her Ph.D. work focuses on the nature of care planning within two NHS Trusts. As a nurse teacher and researcher, she currently serves as a member on the Research and Development Committee of the National Board for Scotland and serves on the Scottish Office Executive CRAG Scoping Group on Mental Health.

Stephan Kirby is currently lecturer/practitioner for Forensic Health and Social Care at The Hutton Centre (Tees and North East Yorkshire NHS Trust) and the University of Teeside (School of Health). He has been in this post for the past two years, having worked within The Hutton Centre for the past 10 years. His main responsibilities (at the moment) are as programme leader for the, multi-disciplinary, ENB A71 Care of the Mentally Disordered Offender and the B.Sc (Hons) Forensic Health and Social Care. Having recently completed his Masters degree he has now undertaken studies for his PhD. This involves implementing and evaluating the effectiveness of a Conceptual Model of Therapeutic Alliance within Mental Health Care Delivery. This will be carried out within the local forensic and generic mental health services. He is a member of the FPNA (Executive Committee member) and the National Forensic Nurses Research and Development Group.

Alison Kuppen has worked as a forensic nurse since 1987. Since 1990 she has been a key-nurse in the forensic unit of the Rheinische Kliniken, Bedburg-Hau in Germany.

Virginia A. Lynch is a forensic clinical nurse specialist with extensive experience and education in the forensic area. She was the founding president of the International Association of Forensic Nurses and continues to be active with IAFN. She currently maintains an independent practice in Colorado, USA and is on the faculty at Beth-El College of Nursing, University of Colorado.

Leah Ousley is presently working as acting lecturer/practitioner at Wathwood Hospital RSU. She is currently conducting research into the supervision and observation of mentally disordered offenders within secure settings, leading to the award of PhD. Leah works part-time within the school of nursing at the University of Sheffield, primarily post basic teaching on psychiatric nursing within secure settings.

Cindy Peternelj-Taylor is a professor of nursing at the University of Saskatchewan, located in Saskatoon, Canada. The focus of her teaching is mental health nursing in general, with clinical and research interests in forensic psychiatry nursing and the impact of mental illness on the family unit. She is Receiving Editor for the Americas, Journal of Psychiatric and Mental Health Nursing; and sits on the Editorial Board of the Journal of Psychosocial Nursing and Mental Health Services. In 1998 she received an Achievement Award from the International

Association of Forensic Nurses, for her contributions to the adcancement of the scientific practice of Forensic Nursing, through research and publications.

David K. Robinson is Ph.D. RNMH Dip. Research Cert. Research Assistant Director of Research at Rampton Hospital Authority and Associate Professor of Forensic Nursing, SCHARR, University of Sheffield. He has been involved in full time research since 1986 at local, national and international levels. He is currently the Chair of the National Forensic Nurses Research and Development Group. He has extensive experience of high secure settings and as such is visiting researcher to the institute of psychiatry, London and the University of Amsterdam. He developed the International Forensic Database with the University of York Centre for Reviews and Dissemination.

Zug G. Standing Bear is an associate professor of sociology at Colorado State University. He is a criminologist with 40 years' experience in criminal justice work as a police officer, criminal investigator, investigations administrator, educator and coroner. He served for 15 years with the United States Army Criminal Investigation Command; was co-ordinator of criminal justice programs and professor of sociology, anthropology and criminal justice at Valdosta State University.

John Swinton worked as a nurse for sixteen years, specialising within the areas of psychiatry and learning disability. He also spent a number of years within the field of hospital chaplaincy, laterally as a community psychiatric chaplain working within a multidisciplinary rehabilitation team. He is presently employed as a lecturer in Practical Theology at the University of Aberdeen.

Carol Watson is the Senior Nurse for Practice Development at the State Hospital Carstairs. She trained as a registered mental nurse and was a staff nurse and ward sister in acute psychiatric care in a large mental hospital throughout the 70's and early 80's before developing her career in education as both a clinical teacher and a tutor. She is one of the Scottish representatives on the National Forensic Nurses Research and Development Group, and with Stephen Kirby was awarded a Kenneth Calman Bursary to explore the impact of different care environments on the perceived role(s) of the forensic nurse. The cohort study included the first Health Service forensic unit in Sydney, Australia, which they visited in January. She is currently seconded as a professional officer to the National Board for Scotland for Nursing Midwifery and Health Visiting, where she is the lead officer for Forensic Nursing.

Edward White is Professor of Nursing at Keele University, United Kingdom. He was the former Director, Health and Social Work Research and Development Unit, Anglia University and, before that, was Senior Research Fellow at the University of Manchester and at Kings College, University of London. He was recently Co-Director of the 4th Quinquennial National Community Mental Health Nursing Census of England and Wales, funded by the Department of Health, London. His present research is a detailed evaluation of an award-winning scheme which accepts mentally ill individuals into adult education services, funded by the National Health Service Executive.

Lawrence A. Whyte is a human being and a nurse.

Phil Woods is a lecturer in nursing at the University of Manchester in the UK and a researcher in the Virtual Institute for Severe Personality Disorder (VISPED). He has many years experience in high secure psychiatric care and extensive research experience. He is collaborating in a European risk assessment project with the Dutch, German and Norwegian forensic services; and violence prediction research in Norway. He runs the Forensic Nursing Resource Homepage which has received international recognition.

Subject Index

Author Index